New Views
OF THE
Constitution
OF THE
United States

CONSERVATIVE LEADERSHIP SERIES

EAGLE PUBLISHING, INC.

Thomas L. Phillips, Chairman
Jeffery J. Carneal, President

Jay Carven, Vice President
J. Brinley Lewis, Vice President
Margory G. Ross, Vice President

Don Poudrier, Director of Operations
Madeline Hopkins, Production Coordinator
Kari Miller, Production Associate

EAGLE BOOK CLUBS, INC.

J. Brinley Lewis, General Manager
John R. Evans, Business Manger

CONSERVATIVE BOOK CLUB

Jeffrey Rubin, Editor
Deborah Weiner, Managing Editor
Bevlin Cleveland, Associate Managing Editor
Michael Gorman, Marketing Director
Frederick A. Ulrich, Marketing Manager

REGNERY PUBLISHING, INC.

Alfred S. Regnery, President
Marjory G. Ross, Vice President and Group Publisher
Harry W. Crocker III, Executive Editor

The Conservative Leadership Series is a joint project of Regnery Publishing, Inc. and Eagle Book Clubs, Inc., divisions of Eagle Publishing, Inc., to make the classics of conservative thought available in hardcover collectors' editions.

New Views
OF THE
Constitution
OF THE
United States

by

JOHN TAYLOR

of Caroline

Edited with an Introduction by

JAMES McCLELLAN

REGNERY PUBLISHING, INC.
Washington, D.C.

Copyright © 2000 by Regnery Publishing, Inc.
First published in 1823 by Way and Gideon, Washington, D. C.

Library of Congress Cataloging-in-Publication Data

Published in the United States by
Regnery Publishing, Inc.
An Eagle Publishing Company
One Massachusetts Avenue, NW
Washington, DC 20001

Distributed to the trade by
National Book Network
4720-A Boston Way
Lanham, MD 20706

Printed on acid-free paper
Manufactured in the United States of America

10 9 8 7 6 5 4 3 2 1

Books are available in quantity for promotional or premium use. Write to Director of Special Sales, Regnery Publishing, Inc., One Massachusetts Avenue, NW, Washington, DC 20001, for information on discounts and terms or call (202) 216-0600.

DISTRICT OF COLUMBIA, *to wit:*

[L. S.] BE IT REMEMBERED, That on the nineteenth day of November, in the year of our Lord one thousand eight hundred and twenty-three, and of the Independence of the United States of America, the forty-eighth, JOHN TAYLOR, of the said District, hath deposited in the office of the Clerk of the District Court for the District of Columbia, the title of a book, the right whereof he claims as proprietor in the words following, to wit:

"New Views of the Constitution of the United States. By John Taylor, of Caroline, Virginia."

In conformity to the act of the Congress of the United States, entitled "An Act for the encouragement of learning, by securing the copies of maps, charts and books, to the authors and proprietors of such copies during the times therein mentioned," and also to the act, entitled "An Act supplementary to an act, entitled "An Act for the encouragement of learning, by securing the copies of maps, charts, and books, to the authors and proprietors of such copies during the times therein mentioned," and extending the benefits thereof to the arts of designing, engraving, and etching historical and other prints."

IN TESTIMONY WHEREOF, I have hereunto set my hand, and affixed the public seal of my office, the day and year aforesaid.

EDMUND I. LEE,
Clerk of the District Court for the District of Columbia.

CONTENTS

Preface . . . . *ix*

Introduction . . . . *xi*

Note on the Text . . . . *lxxi*

1   The Meaning of Certain Primary Words *1*

2   The Journal of the Convention *13*

3   The Subject Continued *19*

4   The Subject Continued *29*

5   The Subject Concluded *41*

6   Yates's Notes *45*

7   The Subject Concluded *63*

8   The Federalist *75*

9   The Subject Continued *87*

10   The Subject Continued *99*

11   The Subject Continued *125*

12   The Subject Concluded *143*

13   Sovereignty *207*

14   One of the People *217*

15   Other Consolidating Doctrines *273*

16   A Federal and National Form of Government
     Compared *291*

17   Construction *365*

Index *391*

PREFACE

THAT many eminent and respectable men have ever preferred, and ever will prefer, a consolidated national government to our federal system; that the constitution, under the influence of this predilection, has been erroneously construed; that these constructions are rapidly advancing towards their end, whether it shall be consolidation or disunion; that they will become a source of excessive geographical discord; and that the happiness and prosperity of the United States will be greater under a federal than under a national government, in any form, are the opinions which have suggested the following treatise. If the survey taken of these subjects is not proportioned to their importance, it yet may not be devoid of novelty, nor wholly ineffectual towards attracting more publick attention towards a question involving a mass of consequences either very good or very bad.

"I once saw a book advertised, entitled *New Views on the Constitution*. I was startled! What right has a man to start *new* views upon it? Speculations upon our Government are dangerous, and should be discountenanced."[1] So exclaimed Justice Joseph Story, the champion of judicial nationalism on the Marshall Court and the leading opponent of states' rights doctrines in the early republic. Story made the remark in a lecture at the Harvard Law School, where he taught from 1829 to 1845, when he was not attending to his judicial duties in Washington and New England. No doubt the eminent jurist would have been even more disturbed about the publication of *New Views of the Constitution* "had he taken occasion to dip into it."[2] For here was one of the most insightful and closely reasoned analyses of the original intent of the Constitution from the states' rights perspective ever written. A neglected classic, it is nowadays considered by some to be "John Taylor's most important work on the Constitution."[3]

That Judge Story probably never read John Taylor's *New Views of the Constitution* is indicated by the fact there is no mention of it in Story's famed *Commentaries on the Constitution*.[4] In his extended discussion of the great constitutional issues that divided the Hamiltonian nationalists from the Jeffersonian states' rightists in the early nineteenth century, Story walked the same ground that had been covered earlier by Taylor. He rejected the view that the states had the right to make final constitutional determinations and defended judicial supremacy, insisting that the Supreme Court was the final interpreter of the Constitution. He also repudiated the compact theory of the union, the doctrines of nullification and secession, and the Jeffersonian concept of strict construction, often citing his own opinions and those of Chief Justice Marshall to support his latitudinarian approach to constitutional interpretation. The only writings of the states' rights school that he cited were St. George Tucker's American edition of Sir William Blackstone's *Commentaries on the Laws of England*,[5] Thomas Jefferson's correspondence, the Kentucky and Virginia Resolutions of 1798, and James Madison's Report of 1800 on the Virginia Resolutions of 1798.[6] Taylor's name came up only once, as the man who introduced the Virginia Resolutions to the Virginia General Assembly.

Taylor's *New Views*, representing his final thoughts on the Framers' intent, was his last book. It was published in Washington in 1823, just a year before his death. Story therefore had ample opportunity to examine Taylor's *New Views*, as well as Taylor's earlier works, inasmuch as his own three-volume treatise on the Constitution did not appear until 1833, a full decade after *New Views* entered the forum.

Whether Story was intimidated by the style and complexity of Taylor's discourse, or was simply distracted by the press of business, are questions that cannot be answered. Given Story's manifest distrust of "artificial reasoning founded upon theory"[7] and his contempt for the "visionary politicians"[8] who espoused the doctrines of states' rights, it is probably the case that Story misjudged the book by its title; erroneously assumed that a refutation of the ideas expressed by Jefferson, Madison, and

Tucker would be sufficient to clinch the case for nationalism, and, in a fit of intellectual arrogance, dismissed Taylor as an armchair philosopher.

Whatever the reason for this cavalier manner, Judge Story most assuredly missed a propitious opportunity to debate the chief architect of states' rights doctrines and challenge Taylor's reading of the Constitution; for John Taylor was "the intellectual leader of the Jeffersonian Republicans."[9] His *New Views* was the *locus classicus* of states' rights jurisprudence. A sustained, point-by-point analysis of Taylor's constitutional interpretations by a jurist of Story's stature and reputation would have given the American public the benefit of an authoritative response to Taylor's powerful indictment of the Marshall Court's constitutional rulings; and it would have gone a long way toward clarifying some fundamental constitutional issues dividing the nation. At the very least, Story's dismissal of Taylor did nothing to enhance the prestige of a beleaguered Court or add credence to its controversial holdings. Story's enigmatic silence is all the more disconcerting in light of the fact much of Taylor's *New Views* was devoted to impugning the supposed neutrality of *The Federalist*, the very work upon which Story would later base his *Commentaries on the Constitution.*

Notwithstanding these considerations, John Taylor's *New Views of the Constitution* plays a distinctive role in the literary history of Southern constitutionalism. A major handicap of the Anti-Federalists and the Republicans who followed in their footsteps in the great constitutional conflicts of the early nineteenth century was the lack of an analytical text, comparable to *The Federalist*, that elucidated the original intent of the Founding Fathers from the states' rights perspective. Patrick Henry, George Mason, and other Virginia Anti-Federalists bequeathed to posterity little more than a mélange of diffuse speeches and pamphlets, which only recently have been collected and bound. Similarly, Republican stalwarts who led the struggle for decentralized government after the Constitution was ratified in 1788, including John Randolph of Roanoke, Nathaniel Macon of North Carolina, and Judges Spencer Roane and St. George Tucker of the Virginia Court of Appeals, produced only fragmentary speeches and writings on states' rights topics. Thomas Jefferson, political leader of the Republican party, wrote often on such matters as state sovereignty, strict construction, and judicial tyranny, all favorite themes of the states' rights movement, but his thoughts were scattered in private correspondence, occasional public pronouncements, and personal memoranda. Jefferson's *Notes on Virginia*,[10] his only methodical work, was written in 1781-82, and barely touched upon the issues that were debated five years later in the Philadelphia Convention.

John Taylor, the only Republican to present a systematic exposition of states' rights doctrines, thus supplied the party with an authoritative treatise that filled the gap and gave meaning and substance to its constitutional policies. Admired and respected by his contemporaries, both Northern and Southern, particularly for his consistency and unwavering devotion to first principles, Taylor was the touchstone of constitutional thought in the Old Dominion, the headmaster of the Virginia school of strict construction, for more than thirty years. Taylor urged Jefferson to prepare a work that laid out his constitutional philosophy, but Jefferson declined, telling Thomas Ritchie, the editor of the *Richmond Enquirer,* that such a work was unnecessary because "Colonel Taylor and myself have rarely, if ever, differed in any political principles of importance"[11]; and John Randolph surmised that Taylor's "disinterested principles" were "the only bond of union among Republicans."[12] As Charles A. Beard would later observe, John Taylor was the "most trenchant and pertinent of all the Republican pamphleteers; and . . . perhaps, the most systematic thinker that his party produced within the two decades which followed the adoption of the Constitution."[13]

Yet it is also the case that John Taylor's fame lies buried with his cause. Until recently, his name was almost forgot; and copies of his writings are exceedingly rare. "In view of the unrivaled comprehensiveness with which Taylor dealt with nearly all aspects of the theory of limited power which played an important part in American history between 1775 and 1861," notes Benjamin F. Wright, "it is somewhat difficult to understand why his writings have received so little attention since his death."[14] Since the Second World War, however, there has been a renewed interest in Taylor, as seen by the publication of two intellectual biographies,[15] the reprinting of most of his writings,[16] and a resurrection of the original intent jurisprudence that he cogently defined and ably defended. These are signs, perhaps, of an increased awareness of Taylor's significance in the history of American political and constitutional thought and of a heightened interest in the timeless principles of limited constitutional government upon which he expounded.

The Sage of "Hazelwood"

Although there is some uncertainty about the exact place and date of his birth, historians are generally agreed that John Taylor was born at "Mill Farm" in Caroline County, Virginia, on

December 19, 1753.[17] Like his friend, John Randolph, who always added "of Roanoke" to his name so as not to be confused with other members of the Randolph family, Taylor identified himself as "John Taylor of Caroline" and proudly affixed the county of his birth and residence to most of the books and pamphlets he wrote.[18] At a very early age, his father died and young John was sent to live with his uncle, Edmund Pendleton, a prominent attorney in the county and aspiring political leader in the state. Pendleton exerted a powerful influence on his nephew, shaping his values and overseeing his moral and intellectual training. Taylor was educated at home by tutors at first, but spent most of his formative years at Donald Robertson's highly acclaimed grammar school located about fifteen miles from his home in a neighboring county. A learned Scotsman, Robertson instilled an enthusiasm for learning in his pupils, who included James Madison (Taylor's distant cousin), and gave lessons in Greek, Latin, French, Spanish, mathematics, geography, and English literature. Taylor last attended Robertson's school in 1763 and went on to complete his formal academic training at the College of William and Mary.

Returning home in 1770, Taylor took up the study of law with his uncle in the town of Bowling Green and gained admission to the Caroline County bar in 1774. Soon, however, both he and Pendleton were caught up in the American Revolution. Eager to get into the fighting, Taylor joined a Virginia regiment of the Continental army in 1775, rose to the rank of major in 1777, and resigned in 1779 after seeing action in northern battlefields.[19] Albeit "there is much evidence that Taylor personally was no sectionalist,"[20] his wartime experience nevertheless gave him his first indication that there were serious underlying sectional differences between the North and South, differences that would become more pronounced and more sinister as antagonism between the regions increased over the years. Writing to Pendleton in 1777, he complained that "the armies of the northern states are really mercenaries, and being foreigners have no attachment to the country."[21] Much to his despair, he also discovered that "enlistments are rare in the provinces north of Maryland, especially in New England; all the stories of regiments complete in New York and New Jersey are utterly false; ours is the fullest regiment in the service. . . ."[22]

Soon after returning to Virginia, Taylor was elected to the Virginia General Assembly in 1779. He quickly became a close political ally of Patrick Henry and supported legislation to enhance the state's prosecution of the rebellion. In 1781, Taylor was also commissioned a lieutenant colonel in the Virginia militia, a title symbolizing his leadership and patriotism in the great War of Independence that the citizen-soldier proudly carried for the rest of his life. When Lord Cornwallis and Benedict Arnold invaded Virginia in the summer of 1781, there was only a small force of American regulars under Lafayette to oppose them. Frustrated by the lack of support from other states, a special committee composed of Patrick Henry, John Tyler, Sr., and John Taylor presented a remonstrance to the General Assembly. It was written by Taylor, who was still smarting from his northern experience in the Continental army. "When we . . . look for our Northern allies," he bitterly declared, "after we had thus exhausted our powers in their defense . . . they are not to be found . . . ."[23] Though not published, "Taylor's statement was one of the first formal expressions of a schism between the northern and southern states in American history."[24] The General

Assembly promptly adjourned in September, and Colonel Taylor took charge of troops from counties on the Eastern Shore. After skirmishing with Hessian forces, Taylor joined Lafayette's command in Gloucester in the weeks preceding Cornwallis's surrender at Yorktown (October 17, 1781) and later in the month returned to the Virginia legislature.

Taylor's first period of service as a legislator extended from 1779 to 1785, except the year 1782, when he declined to stand for election in order to devote more time to his law practice. A year later he married his cousin, Lucy Penn, the daughter of a prosperous lawyer and planter from North Carolina. Taylor rose rapidly in the legal profession and was so successful as a young trial attorney that he was able to retire from the practice of law in a single decade. In 1792, he purchased "Hazelwood," a plantation on the Rappahannock River near Port Royal, where he devoted the remainder of his life to agriculture, politics, writing, and the cause of localism. Sarcastically dubbed the "Oceana of the Rappahannock"[25] by Henry Adams, "Hazelwood" became a favorite stopping place for Southern politicians traveling to and from Washington. One visitor to the plantation in 1814 reported that he "found an old grey-headed gentleman in an old fashion'd dress, plain in his manners, full of politics, and fond of conversational debate. . . He lives . . . on the finest farm I have ever seen. In front of his door he has 800 acres in clover, 300 acres in corn, 2 or 300 in wheat and rye all in perfect plain."[26] At "Hazelwood," John Taylor of Caroline "became the classic figure of 'Old Republican' theory: the exemplar of an almost Roman *virtus*, the Virginia Cato, who soldiers, enforces the law, writes in its defense and of the life it secures, and serves the state well when called to office."[27]

And Taylor was called to office repeatedly. In 1792, the same year he acquired "Hazelwood," Taylor became a two-year replacement for Richard Henry Lee in the United States Senate but refused to accept a six-year term in 1794.[28] Four years later, he was again elected to the Virginia House of Delegates, where he served until 1800. Then in 1803 he was appointed a second time to the Senate to complete the term of the late Stevens T. Mason. He served from June to December 1803 and, much to the consternation of the Virginia Republicans, refused to stand for reelection. Another twenty years would pass before Taylor agreed to serve again in the federal Congress. In 1822, he entered the Senate for a third time to fill the position vacated by James Pleasants, Jr., who became governor of Virginia. He served this term until his death on August 21, 1824.

Despite the brevity and discontinuity that characterized his erratic legislative career, it was universally acknowledged that John Taylor was a commanding presence in the Senate, a skilled debater and stately orator, as effective in a legislative chamber as he was in the courtroom. As early as 1793, James Madison was writing to Pendleton imploring him to encourage Taylor to remain in the Senate. "Permit me," he wrote, "to tell you how much we have been charmed with the successor to Col. R.H.L. and to entreat your cooperation with a number of his other friends in overcoming his repugnance to his present station. His talents during the fraction of time he has been on the Federal theatre have been of such infinite service to the republican cause, and such a terror to its adversaries, that his sudden retirement, on which he is strongly bent, ought to be regarded as a public calamity and counterworked by all the means his friends can use."[29] But Taylor was not the type to strut upon the stage seeking popular acclaim. Notwithstanding the entreaties of his friends and colleagues, he preferred the solitude of plantation life and his private library to the limelight and bustle of Capitol Hill.

When he came out of retirement in 1822 and presented his credentials to the second session of the Seventeenth Congress, Taylor seemed like a ghost from the past. John Randolph predicted that Taylor's quaint attire "will be rather nearer the fashion of the day that his principles."[30] One member of the Senate who befriended Taylor and came to admire his character and principles was Thomas Hart Benton of Missouri. Looking back on Taylor's final term in the Senate, Benton recalled with fond remembrance his lasting impressions:

> All my observations of him, and his whole appearance and deportment, went to confirm the reputation of his individuality of character, and high qualities of the head and heart. I can hardly figure to myself the ideal of a republican statesman more perfect and complete than he was in reality: plain and solid, a wise counsellor, a ready and vigorous debater, acute and comprehensive, ripe in all historical and political knowledge, innately republican—modest, courteous, benevolent, hospitable—a skillful, practical farmer, giving his time to his farm and his books when not called by an emergency to the public service—and returning to his books and his farm when the emergency was over .... He belonged to that constellation of great men which shone so brightly in Virginia in his day ....[31]

John Taylor's Secret Memorandum

It must be admitted, however, that John Taylor's three terms in the United States Senate were all too brief and too sporadic to leave much of a mark on legislative history. Probably the most memorable incident of his Senate career, one that would have rocked the foundations of the union had Taylor made it known to the public, occurred in May 1794, a month before Congress adjourned. Taylor had vigorously opposed most of Hamilton's program as soon as he entered the Senate. He rejected Hamilton's broad interpretation of the Constitution, the Bank of the United States, the funding program, the creation of a national debt, excise taxes, a standing army, and tariffs. He also expressed concern about the growing power of the president and the federal judiciary; and it was no secret that he had opposed the adoption of the Constitution in 1788. Shortly after delivering a speech advocating suspension of the payment of the British debts, Taylor was approached by two of the nation's leading Federalists, Rufus King of New York (formerly of Massachusetts) and Oliver Ellsworth of Connecticut. Both had served as delegates to the Federal Convention of 1787. King invited Taylor into one of the committee rooms of the Senate, where they could converse privately, informing Taylor that he wished to discuss an important subject. When they were alone, King declared that "it was utterly impossible for the union to continue,"[32] that the North and South would never agree on issues of public policy, and that a dissolution of the union by mutual consent was preferable to a forced separation. At this point in the conversation, Ellsworth entered the room, either by accident or design. King repeated what he had been saying, and Ellsworth agreed with him.

Taylor replied that he intended to support the union if possible, but agreed that a peaceful separation would be preferable to a forced one. The cause of the problem, he asserted, was Hamilton's ambitious master plan for solving the nation's economic woes. He thought an effort should first be made to eradicate the cause of the problem before resorting to a permanent separation. King disagreed, however, insisting that the differences went much deeper because Northerners and Southerners "never had and never would think alike."[33] The discussion ended when the parties reached an impasse and could not agree on the cause of the sectional hostility. Taylor left the room convinced that the Federalists were seriously contemplating a dissolution of the union.

Two days later, Taylor wrote a confidential memorandum to James Madison, then serving in the House of Representatives, relating the details of his conversation with King and Ellsworth. Madison was persuaded, however, that they meant simply to warn Taylor that secession was likely if the Anti-Federalists persisted in their opposition to Federalist policies, and the matter was dropped. Whether King and Ellsworth were seriously contemplating a break up of the union is a question that cannot be answered. It is noteworthy, however, that both were close political allies of Federalist leaders of the Essex Junto who would later lead the forces of dissolution in New England, including Harrison Gray Otis, Timothy Pickering, Gouverneur Morris, and Caleb Strong, chairman of the Hartford Convention in 1814.[34]

For reasons that are not explained, neither Taylor nor Madison ever made a public disclosure of the incident, and Taylor's confidential memorandum remained a secret for more than a century. Gaillard Hunt finally discovered it and brought it to light in

1905, after publishing a new edition of James Madison's papers and a new biography of Madison. Hunt's investigation of the matter revealed that Madison had excluded the memorandum from the files of his papers he prepared for posterity. Upon his death in 1836 and the sale of his papers to the Library of Congress, Madison's widow retained possession of the memorandum, whence upon her death it fell into the hands of her nephew, who sold it to Hunt's Washington publisher.[35] We may surmise that both Taylor and Madison were persuaded that it would not have been in the nation's interest to make the memorandum public. Taylor prophesied secession but he did not preach it[36]; and Madison was a unionist to the core of his being. He no doubt believed that the publication of Taylor's memorandum, particularly after 1830, would have served no useful purpose other than to advance the cause of sectionalism and kindle the flames of secession.

The Kentucky and Virginia Resolutions

It was in the Virginia General Assembly rather than the United States Senate, however, where John Taylor made constitutional history. The occasion was his election in 1796 to a four-year term in the House of Delegates, where he contributed as a state legislative leader to the creation and enactment of the famous Virginia Resolutions of 1798. These resolutions, combined with those adopted by Kentucky that same year, and their subsequent embellishment by James Madison in his Report of 1800, mark the birth of the doctrine of states' rights. Although they can be traced back as far as the Articles of Confederation and would later evolve into a more complex and elaborate set of constitutional principles regarding the relationship between the states and the federal government, the "Resolutions of '98" denote the doctrine's formal inauguration and entry into the American political arena. John Taylor of Caroline was not only a witness to the creation, but may truly be said to be the father of the doctrine of states' rights.

By 1798, the Republican party of John Taylor had been out of power at the federal level for nearly a decade. Three Virginia Republicans—Thomas Jefferson, James Madison, and James Monroe—had labored assiduously to establish an opposition party that might effectively challenge the reigning Federalists. In domestic affairs, they fought Hamilton's funding system, the Bank of the United States, and excise taxes, but with limited success. In foreign affairs, they supported neutrality but demanded a policy that was sympathetic toward the new French republic. But there was little public support for such a policy. Alarmed by the excesses of the French Revolution and determined to prevent the spread of French radicalism to American shores, the Federalists rammed four statutes through Congress in the summer of 1798 that came to be known as the Alien and Sedition Acts. The Kentucky and Virginia Resolutions, written in response to these controversial measures, represent the first attempt by a state legislature to challenge the constitutionality of a federal law.

Three of the statutes dealt with resident foreigners. The Naturalization Act made it more difficult to become a citizen by lengthening the period of residence required of aliens before they could be naturalized; the Alien Act authorized the president to expel from the country any alien deemed "dangerous to the peace and safety of the United States"; and the Alien Enemies

Act granted the president power in time of war to restrict, imprison, or deport all subjects of an enemy power in the interest of public safety. The fourth statute, and the most repressive, was the Sedition Act, making seditious libel a federal crime. This act made it a criminal offense, punishable by fine and imprisonment, for any person to conspire to oppose any federal law, to "advise or attempt to procure any insurrection," or publish "any false, scandalous and malicious writing . . . against the government of the United States, or either house of Congress . . . or the President of the United States, with an intent to defame [them] . . . or bring them, or either of them into contempt or disrepute."[37]

The Republicans hotly contested the constitutionality of these laws, particularly the Sedition Act, which in their judgment abridged freedom of the press in violation of the First Amendment and was but a subterfuge to eliminate Republican opposition to Federalist measures. Moreover, they contended, the law in question usurped the reserved powers of the states because Congress had no authority to make laws governing freedom of speech and press in the first place. Added to this, the misdemeanors defined in the act were common law offenses, cognizable in the state courts only. The Constitution had not conferred any common law jurisdiction on the federal courts.

How were these repressive statutes to be overturned? Prospects for relief at the federal level were grim, as the Federalists controlled all three branches of the federal government. The only recourse seemed to be popular resistance. Such was the alternative adumbrated by Republicans when they debated these measures in the House of Representatives. "If we are ready to violate the Constitution," said Edward Livingston of New York, "will the people submit to our unauthorized acts? Sir, they ought not to submit; they would deserve the chains that our measures are forging for them, if they did not resist."[38] A veiled threat of popular revolt, however, was an invitation to mob rule, and the Federalists did not hesitate to accuse Livingston of sedition. Was there no lawful way in which the people might express their opposition to this partisan legislation?

John Taylor of Caroline proposed a simple solution. In a letter to Vice President Jefferson on June 25, 1798, he suggested that, "The right of the state government to expound the Constitution might possibly be made the basis of a movement toward its amendment."[39] Anticipating what came to be known as the compact theory of the Constitution, Taylor went on to assert that, "The people in state conventions are incontrovertibly the contracting parties, and, possessing the infringing rights, may proceed by orderly steps to attain the object."[40] By this he meant that the Constitution was formed when the American people, meeting separately in their state ratifying conventions, agreed among themselves and with each other to accept the document that was proposed by the Federal Convention. The Constitution was thus a compact among the states, resting on the sovereignty of the people as expressed through their state conventions. Being parties to the compact, they had the right to defend their rights under it and seek relief.

As events would later demonstrate, Taylor's understanding of the nature of the federal union became the foundation upon which the doctrine of states' rights was developed, and other Virginia Republicans embraced it wholeheartedly. Even James Madison, who occasionally wandered from the Republican camp on matters involving federal power, subscribed to the compact theory. In a letter dated June 29, 1821, he assured Judge

Spencer Roane of Virginia: "Our government system is established by *compact*, not between the Government of the United States and the State Governments, but between THE STATES AS SOVEREIGN COMMUNITIES, *stipulating* EACH *with* THE OTHER a surrender of certain portions of their respective authorities, to be exercised by a common Government, and a reservation for *their* own exercise, of all the other authorities."[41]

Taylor's suggestion that the states should serve as a check on unconstitutional acts of the federal government was not entirely novel, however, as Alexander Hamilton had earlier assured the states in *Federalist* No. 28 that,

> It may safely be received as an axiom in our political system, that the State governments will, in all possible contingencies, afford complete security against invasions of the public liberty by the national authority. Projects of usurpation cannot be masked under pretences so likely to escape the penetration of select bodies of men, as of the people at large. The legislatures will have better means of information. They can discover the danger at a distance; and possessing all the organs of civil power, and the confidence of the people, they can at once adopt a regular plan of opposition, in which they can combine all the resources of the community. They can readily communicate with each other in the different States, and unite their common forces for the protection of their common liberty.[42]

The task of implementing Taylor's suggestion and writing a constitutional rebuttal to the Alien and Sedition Acts fell on Jefferson and Madison. Jefferson secretly drafted a set of resolutions in November 1798 for the Kentucky legislature, which his friend, John Breckinridge introduced; and Madison secretly prepared the Virginia resolutions a month later for introduction in the House of Delegates by Taylor. The Kentucky and Virginia legislatures adopted the resolutions handily and, in the hope of generating support for the principles they embodied, circulated them among the various state legislatures. To their dismay, not a single state endorsed either resolution, and all of the New England states, where the Federalist party reigned supreme, enacted countermeasures denouncing the resolutions. Seeing no inconsistency, they simultaneously affirmed the constitutionality of the Alien and Sedition Acts and denied the right of a state legislature to interpret the Constitution. The Virginia resolutions, declared the Vermont House of Representatives, are "unconstitutional in their nature and dangerous in their tendency. It belongs not to State legislatures to decide on the constitutionality of laws made by the general government, this power being exclusively vested in the judiciary courts of the Union."[43] Ignoring the resolutions altogether, Virginia's sister states below the Mason–Dixon took no formal action and neither affirmed nor denied their constitutionality. In less than thirty years, however, the "Principles of '98" would become the rallying cry of the states' rights movement throughout the South.

Undaunted, the Kentucky legislature issued a second set of resolves in 1799, reaffirming "its attachment to the Union," but insisting "that the principle and construction contended for by sundry of the State legislatures, that the General Government is the exclusive judge of the extent of the powers delegated to it, stop nothing short of despotism."[44] A year later, the Virginia General Assembly approved Madison's Report (1800), a lengthy and elaborate document intended to prove that each resolution that the legislature had adopted in 1798 was in harmony with the express provisions of the Constitution.[45]

Taken together, the Kentucky and Virginia Resolutions comprise a set of principles that chart the evolution of the states' rights philosophy of the Constitution in the antebellum South. Those principles rested on the basic proposition that the federal system, that is, the division of power between the federal and state governments, was the desideratum of individual liberty in American government, and that the protection of that liberty depended first and foremost not on an energetic federal government or on parchment barriers proclaimed in the Bill of Rights, but upon the balance of power between the federal and state governments. Like John Taylor, the authors of the Kentucky and Virginia Resolutions looked to their states and local communities as the guardians of their liberty, the unwritten assumption being that federal power, in itself, is inherently dangerous unless it is held closely in check. The regime of liberty is that which uses the power of one level of government to restrain the power of the other.

Proceeding upon this basis, the Kentucky and Virginia Resolutions hold that the federal union rests upon a compact. This is the first principle of the Constitution. The Kentucky Resolutions claimed "that by compact" the states "constituted a General Government,"[46] and the Virginia Resolutions declared that "the powers of the federal government" are the result of a "compact to which the states are parties."[47] No further explanation was offered, and it would thus appear that the compact theory was everywhere asserted, but nowhere demonstrated. The question, at bottom, was one of original understanding and historical investigation: what is the nature and origin of the federal union? Was it formed, as the wording of the Preamble indicates, by "We the people," abstractly considered in their constituent capacity, or was it the result of a compact among the states in their sovereign capacity? John Taylor single-handedly addressed the issue while leading the debate on the Virginia Resolutions. Critics of the Resolutions, he noted, had argued that the states have no right to challenge the constitutionality of a federal law "because the people alone are parties to the compact." But, said Taylor, that was not exactly the case. "Although the framers of the Constitution chose to use the style, 'We the people,'" it may be seen

that in every step, from its commencement to its termination; the sense of the people respecting it, appeared through the medium of some representative State assembly, either legislative or constituent. That the Constitution itself, in many parts, recognizes that states as parties to the contract, particularly in the great articles of amendment, and that of admitting new states into the Union without a reference to the people; and that even the government of the Union was kept in motion as to one House of the legislature, by the act of the state sovereignties. That added to these incontestable arguments to show that the states are parties to the compact, the reservation of powers not given, was to the states as well as to the people, recognizing the states as a contracting party, to whom rights were expressly reserved. From all which it followed, though it be not denied that the people are to be considered as parties to the contract, that the states are parties also, and as parties, are justifiable in preserving their rights under the compact against violations; otherwise their existence was at an end; for, if their legislative proceedings could be regulated by Congressional sedition laws, their independency, and of course their existence, were gone.[48]

The union, then, was a compact formed not by "the people" in the abstract, but by the people organized politically in the several states.

At the Virginia ratifying convention of 1788, it will be recalled, Patrick Henry had criticized the wording of the Preamble to the Constitution. "What right," he asked, did the delegates to the Federal Convention have in saying *"We the people"*? "Who authorized them to speak the language of *We, the People,* instead of *We, the states?* States are the characteristics and the soul of a confederation. If the states are not the agents of this compact, it must be one great consolidated government, of the people of all the states."[49] Edmund Randolph and Edmund Pendleton had struggled to answer Henry, but it was James Madison who gave the most satisfactory reply. The people, to be sure, said Madison, were parties to the compact, but "not the people as composing one great body." Rather, it is "the people as composing thirteen sovereignties." Moreover, he added,

Were it . . . a consolidated government, the assent of a majority of the people would be sufficient for its establishment: and, as a majority have adopted it already, the remaining States would be bound by the act of the majority, even if they unanimously repro- bated it . . . . But, sir, no state is bound by it, as it is, without its own consent.[50]

This was essentially the same explanation offered by Taylor in support of the Virginia Resolutions. Ironically, Taylor, who had opposed the Constitution and was excluded from the Virginia ratifying convention, and Madison, a Framer of the Constitu- tion who led the fight for its ratification, were of the same mind respecting the origin and nature of the union.

Assuming that the union was thus a compact to which the people and the states were parties, it necessarily followed that the states were justified, as Taylor put it, "in preserving their rights under the compact against violation."[51] But who had the right under the Constitution to determine whether there had been a violation? Was the adjudicatory task the exclusive prerogative of the federal courts, or might not the states also perform this func- tion? To the modern mind, this would seem to be a frivolous question; but it must be remembered that in the early republic the federal judiciary, including the Supreme Court, had not yet assumed the power of resolving every question about the mean- ing of the Constitution. The forum for discussing or settling constitutional disputes was most often the halls of Congress, although the executive branch also presumed to exercise an interpretive power as occasion permitted. In any event, the Con- stitution is silent as to which government, state or federal, has the right to interpret the document. The supremacy of the

Constitution is freely acknowledged, but there is no accompanying language to indicate that one particular branch of the state or federal governments is obliged to submit to the interpretation of another branch. Accordingly, the Kentucky and Virginia legislatures took the position that they had a coequal right to determine the constitutionality of federal laws, and denied that the federal government had the exclusive power to judge the extent of its own powers. Judicial supremacy, or the practice of deferring to the Supreme Court in constitutional disputes and rendering Supreme Court interpretations binding on the states was to Taylor and the states' rightists inconsistent with the republican principle of popular sovereignty, the original understanding of both the framers and ratifiers of the Constitution, and plain common sense. *Quis custodiet ipos custodes.* Who will watch the watchdogs? As stated in the Kentucky Resolutions, "the Government created by this compact was not made the exclusive or final *judge* of the extent of powers delegated to itself; since that would have made its discretion, and not the Constitution, the measure of its powers." And, "as in all other cases of compact among parties having no common Judge, each party had an equal right to judge for itself, as well of infractions as of the mode and measure of redress."[52]

A corollary principle to the compact theory, it may thus be seen, was the proposition that a party to the compact has a coequal right "to judge for itself" whether a federal law conforms to the Constitution. If it does not, what is "the mode and measure of redress"? On this point the Kentucky and Virginia Resolutions lacked both clarity and consistency. The former provided simply that "whensoever the General Government assumes undelegated powers, its acts are unauthoritative, void, and of no force."[53] Kentucky's second resolves, adopted in 1799, went further, however, and asserted "*That a nullification . . . of all unauthorized acts done under color of that instrument is the rightful remedy.*"[54] The Virginia Resolutions, on the other hand, spoke of "interposition," declaring "that in case of a deliberate, palpable, and dangerous exercise of other powers, not granted by the said compact, the States who are parties thereto, have the right, and are duty bound, to interpose for arresting the progress of the evil . . . ."[55]

Madison's reference here to a "right to interpose" is vague, for the term encompasses a wide range of remedies, including state protest, remonstrance, objection, and intervention. The word "nullification" preferred by Jefferson in the Kentucky Resolutions suggests even stronger action, and both terms seem to imply the use of force. What Madison and Jefferson actually intended is a question that has been debated for years. Certainly secession was not contemplated; and there is even some doubt whether the nullification doctrines espoused by John C. Calhoun accurately reflected Jefferson's use of the term. Adding fuel to the controversy, one modern writer has suggested that, in the final analysis, the terms "interposition" and "nullification" are essentially convertible, leading to the same result.[56] The better view seems to be that Madison and Jefferson, ever prone to rhetorical flourishes, had in mind a peaceful settlement of the dispute, one that preferred the convention method to state legislative action. Their primary objective, after all, was repeal of the Alien and Sedition Acts. Even repeal soon became moot, however, because these laws expired by their own terms at the end of the Adams administration in March 1801. They were not renewed, and a major constitutional crisis in the early republic thus came to an abrupt end, leaving the constitutional issues unresolved.

As a harbinger of things to come, however, a close reading of the Kentucky and Virginia Resolutions and Madison's Report revealed that Madison's constitutional theories did not fully comport with those espoused by Jefferson and Taylor. Madison's more temperate Virginia Resolutions, as we have seen, call for interposition rather than nullification, and his Report also indicated that there were disagreements regarding the principle of judicial review.[57] Although he acknowledged the need for state legislatures to seek constitutional redress through petitions to Congress and the amendment process, he hesitated in asserting the right of state legislatures to judge constitutional issues with any finality. At the same time, he affirmed the right of the federal judiciary to review acts of Congress and the president, while denying that its power of judicial review extended to state laws and the "rights of the parties to the constitutional compact."[58]

Madison's constitutional disagreements with fellow Republicans, particularly the more conservative members of the party, became more pronounced as the years passed, contributing significantly to the schism that plagued the party of Jefferson after it come into power in the elections of 1800. Though Taylor was critical of Jefferson's constitutional lapses into nationalism in his second administration and frustrated by his accommodating compromises with the Federalists, Taylor and Jefferson maintained a friendly relationship in the years that followed. Such was not the case with Madison. Among the Old Republicans, he soon acquired the reputation of being a "trimmer." By 1806, Taylor was persuaded that Madison was "too much of a Federalist"[59] to warrant his continued support, and in the 1808 campaign for the presidency he served as a Monroe elector. The congressional elections of 1810, providing 63 new faces in a House of 142 members, gave new leadership to the party, further isolating the Old Republicans with whom Taylor identified. Many, including newcomers Henry Clay and John C. Calhoun, had little respect at this time for the doctrines of '98 and "cared little for Jeffersonian or Madisonian dogmas."[60] Although Madison would later redeem himself from time to time, as when he vetoed the Bonus Bill in 1816 on constitutional grounds, he and Taylor remained estranged. Calhoun would later come around to Taylor's view of the Constitution. By 1832, however, Madison was disavowing Calhoun's interpretation of the Kentucky and Virginia Resolutions.

As his writings would later demonstrate, it is John Taylor of Caroline, rather than the authors of the Kentucky and Virginia Resolutions, who deserves the most credit for carrying the legacy of the "Principles of '98" into the nineteenth century. More than that, Taylor alone refined and expanded the rudimentary concepts expressed in the Resolutions by adding meaning and substance to them. This he accomplished through a careful scrutiny of the founding documents and the intent of the Framers, a task that Madison could have undertaken with his own *Notes of the Debates in the Federal Convention.*[61]

The Writings of John Taylor

Having already forsaken the practice of law, Taylor abandoned public life after 1800 and, with the exception of a brief stint in the United States Senate in 1803, did not again serve in office until 1822. Retiring to "Hazelwood," he dabbled in local politics but devoted most of his remaining years to agricultural pursuits, family life, and serious writing.

During his first years in office, Taylor had written a number of pamphlets, most of them in opposition to Alexander Hamilton's ingenious financial schemes: the funding of the debt of the general government, the assumption of state debts, a new excise tax, and the establishment of a national bank. These writings included *Definition of Parties; or, The Political Effects of the Paper System Considered* (1794); *An Enquiry into the Principles and Tendency of Certain Public Measures* (1794); and *An Argument Respecting the Constitutionality of the Carriage Tax* (1795). More ambitious was his 136-page encomium on President Jefferson's first term of office. Entitled *A Defence of the Measures of the Administration of Thomas Jefferson* (1804), and written under the pseudonym of the Roman historian "Curtius," this extended work covered a variety of subjects, including the Judiciary Act of 1801, the Twelfth Amendment, and the Louisiana Purchase, as well as laudatory sketches of the men who served in Jefferson's cabinet. James Madison, singled out for special praise as the moving force behind the Constitution, author of the Virginia Resolutions, and Jefferson's talented secretary of state, was hailed as a man of superior talents for "the penetration of his genius, the soundness of his judgment and the extensiveness of his information . . . ."[62]

More circumspect were Taylor's remarks concerning the Louisiana Purchase. On April 30, 1803, the United States entered into a treaty with France, whereby the United States obtained more than one million square miles of land in the Louisiana Territory for $15 million. The proposed annexation, however, raised a serious constitutional problem: there was no specific grant of power in the Constitution authorizing the acquisition of territory by the federal government. Taking the Senate floor in defense of the treaty, Taylor invoked the principle of state sovereignty to justify the exercise of federal power. Prior to the formation of the union, he reasoned, each state, being sovereign, enjoyed the right to acquire territories. Under the new Constitution, however, the states surrendered this power to the general government, as shown by Section 10, Article I, which prohibits the states from engaging in war or entering into compacts with another state or with a foreign country. The fact that neither the means nor the right of acquiring territory was forbidden to the general government was further evidence that the acquisition was constitutional. This interpretation was further supported by Article IV of the Constitution, which empowers Congress "to dispose of and regulate the territory belonging to the United States" and affirms the right of the United States to hold territory. Territory may be acquired by means of war or compact. Inasmuch as both means were expressly delegated to Congress and prohibited to the states, it necessarily followed that these attributes of sovereignty formerly possessed by each state had been transferred to the federal government and annexed to both the treaty-making power and the power to make war.

Thus did Taylor summon forth the states' rights doctrine of state sovereignty to justify a questionable exercise of federal power. This is apparently one of the few instances in which he departed from a strict constructionist premise, and it has been suggested that Taylor's legal apology for the Louisiana Purchase may have been based more on his friendship with Jefferson than on solid conviction. That Jefferson understood as well as Taylor that their constitutional position was precarious is suggested by Jefferson's pursuit of an amendment to the Constitution that would have sanctioned the purchase. If it is true that Jefferson and Taylor compromised their principles, it is also fair to say that the digression was nominal at best; for the Louisiana Purchase was a foreign rather than a domestic matter. It did not involved federal-state relations, had no discernible impact on the reserved powers of the states, and resulted in no aggrandizement of federal power at the expense of the states. What mattered most to Jefferson and the states' rights school was the context of a particular constitutional provision within the overall purpose of the Constitution, and not the text of the provision alone. Jefferson, for example, "was a strict constructionist with regard to most of the powers granted Congress in Article I, Section 8, especially where federal powers could preempt state law. Nevertheless, he could interpret federal powers under the Constitution quite liberally in matters involving foreign affairs."[63] Taylor prudently avoided mention of the constitutional controversy surrounding the Louisiana Purchase in his *Defence of the Measures of the Administration of Thomas Jefferson*, however, and defended the transaction on practical grounds—as an improvement of trade, better protection of navigation rights on the Mississippi River, and, above all, as a necessary alternative to war.[64]

No sooner was the Louisiana Purchase Treaty ratified than John Taylor returned once again to his plantation to devote all of his energies to farming. Deemed "the philosopher and statesman of agrarianism," Taylor seemed at times to be as deeply interested in agriculture as he was in the constitutional, political, and economic issues of the day. A planter's planter, Taylor once admitted that there was "a spice of fanaticism in my nature upon two subjects—agriculture and republicanism, which all who set in motion, are sure to suffer by."[65] From the time he acquired

"Hazelwood," he was acutely aware that his land, like much of the surrounding area, was exhausted and would no longer support tobacco and other remunerative crops. Determined to make his homeplace a model plantation, he inaugurated an ambitious land reform through research and experimentation, adopting innovative practices to improve seeds, plowing methods, and the fertility of the land. Soon he was recognized as one of the state's leading agricultural authorities, becoming president of both the Virginia Agriculture Society and the Richmond Agricultural Society, and a lifetime member of the Philadelphia Society for Promoting Agriculture.

In 1803, the same year as the Louisiana Purchase, Taylor began publishing a series of articles in a local newspaper, which he collected and finally published in 1813 under the title *Arator: Being a Series of Agricultural Essays, Practical and Political.*[66] As M.E. Bradford has observed, "Taylor is like Cato . . . in treating advice on farming as a species of moral instruction . . . [for] *Arator* is about the social order of an agricultural republic, and not just about farming."[67] Much of the book dealt with the agricultural reform and plantation management problems with which he was intimately familiar—better seed and fertilizers, crop rotation, care of livestock, and the like—but a considerable portion also discussed "the political state of agriculture." Agriculture, he believed, was "the guardian of liberty, as well as the mother of wealth."[68] Lamenting the decline of agricultural life in America, when government was decentralized and local leaders governed human affairs, Taylor found that conditions in rural America since independence had deteriorated to such an extent as to threaten "the liberty and prosperity" of a country, "whose hostage for both is agriculture. An order of new men, *earning a bare subsistency in low circumstances, and whose inferior rank is wretched in the extreme* cannot possibly constitute a moral force, adequate to either object."[69] Everywhere he looked he saw impoverished soil, declining production, lower profits, and "the decay . . . of small towns," abandoned "by the promise of the manufacturing mania." Indeed, "the miserable agricultural state of the country," he concluded, was "a national calamity of the highest magnitude."[70]

The solution, he surmised, was agricultural and political reform, that is, "practical improvements" in the science of farming and "preserving those we had already made" in the science of politics. At the source of the agricultural malaise was legislative indifference to the plight of the rural community, or simply bad legislation that failed to meet the needs of the farming population. But "Legislatures must begin to notice and discuss the state of agriculture before they can discover or remove the causes of the cadaverous countenance exhibited by the soil."[71] Likewise, there must be changes at the federal level regarding the system of taxation, banking, duties, and patronage that discriminate against agriculture. "A healthy state of society," he asserted, "must consist in that equable pulsation throughout all its parts, produced by an equipoise of justice, favour and protection among its several interests."[72] Enlightened legislation, then, would go a long way toward restoring the rural economy and the balance between city and country. *Arator* attracted a considerable following and proved to be Taylor's most popular work. By 1818, it had gone through six editions. Edmund Ruffin, Taylor's successor as a leader of scientific improvements in agriculture and defender of states' rights, printed a seventh edition in 1840.[73]

A companion volume to *Arator*, designed to restore the political principles of agrarian republicanism, appeared a year later, in

1814. *Arator*, he explained, "is chiefly confined to agriculture, but it contains a few political observations. The *Inquiry*, to politics; but it labours to explain the true interest of the agricultural class."[74] Regarded by some scholars as Taylor's magnum opus, *An Inquiry into the Principles and Policy of the Government of the United States*[75] was in the making for twenty years. Taylor began the book in 1794, writing when leisure permitted; but his admittedly "wild, careless, and desultory way"[76] of writing delayed publication far longer than he intended. A massive work, extending to nearly 700 pages, Taylor's *Inquiry* has been heralded as "a brilliant statement of the doctrine of separation of powers," and as "the most sustained and comprehensive defense"[77] of the pure separation of powers theory ever written. One of the few original treatises on government written by an American, the *Inquiry* has been ranked with *The Federalist* and John C. Calhoun's *Disquisition on Government* as a classic in the history of American political theory. To be sure, John Taylor of Caroline may be "the most impressive political theorist that America has produced."[78]

In essence, Taylor contended that the American political tradition is based on certain principles of government inherited from the American Revolution. The most important and fundamental of these is the principle of popular sovereignty, or the right of self-government declared in the Declaration of Independence. That principle was best embodied in the Articles of Confederation and in the constitutions of the separate states. The federal Constitution, as ratified by the people through conventions, sought to protect the sovereignty of the people by means of a division of power between the federal and state governments. The federal system, in other words, served as the principal guardian of the people's liberties.

The tripartite separation of powers system providing for three branches of government at the federal level, instead of complementing and reinforcing the division of powers so as to give added protection to the people's liberties, had actually served to subvert their liberties and undermine popular sovereignty. This had been accomplished through the growth of executive and judicial power. In Taylor's view, the separation of powers arrangement had vitiated the principle that the executive and judicial power should be subordinated to the people. The president could create judges, but the people could not remove them. Moreover, the Supreme Court's power to make or abolish laws by creating or manipulating precedents, or by arbitrary construction, blurred the separation of powers. It was exceedingly strange, thought Taylor, that "judicial power has never appeared in any political system, completely independent of the sovereign power, except under the Constitution of the United States."[79] The conclusion seemed inescapable, that even though the republican principle stipulated that only the people may alter the constitution, in reality, the people's Constitution was subject to a power of construction that was not responsible to the people. The Constitution was fundamentally flawed.

What was the source of this separation of powers problem, and how might it be corrected? At bottom, reasoned Taylor, the elaborate check and balance system engrafted onto the separation of powers scheme at the Federal Convention was the culprit. More specifically, the cause of the mischief was John Adams's three-volume *Defence of the Constitution of the United States* (1787), which provided the inspiration and rationale for the checks and balances arrangement finally adopted. Taylor believed that Adams's basic mistake was classifying governments into monarchy, aristocracy, and democracy, structuring government around social classes, and seeking to limit power by balancing one order against another. The authors of *The Federalist*, who perpetuated these foreign anachronisms, had paid too much attention to "political skeletons" constructed with fragments torn from the illusory monarchy, aristocracy, and democracy model or what Taylor described as "the numerical analysis." These "rude almost savage political fabrics," said Taylor, had no application in America and could hardly be expected to provide the materials for an American system of government. To create a government in the New World based on this design was "like that of erecting a palace with materials drawn from Indian cabins."[80]

Adams's mistake was assuming that an aristocracy was "natural," thereby committing us to an acceptance of its evil characteristics. In America, there was no reason to accept the aristocratic yoke. Taylor condemned both the feudal aristocracy and the new aristocracy of "paper and patronage," *i.e.*, the bank and moneyed interests and the president's patronage system. Neither was inevitable or desirable. Governments ought to be constructed, he insisted, on the basis of man's moral qualities, not fixed orders. Since the American political tradition was "rooted in moral or intellectual principles, not in orders, clans or casts, natural or factitious," Adams was wrong in assuming that we are necessarily governed by a natural aristocracy, and therefore wrong again in calling for a king or single independent executive power and a house of popular representatives to balance it. In short, Adams's peculiar blend of a mixed and balanced constitution was "bottomed upon a classification of men, our [state] constitutions upon an application of moral principles to human nature."[81] The basic distinction between Taylor and

Adams, as Taylor put it, was that "our policy divides power, and
unites the nation in one interest; Mr. Adams's divides a nation
into several interests and unites power." Thus, "instead of balancing power, we divide it and make it responsible, to prevent the
evils of its accumulation in the hands of one interest."[82]

What was to be done? Our only recourse, Taylor concluded,
was to amend the Constitution and restore the sovereignty of the
people. This entailed limiting the president to one brief term, in
order to reduce his incentive for amassing a legislative following; elimination of executive privilege, secrecy being anathema to
democratic republics; and curtailing his patronage power, his military and diplomatic powers, and his power to appoint judges.

The *Inquiry* also proposed reform of the judiciary in order to
protect the sovereignty of the people. The judicial branch of the
federal government should therefore become elective, and judicial review of legislation should be abolished. The proper role of
the judiciary, noted Taylor, is to enforce the law, but "admitting
that a power of construction is nearly equivalent to a power of
legislating, why should construction of law be quite independent
of sovereign will, when law itself is made completely subservient
to it?"[83]

Taylor provided Adams with sections of the book as they came
from the presses, but without signature or explanation until the
entire work had been forwarded. "Who he is, I cannot conjecture," wrote Adams to Jefferson. "The Honorable John Taylor, of
Virginia, of all men living or dead, first occurred to me."[84] Adams
had paid little attention to the attacks on his *Defence* in years
past, but he was probably as flattered as he was surprised that
someone of Taylor's "high rank, ample fortune, learned education, and powerful connections"[85] had endeavored to refute him

more than a quarter century after the *Defence* was published. Thus began an extended correspondence between Adams and Taylor, who maintained a friendly and respectful relationship despite their differences. Adams complained–and with some justification–that Taylor had misread parts of the book, and proceeded to offer "a few explanations and justifications of a book that has been misunderstood, misrepresented, and abused, more than any other, except the Bible,"[86] ever since it was published. In a series of thirty-two letters written over a five-year period, Adams proceeded to enlarge upon his views and expound upon his philosophy of government. By the time he wrote his thirtieth letter, however, he had reached only the twelfth page. Adams insisted, nevertheless, that he should have as long to answer as Taylor had to write the criticisms.[87] Adams finally abandoned the project in his eightieth year when his hand trembled so much that he could not hold a pen.

Who besides John Adams read John Taylor's *Inquiry*? Henry Adams wishfully reckoned that it "was probably never read,—or if read, certainly never understood,—north of Baltimore by any but curious and somewhat deep students . . . ."[88] We know, however, that leading political figures of the day examined the work. Thomas Jefferson, although he had endorsed Adams's *Defence* in 1787, heartily approved of the *Inquiry*, found parts of it very absorbing, and thought John Taylor had "completely pulverized"[89] Adams's separation of powers theory. There is no question, however, that Taylor's convoluted and tediously prolix literary style rendered the *Inquiry*, as well as his other writings, a formidable challenge to the reader and undermined his influence. Even Taylor's friends were exasperated with his diffuse, sometimes incoherent ramblings. Thomas Hart Benton found his writings dressed "in a quaint Sir Edward Coke style,"[90] and John Randolph was given to remark, after taking up the *Inquiry*: "For heaven's sake, get some worthy person . . . to do a second edition in *English*."[91] Some modern scholars, however, have a more generous view, and the advice of a British scholar, who is persuaded that Taylor "was in some ways the most impressive political theorist that America has produced,"[92] seems well taken. Taylor's style, he concludes, "was loose and undisciplined, and the length and repetitiveness of his works was hardly designed to make him a truly popular author. Yet if the initial effort is made to overcome the barrier of his prose style, the ultimate impression is one of great clarity and consistency, together with a certain charm."[93]

New Views of the Constitution

From 1800 to 1824, Virginia Republicans, in the persons of Thomas Jefferson, James Madison, and James Monroe, monopolized the presidency. "The history of the Antebellum Period," as a noted student of American political thought has observed, "reveals that in all but twenty of the seventy years of Union under the Federal Constitution, a Southern president occupied the White House. And for a good percentage of those remaining years, the Northern president was a man with Southern sympathies."[94] In this political climate, John Taylor's self-imposed exile to the Virginia countryside, and preoccupation with plantation life, agricultural affairs, and political theory, seemed altogether prudent and reliably secure. There were, of course, important political events demanding attention, including elections, the War of 1812, and the Hartford Convention of 1814, which brought New England to the brink of secession. Then, too, momentous constitutional issues involving such matters as the power of Congress to recharter a national bank and provide for internal improvements were the common, almost daily order of affairs in Washington.

But the situation in 1815 from Taylor's perspective was reasonably under control. Jefferson, Madison, and Monroe had all applied the yardstick of strict construction to defeat internal improvements legislation. The Supreme Court was still in a passive state, the war with Great Britain had ended, sinking the Hartford Convention and humiliating the Essex Junto in Massachusetts. Even Madison had vetoed the bill to recharter the Bank of the United States. With the election of Monroe in 1816, and the Federalists too weak to be an effective minority, the United States seemed to be entering what the historians would later call the "Era of Good Feeling." What better time for John Taylor to debate John Adams on questions of political theory instead of arguing with members of Congress on public policy issues.

It is commonly assumed that the Missouri Compromise of 1820 and the sudden emergence of the increasingly dominant issue of slavery in the territories—the "fireball in the night," as Jefferson put it–marked the great turning point in the sectional conflict that led to the War Between the States. A closer examination of the period suggests, however, that the watershed year was 1816. That was the year President Madison, shortly before leaving office, changed his stance and signed the bill to recharter the Bank of the United States. That was also the year a Republican Congress passed a new tariff law. Since the beginning of Washington's administration, the tariff had been gradually raised until by 1812 it had reached a level of about twelve and a half percent. During the war, the rate was raised to twenty-five percent, with the expectation that it would be lowered with the coming of peace. The Tariff Act of 1816, in anticipation of the "Tariff of Abominations" of 1828, not only retained the war rate but even raised it on some articles.

No less foreboding was the sudden turnabout of the Supreme Court, and the new onslaught of unprecedented decisions expanding the powers of the Congress and the federal judiciary. The first of these, and in many respects the most damaging to states' rights, was Justice Story's ruling in 1816 in the case of *Martin v. Hunter's Lessee*,[95] in which the Court upheld the constitutionality of section 25 of the Judiciary Act of 1789, a statute enacted by the Federalists in the First Congress that authorized the Supreme Court to review decisions of the state courts. The impact of the decision on federal-state relations was revolutionary, and over the years has proved to be "the keystone of the whole arch of Federal judicial power."[96] *Cohens v. Virginia*,[97] decided a few years later through an opinion by Chief Justice John Marshall, affirmed *Martin* and extended the principle of judicial review of state court decisions to include criminal cases. Even more controversial was Marshall's opinion in the landmark case of *McCulloch v. Maryland*,[98] in which the Supreme Court established a broad interpretation of Congress's implied powers under the Necessary and Proper Clause of the Constitution.

These decisions, as well as the actions of Congress, drew Taylor out of retirement. Though back in the Senate, where he was once again in active opposition to the nationalists, events would prove that "it is as a thinker and author, and not as an active statesman, that Taylor's career was most significant."[99] In rapid succession, he produced three books in the space of four years. In 1820, he published *Construction Construed and Constitutions Vindicated*,[100] an assault on the constitutionality of both Marshall's decision in the *McCulloch* case and the Missouri Compromise. Much of his commentary on the Missouri Compromise is an insightful prophecy anticipating the heightened sectional hostilities that swept across the land and the Supreme Court's decision in the Dred Scott case.[101] Particularly striking were his concluding remarks:

> There remains a right, anterior to every political power whatsoever, and alone sufficient to put the subject of slavery at rest; the natural right of self-defence. . . . It is allowed on all hands, that danger to the slave-holding states lurks in their existing situation, however it has been produced; and it must be admitted, that the right of self-defence applies to that situation, of the necessity for which the parties exposed to the danger are the natural judges: otherwise this right, the most sacred of all possessed by men, would be no right at all. I leave to the reader the application of these observations.[102]

In 1822, Taylor published a repudiation of the new tariff legislation under the sensational title of *Tyranny Unmasked*.[103] It has been described as "the first extensive argument against protectionist theory in the United States."[104] Taylor offered the work at a time when Hamilton's *Report on Manufactures* was being resurrected, and most of the text is devoted to assailing the Report of the House Committee on Manufactures (January 15, 1821) calling for tariffs to help expand industry. The third and last section of the book, however, is a vigorous assault on the new judicial activism of the Marshall Court, culminating in an extended list of inconsistencies produced by the Supreme Court between established principles of the Constitution and the Court's arbitrary interpretation of them. Taylor's complaint that "no effort has ever been made by Congress to defend State rights against judicial construction"[105] was taken to task by conservative Republicans, who almost succeeded in the 1820s in repealing section 25 of the Judiciary Act of 1789.[106]

Taylor's third and final work on the Constitution, which should be read in tandem with the *Inquiry, Construction Construed,* and *Tyranny Unmasked* in order to see the full panoply of Taylor's constitutional philosophy, was his *New Views of the Constitution of the United States*, published in 1823. This book differs considerably from Taylor's other writings on the Constitution and is not a reconsideration of his earlier thoughts, but the introduction of new materials into the debate on the proper interpretation of the Constitution. From 1789 down to the publication of *New Views*, American political leaders and members of the bar had struggled with the fact that the original intent of the Framers was, in many cases, a mystery. The proceedings of the Federal Convention, it will be recalled, were held in secrecy. The Journal that was kept during the course of the deliberations, recording only the votes taken, had been given to Washington when the Convention adjourned. Washington in turn deposited the Journal with the Department of State. A few members of the Convention, including Madison, had kept notes on the debates, but by the common agreement on secrecy withheld them from the public.[107]

Hence, the only original founding documents extant for a number of years were the debates of the state ratifying conventions. Only five states kept a record of their proceedings, however, and many of these were incomplete and fragmentary. But not until 1836, when Jonathan Elliott published the *Debates in the Several State Conventions on the Adoption of the Constitution*,[108] did interested parties have ready access to the ratification debates. This left only the essays written by the Federalists and Anti-Federalists during the ratification struggle as sources–and secondary at that–of information on the thinking of those who framed and adopted the federal Constitution. Since the Anti-Federalist essays were never collected and reprinted, the Federalist papers written by Hamilton, Madison, and Jay were virtually the only materials available in the early republic that shed light on the original intent and meaning of the Constitution, other than the document itself.

What occasioned the publication of John Taylor's *New Views of the Constitution*, and gave it its title, was the decision of Congress in 1818 to break the pledge of secrecy and publish the Journal. Once the seal of secrecy was broken, the notes taken by Robert Yates, a delegate to the Federal Convention from New York, were also released and published in Albany (1821) under the title of *Secret Proceedings and Debates of the Convention Assembled at Philadelphia, in the Year 1787, for the purpose of forming the Constitution of the United States of America. From Notes taken by the late Robert Yates, Esq. Chief Justice of New York, and copied by John Lansing, etc.*[109] Unfortunately, Yates's notes ceased with the fifth of July. Only Madison, of course, had notes on the entire Convention. He steadfastly refused to release them, however, and it was not until 1840 that the public had an opportunity to see his notes or review the Convention debates in their entirety. In retrospect, it is no exaggeration to say that Madison's decision to withhold his convention notes may have seriously undermined the states' rights movement, or possibly doomed it. As Taylor observed, if "the journal of the convention [had] been published immediately after the ratification . . . it would have furnished lights towards a true construction sufficiently clear to have prevented several trespasses upon its principles. . . ."[110]

Armed now with original source material on the intent of the Framers, Taylor proceeded in *New Views* to examine the constitutional law of the Supreme Court and the essays in *The Federalist* in the light of the Journal and Yates's notes. What he discovered were distortions of original meaning and a nationalistic bias permeating *The Federalist*. The reader is invited to follow him on his search for truth, and to judge the veracity of his findings.

That Taylor's *New Views of the Constitution* had an impact on the thinking of his generation–and may now exert an even greater influence–seems clear enough. The only question is the degree to which his work affected others. Though it was largely ignored in the Northern journals, *New Views* was welcomed in *The Southern Review* (1830) in a review essay appearing under the title "The Tribunal of Dernier Resort."[111] The anonymous author, believed to have been a South Carolina judge, wrote a thoughtful review that also included a critique of Justice Story's opinion in *Martin v. Hunter's Lessee*. In substantial agreement with Taylor, he recommended the book as "a body of valuable information and considerable original thought."[112]

It is also apparent that Jefferson read the book, and that John C. Calhoun relied upon Taylor during the course of his gradual transformation from a nationalist to a states' rightist–particularly after he turned to intensive constitutional studies in the summer and fall of 1828. It has been pointed out, for example, that Calhoun adopted and elaborated upon Taylor's doctrine that the central and state governments possess the right to veto the acts of each other.[113] Calhoun, in fact, visited Taylor at "Hazelwood" in April 1823, just months before his death. "I have no more decided friend that Colo. Taylor, " he told one correspondent, "who I was happy to find knew very accurately the course of political events for the last 2 years. His differing with me on constitutional points will only add to the weight of his opinion."[114] Writing to another friend a month later, he reported that "I was much gratified with my visit to Colo. Taylor . . . [H]e is my decided friend, tho' we differ on constitutional points. No man except Mr. Jefferson has more weight in Virginia . . . ."[115] In 1842, some twenty years later, after Calhoun had decided to reduce his views to a systematic form and write a book on government, he was asked by William H. Roane, while Calhoun was passing through Richmond on his way to Washington, about the nature of his projected treatise. Calhoun is reported to have "discussed the project freely, giving Roane the impression that the result was to be 'John Taylor of Caroline with metaphysical variations.'"[116]

On another occasion, a friend and supporter from New York, writing to tell Calhoun that his Senate speech and his exposition of the federative system reminded him of John Taylor, recalled:

I read many years ago "New Views of the Constitution" by John Taylor of Caroline Va. and one remark of
the author in that work was so evidently clear to me,
that I have been a states rights Republican ever since.
It was in substance that if any state of the confederation opposed or resisted an unconstitutional act of the
General Government, the opposition in such a case
would be the act of the sovereign state, and as such
command consideration and respect, while if the
Government was national and a consolidated one, the
conduct of the State would be rebellion and treason.[117]

It is interesting to speculate on the fate of Judge Story, and of
the United States, had he read John Taylor's *New Views of the Constitution*. Like Taylor, he read the Journal of the Federal Convention and Yates's *Minutes*, but not as carefully, and with different
results. In his *Commentaries on the Constitution*, published in 1833,
he incorporated material from these sources into his analysis, and
cited them liberally to support his interpretations. Perhaps the
most important piece of information that he gleaned from them,
and used as the cornerstone in his edifice of nationalism, was that
"the very first resolution adopted by the Convention (six states
to two states) was that a national government be set up with a
supreme legislature, judiciary and executive." This, said Story,
was proof enough that the Framers intended to establish "a
national constitution," and that the vote for the resolution was
"plainly showing that it was a national government, not a com
pact, which they were about to establish. . . ."[118] Had Judge Story
read a little further into the Journal or into Yates's *Minutes*, or

better still, consulted John Taylor's *New Views*, he would have learned that this resolution was later expressly revoked.

Such are the consequences of ignoring John Taylor of Caroline and his startling revelations in this powerful little book.

James McClellan
James Bryce Visiting Fellow in American Studies
Institute of U.S. Studies
University of London

Notes

1. *Life and Letters of Joseph Story*, ed. by William W. Story (Boston: Little Brown, 1851), II: 506. Story's remark is taken from memoranda left by one of his students, and was apparently made toward the close of his career.
2. Elizabeth K. Bauer, *Commentaries on the Constitution, 1790–1860* (New York: Columbia University Press, 1952), 194.
3. *Ibid.*
4. Joseph Story, *Commentaries on the Constitution of the United States*, 3 vols. (Boston: Little Brown, 1833).
5. St. George Tucker, *Blackstone's Commentaries: With Notes of References to the Constitution and Laws of the United States and of the Commonwealth of Virginia*, 5 vols. (Philadelphia: William Birch Young and Abraham, 1803). Tucker's commentary on the American Constitution, originally in an appendix to this work, has now been published separately. See St. George Tucker, *View of the Constitution of the United States*, ed. by Clyde Wilson (Indianapolis: Liberty Fund, 1999).
6. The Kentucky and Virginia Resolutions of 1798 and Madison's Report of 1799-1800 on the Virginia Resolutions are published in Jonathan Elliot, ed., *The Debates in the Several State Conventions on the Adoption of the Federal Constitution* (Philadelphia: J.B. Lippincott, 1836), IV: 528-580. A later and better edition that includes the debates on the Virginia Resolutions in the House of Delegates, the House's Instructions to Virginia Senators, and letters from James Madison explaining his apparent inconsistencies was published under the title of *The Virginia Report of 1799–1800 Touching the Alien and Sedition Laws, Together with the Virginia Resolutions of December 21, 1798* (Richmond: J.W. Randolph, 1850), reprinted by Da Capo Press, 1970). This edition also contains the Kentucky Resolutions of 1798, but unfortunately omits Kentucky's second set of resolutions in 1799. See also *Resolutions of Virginia and Kentucky Penned by Madison and Jefferson in Relation to the Alien and Sedition Laws, and Debates in the House of Delegates of Virginia, 1798* (Richmond: Robert I. Smith, 1832); Ethelbert Dudley Warfield, *The Kentucky Resolutions of 1798: An Historical Study* (New York: G.P. Putnam's Sons, 1894). As Warfield notes, Elliot's edition omits an

important clause from the Kentucky Resolutions. See his account of the confusion, *ibid.*, 183.

7. Story, *Commentaries on the Constitution*, I: 343.

8. *Ibid.*, 442.

9. Vernon Parrington, *Main Currents in American Thought, 1800–1860* (New York: Harcourt Brace, 1927), II: 14.

10. Thomas Jefferson, *Notes on the State of Virginia*, ed. by William Penden (Chapel Hill: University of North Carolina Press, 1955). This work was originally published in 1785, without the author's name, by a French printer. He printed only two hundred copies for private distribution. The first edition in English was published in London in 1787. The first edition to include Jefferson's annotations was the Randolph edition, published in 1853 in Richmond, Virginia.

11. As quoted in Benjhamin F. Wright, "The Philosopher of Jeffersonian Democracy," XXII *American Political Science Review* 870 (1928).

12. William Cabell Bruce, *John Randolph of Roanoke* (New York: G.P. Putnam's Sons, 1922), II: 235. Although Randolph and Taylor were good friends and close political allies, Taylor found the relationship somewhat painful at times because of Randolph's eccentricities and vitriolic attacks on Thomas Jefferson. See Robert E. Shalhope, *John Taylor of Caroline: Pastoral Republican* (Columbia: University of South Carolina Press, 1980), 124.

13. Charles A. Beard, *Economic Origins of Jeffersonian Democracy* (New York: Free Press, 1943), 323.

14. Wright, "Philosopher of Jeffersonian Democracy," 892.

15. C. William Hill, Jr., *The Political Theory of John Taylor of Caroline* (Rutherford: Fairleigh Dickinson University Press, 1977); Robert E. Shalhope, *John Taylor of Caroline: Pastoral Republican* (Columbia: University of South Carolina Press, 1980). Three notable earlier studies are William E. Dodd, "John Taylor, Prophet of Secession," *The John P. Branch Historical Papers of Randolph-Macon College*, II: 214-52; Henry H. Simms, *Life of John Taylor* (Richmond: The William Byrd Press, 1932); Eugene Tenbroeck Mudge, *The Social Philosophy of John Taylor of Caroline* (New York: Columbia University Press, 1939).

16. These include *A Defence of the Measures of the Administration of Thomas Jefferson* (Union, New Jersey: The Lawbook Exchange,

1999); *Arator; Being a Series of Agricultural Essays, Practical and Political in Sixty-Four Numbers*, ed. by M.E. Bradford (Indianapolis: Liberty Fund, 1977); *An Inquiry into the Principles and Policy of the Government of the United States*, ed. by Loren Baritz (Indianapolis: Bobbs-Merrill, 1969); *Tyranny Unmasked*, ed. by Thornton Miller (Indianapolis: Liberty Fund, 1992); *Construction Construed and Constitutions Vindicated* (New York: Da Capo Press, 1970). Da Capo also published a facsimile reprint of *New Views of the Constitution of the United States* in 1971.

17. Dodd, for example, claims that Taylor was born near James Madison in Orange County in 1754. William E. Dodd, "John Taylor of Caroline, Prophet of Secession," 214. Benjamin F. Wright also says he was born in Orange County, but in 1750. See Shalhope, *John Taylor of Caroline*, 14 n.2; Hill, *The Political Theory of John Taylor of Caroline*, 36 n.19, 20.

18. Taylor apparently assumed the name "John Taylor of Caroline" in 1781, when he returned to the Virginia Assembly, in order to distinguish himself from a Southhampton delegate bearing the same name. Shalhope, *John Taylor of Caroline*, 31.

19. Influenced by Patrick Henry and Richard Henry Lee, who were dissatisfied with Washington's command, and believing the revolutionary effort was being mismanaged, Taylor resigned his commission to return to Virginia and run for the House of Delegates. Washington was nevertheless impressed with Taylor's character and ability as an officer. Shalhope, *John Taylor of Caroline*, 25.

20. Hill, *The Political Theory of John Taylor*, 223.

21. Simms, *Life of John Taylor*, 11.

22. *Ibid.*, 12

23. Shalhope, *John Taylor of Caroline,* 30.

24. Baritz, Introduction to Taylor's *Inquiry into the Principles and Policy of the Government of the United States*, xiii.

25. Henry Adams, *History of the United States during the Administration of James Madison*, IX (New York: Charles Scribner's Sons, 1890), 197. "John Taylor," said Adams, "might without irreverence be described as a *vox clamantis*,—the voice of one crying in the wilderness." *Ibid.*, 195.

26. Baritz, Introduction to Taylor's *Inquiry into the Principles and Policy of the Government of the United States*, xii.

27. M.E. Bradford, "A Virginia Cato: John Taylor of Caroline and the Agrarian Republic," in *The Reactionary Imperative* (Peru, Illinois: Sherwood Sugden, 1990), 159.

28. Richard Henry Lee, a signer of the Declaration of Independence and a lifelong friend of both John and Samuel Adams, refused to attend the Constitutional Convention and opposed ratification. With Taylor's support, he became Virginia's first senator in 1789 but was incapacitated because of tuberculosis and resigned in 1792. Lee died in 1794.

29. James Madison to Edmund Pendleton, February 23, 1793, *The Papers of James Madison*, ed. by Robert Rutland *et al.* (Charlottesville: University of Virginia Press, 1983), XIV: 451.

30. As quoted in Shalhope, *John Taylor of Caroline*, 206.

31. Thomas Hart Benton, *Thirty Years' View; or, a History of the Working of the American Government for Thirty Years, from 1820 to 1850* (New York: D. Appleton, 1854), I: 45. In his obituary (August 24, 1824), Thomas Ritchie, editor of the Richmond *Enquirer* and conservative Republican, described Taylor as "The great lawyer—the profound politician—the *friend of the Constitution in its original purity* . . . who by precept and example has scattered a flood of light over agriculture. . . . Let Virginia weep over the ashes of the illustrious patriot." As quoted in Simms, *Life of John Taylor*, 210. (Emphasis supplied.) Ritchie wrote the preface to Taylor's *Construction Construed and Constitutions Vindicated* (1820), informing the reader that "we have arrived at a crisis, when the first principles of the government and some of the dearest rights are threatened with being utterly ground into dust and ashes. . . . The period is, indeed, by no means an agreeable one. It borrows new gloom from the apathy which seems to reign over so many of our sister states. The very sound of the State Rights is scarcely ever heard among them; and by many of their eminent politicians, it is only heard to be mocked at. But a good citizen will never despair of the republic. Among these good citizens is John Taylor, of Caroline." ii-iii. In 1808, Ritchie and Taylor quarreled over the election of Madison and related political issues, but soon settled their differences. See Simms, *Life of John Taylor*, 122-25.

32. *Disunion Sentiment in Congress in 1794: A Confidential Memorandum Hitherto Unpublished Written by John Taylor of Caroline . . .* , ed. by

Gaillard Hunt (Washington, D.C.: W.H. Lowdermilk, 1905), 11. Taylor's memorandum, omitting Hunt's introduction, is also published in *The Papers of James Madison*, ed. by Thomas A. Mason *et al.* (Charlottesville: University of Virginia), XV: 328-31.

33. *Disunion Sentiment in Congress*, 13.

34. The Hartford Convention, called at the invitation of the Massachusetts legislature, was a secret meeting of twenty-six leading Federalists from Massachusetts, Connecticut, and Rhode Island, who met in Hartford, Connecticut in 1814–1815 for the declared purpose of calling a convention to revise the Constitution, with a view in the minds of some delegates toward New England secession. The convention was promoted by New England opposition to "Mr. Madison's War" and frustration by the continued domination of the Virginia Republicans in national affairs. The delegates included Nathan Dane, a prominent lawyer and friend of Joseph Story who helped to found the Harvard Law School and endowed Story's professorship. Two representatives from New Hampshire and one from Vermont were also admitted. When it adjourned, the Convention published a report, using some of the exact language that Madison had used in the Virginia Resolutions of 1798. The Journal of the Convention was not published until 1833. A committee was appointed to present the Convention's resolutions to Congress, but abandoned its mission when news reached Washington of General Jackson's victory in New Orleans. See Timothy Dwight, *History of the Hartford Convention* (New York: N&J White, 1833); James M. Banner, Jr., *To the Hartford Convention: The Federalists and the Origins of Party Politics in Massachusetts, 1789–1815* (New York: Alfred A. Knopf, 1970).

35. *Disunion Sentiment in Congress*, 1.

36. Responding to a letter from Taylor that has apparently been lost, Jefferson indicated that Taylor advised him to consider the separation of Virginia and North Carolina from the union in the wake of the Alien and Sedition Acts. Though seriously alarmed by this oppressive legislation, Jefferson cautioned patience, correctly anticipating the electoral defeat of the Federalists in 1800 and the end of the "reign of witches." Thomas Jefferson to John Taylor, June 1, 1798, *The Writings of Thomas Jefferson*, ed. by Andrew Lipscomb and Albert Bergh (Washington, D.C.: Memorial edition, 1905),

X: 44–47. Less than a month later, Taylor conceived the idea of the Virginia Resolutions. See note 39, *infra*.

37. *The Virginia Report . . . Together with the Virginia Resolutions,* 20.

38. As quoted in Norman K. Risjord, *The Old Republicans: Southern Conservatism in the Age of Jefferson* (New York: Columbia University Press, 1965), 15. Albert Gallatin agreed, and endorsed Livingston's concept of resistance to unconstitutional measures as a "doctrine" that is "strictly correct and neither seditious nor treasonable." *Ibid.*

39. John Taylor to Thomas Jefferson, June 25, 1798, in William Dodd, ed., "John Taylor Correspondence," *John P. Branch Historical Papers of Randolph-Macon College,* II: 276.

40. *Ibid.*

41. As quoted in Jesse T. Carpenter, *The South as a Conscious Minority, 1798–1861* (New York: New York University Press, 1930), 209. Reprinted by University of South Carolina Press, 1990.

42. *The Federalist,* ed. by George W. Carey and James McClellan (Dubuque, Iowa: Kendall-Hunt, 1990), 141.

43. *The Virginia Report . . . Together with the Virginia Resolutions,* 177. The most extensive reply came from the Senate of the Massachusetts legislature, which asserted that it "cannot admit the right of the state legislatures to denounce the administration of that government to which the people themselves, by a solemn *compact,* have exclusively committed their concerns." *Ibid.*, 170 (Emphasis supplied.)

44. Elliot, *Debates,* IV: 545.

45. *The Virginia Report . . . Together with the Virginia Resolutions,* 178–237.

46. *Ibid.,* 162.

47. *Ibid.,* 22.

48. *Ibid.,* 120.

49. Elliot, *Ibid.,* III: 22.

50. *Ibid.,* 94. See also James Jackson Kilpatrick, *The Soverign States* (Chicago: Henry Regnery, 1957), 13–18.

51. *The Virginia Report . . . Together with the Virginia Resolutions,* 112.

52. *Ibid.,* 162.

53. *Ibid.*

54. Elliot, *Debates,* IV: 545. Jefferson had included the specific remedy of "nullification" in his original draft of the first Kentucky Resolutions, but it was stricken by the legislature. What the legislature

meant by "nullification" is not entirely clear, given the assurance in the last paragraph of the 1799 Resolutions that Kentucky "will not now, or ever hereafter, cease to oppose in a constitutional manner every attempt . . . to violate that compact."

55. *The Virginia Report . . . Together with the Virginia Resolutions*, 22. In *Federalist No. 46*, Madison explained the means by which encroachments by the federal government might be resisted under the new Constitution, in language which resembles the invocation of the "interposition" in the Virginia Resolutions. If Congress passes an objectionable act, he wrote, "the means of opposition to it are powerful and at hand. The disquietude of the people; their repugnance and, perhaps, refusal to cooperate with the officers of the Union; the frowns of the executive magistracy of the State, the embarrassments created by legislative devices, which would often be added on such occasions, would oppose, in any State, very serious impediments; and where the sentiments of several adjoining States happened to be in unison, would present obstructions which the Federal government would hardly be willing to encounter." *The Federalist*, 242-43 (note Madison's use of the term "interposition" in this essay, at 242).

56. See Kilpatrick, *The Sovereign States*, 96.

57. *The Virginia Report . . . Together with the Virginia Resolutions*, 230-31.

58. *Ibid.*, 192. On the differences between Madison and Jefferson as reflected in the Kentucky and Virginia Resolutions, see Saul Cornell, *Anti-Federalism and the Dissenting Tradition in America, 1788–1828* (Chapel Hill: University of North Carolina Press, 1999), 240-45.

59. As quoted in Shalhope, *John Taylor of Caroline*, 124. See also Kevin R. Gutzman, "A Troublesome Legacy: James Madison and the 'Principles of '98,'" *Journal of the Early Republic*, XV: 569-89 (1995).

60. Henry Adams, as quoted in Risjord, *The Old Republicans*, 121.

61. The members of the Federal Convention pledged themselves to maintaining the secrecy of their proceedings after adjournment. Those delegates who took notes on the debates, including Madison, therefore declined to make a public disclosure of their personal recordings. This situation radically changed in 1819, however, when Congress ordered the Journal to be printed. See p. lii, *infra*.

62. John Taylor [Curtius], *A Defence of the Measures of the Administration of Thomas Jefferson* (Washington: Samuel M. Smith, 1804), 15. While

serving in the Senate, Taylor was instrumental in the creation of the Twelfth Amendment to the Constitution, providing for separate ballots for president and vice president. The Amendment was ratified in 1804.

63. David N. Mayer, *The Constitutional Thought of Thomas Jefferson* (Charlottesville: University of Virginia Press, 1994) 194, 215. For a discussion of the constitutional issues attending the Louisiana Purchase, see Everett S. Brown, *The Constitutional History of the Louisiana Purchase, 1803–1812* (Berkeley: University of California Press, 1920). Jefferson's rules of interpretation, criticized by Judge Story in his *Commentaries on the Constitution*, I, § 407, 390–92, asserted that "The capital and leading object of the Constitution was, to leave with the states all authorities, which respected their own citizens only, and to transfer to the United States those, which respected citizens of foreign or other states; to make us several to ourselves, but one to all others. In the latter case, then, constructions should lean to the general jurisdiction, if the words will bear it; and in favour of the states in the former, if *possible*, to be so construed." *Ibid.*, 390 n.1. Taylor's constitutional interpretations of the issue are in Brown, *Constitutional History of the Louisiana Purchase*, 57. John Randolph also saw no states' rights interests at stake. "Upon the question of the right to acquire territory, Randolph of Virginia stood, in the House, as the champion of broad construction of the Constitution." *Ibid.*, 63. Even many Federalists, including John Adams, admitted that the constitutional objections raised by some members of their party were groundless. Senator Timothy Pickering of Massachusetts, for example, "had never doubted the right of the United States to acquire new territory either by purchase or conquest and to govern the territory so acquired as a dependent province." *Ibid.*, 56.

64. Taylor, *Defence of the Measures of the Administration of Thomas Jefferson*, 132.

65. John Taylor to Thomas Jefferson, March 5, 1795, as quoted in Shalhope, *John Taylor of Caroline*, 108.

66. John Taylor, *Arator; Being a Series of Agricultural Essays, Practical and Political in Sixty-Four Numbers*, ed. by M.E. Bradford (Indianapolis: Liberty Fund, 1977).

67. *Ibid.*, 37.

68. *Ibid.*, 58

69. *Ibid.*, 66. *Arator* was inspired to a very large extent by William Strickland's *Observations on the Agriculture of the United States* (London, 1801). Reissued with *Journal of a Tour of the United States of America, 1794–1795* in an edition prepared by the Rev. J.E. Strickland (Charlottesville: University of Virginia Press, 1976). An Englishman, Strickland toured the United States, from New England as far South as Virginia, and found that agricultural decline "has pervaded all the states," and that "Land in America affords little pleasure or profit, and appears in a progress of continually affording less."Virginia, in particular, he wrote "is in a rapid decline," where agriculture has "already arrived at its lowest state of degradation." As quoted in *Arator*, 66.

70. Taylor, *Arator*, 73.

71. *Ibid.*, 50, 54.

72. *Ibid.*, 56.

73. Edmund Ruffin of Virginia (1794–1865), a pioneer in agricultural reform who followed in the footsteps of John Taylor, published a number of scientific studies, including a highly acclaimed *Essay on Calcareous Manures* (1832). Also active politically, he founded the League of United Southerners and served in three secession conventions. As a volunteer with the Charleston Palmetto Guard in South Carolina, he was given the honor of firing the first shot against Fort Sumter. Rather than live under Yankee rule, he took his own life in 1865 when the Confederacy collapsed.

74. Taylor, *Arator*, 50.

75. John Taylor, *An Inquiry into the Principles and Policy of the Government of the United States*, ed. by Loren Baritz (Indianapolis: Bobbs-Merrill, 1969).

76. John Taylor to Aaron Burr, as quoted in Baritz, *ibid.*, xxiv.

77. M.J.C. Vile, *Constitutionalism and the Separation of Powers*, 2d ed. (Indianapolis: Liberty Fund, 1998), 183.

78. *Ibid.*

79. Taylor, *An Inquiry into the Principles . . . of the United States,* 188.

80. *Ibid.*, 4.

81. *Ibid.*, 79.

82. *Ibid.*, 82

83. *Ibid.*, 203

84. John Adams to Thomas Jefferson, September 15, 1813, *The Works of John Adams*, ed. by Charles Francis Adams (Boston: Little Brown, 1851), X: 70.

85. John Adams to John Taylor, April 15, 1814, *Works of Adams*, VI: 447.

86. *Ibid.*

87. For a discussion of John Adams's separation of powers theory and his *Defence of the Constitutions of the United States*, see C. Bradley Thompson, *John Adams and the Spirit of Liberty* (Lawrence: University Press of Kansas, 1998), *passim.*

88. Henry Adams, *History of the United States during the Administration of James Madison*, X: 194–95.

89. Thomas Jefferson to John Taylor, May 23, 1816, *Writings of Thomas Jefferson*, XV: 19.

90. As quoted in Parrington, *Main Currents in American Thought*, 15. This may explain Justice Story's apparent lack of interest in Taylor's work. As a law student, Story found *Coke on Littleton* almost incomprehensible. "I took it up," recalled Story, "and after trying it day after day with very little success, I sat myself down and wept bitterly. My tears dropped upon the book, and stained its pages." As quoted in McClellan, *Joseph Story and the American Constitution*, 13–14.

91. As quoted in Bruce, *Randolph of Roanoke*, II: 622.

92. Vile, *Constitutionalism and the Separation of Powers*, 183.

93. *Ibid.* Norman Risjord dissents, however, and argues that Taylor's *Inquiry* was "written in a prosaic, discursive style," and that his "ideas were so obscured by dull and unnecessary verbiage as to be all but unreadable .... It is unlikely that it was read by anyone except a few interested Virginians." *The Old Republicans*, 150.

94. Carpenter, *The South as a Conscious Minority*, 90.

95. *Martin v. Hunter's Lessee*, 1 Wheaton 304 (1816).

96. Charles Warren, *The Supreme Court in United States History* (Boston: Little Brown, 1922), I: 449. For a discussion of the significance of the *Martin* case respecting federal-state relations, see James McClellan, *Joseph Story and the American Constitution* (Norman: University of Oklahoma Press, 1990), 240–52.

97. *Cohens v. Virginia*, 6 Wheaton 262 (1821).

98. *McCulloch v. Maryland*, 4 Wheaton 316 (1819). One of the most vigorous critics of *McCulloch* was Judge Spencer Roane of Virginia.

See his essays, and Marshall's rejoinder, in *John Marshall's Defense of McCulloch v. Maryland*, ed. by Gerald Gunter (Stanford: Stanford University Press, 1969).

99. M.E. Bradford, *Arator*, 31.
100. John Taylor, *Construction Construed and Constitutions Vindicated* (Richmond: Shepherd & Pollard, 1820).
101. *Scott v. Sandford*, 60 U.S. 393 (1857).
102. Taylor, *Construction Construed and Constitutions Vindicated*, 314.
103. Taylor, *Tyranny Unmasked*, ed. by F. Thornton Miller (Indianapolis: Liberty Fund, 1992).
104. Wright, "The Philosopher of Jeffersonian Democracy," *American Political Science Review*, 885.
105. Taylor, *Tyranny Unmasked*, 223.
106. In 1831, the House Judiciary Committee reported a bill to abolish section 25 of the Judicairy Act of 1789. See *House Report No. 43*, January 24, 1831 (21st Cong., 2d Sess.). The majority cited the Kentucky and Virginia Resolutions at 4-5, and the minority cited *The Federalist* in opposition to the proposed repeal, at 17.
107. *The Records of the Federal convention of 1787*, ed. by Max Farrand (New Haven: Yale University Press, 1937), I: xi.
108. *The Debate in the Several State Conventions on the Adoption of the Federal Constitution*, ed. by Jonathan Elliot, 4 vols. (Philadelphia: J.B. Lippincott, 1836). A fifth volume, containing James Madison's Notes of the Debates in the Federal Convention, was added in 1840.
109. Yates's Notes were reprinted in Elliot, *Debates*, I: 389-479. Luther Martin's *Genuine Information*, another Anti-Federalist account of the Convention's proceedings that Martin presented to the Maryland legislature in 1788, was printed with Yates's Notes in 1821, and reprinted in Elliot, *Debates*, I: 344-89. See also James Hutson, "Robert Yates's Notes on the Constitutional Convention of 1787," *Quarterly Journal of the Library of Congress*, LXV: 1-39 (1986). James Madison contended that there were "egregious errors" in Yates's Notes, and that it contained partisan "prejudices" against strengthening the federal government. See Drew R. McCoy, *The Last of the Fathers: James Madison and the Republican Legacy* (Cambridge: Cambridge University Press, 1989), 85. Regarding the influence among states' rightists, Taylor's *New Views*, and use of Yates's Notes, see Cornell, *Anti-Federalism and the Dissenting Tradition*, 288-94.

110. Taylor, *New Views of the Constitution* (Washington: Way and Gideon, 1823), 11.
111. Anonymous, "The Tribunal of Dernier Resort," *The Southern Review* (August and November, 1830), VI: 421-513. The author of this insightful review is thought to be Judge Samuel Prioleau of Charleston, South Carolina (1784–1839), who often contributed to this journal. His wife, Hannah, was the daughter of James Hamilton. "In South Carolina," he observed, "the people are at this moment so enlightened on the subject of our political institutions, and understand so fully the nature of the compact, that it would be a waste of time to reply to observations, founded on premises affirmed to be false by our legislature, and, of course, generally repudiated by our citizens." *Ibid.*, 470.
112. *Ibid.*, 464.
113. Walter Bennett, *American Theories of Federalism* (Tuscaloosa: University of Alabama Press, 1964), 121.
114. John C. Calhoun to V. Maxcy, April 24, 1823, *Papers of John C. Calhoun*, ed. by W. Edwin Hemphill (Columbia: University of South Carolina Press, 1975), VIII: 28.
115. John C. Calhoun to Ogden Edwards, May 2, 1823, *ibid.*, 45.
116. As quoted in Charles M. Wiltse, *John C. Calhoun: Sectionalist, 1840–1850* (Indianapolis: Bobbs-Merrill, 1951), 411. It is noteworthy that one of Taylor's main criticisms of *The Federalist*, as expressed in *New Views of the Constitution*, was Publius's erroneous description of the general government as a *national* rather than a *federal* government. This thesis reappears in the writings of Calhoun, as indicated by the following:

> How the distinguished and patriotic authors of this celebrated work fell—against their own clear and explicit admissions—into an error so radical and dangerous [as that the Constitution established a national government]—one which has contributed, more than all others combined, to cast a mist over our system of government, and to confound and lead astray the minds of the community as to a true conception of its real character, cannot be accounted for, without adverting to their history and opinions as connected with the formation of the constitution. The two principal writers were prominent members of the convention; and leaders, in that

body, of the party, which supported the plan for a national government. The other, although not a member, is known to have belonged to the same party. They all acquiesced in the decision, which overruled their favorite plan, and determined, patriotically, to give that adopted by the convention, a fair trial; without, however, surrendering their preference for their own scheme of a national government. It was in this state of mind, which could not fail to exercise a strong influence over their judgments, that they wrote the Federalist: and, on all questions connected with the character of the government, due allowance should be made for the force of the bias, under which their opinions were formed.

John C. Calhoun, *A Discourse on the Constitution and Government of the United States,* in *The Essential Calhoun,* ed. by Clyde N. Wilson (New Brunswick: Transaction, 1992), 70-71.

117. Fitzwilliam Byrdsdale to John C. Calhoun, March 1, 1847, *Papers of John C. Calhoun,* ed. by Clyde Wilson (Columbia: University of South Carolina Press, 1998), XXIV: 228.

118. Story, *Commentaries on the Constitution,* §355, n.1 at p. 322. Joseph Story, it is interesting to note, was appointed to the Supreme Court in 1811 by President James Madison, over the objection of Thomas Jefferson. See McClellan, *Joseph Story and the American Constitution,* 39-40.

Note on the Text

Except for a facsimile reprint published by Da Capo Press of New York in 1971, this new edition of John Taylor's *New Views of the Constitution* is the only republication of the work since 1823. Regnery Publishing has remained faithful to the original text, which is reprinted here, in a new design, in its entirety. Typography has been silently modernized. The introduction and the index are new.

As the reader will note, Taylor's references to essays in *The Federalist* are abbreviated throughout the book. Those essays attributed to Alexander Hamilton, appear as *H* and those to James Madison as *M*, with the number of the essay following the letter—for example, "H. No. 33" or "M. No. 39."

There is one obscure reference in the book that warrants clarification. This is the pamphlet entitled "One of the People" to which Taylor frequently refers in section XIV of the book. This is George McDuffie's, *National and States Rights Considered by "One of the People," In Reply to "Trio"* (Charleston, 1821). A vehement Calhoun nationalist in the 1820s, and an equally passionate Calhounite nullifier in the 1830s, McDuffie was a lawyer and member of the House of Representatives. He published the pamphlet in response to a series of essays appearing in the *Milledgeville Gazette* by a "Trio" of Georgia Crawfordites who considered nationalism a folly. Writing in the *Georgia Advertiser*, McDuffie assumed the task of repudiating his opponents in vitriolic terms. Colonel William Cummings, the leader of "the Trio," demanded satisfaction, and a duel ensued. McDuffie was seriously wounded in the spine and remained physically impaired for the remainder of his life. He later served as Senator and as Governor of South Carolina. His fiery speech of May 19, 1831, in Charleston is often said to have brought John C. Calhoun to open advocacy of nullification.

The reader will find that reading this book is like embarking on a treasure hunt. The path is long and winding, with annoying digressions and difficult terrain impeding the search. With perseverence and patience, however, the reader will discover in these pages many gems of wisdom that can be found in no other work on our Constitution.

James McClellan

The Meaning of Certain Primary Words

I shall attempt to ascertain the nature of our form of government, and the existence of a project to alter it. Principles and words are the disciplinarians of construction, but the latter require definitions to come at truth.

The word union is inexplicit. It may imply either a perfect consolidation; or an association for special purposes, reaching only stated objects, and limited by positive restrictions. Of civil unions, the matrimonial is the most intimate; and yet the parties to it are invested with separate and independent rights. The ancient union of the independent kingdoms of Spain, effected by marriage or conquest, left to each many local privileges. The union of England and Scotland, effected by compact, contains stipulations beyond the power of the united government to alter, especially that in relation to the religion of the latter kingdom. That between England and Ireland is a political consolidation. The latter kingdom did not obtain an establishment of the Roman Catholick religion. Had the majority of the people possessed free will, they would have reserved this local right; and the Roman Catholick religion, like the Presbyterian, would have been placed beyond the reach of the united representation in parliament; just as the reserved rights of the states are placed beyond the reach of our united representation in Congress; because political unions for special purposes, cannot be defeated by inferences from the form adopted for their execution. In order to determine whether the United States meant by the term *union,* to establish a supreme power or a limited association, we must commence our inquiry at their political birth, and accommodate our arguments with the principles they avowed in proclaiming their political existence. These are stated in the declaration of independence: "We the *representatives of the United States* of America, in *general Congress* assembled, appealing to the Supreme Judge of the world, for the rectitude of our intentions, do, in the name and by the authority of the good *people of these colonies,* solemnly publish and declare, that these United Colonies are, and of right ought to be, *free and independent states;* and that as free and independent states, they have full power to levy war, conclude peace, contract alliances, establish commerce, *and do all other acts and things,* which independent states may of right do." Such is the origin of our liberty, and the foundation of our form of government. The consolidating project ingeniously leaves unexamined the arguments suggested by this declaration, and commences its lectures at the end of the subject to be considered. If the declaration of independence is not obligatory, our intire political fabrick has lost its magna charta, and is without any solid foundation. But if it is the basis of our form of government, it is the true expositor of the principles and terms we have adopted. The word "united" is used in conjunction with the phrase "free and independent states," and this association recognises a compatibility between the sovereignty and the union of the several states. The regulation of commerce is enumerated among the rights of sovereignty, and this right having been exercised by each state under their first confederation, because it was not surrendered, is an evidence of what was meant by the sovereignty of the states, and a proof that the separate sovereignty of each, and not a consolidated sovereignty of all, was established by the declaration of independence. The same observation applies to the sovereign rights of the states, not surrendered by the existing federal constitution. Take from the states the political character they assumed by the declaration of independence, and they could not have united. To contract, to stipulate, to unite, are among the "acts and things which independent states may of right do." The first confederation or union recognises the compatibility between the union and the sovereignty of the states. The existing union adheres to the same idea, professes to establish a more perfect union of states created by the Declaration of Independence, and contains many provisions incapable of being executed except by state sovereignty. It uses the words "United States," taken by the first confederation from the declaration of independence, and transplanted from both these instruments, in which they are associated with positive assertions of the independence and sovereignty of each state; and therefore the last instrument, like the others, recognises the compatibility between the union and the sovereignty of the several states.

The notion that the "freedom and independence of the states" refers to a consolidation of states, admits of a perfect refutation. It would render the language of the declaration of independence ungrammatical, because had this been intended, it ought to have recognised the rights of sovereignty as residing in one consolidated state, and not in several states. It would have rendered the confederation unnecessary; because, had the declaration of independence invested a consolidation of states with a power to do "all acts and things which a free and independent state may of right do," there would not have existed the least reason for delegating powers to a federal Congress. It would have divested each province or state of the right to make and alter its own constitution and its own laws; and it would have converted the exercise of any sovereign power by a state, subsequently to the declaration of independence, into usurpation. The contemporary construction of the declaration of independence was completely adverse to the idea that it had conferred any sovereign power, whatever, upon a consolidation of states. Hence a confederation became necessary; and hence the several states exercised, among others, the sovereign powers of raising armies, imposing taxes, and regulating commerce. The language used in the declaration of independence was adopted and explained by the confederation framed in 1777. It is entitled a "perpetual union," its style was "The United States of America," and it declares that "each state retains its sovereignty." So far state sovereignty is explicitly recognised, and no idea existed that it had been lost by a union of states. Upon trial, it being discovered that the powers bestowed upon Congress by the first confederation, were insufficient "for their common defence and general welfare," the ends it expresses; another union was framed by the constitution of 1787, rendered more perfect by enlarging federal powers, and repeating the same words of "common defence and general welfare" as its chief ends. If this phrase was understood, as neither creating a supreme national government, nor extending the powers delegated by the confederation of 1777, it must have been also understood in the same sense when used in the constitution of 1787. Its meaning is ascertained by the tenth section of the latter instrument. The individual states are prohibited from exercising certain attributes of sovereignty, particularly those of making war, treaties, and regulating commerce, because, except for the prohibition, they would have retained them, as adjuncts of sovereignty. The prohibition is therefore a construction of this phrase, corresponding with the construction it received when used in the confederation of 1777, and uniting both instruments with the public opinion, that neither the word union, nor this specification of its objects, extended delegated powers, created a general government or supremacy, or deprived the states of any attributes of sovereignty except those prohibited.

The word consolidation, colloquially adopted, expresses an idea opposite to that universally supposed to be conveyed by a political union of sovereign and independent states, and inconsistent with limited powers, or positive restrictions. It implies a fusion of the state sovereignties into one mass, so that each would lose its individuality. Had this event taken place, the aggregate sovereignty would certainly have imbibed all the powers annexed to the materials of which it was compounded, and the several states would not have retained a single power. We must therefore either conclude that a consolidated sovereignty was established, or that every attribute of sovereignty remained with the states, except the attributes prohibited, because these prohibitions are the only rule by which those they surrendered can be distinguished from those they retained. Had a concentrated sovereignty or supremacy been contemplated by either of our three political instruments, it would have been expressed by consolidation or an equivalent word. As this was not the case at either era, the declaration of independence, the confederation of 1777, and the constitution of 1787, have used the same words and phrases to express the publick opinion; and if the Jesuit, construction, can extract a consolidated supremacy or sovereignty out of the last of these instruments, it must have been created by the two former.

The word Congress requires attention. It was adopted by the provinces, and the declaration of independence was framed "by the representatives of *the United States in Congress assembled.*" The representative character, was common to the Congress of the provinces, of the states under the confederation of 1777, and of the states under the constitution of 1787; but neither this character, nor the intrinsick meaning of the word, were supposed to convey any powers until very lately. If the phrase "Congress of the United States," or the representative character of one branch of that body, had conveyed implied powers, it would have been useless to grant specified legislative powers to this "Congress of the United States" by the first article of the constitution. The numerous sovereign powers not granted by this article, must either pass by implication, or not pass at all. If they did not pass by this mode of conveyance, they remained with the states. The implication or inference is obviated by selecting the word "Congress" in preference to the words parliament or assembly, to the comprehensiveness of which the states had been accustomed. It was the precise word used to express a congregation of deputies from independent states or governments. In that sense it was adopted by the provinces, used in the confederation of 1777, and repeated in the constitution. No word could have been selected with equal felicity, to convey the idea contemplated by a federal system. It avoided the implications which the usual words parliament or assembly might have furnished, and demonstrated that a body of men invested with powers equivalent to those exercised by such denominations, was not intended to be established. And it intimated the independence of the several states as being similar to the independence of the several provinces of each other, as well as to that of distinct kingdoms. The assemblage of men which framed the constitution, was called "A convention of deputies from the states of New-Hampshire, Massachusetts, Connecticut, New-York, New-Jersey, Pennsylvania, Delaware, Maryland, Virginia, North-Carolina, South-Carolina, and Georgia." By what authority did the states appoint these deputies, if not in virtue of their respective sovereignties, existing in common with a "Congress of the United States?" If a Congress did not destroy the sovereignties of the states at that time, is it reasonable to suppose that the present "Congress of the United States" was constituted to destroy them? The deputies of the states in the convention, though representatives, could not have enacted a constitution, because it would have violated the limited powers which they received from state sovereignties; and in like manner, the deputies of the states now composing a Congress, though representatives, cannot exceed their powers. It is upon this principle, that Congress cannot alter the terms of the union.

The word "federal," also adopted into our political phraseology, is a national construction of the terms used in forming our system of government, comprising a definite expression of publick opinion, that state sovereignties really exist. It implies a league between sovereign nations, has been so used by all classes of people from the commencement of our political existence down to this day, and is inapplicable to a nation consolidated under one sovereignty.

The meaning of the word "state" accords with that of the words associated with it. Used in reference to individuals, it comprises a great variety of circumstances, but in reference to the

publick, it means a political community. Johnson thus expounds
it, and adds, that it implies a republick, or a government not
monarchical. What other word was more proper to describe the
communities recognised by the declaration of independence,
the union of 1777, and the union of 1787? Can the same word
have been intended to convey an idea in the last, inconsistent
with the idea it conveys in the two first instruments? Neither
monarchy nor aristocracy would have fitted the case, and the
word republick itself would have been exposed to uncertainties,
with which the word state is not chargeable; because it has been
applied to governments discordant with those which were established by our revolution. As no word more explicitly comprises
the idea of a sovereign independent community; as it is used in
conjunction with a declared sovereignty and independence; as it
is retained by the union of 1787, and in all the operations of our
governments; and as sovereign powers only could be reserved
by states; there seems to be no sound argument by which it can
be deprived of its intrinsick meaning, contrary to these positive
constructions.

Against this concomitancy of interpretation, the consolidating school takes refuge under the word "people," and contends
that it is susceptible of a meaning which inflicts upon many of
its associates the character of nonsense, and deprives them of
their right to assist in the construction of the constitution. Let
us therefore endeavour to defend it against the aspersion of
hostility to its best friends, and to save it from the crime of self-
murder. In all ages metaphysicians have been so skilful in splitting
principles, as to puzzle mankind in their search after truth; and
morality itself would be lost by the minuteness of their dissec-
tions, except for the resistance of common sense, and the dictates

of unsophisticated conscience. But the achievement of losing twenty-four sovereign states by the acuteness of construction, and getting rid of a people in each, by means of the word necessary to describe them, was reserved for the refined politicians of the present day; and is equivalent to the ingenuity of a fisherman, who should lose a whale by a definition of his name, which would destroy his qualities.

At the commencement of the revolutionary war, emergency dictated temporary expedients, and delayed the formal adoption of measures for constituting a people in each province. A Congress was therefore appointed by provincial legislatures, by one branch of these legislatures, or by districts in a province; but when disorder was exchanged for independence, it was appointed, and its powers were derived from the state governments, who were deemed sufficient to ratify the declaration of independence, because they represented a people circumscribed within each state territory. The same species of sanction was resorted to, for the ratification of both the union of 1777 and the union of 1787. The ratification of the first was to be made by "the legislatures of all the United States," and of the latter by "the conventions of nine states." The reference to their representatives in both cases, far from acknowledging that each state was without a people, acknowledged the contrary. The differences between the two modes of ratification, consisted in the distinction between the words "legislatures and conventions," and between the necessity for unanimity in one case, and the sufficiency of nine states in the other, to establish the proposed unions. In neither, could the object be effected by a majority of the people of the United States. Whatever may be the difference between the words legislatures and convention, in other cases, there is none in this, because both were representatives of the same people. Why did the first union require a unanimity of states? Because a people of each state had been created by the declaration of independence, invested with sovereignty, and therefore entitled to unite or not. Why were the ratifying nine states only to be united by the second? For the same reason; demonstrating, that as to the ratification of both, no distinction was made between legislatures and conventions; and that a concurrence or rejection of either, was considered as a sovereign act of a state people by their representatives. This principle is confirmed beyond all doubt, by the different modes in which men act when framing a constitution for a consolidated people, or creating a federal union between distinct states. In the first case, neither the consent of every individual, nor of every county, is necessary, because no individual possesses sovereign power, and because no county comprises a people politically independent. If there are thirteen counties in a state, and the deputies of four dissent from a constitution, it is yet obligatory upon all, because all are subject to the sovereign power of one people. The constitution of the United States was only obligatory upon the ratifying states, because each state comprised a sovereign people, and no people existed, invested with a sovereignty over the thirteen states. This consent, whether expressed by state legislatures or state conventions, was the consent of distinct sovereignties, and therefore the consent of nine states could not bind four dissenting states, or even one. A majority of a state legislature or convention dictates to a minority, because it exercises the sovereignty of an associated people over individuals. If state nations had not existed, they could not have exercised this authority over minorities, and therefore it is necessary to admit their existence in order to bestow validity upon the federal constitution.

The establishment of state governments, demonstrates the existence of state nations. No act can ascertain the existence of a sovereign and independent community more completely, than the creation of a government; nor any fact more completely prove that these communities were each constituted of a distinct people, than that of their having established different forms of government. If the art of construction shall acquire the power both of dispensing with the meaning of words, and also with the most conclusive current of facts by which these words have been interpreted, it will be able, like the dispensing power of kings, to subvert any principles, however necessary to secure human happiness, and to break every ligament for tying down power to its good behaviour.

SECTION II

The Journal of the Convention

Had the journal of the convention which framed the constitution of the United States, though obscure and incomplete, been published immediately after its ratification, it would have furnished lights towards a true construction, sufficiently clear to have prevented several trespasses upon its principles, and tendencies towards its subversion. Perhaps it may not be yet too late to lay before the publick the important evidence it furnishes.

A short history of the convention itself will enable us to understand its proceedings. A meeting of deputies from several states, in 1786, at Annapolis, recommended the appointment of commissioners to devise such *further* provisions, as shall appear to them necessary to render *the constitution of the federal government,* adequate to the exigencies of the *union;* and Congress, in 1787, recommended a convention of delegates to be appointed by the several states, as the most probable mean of establishing in these states a firm *national* government; and resolved that a convention of delegates, who shall have been appointed by the *several states,* be held at Philadelphia for the *sole and express purpose* of revising the articles of the confederation, and reporting to Congress and the several legislatures, such alterations and provisions therein, as shall, when agreed to in Congress and *confirmed by the states,* render the *federal constitution* adequate to the exigencies of government and the preservation of the union. In these proceedings the word convention is used to describe the deputies of a state, and the word constitution as equivalent to the word confederation.

The confederation of 1777 had declared that "no alteration should be made in its articles, unless such alteration should be agreed to in a Congress of the United States, and be afterwards confirmed by the legislatures of every state." Accordingly the constitution framed by the convention, was referred to Congress, by Congress to the state legislatures, and by a law of each state legislature to a state convention. Each ratification was returned to Congress, and it passed a resolution for putting the new constitution into operation. This process was pursued in conformity with the existing compact between the states, proving that the states were at this time considered as the only parties to their federal union. If the ratification of the new compact was made according to the injunctions of the old compact, it was the act of separate states required by that old compact, and not the act of a consolidated American nation; and it recognised the states as the parties to the constitution. Both unions were ratified in a federal mode; and no state suspected, that by exercising its independent right of assenting or rejecting, it was exercising an usurped authority, and moreover acknowledging its subordination to an aggregate American nation.

The ratification of amendments by the confederation and the constitution, was to be made by states. In both the word "states" must have been used in the same sense, because no American nation had appeared in the interval. Had these instruments, or either of them, been ratified by an American nation, they would not have been thereby made obligatory on the states; and should an American nation now attempt to amend the constitution, it would be a usurpation, because no such nation exists invested with a supremacy over the states; and it would violate the mode of amending the constitution, agreed upon by the parties to the union. Any species of per capita supremacy over all the states, would establish an oligarchy of a minority of states, and if such a supremacy does not exist as a consequence of national sovereignty, with a power of altering the constitution, a supremacy in construing it cannot find any basis upon which it may be erected. A per capita supremacy of construction would be equivalent to a per capita supremacy of amendment, and the same oligarchical power in a minority of states containing a majority of people, would be the consequence.

To avoid this identical misfortune, the convention required the same sanction for both unions, and for the amendments of both, namely, state ratifications. If a constructive supremacy can alter the intention of the constitution, then it would have been necessary to subject the constructions of Congress, as well as more direct alterations of the constitution, to the prescribed mode of ratification, or that mode would be soon rendered of little use by resorting to the constructive mode of amendment. By wholly neglecting to guard against a constructive supremacy, so evidently destructive of the federal supremacy by which the constitution was framed, ratified, and is to be amended, it seems certain that the convention did not entertain the least suspicion, that a constructive supremacy would be pretended to.

In the mode of amending the constitution of 1787, as well as in the necessity for the ratification of a state, to make it binding upon that state, we discern distinctly the opinion of the convention, that no American nation existed. Had it been made by an American nation, it would be a rare anomaly, that state nations should have the power to reject and alter it.

As a difference of meaning between "a confederation and a constitution" has been contended for, it ought not to be overlooked, that the deputies at Annapolis, applied the term constitution to the confederation of 1777.

It is very remarkable, that the Congress of 1787 introduced the word *national* into the resolve recommending a convention. It expressed an opinion "that a convention was the most probable mean of establishing in these states a firm *national government*." So far it unequivocally advocated the exchange of a federal for a national form of government; but an intimation so plain and positive, that the state governments ought to be destroyed, might not have been received with applause, and might have obstructed the removal of the defects of the existing federal union. The expedient of complexity was therefore practised to flatter the opinion of the states, and yet to supply a text for the advocates of a national government. After suggesting this form as one propositum, towards which the convention might direct its attention, Congress subjoined another, namely, "that the convention shall render the *federal* constitution adequate to the exigencies of government." Except for the restriction comprised in the word federal, this part of the resolve would have been as capacious as the expression "national government," because a limitation of power to the exigencies of government, of which the government itself must judge, is no limitation at all. But it adds, "and the preservation of the union." The recommendation of Congress comprises "a *national* government, a *federal* constitution, the *preservation of the union,* and a convention for the *sole purpose of revising the articles of the confederation.*" These recommendations are at discord with each other, as a national and a federal form of government are not the same form. By planting the word *national* among them, as a scion to be watered up to a tree, a concert between individuals, unfriendly to the political existence of the states, appears at this period to have existed.

Let us see how these recommendations were received by a concert of states, and by the concert of individuals. Twelve states appointed deputies to assemble at Philadelphia, and each gave its deputies credentials specifying their powers. The idea that the recommendation of Congress was addressed to an American nation or people, no where appeared, and that of a national government was rejected by every state. The powers to these deputies were the following:

By New-Hampshire, "to discuss and decide upon the most effectual means to remedy the defects of the *federal* union."

Massachusetts, "in conformity with the resolution of Congress recommending a convention for the *sole purpose* of revising the articles of confederation, to render the *federal constitution* adequate to the preservation of the *union.*"

Connecticut, "for the *sole* and express purpose of revising the articles of confederation, to render the *federal* constitution adequate to the exigencies of government and the *preservation of the union.*"

New-York, in the same words.

New-Jersey, "for the purpose of taking into consideration the state of the *union,* as to trade and other important subjects, and of devising such *other provisions,* as shall appear to be necessary, to render the constitution of the *federal* government adequate to the exigencies thereof."

Pennsylvania, "to devise such *alterations and further provisions,* as may be necessary to render the *federal* constitution fully adequate to the exigencies of the *union.*"

Delaware, in the same words, with a proviso, that each state shall have one vote in Congress.

Maryland, in the same words, without the proviso.

Virginia, in the same words. This state passed the first law for appointing delegates to the convention.

North-Carolina, "for the purpose of revising the *federal* constitution."

South-Carolina, "to devise such *alterations* as may be thought necessary, to render the *federal* constitution entirely adequate to the actual situation and future good government of the *confederated states.*"

Georgia, "to devise such alterations as may render the *federal* constitution adequate to the exigencies of the *union.*"

Thus the states unanimously rejected the recommendation of a *national* government, and by excluding the word national from all their credentials, demonstrated that they well understood the wide difference between a *federal* and a *national* union. The distinction was enforced in Massachusetts and Connecticut by the words "sole purpose." The reference of sole, is to the word national, used by Congress, and in all the credentials the word federal is used also in opposition to the word national. There existed no other object but the suggestion of a national government, for the restrictions in the credentials of the states to operate upon; and their unanimity, without consulting each other, is a complete proof that they all comprehended the difference between a federal and a national form of government. The word constitution is also uniformly considered by the states as equivalent to the word confederation. Having seen what was the unanimous opinion of the states, let us next inquire how far it was regarded by a concert between individuals.

The Subject Continued

O n the 29th of May, 1787, the convention was organized, and Mr. Randolph, of Virginia, offered sundry
resolutions resuming the word national, though it had
been rejected by all the states, and proposing "that a *national*
legislature shall have the right to legislate in all cases in which the
harmony of the United States may be interrupted by the exercise
of *individual legislation, and to negative all laws passed by the several
states, contravening, in the opinion of the national legislature, the articles
of the union,* or any treaty under the union." The resolutions also
proposed "a *national* executive and a *national* judiciary; that the
executive and a convenient number of the *national* judiciary
ought to compose a *council of revision,* with authority to examine every act of the national legislature, before it shall operate, and
every act of a *particular legislature,* before a negative thereon shall
be final; and that the *dissent* of the said council shall amount to a
rejection, unless the act of the national legislature be again passed,
or that of a particular legislature be again negatived by _____ of
the members of each branch."

It is worthy of particular observation, that in this project, the
constructive supremacy now claimed for the federal government
"over the articles of the union," was proposed to be given to a
national government; because the actual consideration of this
identical power, and its absence from the constitution as it was
finally adopted, seems to be irresistible evidence that it does not

exist. Throughout Mr. Randolph's resolutions, fifteen in number, the word national is adopted, and the word Congress rejected, except in reference to the Congress under the confederation of 1777, proving that the word was applicable to a federal union, but not to a national government.

The proposed national form of government was ultimately renounced or rejected, but the negative power over state laws with which it was invested, was much less objectionable than that now constructively contended for on behalf of the federal government. The president was to be one of a council of revision, and the influence of the states in his election might have afforded to them some feeble security, a little better than could be expected from a council of revision composed of a few federal judges. Both the legislative branches which were to pronounce the first veto upon state laws, were also to be exposed to popular influence, and might feel all the responsibility of which a body of men are susceptible in extending its own power by its own vote. A judicial veto, as now contended for, is exposed to no responsibility whatever. The council of revision, with the president at its head, were only to be controlled by more than a majority of the national legislature. This was evidently a better security for the small states, than a power in a majority of Congress to abrogate state laws. But all these alleviations of the power in a national form of government to negative state laws, were unsuccessful, because the principle itself, however modified, was inconsistent with the federal form adopted. It can never be conceived that the principle of a negative over state laws, audibly proposed and rejected, had silently crept into the constitution. This was quite consistent with the national form of government proposed, but quite inconsistent with the federal form adopted.

The project for a national form of government was deduced from the doctrine, as we shall hereafter see, that the declaration of independence had committed the gross blunder of making the states dependent corporations; that it was in fact a declaration of dependence. When this doctrine failed in the convention, the national negative over state laws died with it. Revived by construction, it assumes a far more formidable and consolidating aspect than as it was originally offered, because the usurped negative over state laws, by a majority of a court or of Congress, would not have its malignity to the states alleviated by the checks to which the project itself resorted. Without these checks, even the advocates for a national form of government thought such a negative intolerable. The project contemplated a mixed legislative, executive, and judicial supremacy over state laws, so that one department of this sovereignty, like that of the English, might check the other, in construing "the articles of the union," and did not venture even to propose, that a government should be established, in which a single court was to be invested with a supreme power over these articles, or the constitution. The idea seems to be a political monster never seen in fable or in fact.

On the same day, Mr. C. Pinckney offered a draft for a federal "constitution." It recognised the people of the several states; proposed "that the style of the government should be the *United States of America;* that the legislative power should be vested in a *Congress,* to be chosen by the people of the several states; enumerated limited powers to be exercised by this Congress; proposed a president of the United States; *and that the legislature of the United States should have power to revise the laws of the several states that may be supposed to infringe the powers exclusively delegated to Congress, and to negative and annul such as do.*"

This project for a form of government being somewhat at enmity with the resolutions, hostilities between them forthwith commenced, and the resolutions obtained successive victories over a nominal rival, during the greater portion of the time expended by the convention. The journal, however, is too obscure to supply us with a history of a controversy which related only to the form of a national government mutually advocated. We do not find in the constitution the negative over state laws proposed both in the resolutions and the draft. As it was distinctly proposed by both, it must have been maturely considered and doubly rejected. The reasons of these rejections were, that though a supreme power of construction, was consistent with, and might have been intrusted to a government throughout responsible to one people or nation, it was inconsistent with and could not therefore be intrusted to a federal form of government, or any of its departments. And hence when the federal form of government prevailed over the national form, the alteration of the federal articles was exclusively limited to the modes prescribed, and not extended to a supreme power of construction in the federal government or any of its departments. The constitution was not intended to be an alembick, fraught with heterogeneous principles, to condense the tortuosities of construction, and distil from taciturnity a supreme power of construction, and consequently a negative upon state legislation.

May 30, Mr. Randolph, seconded by Mr. G. Morris, moved "that an union of states merely federal, will not accomplish the objects proposed by the articles of confederation, namely, common defence, security of liberty, and general welfare;" and by Mr. Butler, seconded by Mr. Randolph, "that a *national* government ought to be established, consisting of a *supreme* legislative, judiciary, and executive." In opposition to this resolution it was moved, "that in order to carry into execution the design of the states in *forming this convention,* and to accomplish the objects proposed by the confederation, a more effective government, consisting of a legislative, judiciary, and executive, ought to be established," excluding the words national and supreme. But it was resolved "that a *national* government ought to be established, consisting of a *supreme* legislative, judiciary, and executive." The collision between these resolutions, and consequently the debate, was produced by the words national and supreme. Massachusetts, Pennsylvania, Delaware, Virginia, North-Carolina, and South-Carolina, voted for this resolution, Connecticut against it, and New-York was divided; so that a convention of only eight states decided by a majority of six, that the states should be annihilated. It was late in the session before twelve states assembled; but whether an accession of votes, or the repentance usually attached to precipitancy, produced the ultimate discomfiture of the resolution to establish a supreme national government, can only be conjectured by computing the consequences likely to result from an excessive zeal for this consolidating policy, and from a refrigeration inculcated by an accession of votes or a firm opposition.

However this may be, it is plain that some members of the convention came with preparatory impressions that the distinction of states ought to be destroyed, and availed themselves of a thin convention to obtain a footing for the opinion. On the first day of the session, two projects are offered, both founded upon the principle of a supreme national government, and on the second, the deputies of six states resolve to annihilate thirteen. The hastiness of this movement indicates a design to obtain a victory by surprise, ascertains the existence of a concert unfaithful to

credentials, and displays a rooted hostility to the state governments. A blow so unexpected and violent was endeavoured to
be suspended by succinctly urging in the adverse resolution,
that it was the duty of the convention "to carry into execution
the design of the states," but not a single day is allowed for
consideration, and the treachery of sacrificing duty to prepossession is instantly perpetrated. The states and the duty are
entombed together, by a resolution to establish a supreme
national government.

At the threshold of the business, we clearly discern that the
convention was apprized of the meaning of words. One resolution asserts that a government merely *federal* would not answer,
and that a *supreme national* government ought to be established.
The rival resolution rejects the words national and supreme, as
incompatible with a federal union. One avails itself of the intimation from Congress in favour of a national government, and
rejects the intimations of the same Congress in favour of a federal government; the other prefers the latter intimations, because
they were legitimated by the states, and rejects the former,
because it was rejected by the states. These adverse opinions were
evidently dictated, one by the political opinion already invented,
of a consolidated nation; the other, by the actual existence of
United States. The contrast between the two preliminary resolutions in a very important view, depends on a single word. One
proposed "a *supreme* legislative, judiciary, and executive," the other
"a legislative, executive, and judiciary," excluding the word
supreme. This word was adopted as suitable for the proposed
national government, and rejected, as inconsistent with the federal form of government, to which the states had confined their
deputies. The adoption and rejection conspire to furnish us with

a definition of this formidable word, both by the national and federal parties in the convention. The sense in which both of these parties understood it, caused its exclusion from the constitution, as inapplicable to a federal government. The advocates for a national government proposed to invest that form of government with a supreme power to "construe the articles of the union." The advocates for a federal government originally proposed to withhold supremacy from the legislative, judiciary, and executive, and though they at first failed, finally succeeded. As applied by the successful federal party to the supreme court, it evidently refers to inferior federal courts. Instead of a judiciary, invested with a supreme power to construe the articles of the union and to negative state laws, a limited judiciary is found in the constitution. To reject a supreme legislature and executive, and yet to retain a supreme judiciary, was never even suggested by either the national or federal party in the convention. As the project for a national form of government, bestowed the supremacy of construing the articles of the union and negativing state laws, upon all its departments, by plain words; and the project in favour of a federal form intirely rejected this supremacy, it is doing the utmost violence to probability to imagine, that the constitution by inference without plain words, and without its having been proposed in the convention, should have both deprived the federal legislature and executive of a power to settle the construction of our federal articles and to negative state laws, and also have bestowed this enormous power exclusively on one federal court.

The word supreme is used twice in the constitution, once in reference to the superiority of the highest federal court over the inferior federal courts, and again in declaring "that the constitution, and laws made in pursuance thereof, shall be the supreme law of the land, and the judges in every state shall be bound thereby." Did it mean to create two supremacies, one in the court, and another in the constitution? Are they colateral, or is one superior to the other? Is the court supreme over the constitution, or the constitution supreme over the court? Are "the judges in every state" to obey the *articles of the union,* or the construction of these articles by the supreme federal court?

The project for a national government, gave a supremacy over the articles of the constitution it advocated, to the legislative, judiciary, and executive, and did not propose that the constitution should be supreme over these departments, because it would have involved a contradiction. As they were to have had a supreme power of construing its articles, these articles could not possess a supreme power over their constructions. But a federal system required that the articles of union should be invested with supremacy, over the instruments created to obey and execute them. Hence they are declared to be so in reference to all these instruments, without excepting the federal court. And hence the right of altering these articles is retained by these parties. In all treaties, the right of construction must be attached to the right of alteration, or the latter right would be destroyed. No right of alteration was proposed to be reserved to the states by the project for a national government, nor any supremacy of the constitution recognised; and in lieu of such articles it was proposed to invest the government itself with a supremacy of construction; because, if a national government resulted from a consolidated people, collateral state and federal departments would not have existed mutually to enforce the supremacy of the constitution; and a national government must necessarily have possessed an absolute power of construing, under the sole control of the consolidated people, by election, in whom the right of alteration resided. But the right of alteration being placed in the states, because they made it, and not in a consolidated people, because such a people did not make it; the right of construction is attached to the altering power, and not given to its own agents under the fictions assumed to sustain a national government, namely, that a consolidated people existed; that this people possessed a right to make and alter a constitution for the union of states; and that a national government established by their authority, ought not therefore to be controlled by states in the construction of its articles.

The supremacy of the constitution is an admonition to all departments, both state and federal, that they were bound to obey the restrictions it imposes. In relation to the federal government, it literally declares that its laws must conform to its exclusive and concurrent powers; and in relation to the state governments, it implies, that theirs must also conform to their exclusive and concurrent powers. It neither enlarges nor abridges the powers delegated or reserved. And it is enforced, not by an oath to be faithful to the supreme constructions of the federal departments, but by an oath to be faithful to the supremacy of the constitution.

SECTION IV

The Subject Continued

I shall select a few other extracts from the journal of the convention, proving that the words "national and supreme,"
constituted the great subject of debate; that they were well
considered by the respective advocates for a national or a federal
form of government; that both were annexed to the departments
of a national form, and neither to the departments of the federal
form; and that their insertion in the constitution can only be
effected by reviving the fictions upon the strength of which they
were proposed.

The battle between a national and federal form of government
began now to wax warm. June 6th, Mr. Pinckney gave notice
"that to-morrow he should move for the reconsideration "of that
clause in the resolution adopted by the committee, which vests
a negative in the *national* legislature on the laws of the several
states. Friday assigned to reconsider."

"June 8th, Mr. Pinckney, seconded by Mr. Madison, moved
to strike out the following words in the sixth resolution: negative
all laws passed by the several states contravening, in the opinion
of the national legislature, the articles of the union, or any treaties
subsisting under the authority of the union," and to insert the
following words in their place, namely, "*to negative all laws which to
them shall appear improper.*" This motion was rejected, only Massachusetts, Pennsylvania, and Virginia, voting in the affirmative. It
comprised the precise negative over state laws now claimed by

the supreme court. This trivial advantage seems to have been the first gained by the party adverse to a national government; but they speedily lost it.

June 13. It was moved by Mr. Randolph, seconded by Mr. Madison, to adopt the following resolution respecting the *national* judiciary, namely, "that the jurisdiction of the national judiciary shall extend to cases which respect the collection of "the national revenue, impeachments of any national officers *and questions which involve the national peace and harmony.*" It passed in the affirmative. These resolutions ought to be kept in mind, until we come to the consideration of the Federalist, as the origin of a construction of the constitution by Mr. Madison, upon which the pretension of the federal court to a supremacy over the laws of states and the articles of the union is founded. The jurisdiction of the federal judiciary is extended by the constitution to cases of revenue, but not to cases of impeachment, or to *questions which involve the national peace and harmony.* It is very remarkable that the very jurisdiction now claimed was actually proposed, considered, and rejected, together with the jurisdiction proposed in cases of impeachment as appears from the absence of both in the specifick statement of federal jurisdiction.

June 15, Mr. Patterson offered sundry federal resolutions among them "that a *federal* judiciary be established," which with all the resolutions previously agreed to, were referred to a committee of the whole house.

June 18, it was moved by Mr. Dickinson, and resolved "that the articles of confederation ought to be revised and amended "so as to render the government of the United States, adequate to the exigencies, the *preservation* and the prosperity of the *union.*" This was the first resolution in favour of a federal government in opposition to a national government, but it was speedily revoked.

On the same day, Colonel Hamilton read a plan of government, containing, among others, the following proposals: "The *supreme* legislative power of the United States of America to be vested in two distinct bodies of men, the one to be called the assembly, and the other the senate," excluding the word Congress, "with power to *pass all laws whatsoever,* subject to the negative hereafter mentioned. The senate to consist of persons elected to serve during *good behaviour.* The supreme executive authority of the United States to be vested in a governor, to be elected to serve during *good behaviour.* To have a negative upon all laws about to be passed, and the execution of all laws passed. To have the *intire direction* of war when authorized or begun. To have the power of pardoning all offences, except treason, which he shall not pardon without the approbation of the senate. The senate to have the sole power of declaring war. All laws of the particular states, contrary to the constitution or *laws* of the United States, *to be utterly void.* And the better to prevent such laws being passed, the governor or president of each state shall be appointed by the *general government,* and shall have a *negative* upon the laws about to be passed in the state of which he is governor or president."

It is needless to waste time in proving, that this project comprised a national government, nearly conforming to that of England; but it furnishes other remarks particularly applicable to our subject. Had it succeeded, would the proposed general governor of the United States, have been invested by "the intire direction of war," with powers to raise supplies, impress men, send militia out of the states, and make roads and canals. If any of the doctrines "that a power includes whatever may be necessary or convenient in its execution; that great power implies small power; or that power has a right to use all auxiliaries it may judge proper for advancing its designs, and to destroy all obstructions in its way," are true, then a power of *intirely directing war,* would have comprised many more powers than those hitherto supposed to have been tacitly annexed to the limited powers delegated by the constitution. But had this project been adopted, its prototype would have furnished many proofs that none of these doctrines are true, and might have defeated the usurpations of this great and powerful governor-*general,* upon the pretence that they were so. The political department, called king, in England, is invested with many very great powers, and among them, those both of declaring and directing war; and although many English kings have attempted, under cover of the appurtenances added by these doctrines to power, to extend their legitimate powers, such attempts, after producing resistance and sanguinary conflicts, have failed. One king may have lost his head for raising money unconstitutionally to build ships of war, and no king pretended he could appropriate the publick treasure to roads and canals, as deeming them appurtenant powers to his rights of declaring and directing war. These would have been formidable precedents towards preventing Colonel Hamilton's great governor-general from absorbing the powers of less powerful departments, and it seems to me that they are equally, and even more forcibly, applicable to our federal form of government. The integrity of our political departments is undoubtedly as necessary to preserve that form, as the integrity of the English departments can be to preserve a limited monarchy. Our specifications and restrictions of powers are more literal and intelligible than the English; and liberty at least, as essentially depends here, as it does in England, upon a resistance by one department against the encroachments of another.

By Colonel Hamilton's project, the states were fairly and openly to be restored to the rank of provinces, and to be made as dependent upon a supreme national government, as they had been upon a supreme British government. Their governors were to be appointed by the national government, and invested with a negative upon all state laws; and all their laws, contrary to the laws of the supreme government, were to be void. The frankness of this undisguised proposition was honourable, and illustrates the character of an attempt to obtain a power for the federal government, substantially the same, not by plain and candid language, like Colonel Hamilton's, but by equivocal and abstruse inferences from language as plain, used with the intention of excluding his plan of government entirely. A power in the supreme federal court to declare all state laws and judgments void, which that court may deem contrary to the articles of the union, or to the laws of Congress; and also to establish every power, which Congress may infer from those delegated; comes fully up to the essential principle of Colonel Hamilton's plan; except that the court will both virtually, and directly, control the legislative, executive, and judicial state departments, by a supremacy exactly the same with that exercised by the British king and his council over the same provincial departments.

June 19. The day after Colonel Hamilton's plan was promulgated, Mr. Dickinson's resolution for a federal form of government was taken up and rejected. "For it, Connecticut, New-York, New-Jersey, Delaware. Against it, Massachusetts, Pennsylvania, Virginia, North-Carolina, South-Carolina, Georgia. Maryland divided." Even yet, only eleven states had appeared, and five refused their concurrence to a national government, which now began to totter.

June 23. The deputies of New-Hampshire first appeared, and New-York never afterwards seems to have given a vote in the convention.

June 25. "It was proposed and seconded to erase the word *national*, and to substitute the words *United States* in the fourth resolution, which passed in the affirmative." Thus we see an opinion expressed by the convention, that the phrase "United States" did not mean "a consolidated American people or nation," and all the inferences in favour of a national government from the style "We, the people of the United States," are overthrown, as that style was adopted, not to establish the idea of an American people, but to defeat it.

July 23. "The proceedings of the convention for the establishment of a *national* government, except what respects the *supreme* executive, were referred to a committee, and the next day the propositions of Mr. C. Pinckney, and of Mr. Patterson, were referred to the same committee."

August 18. It was proposed to empower the legislature of the United States, (the word national is now dropt,) "to grant charters of incorporation in cases where the publick good may require them, and the authority of a single state may be incompetent; to establish a university; to encourage, by proper premiums and provisions, the advancement of useful knowledge and discoveries; to establish seminaries for the promotion of literature and the arts and sciences; to grant charters of incorporation; to establish institutions, rewards, and immunities, for the promotion of agriculture, commerce, and manufactures; and to regulate stages on the post-roads," which, with other propositions, were referred to the committee of July 23d.

August 27. It was moved and negatived, that "in all other cases before mentioned, the judicial power shall be exercised in *such manner as the legislature may direct.*"

September 14. "Question. To grant letters of incorporation for canals, et cetera; negatived. To establish a university; negatived."

The propositions of August the 18th, seem to have been the last considerable struggle for a national government; but the residue of the journal is so concise and imperfect, that their rejection is only discoverable by a reference to the constitution, in which not a single one of them is to be found.

Their rejection was a necessary consequence of substituting a federal for the national government zealously contended for, from the 29th of May to the 14th of September. It was obvious that powers to establish corporations, prescribe the mode of education, patronise local improvements, and bestow rewards and immunities for the promotion of agriculture, commerce, and manufactures, would certainly swallow up a federal, and introduce a national government. When, therefore, a federal system obtained the preference, it would have been inconsistent with the high degree of intelligence possessed by the members of the convention, to have permitted their determination to be defeated by these indirect attempts. This intelligence was assailed by the soothing but insidious restriction, that the powers to incorporate, grant exclusive privileges, and exercise every species of patronage, were only to be exercised "in cases where the *publick good* may require it." The same soothing but insidious argument is now addressed to the intelligence of the publick, to justify an exercise of the very powers which the intelligence of the convention withheld from a federal government; and

whether the promise of publick good, has been fallacious or fulfilled by the monopolies of currency, of manufactures, and the
extension of federal patronage, the publick can decide. Yet, whatever may have been their temporary effect, it is obvious that the
enlightened framers of the constitution considered the condition
of publick good, as an enlargement and not a restriction of
power; and that it would defeat all the limitations of the constitution, by which a federal government could be formed or sustained. It was a pretext which would fit every encroachment or
usurpation; and no powers could be more indefinite and sovereign than those of granting exclusive privileges, bestowing
rewards and immunities upon the three comprehensive interests
of society, agriculture, commerce, and manufactures, and patro-
nising capitalists, paupers, knowledge, and ignorance. Such a nest
of powers, though exhibited as sleeping in the *bed of publick good,*
bore so strong a resemblance to the old *bed of justice* in France,
which was the repository of evil as well as good, that they were
all rejected. It was evident that they would be sufficient to re-
hatch the strangled *national* form of government; and the convention having finally preferred the federal form, thought that no
good to the publick could result from such powers, which would
recompense it for the evils it would sustain from the subversion
of that form. The convention saw, that if Congress could exercise such powers, *for the publick good,* it might, upon the same
ground, usurp any powers whatsoever, and in rejecting the
propositions, decided between investing that body with a general
or a limited federal authority. Hence the power to regulate commerce was not intended to revive the rejected proposition to
empower Congress to bestow rewards upon agriculture, commerce, and manufactures. Hence the rejected proposition, to

empower Congress to direct the exercise of the judicial power, cannot enable it to extend the jurisdiction of the supreme court. And for the same reason, a power to make war, cannot revive the rejected power to make canals, or to perform any of those et ceteras, whatever they were, referred to by the journal. If these sweeping and indefinite sovereign powers, or all powers thought by those who exercise them to be necessary for the publick good, with an et cetera besides, though proposed and rejected, do yet pass to Congress under the constitution; then the battle between the national and federal parties in the convention, terminated quite contrary to the usual course of things; the vanquished were victorious, and the victorious were vanquished; and if they were now alive, one party would be as much surprised to discover, that it had carried the consolidating propositions which it had lost, as the other, that it had lost the federal principles which it carried. The spectacle of the slain rising up alive, and the living falling down dead, could not have been expected by either.

No powers can be more sovereign and arbitrary, than those of deciding and doing whatever may administer to the public good, and of pilfering private property by privileges, partialities, premiums, monopolies, rewards, and immunities; nor more capable of reaching any end. Had the rejection of such powers been unnecessary for the security of a federal form of government, the convention might have still been justifiable for the act, as deeming them tyrannical, fraudulent, and oppressive. Did the convention reject them in fact, and re-plant them in masquerade? I discern no evidence in the journal to excite such a suspicion. Colonel Hamilton, far from discerning the supposed ingenuity of sinking a national form of government in a lake of obscurity,

to be fished up by a long line of constructions, when it might
be safer to avow the intention, seems to have quitted the convention in despair, soon after the failure of his project. Mr. Randolph, undoubtedly influenced by having lost his plan also,
refused to sign the constitution. And though Mr. Madison and
Colonel Hamilton both signed it, and Mr. Randolph supported
it in the Virginia convention, they must have been influenced
by the patriotick motive of effecting some good, though they
could not accomplish all which they attempted. These are strong
reasons to prove, that the gentlemen who had contended for a
supreme national government, and of whose propositions for
that purpose, not one was adopted by the constitution, did not
imagine they had succeeded.

The journal of the convention states "that the constitution was
transmitted to Congress, and by it to the state legislatures; that
these legislatures, by separate laws, appointed state conventions
for the consideration of the constitution; and that it was ratified
by the delegates of the people of each state." Every step in its
progress, from beginning to end, defines it to be a federal and not
a national act. The deputies who framed it were federal and not
national deputies. They transmitted it to Congress, because the
assent of that body was required by the federal union of 1777. It
was transmitted by Congress to the state legislatures, because
the federal principle required it. And it was ratified by each state,
because each state was sovereign and independent.

"The conventions of each state, reported to Congress their
ratifications. That of South-Carolina subjoined to theirs a declaration, that no section or paragraph of the constitution warrants
a construction, that the states do not retain every power, not
expressly relinquished by them, and *vested* in the general govern-

ment of the union"; and the conventions of other states subjoined declarations of the same import, or still more explicit, to
their ratifications. The various efforts in the convention to invest
a federal government, or some department thereof, with a negative upon state laws, though generally unknown, were known to
its members. It was natural that the obstinacy with which they
had been persevered in, and the vehement desire to establish a
national government, unequivocally disclosed, should inspire a
jealousy, lest the same design should be attempted by constructions. The great talents and weight of character by which it was
advocated, probably increased this apprehension, and suggested
the necessity for these declarations to those members who knew
the fact, and could estimate the danger. They were a contemporaneous federal construction of the constitution, intended to
counteract and defeat any future construction, by which the
rejected national government might be reinstated. A negative in
the government of the union, or in some of its departments,
upon state legislation, had been strenuously urged and resisted
in the convention, on the same ground; by one party, because it
would establish a national government; by the other, because
it would destroy a federal government.

The convention of New-York prophetically declared "that the
jurisdiction of the supreme court of the United States, or of any
other court to be instituted by Congress, is not in any case to be
increased, enlarged, or extended, by any fiction, collusion, or
mere suggestion."

These contemporary constructions of the states, produced
the amendment, made by the parties to the union, reserving to
the states or to the people, the powers not delegated to the
United States. No negative upon state laws was delegated to

the federal government, or any department thereof, and the absence of such a power had been enforced by its rejection. The right of state legislation without being subject to this negative, not being prohibited to the states, is among the rights reserved. It is in vain to say, that the constructive negative contended for, only extends to such state laws as are contrary to the articles of the constitution, because that very modification of a negative power in the federal government was proposed and rejected. It would have as effectually defeated a federal and established a national government, as a negative in any other form over state laws. The mutual checks established for the security of a federal government, between the state and federal departments, are positively established, by the exclusion of a supreme negative power in either over the other, for the purpose of inspiring that mutual moderation, which is an end of a division of power, and one of the securities for a free government. And the guardianship of this desirable moderation, is deposited in three-fourths of the states. Co-ordinate and independent powers alone, can beget mutual moderation; an unchecked supremacy uniformly inspires arrogance, and causes oppression. To defeat or weaken federal checks by a substitution of constructive national checks, is therefore not less hostile to the freedom of the states, than to the sufficiency of facts and words for establishing a federal form of government.

SECTION V

The Subject Concluded

Let us suspend the consideration of contemporaneous testimony, and concisely review the ground we have passed over. Suppose the proceedings of the convention had been publick, and that all the panoply for the establishment of a national government, had been displayed in the newspapers. Suppose the states to have been alarmed by the exhibition, and to have remonstrated against the project. That this would have been the case, is demonstrated by the credentials to their deputies, and the opinions annexed to their ratifications. Suppose the states, after the publication of the constitution, to have retained fears inspired by the attempts to establish a national government, and that a great number of eminent men had assured them that these fears were groundless. And suppose that the states, still unsatisfied, had, for conclusive security, insisted upon the amendments which they added to the constitution; particularly that reserving all their rights not delegated. Had the proposals for a national government, and for negatives over state laws and judgments, been published when they were made, there is no doubt but that they would have provoked the irresistible remonstrances of every state. Now imagine, that in consequence of state oppositions, these projects had been abandoned exactly as they were, in consequence of the opposition by state deputies; that the federal constitution had been substituted for them; and that the states had, under the impression which the projects had made, subjoined to it the amendments. Could the states have been honestly told, after all this process, that the apparent rejection of a national government and its supreme negatives, was only a delusion to appease their fears, and a bait to allure them within the trap, hypocritically abandoned?

Now this very case is that under consideration. The proposals for a national government and its negative over the state acts, were really made. They were opposed by the state deputies, who had a knowledge of them. They were rejected. A different form of government was promulgated. It contained no such negative. The states expounded its meaning to be federal, by a positive reservation of rights not delegated. And now they are told that the devil, thus repeatedly exorcised, still remains in the church.

The notoriety of this deception is fully illustrated by recollecting, that the states, by their deputies (and they could only do it by deputies), had made themselves sovereign and independent; that they had already united in virtue of that character; that in virtue of that character, they had appointed deputies to frame a more perfect union; that by these deputies they voted as states; that they ratified the constitution as states; that they immediately amended it as states; that they reserved the supreme power of altering it as states; that they vote in the senate as states; and that they are represented as states in the other federal legislative branch. Further, the declaration of independence was never repealed. Its annual commemorations demonstrated, and continue to demonstrate, a publick opinion, that it still lives; and the constitution did not confer sovereignty and independence upon the federal government, as the declaration of independence had done upon the states. On the contrary, by the constitution, the states may take away all the powers of the federal government, whilst that government is prohibited from taking away a single power reserved to the states. Under all these circumstances, is it possible that any one state of the union, in ratifying the constitution, which literally conformed to previous solemn acts, to previous words and phrases, and to the settled rights of the states, entertained the most distant idea, that it was destroying itself; betraying its people; establishing a national government; and creating a supreme negative over all its acts, political and civil, or political only, with which the federal government, or one of its departments, was invested by implication.

Sovereignty is the highest degree of political power, and the establishment of a form of government, the highest proof which can be given of its existence. The states could not have reserved any rights by the articles of their union, if they had not been sovereign, because they could have no rights, unless they flowed from that source. In the creation of the federal government, the states exercised the highest act of sovereignty, and they may, if they please, repeat the proof of their sovereignty, by its annihilation. But the union possesses no innate sovereignty, like the states; it was not self-constituted; it is conventional, and of course subordinate to the sovereignties by which it was formed. Could the states have imagined, when they entered into a union, and retained the power of diminishing, extending, or destroying the powers of the federal government, that they who "created and could destroy," might have this maxim turned upon themselves, by their own creature; and that this misapplication of words was able both to deprive them of sovereignty, and bestow it upon a union subordinate to their will, even for existence. I have no idea of a sovereignty constituted upon better ground than that of each state, nor of one which can be pretended to on worse, than that claimed for the federal government, or some portion of it. Conquest or force would give a much better title to sovereignty, than a limited deputation or delegation of authority. The deputations by sovereignties, far from being considered as killing the sovereignties from which they have derived limited powers, are evidences of their existence; and leagues between states demonstrate their vitality. The sovereignties which imposed the limitations upon the federal government, far from supposing that they perished by the exercise of a part of their faculties, were vindicated, by reserving powers in which their deputy, the federal government, could not participate; and the usual right of sovereigns to alter or revoke its commissions.

If, under all these circumstances, the states could never have conceived that they had, by their union, relinquished their sovereignties; created a supreme negative power over their laws; or established a national government; their opinion ought to be the rule for the construction of the constitution. And if the constitution has, by implication, effected all these ends without their knowledge or consent, it is certainly the most recondite speculation that was ever formed, and the states of all cullies, the most excusable.

Yates's Notes

It is obvious to the reader, that my chief object is to exhibit facts, generally unknown, for the purpose of enabling the state republicks, the federal republick, and the people, to compare the federal division of power, with its concentration in one supreme national government; and that though I subjoin to the history, observations in relation to the preference of one system, it is with a deep conviction of my inability to do justice to this part of the subject, and a sincere reference to the tribunal of publick opinion.

In pursuance of this historical design, I shall now advert to Judge Yates's notes of the secret debates, preceded by Mr. Luther Martin's statement of explanatory facts; one, chief justice of the state of New-York; the other, an eminent lawyer of the state of Maryland. Both these gentlemen appear to have been as thoroughly convinced of the superiority of a federal, as other gentlemen were of the superiority of a monarchical or national, form of government; and both left the convention under a conviction that the latter would be established. They unfortunately abandoned their opposition to the national form, at the juncture when the New-Hampshire delegates arrived, and before the federal system prevailed; carrying with them a belief, that the former would maintain its ground, and that whatever gloss it might receive to conciliate or deceive publick opinion, it would yet contain hidden seeds of consolidation. Subsequently to their departure, the plan of government was changed from a national to a federal form. Whether this was effected by the accession of New-Hampshire, or by the refusal of the states, hitherto in the minority, to accede to a national form of government; or whether the change was radical and sincere, or only superficial and delusive; these gentlemen were prevented from discerning, by their absence. They therefore viewed the constitution under the prepossession inspired by the eagerness for a national government, displayed in the convention before they left it; and were influenced in their construction by the suspicion, that the majority, whose success they had deplored, would endeavour to conceal in a labyrinth, the design which could not succeed if distinctly disclosed. Under this prepossession, they construed the constitution, and their constructions must of course be erroneous. But the same candour which estimates the prepossessions of these two gentlemen, will also estimate those of Mr. Madison and Mr. Hamilton. If the constructions of the two first were liable to be influenced by their fears, those of the two last were as liable to be influenced by their wishes; and a prepossession in favour of a national government was an authority, at least as suspicious for ascertaining the meaning of the constitution, as a prepossession against it. On this ground, I shall reject all the opinions of Mr. Martin and Mr. Yates, asserting that the constitution would be construed with a view to make it the matrix of a national government; and on the same ground, those of Mr. Madison and Mr. Hamilton, asserting that it was really intended for this matrix, ought also to be rejected.

But there is a great difference between the facts asserted by all these honourable men, and their speculative opinions. Prejudice is less able to conceal plain truth, than to invent incorrect constructions. Facts may be sustained or contested by other facts; but speculative opinions can avail themselves of all the defects of language. I shall therefore only select the facts asserted by Mr. Martin and Mr. Yates, which are sustained by the journal of the convention, or by other evidence.

Secret proceedings of the convention, page 12. Mr. Martin. "So extremely solicitous were they, that their proceedings should not transpire, that the members were prohibited even from taking copies of resolutions, on which the convention were deliberating, or extracts of any kind from the journals, without formally moving for, and obtaining permission, by a vote of the convention, for that purpose."

The fact of this jealous secrecy is ascertained by the journal, and the perseverance in it for years. Even now, the veil is imperfectly removed; the journal has not come to the general knowledge of the publick, and it appears in a mutilated state. It stops or is impenetrably obscure, precisely at the period when the projected plan for a national form of government was supplanted by the federal system; and a suppression of the important steps by which this radical change was effected, must have taken place in the convention, or subsequently. Thus the vindicators of a federal construction of the constitution are deprived of a great mass of light, and the consolidating school have gotten rid of a great mass of detection. Secrecy is intended for delusion, and delusion is fraud. If it was dictated by an apprehension, that a knowledge of the propositions and debates, would have alarmed the settled preference of the states and of the publick, for a federal form of government, it amounts to an acknowledgement that these propositions and debates were hostile to that form and to the publick opinion. If, by an apprehension that a publication of the journal and debates, would produce a construction hostile to the rejected national form of government, it is an acknowledgment that constructions in favour of that form, are hostile to the constitution adopted. To avoid these consequences, and no others that I can discern, it was necessary to keep the people in the dark, and this stratagem to obtain a victory over their most sacred right in the ambuscade mode, can only be accounted for upon a supposition, that a real hostility of opinion existed between the publick and a party of politicians behind the curtain, which rendered it necessary that the people should be worked as puppets, first by the wire of concealment, and secondly by the wire of construction, into the catastrophe of a consolidated government, either national or monarchical.

Page 13. L. Martin. "The resolutions of the members from Virginia were discussed with great coolness in a committee of the whole house, and hopes were formed that the farther we proceeded in their examination, the better the house might be satisfied of the impropriety of adopting them, and that they would be finally rejected. Whilst they were under discussion, a number of the members who disapproved them, were preparing another system, such as they thought more conducive to the happiness and welfare of the states. The committee, by a *small majority,* agreed to a report, declaring, among other things, that a *national* government ought to be established, consisting of a *supreme legislative, judiciary, and executive.* That the national legislature ought to be empowered to legislate in all cases to which the separate states are incompetent, or *in which the harmony of the United States may be interrupted* by the exercise of individual legislation, and to *negative all laws* passed by the several states, contravening, in the opinion of the legislature of the United States, *the articles of the union.* And that the jurisdiction of the *national* judiciary, shall extend to questions which involve the *national peace and harmony.* There were three parties in the convention. One, whose object it was to abolish and annihilate all state governments, and to bring forward one *general* government over this extensive continent, of a *monarchical nature,* under certain restrictions and limitations. The second party was not for the abolition of the state governments, nor for the introduction of a monarchical government under any form; but they wished to establish such a system, as would give their own states undue power. A third party was what I considered truly federal and republican, which were unwilling to act contrary to the purpose for which they were elected. The first party, *conscious that the people of America* would reject their system, if proposed, joined the second, well knowing that by departing from a federal system, they paved the way for their favourite object, the destruction of the state governments, and the introduction of monarchy. Parts of the proposed system were warmly and zealously opposed."

I premise, that in using the words monarchist, suprematist, consolidator, republican, federalist, or any equivalent expressions, neither praise nor imputation is designed to be insinuated in relation to any person or party; and that they are only employed to explain political opinions, and to display the force of extracts. My wish is to exhibit a fair history of political tenets, to assist the publick in deciding upon their respective merits; for with great satisfaction I declare that I have met with many persons, belonging to all these political sects, of unsullied integrity and great talents, with whom I wished to reciprocate the most cordial friendship; nor do I claim any right of private judgment for myself, which I am not perfectly willing should be enjoyed by them.

The facts stated by Mr. Martin are completely sustained by the journal of the convention, and far from being aggravated, are related in a softer tone than it would have justified; probably from a fear of exceeding the truth; as the vouchers necessary to refresh his memory, were locked up in the strong box of secrecy. It is evident from the journal, that the difference between a national and a federal government was earnestly debated, thoroughly considered, and well understood, in the convention. Both from the journal and Mr. Martin's assertion, it appears, that the identical two points of difference between these two forms of government, which comprise the question now in debate, were considered and determined. It was proposed to invest a *national Congress* with an unlimited negative over *all laws* of the states, contravening, in its opinion, the *articles of the union*. It was determined to confine the negative of a *federal Congress to specified cases*. It was proposed to extend the jurisdiction of a *national judiciary*, to questions which involve the *national peace and harmony*. It was determined to confine the jurisdiction of a *federal judiciary*, to *specified cases* also. Controversies between the federal and state departments would certainly arise, and might contravene the articles of the union, so as to involve the national peace and harmony. Propositions to invest a national legislature and a national judiciary with powers to settle such controversies, accorded with the plan of a national government, and must have been adopted had that plan succeeded. But when the federal plan was preferred, the attributes of the national plan were necessarily abandoned; and a federal balance was of course substituted for a national supremacy. The power proposed to be given over state rights to a national legislature and judiciary, could not be given to a federal legislature and judiciary, because it would have made them national. Therefore this supreme power was approved of in connexion with a national, and rejected in connexion with a federal, form of government. The reason for the approbation was, that a national government could not exist without a supreme controlling power over the states; and the reason for its rejection was, that a federal government could not exist with it. A mutual controlling power between the federal and state departments, was as necessary for a federal, as an abolition of this principle was for a national, government.

Mr. Hamilton's selection of one half of these attributes of a national form of government, and Mr. Madison's selection of the other, to be constructively reinstated in the constitution, produces a curious anomaly. The convention, so long as it contemplated a national government, determined that a concurrent power of preserving the articles of the union and its peace and harmony, ought to be lodged in a national legislature and judiciary. Mr. Hamilton gives this power to Congress exclusively. Mr. Madison gives it exclusively to the federal judiciary. Thus neither of these gentlemen adheres to the national system with which a supreme power was associated in the convention, nor to the federal system from which it was dissevered by the same body; but yet their two halves make up a whole national government, of which both approved. The plan for a national government, proposed to invest a national legislature with a negative power over state laws contravening "the articles of the union or treaties," and as a jurisdiction in the case of treaties was given by the constitution to the federal judiciary, but not in the case of contraventions to the articles of the union, a violent presumption arises, that the latter power, only contemplated for a national legislature, was never intended to be given to a federal judiciary. We do not discern in the journal of the convention, in the secret debates, or in the constitution, the most distant idea of placing the *articles of the union* exclusively under the guardianship of a judicial department, either when a national or federal government was contemplated; and such a proposition would not have obtained the least countenance, because it would not have accorded with either of the three forms, national, monarchical, or federal. Mr. Hamilton's construction is more consistent with the national system proposed, and the federal system adopted, and also more republican, than Mr. Madison's, because a supremacy in Congress would be more national, as the house of representatives is elected by the people; more federal, as the senate is appointed by the state legislatures; and more republican, if that word embraces popular influence; than a supremacy in the judiciary, or a single court. A judiciary is associated with all governments, monarchical, aristocratical, or republican, and contains no innate principle for discriminating between those which are despotick, and those which are free. The nature of a government is defined by the structure of the legislative and executive departments. These contain the essential distinctions between free and despotick, and between federal and national governments. Whether therefore it was the intention of the constitution to establish a free or a despotick, a federal or a national, government, the departments most essential for effecting either object, must have been the means used, and not a department never contemplated as possessing any such capacity.

The last paragraph extracted from Mr. Martin's statement, proposes a subject for public consideration, yet more important, as being more deeply connected with the preservation of a free, fair, and moderate form of government. If the parties he describes did exist, yet exist, and will for ever exist, it is evident that civil liberty can only be preserved by a constant attention to their movements, and a perpetual counteraction of their efforts. Monarchy, its hand-maid, consolidation, and its other hand-maid, ambition, all dressed in popular disguises, require the utmost watchfulness from those who do not love them, and prefer a republican government.

History and human nature both demonstrate, that in all nations a party invariably exists, disposed to elevate the powers of a government to a pitch graduated by personal motives, and to tighten a magical cordage about the people, until it must break or be made of iron. Ambition and avarice are rope-makers constantly at work, and they unfortunately inlist the most skilful workmen, by offering the highest wages. Hence popular rights are forced to enter the list under great disadvantages, as is evinced by the humble instrument they have used in this instance. Superiorities of wealth and talents meet their struggles, and have almost universally defeated their efforts. Poor and rich men of great talents generally unite in fostering principles, which will afford them the best markets; and the best understandings are often the worst authorities, because they are exposed to the highest temptations. History and human nature are therefore credible witnesses, united with the journal, for confirming the truth of Mr. Martin's formidable assertion.

Waiving foreign, it may be sufficient to adduce the most prominent domestick events, by which this bias of human nature is established. The respectable and well-informed party called tories, at the epoch of our revolution, contended for the supremacy of the British parliament. National splendour, national strength, and a national government, were the arguments they used; but personal considerations, suggested by the prominence of their stations, or the hopes suggested by their talents, really forged their opinions. If the war of words between the whigs and tories, preceding the war with swords, could be correctly related, it would be seen that the topicks and arguments now used by the parties in favour of a federal or national government, had been anticipated; and that the similitude between the cases had produced a similitude between the reasonings. The tories loudly insisted upon the benefits of a supreme power in the British parliament and judiciary over the provincial legislatures and judiciaries, as sufficient compensations for the ignorance and partiality of these British supremacies as to the local interest of the provinces; and that local oppressions would beget national prosperity. They considered a British power of controlling provincial patriots and demagogues, as an instrument, not of tyranny, but of liberty; and they insisted that the precedents established by these supremacies, though usurpations, were constitutional laws. The whigs, more loudly as it proved, urged the oppressive consequences certainly resulting from a supremacy, incapable, from the supremacy of nature, of ascertaining what was good or bad for the provinces, locally. That the pretended national prosperity, was only a pretext of ambition and monopoly. That by unprincipled precedents, and the pretext of restraining provincial demagogues, it was intended to feed avarice, gratify ambition, and make one portion of the nation tributary to another. And that precedents for subjecting liberty to tyranny did not become sacred, because they were unheeded or could not be successfully resisted. The whigs did not consider time as an ocean, in which, should the principles of liberty be once overwhelmed, there would be no buoy for finding them again. The same arguments are now revived. The natural impossibility that the supremacies now contended for, should understand the laws, manners, and local interests of each state, will, it is said, be recompensed by the same benefits shed over the provinces by the British supremacy. Demagogues are yet so terrible, that their suppression, at the expense of losing state rights, will still be a good bargain; and precedents so holy as to be more valuable than principles or constitutions. Reformers are justly objects of suspicion, because some secret design too often lurks under their professions, and dictates their attempts. Sensible of this, the whigs and tories charged each other with innovation; and the justice of the allegation on either side, depended on the question, whether British supremacy over the provinces internally, could be legitimately exercised; or whether the provinces possessed a birth-right title to local self-government. The same mutual charge of innovation is revived in discussing the same question. The declaration of independence is a more visible birth-right of the states, than any the provinces could produce. But the states are reduced to corporations by the suprematists, as the provinces were by the tories, to evade the charge of innovation. It is very remarkable, that the same doctrine which was used as a justification of the British legislative and judicial supremacy over the provinces, is now used to justify a federal legislative and judicial supremacy over the states. It is said to be no innovation, and only a vindication of the ancient political subordination of the provinces. If the argument is sound, it proves that the claim of British supremacy was well-founded; and that it is yet the best, because it is the oldest, title, which could not be vacated vi et armis, as the lawyers say. Whether the revived doctrine will be more successful than its lineal ancestor, or less likely to terminate in civil war or disunion, may be doubtful; but there is no doubt that it is a further confirmation of Mr. Martin's account of the parties in the convention.

If more was known of the intrigue suppressed by General Washington, about the end of the revolutionary war, it might illustrate the existence of such parties as Mr. Martin describes. Its object must have been formidable, both from the weight of the characters by whom it was conceived, and also from having called forth the powerful opposition of a man, too modest to become prominent without an urgent occasion, and too respectable to waste his energy upon slight occurrences. It could have been nothing less than a political revolution, either to a national or monarchical form of government; and if it contemplated either, it establishes the previous existence of the parties which appeared in the convention.

Historical truth requires a reference to Mr. Adam's volumes in defence of the American constitutions, published during the confederation of 1777. They appear to be the result of profound literature in ancient political lore, and a deep conviction imbibed from that source. They were a manly, candid, and independent vindication of his own opinions, by a gentleman too honourable to advance them by secret or indirect modes, and too strongly impressed with their truth, to suspect that they were unable to encounter our modern improvements in the science of government. These learned volumes had their effect upon those whose object was power or wealth. They opened a rich and tempting British perspective to talents, ambition, and avarice, and they effected a combination of these powerful agents; but they failed in a plain contest with republican principles. Their impression however remained, and the eternal party, though foiled, was not subdued. After waving its crest in the convention, with all the candour inspired by secrecy, and all the energy inspired by conviction; and after having sustained a signal defeat; it is again recruited by aspirants from the republican ranks, throws down the gauntlet in open day, and challenges its antagonist to renew the combat.

But all these confirmations of Mr. Martin's assertions are surperfluous. They are established by the journal of the convention. In this we see the very parties described by Mr. Martin, and foretold by experience. Did they die with the convention, and could the lectures of the constitution repeal the laws of nature, and obliterate passions destined to live for ever? The preceding events, the journal, and the testimony of Mr. Martin, concur in proving the existence of the parties which yet divide us, although their creation has been ascribed to Mr. Jefferson. Can any assertion be more groundless, than one which cannot be true, without denying the well-known qualities of human nature, and without postponing previous events to subsequent periods? Irrevocable laws have as absolutely decided, that a perpetual struggle shall exist between liberty and tyranny, as between virtue and vice; and it is equally unjust to charge the advocates of a free form of government, or the advocates of moral rectitude, with the introduction of party spirit. Mr. Jefferson was in Europe, when our parties appeared in the convention. Subterfuges from historical truth, and local facts, indicate a consciousness of frailty, or a supremacy of prejudice.

The principles of limited monarchy were eulogized in the convention, and an attempt to establish a national government, was persevered in during the greater part of its session. These two parties are therefore unequivocally defined. The third party, called federal and truly republican, by Mr. Martin, could not be so clearly identified, because the various interpretations of the words federal and republican, enable political parties to decorate principles essentially different, with these robes admired by the publick. Like stars and garters, they may be used to adorn the most opposite characters, and the beholder who is content with their imposing surface, to ascertain patriotism or ambition, will act like one who ascertains the principles of individuals by the richness of their dress. But however indefinite may be the terms used by Mr. Martin to describe it, the journal demonstrates that a third party did exist in the convention, and that this third party successfully resisted both a monarchical and national form of government.

So far the journal literally sustains Mr. Martin's statement of facts, and to establish the last, namely, that the monarchical and national parties united, the evidence is not less conclusive. It is obvious from the journal, that the majority so long prevalent, was produced by a coalition between these two parties; and that had each of the three parties persisted separately to insist upon its own principles, the federal republican party would have been the strongest, although it received the aspect of a minority from the union of the other two. Of this union, the events between the formation and ratification of the constitution afford proofs. What became of the monarchical and consolidating parties on the dis-solution of the convention? Were their principles also dissolved, and did they become adverse to their own creeds? or did they, from the same policy which dictated their junction in the con-vention, and the same consciousness that the people of the states were not ripe for either of their systems, melt up themselves with the strong federal party, as a safer step towards their ultimate designs, than an open avowal of their principles? It is not as evident that this fusion of the monarchical and consolidating parties into one mass, took place to procure the ratification of the constitution, as that it was designed in the convention to introduce a national government? There are some metals of properties so very similar, that their mutual attraction is highly amicable, and their amalgamation easy. Mr. Madison and Mr. Hamilton, the champions of the national and monarchical systems, liberally yielded to the example established in the convention, and renewed the same conciliatory treaty. The publick indeed was not edified by the arguments used by one of these accomplished men, for reducing the states to corporations, and establishing a supreme national government; nor by the eulogies of a limited monarchy, expressed by the other; and with unexampled felicity both substituted for the consolidating and monarchical dialect, used in the convention, a federal one, ingeniously constructed to accommodate itself with publick opinion, and also with the prepossessions of their respective partisans. Monarchy and consolidation disappeared from the question, conspicuous as they had been in the journal, and the term federal was adopted, because it would embrace the parties inclined to either, and also the party adverse to both, but friendly to a federal system. If this new dialect, so different from that used in the convention, was policy, the monarchical and consolidating parties will of course adhere to the same policy; if it was the consequence of an essential difference between a national and a federal government, a national dialect cannot be proper for construing the constitution, since a federal dialect was necessary to procure its ratification. If these gentlemen were sincere in the convention, the arguments they used in opposition to a federal system, cannot be applicable

in defence of it; if they were ingenious in procuring the ratification of the constitution, the ingenuity consisted in copious solicitations of publick opinion by federal doctrines, mixed with tints
transfused from the conclave, too faint to alarm the federal party,
and yet sufficiently perceivable to obtain the concurrence of the
consolidating and monarchical parties. The intimations that
supremacy or sovereignty was lodged in Congress or the
supreme federal court, enveloped in clouds of sound federal reasoning, was a profound or lucky piece of dexterity to effect both
objects.

Truth has compelled me to admit, however it is to be
deplored, that a superiority of talents will for ever appear on the
side of a high-toned system of government. The adoption of the
word federal as a political badge is an illustration of this fact. I
do not recollect whether the Federalist was entitled to the
applause merited by this proof of genius; but whoever was its
author, it was most happily contrived for covering the monarchical, consolidating, and federal parties. The last, at the time the
constitution was ratified, was, and yet is, the most numerous.
But unfortunately, both then and since, no test existed for
expelling heterogeneous mixtures. The genuine federal party in
the convention, proceeded upon two principles, one, that a
republican equality between the states ought to be established;
the other, that each state ought to enjoy the exclusive power of
managing its local interests. Could not some device be invented
emblematical of such principles? We do not discern, except in
the convention, and avowed hostility to them. So far as this hostility can insinuate itself into the councils of a genuine federal
party, it must corrupt or warp its principles, just as monarchical
principles may corrupt republican. Monarchical or consolidat-

ing parties, whilst they pretend to fight under federal colours, will fight for their own principles. They are seeds of disease in a federal union, which will be for ever sprouting, and if they are not eradicated as they appear by genuine federal principles, they will over-shadow and kill them.

A party "federal and truly republican," being thus deprived of half its motto, was forced to take the other half, and hoisted an ensign called republican; a definition which expelled from its ranks both the monarchical and consolidating parties. Ambitious and avaricious people were all disgusted with it. Many of the genuine federal party suspected it of a design to destroy the union, and therefore united with it slowly. The consolidating and monarchical parties, with more acuteness, perceived the devotion to a federal system, and therefore labored to keep this suspicion alive. The monarchical party, without much acuteness, could see that its object was infinitely more likely to be effected by consolidating constructions of the constitution, than by the federal constructions which obtained its ratification.

The political tactician who displayed a banner, with only the word federal written upon it, ably copied the policy by which a conqueror makes a nation subservient to its own destruction. Federalists and republicans were engaged in hostilities by monarchists and consolidators, who derived strength from their conflicts, and expected victory from their divisions.

Between the monarchical party in the convention, which wished for a suppression of the state governments; and the national party, which proposed that they should be made dependent upon a supreme legislature, judiciary, and executive, a chink is undoubtedly discernible, and this chink is now said to be the place, not for crushing, but for securing a federal system, because it is baited with didactick federalism, just as certain traps, baited with honey, are contrived to catch bears. But the chasm made by the ridiculous quarrel between the words federal and republican, as if they were not twins which must die or live together, seems to be well contrived for entrapping, not bears, but sovereign states.

The Subject Concluded

Whether Yates's notes of the secret debates in the convention, are to be considered as explanatory of the secret journal, or the journal as explanatory of the notes, the connexion between them is so intimate, necessary, and uniform, as to stamp both histories with unquestionable veracity. Every speech recorded by Yates, accords with some proposition recorded in the journal. His notes coincide with Mr. Martin's account of parties. When Mr. Martin wrote, he could not have had any knowledge of the notes; and when Mr. Yates made his notes, Mr. Martin's observations were not written. The reader can compare the following extracts both with the journal, and Martin's statements.

Yates, page 97. "Governor Randolph candidly confessed, that his resolutions were *not intended for a federal government, he meant a strong consolidated union, in which the idea of states should be nearly annihilated.*"

"Mr. Pinckney read his system, and confessed that it was grounded on nearly the same principle as Mr. Randolph's resolutions."

106. "Mr. Dickenson is for combining the state and national legislatures in the same views and measures."

"Mr. Madison is of opinion, that when we agreed to the first resolve of having a *national government,* consisting of a *supreme* executive, judicial, and legislative power; it was then intended to

operate the exclusion of a federal government, and the more extensive we made the basis, the greater probability of duration,
happiness, and good order."

107. "Mr. Wilson. The state governments ought to be preserved; the freedom of the people and their internal good police,
depends on their existence in full vigour; but such a government can only answer local purposes. That it is not possible a
general government, as despotick as even that of the Roman
emperors, could be adequate to the government of the whole
without this distinction."

108. "Mr. Pinckney moved that the national legislature should
have the power of *negativing all laws* to be passed by the state
legislatures, which they may judge to be improper. Mr. Madison
wished that the line of jurisdiction could be drawn, he would
be for it, but upon reflection, he finds it impossible, and therefore
he is for the amendment."

110. "The question put on Mr. Pinckney's motion, 7 states
against, Delaware divided, Virginia, Pennsylvania, and Massachusetts for it."

112. "Mr. Patterson. Let us consider with what powers we are
sent here. By our credentials we see, that the basis of our present
authority is founded on a revision of the articles of the present
confederation, and to alter and amend them in such parts where
they appear defective. Can we on this ground form a *national*
government? We are met here as the deputies of thirteen *independent and sovereign states for federal purposes.* Can we *consolidate
their sovereignty and form one nation;* and annihilate the sovereignties of our states who sent us here for other purposes?"

117. "Governor Randolph. If the state judges are not sworn
to the observance of the new government, will they not judi-

cially determine in favour of their state laws? We are erecting a *supreme national government;* ought it not to be supported, and can we give it too many sinews?"

"Mr. Gerry rather thinks that the national legislators ought to be sworn to preserve the state constitutions, as they will run the greatest risque to be annihilated; and therefore moved it. For Mr. Gerry's amendment, 7 ayes, 4 noes."

122. "Mr. Lansing. Had the legislature of the state of New York, apprehended that their powers would have been construed to extend to the formation of a *national government,* no delegates would have appeared on the part of that state. *New plans, annihilating the rights of the states* (unless upon evident necessity), can never succeed."

124. "Mr. Patterson. When independent societies confederate for mutual defence, they do so in their collective capacity; and then each state for these purposes must be considered as one of the contracting parties. Destroy this balance of equality, and you endanger the rights of the lesser societies, by the danger of usurpation in the greater."

Mr. Patterson's was a plan for a federal government, supported by many other arguments.

128. "Governor Randolph. The question now is, which of the two plans is to be preferred. The resolutions from Virginia must have been adopted on a supposition that a *federal government was impracticable.*"

129. "Mr. Hamilton. I have well considered the subject, and am convinced that no amendment of the confederation can answer the purpose of a good government, so long as state sovereignties do in any shape exist; and I have great doubts whether a national government on the Virginia plan can be made effec-

tual. From the lessons of experience results the evident conclusion, that all federal governments are weak and distracted. To
avoid the evils deducible from these observations, *we must establish a general and national government, and annihilate the state distinctions and state operations. I believe the British government forms the
best model the world ever produced,* and such has been its progress
in the *minds of many,* that this truth *gradually gains ground.* This
government has for its object publick strength and individual
security. It is said with us to be unattainable. *If it was once formed
it would maintain itself.* See the excellence of the British executive.
He is placed above temptation. He can have no distinct interests
from the publick welfare. *Nothing short of such an executive can
be efficient.* I would give the legislature *unlimited power of passing
all laws* without exception, and to appoint courts in each
state, so as to make the state governments unnecessary to it. *I
confess that this plan, and that from Virginia, are very remote from the
idea of the people."* Mr. Hamilton acknowledges that state sovereignties did exist, and proposes to destroy them, as is now
attempted.

184. "Judge Read. I would have no objection if the government was more national. *A state government is incompatible with a
national government.* The plan of the gentleman from New-York
(Mr. Hamilton's) is certainly the best."

"Mr. Madison. Some gentlemen are afraid that the plan is not
sufficiently national, while others apprehend that it is too much
so. If this point of representation was once well fixed, we should
come nearer to one another in sentiment. The necessity would
then be discovered of circumscribing more effectually the state
governments, and enlarging more effectually the bounds of the
general government. *Some contend that the states are sovereign, when*

in fact they are only political societies. The states never possessed the essential rights of sovereignty. *They were always vested in Congress.* Their voting as states in Congress is no evidence of their sovereignty. The state of Maryland voted by counties. Did this make the counties sovereign? The states, at present, are only great *corporations,* having the power of making by-laws, and these are effectual only if they are not contradictory to the general confederation. *The states ought to be placed under the control of the general government, at least as much as they formerly were under the king and the British parliament.* The arguments, I observe, have taken a different turn, and I hope may convince all of the necessity for a strong energetic government, which would equally tend to give energy to, and protect, the state governments."

188. "Mr. Gerry. It appears to me that the states never were independent."

190. "Mr. Madison. *The great danger to our general government, is the great southern and northern interests of the continent being opposed to each other. Look at the votes in Congress, and most of them stand directly divided by the geography of the country, not according to the size of the states.*"

200. "Judge Ellsworth. I am asked by my honourable friend from Massachusetts, whether by entering into a national government, I will not equally participate in national security? I confess I should; but I want domestick happiness, as well as general security. *A general government will never grant me this, as it cannot know my wants or relieve my distress.*"

201. "Mr. Sherman. It seems we have gotten to a point, that we cannot move one way or the other." This happened on the 2d of July, and Messrs. Yates and Lansing left the convention on the 5th, which was not dissolved until the 17th of September.

"Mr. Morris. It is confessed on all hands, that the second branch ought to be a check on the first, for without its having this effect, it is perfectly useless. The first branch, originating from the people, will ever be subject to precipitancy, changeability, and excess. This can only be checked by the ability and virtue in the second branch. The second branch ought to be composed of men of great and established property; an aristocracy; and to make them completely independent, they must be chosen for life, or they will be a useless body. Such an aristocratic body will keep down the turbulency of a democracy. But if you elect them for a shorter period, they will only be a name, and we had better be without. Thus constituted I hope they will shew us the weight of an aristocracy."

"History proves, I admit, that the men of large property will uniformly endeavour to establish tyranny. How then shall we ward off the evil? Give them the second branch, and you secure their weight for the publick good."

"The wealthy will ever exist; and you never can be safe unless you gratify them as a body, in the pursuit of honour and profit. Prevent them by positive institutions, and they will proceed in some left-handed way. It is good policy that the men of property be collected in one body. Let vacancies be filled up as they happen, by the executive. If you choose for seven years, whether chosen by the people or by the states; whether by equal suffrage or in any other proportion, how will they be a check? They will have local and state prejudices. *A government by compact is no government at all.*" This extract discloses the influence of Mr. Adams's political system. All these ideas are borrowed from it.

From the 5th of July to the 17th of September, nothing is to be found, either in the journal of the convention or Yates's notes, by which the change from a national to a federal government can be traced; but in addition to the wide difference between the national form proposed, and the federal form adopted, we have the highest authority of which the case was susceptible, that this radical alteration was effected.

In the appendix to Yates's notes, page 265, is the letter dated on the 17th of September, written by the unanimous order of the convention, signed by its president, and addressed to the president of Congress; containing the following passages:

"It is obviously impracticable, in the *federal government* of these states, to secure *all the rights* of independent sovereignty to each. It is at all times difficult to draw with precision the line between those *rights* which must be surrendered, and *those* which may be *reserved*."

By this solemn document the constitution was offered to the states as a federal form of government; the independent sovereignty of each state was explicitly acknowledged; the impracticability of securing to the states all the rights of their independent sovereignty in conjunction with a federal government, and the practicability of reserving some of these rights, is stated as comprising the character of the constitution; and the difficulty of drawing a precise line between such of these rights as were surrendered, and such as were reserved, is urged as an apology for any imperfection in the attempt. It expressly announced to the states, that the constitution was federal and not national, and that it had drawn a line between rights of sovereignty surrendered and reserved; and it constituted the unanimous decision of the convention, of the two great questions now disputed. The imperfection of this line might apply to both classes of these rights, but it could not destroy either, nor transfer one class of rights to the other, so as to obliterate the line intirely. The line drawn by the constitution, though imperfect, was the only criterion by which a federal, could be distinguished from a national, government; nor could a federal union be contrived, except by the concurrent means both of surrendering and reserving sovereign rights.

Is it possible to imagine that a respectable convention and its magnanimous president, should have combined to deceive the states, by telling them, that the proposed government was federal, and that the constitution divided by a line the delegated federal rights, from the sovereign state rights reserved? The indignity of such a suspicion, and the absurdity of supposing that every member who had contended for a federal government, had renounced his opinion and subscribed to a falsehood, are the foundations upon which the doctrine, "that the government is national," must rest.

The journal and Yates's notes unequivocally discover, that the difference between a federal and national government, was thoroughly understood in the convention, and that the members unanimously admitted, that the two forms were incompatible. The national form was honestly allowed by its advocates, as *nearly annihilating the idea of states, and as not intended for a federal government.* It was admitted that a national government, consisting of a *supreme* executive, judicial, and legislative power, would *operate the exclusion of a federal government.* That the resolutions for the national plan were adopted, upon a supposition that a *federal government was impracticable. That a general and national government would annihilate the state distinctions and operations;* and that such a government once established, would maintain itself. To prevail with the convention to propose a national government, the several doctrines "that the states were never sovereign and independent; that they were only corporations; that they were like counties; that the rights of sovereignty were always vested in Congress; that the rich ought to have aristocratical powers; and that a government by compact, is no government at all," were urged. These admissions and doctrines candidly stated the question, then secretly debated, and now openly, but with less candour, renewed. If a national and a federal government were then incompatible, as the whole convention believed, they must be so still. If the former would then annihilate the latter, it will yet do so. If a national government was then very remote from the idea of the people, such may still be the case. And if the people were not prepared to surrender their principles then, an attempt to overturn them now, by construction, may produce the convulsion than apprehended.

There was no substantial difference between the Virginia plan and Mr. Hamilton's. One proposed that states should continue to exist as corporations or counties, but as subjects of a government invested with *supreme* legislative, executive, and judicial powers; the other, that the state governments should be directly and not indirectly abolished. One gave them rights upon paper, subject to supreme negatives, without any means of defending those rights; the other more candidly denied to them any rights at all. The two plans resemble two plans for defending a country; one, by a mercenary army combined with a militia, but refusing to intrust the militia with arms, lest they should use them against the army; the other, by a mercenary army alone. The Virginia plan opposed paper to power; Mr. Hamilton's tore the frail sanction to pieces, to save power the trouble of disorganizing conflicts, or of quelling abortive oppositions whilst doing the same thing gradually. Those

who approved of but could not carry Mr. Hamilton's plan, saw
in the Virginia plan a kindred alternative; and deriding its federal
preachment, adopted its circuitous and strifeful mode of effecting their object, because they could effect it in no other. Although
neither the Virginia plan nor Mr. Hamilton's succeeded in the
convention, they embraced a mass of talents, too proud and powerful for humility and submission; and they resorted to the engine
of construction, to be directed by many an Archimedes. But at this
point the two parties began to split. Encroachments upon the
paper rights of the states soon appeared, and then Mr. Hamilton
and Mr. Madison divided. One acted and the other preached, each
in accordance with his own principles as displayed in the convention. The gentlemen who first contended for a federal
supremacy over state rights, but yet sincerely wished that this
supremacy should preserve these rights, bethought themselves of
lodging it exclusively in the supreme federal court, insisted that
this court should use it impartially, and that Congress should have
no share of it. Their later associates laugh at these paper chains, as
only the scruples of good souls; and Congress soon believed, that
which is unquestionably true, that its right to supremacy was as
good, and indeed better, than that of the judiciary. In virtue of this
supremacy, contended for by Mr. Hamilton, in the Federalist,
Congress construed the constitution in one way, and Mr. Madison's didactick federalism, construed it in another; as in the cases
of the bank law, the sedition law, and the decision of the supreme
court, that the supremacy of Congress has a right to remove every
obstruction in its way. And a union between federal legislative and
judicial supremacy, has composed an imperative high mightiness,
subject to no check, and equivalent to the monarchical and
national projects, advocated in the convention.

The origin of the coalition between the monarchists and consolidators in the convention, is visible in the journal. It arose from the question of representation. The deputies from the most populous states naturally contended for an absolute preponderance of numbers; those from the small states, for the moral equality of sovereignties. The gentlemen in favour of monarchy or consolidation, united with great address, to use this contest, as the means for effecting their object; and acted with more skill and foresight, than the didactick federalists. They aimed at a possibility; the didactick federalists entertained the hopeless idea of reconciling contradictions. A monarchy or a consolidated government might be established; but a union of states in conjunction with either, was an impossibility. If we believe that a substantial distinction between different forms of government exists, we must conclude that a national government, and a union of states, cannot subsist together, however the appearance of such a fellowship may for a time be kept up, by the courtesy or policy of the supreme associate; just as Augustus retained republican words to confirm imperial power. The verbal federalists however advocated this hopeless experiment, and the advocates of a monarchical or national government, profiting by the example of the Roman triumvir, gladly joined them, as knowing that the experiment would accelerate one of these ends. Happily the experiment was defeated by the establishment of a federal form of government; but we are again told by the gentlemen who prefer monarchy or a national government, that a national and federal government may be made to subsist together, by giving to Congress and its court an absolute supremacy over the state governments, and securing the states by federal words, just as the Roman republick was secured by republican words.

If we should even admit, with Mr. Madison, that the government is semi-federal, and semi-national, the question arises, by
what means can it be kept so? These are ascertained by the means
necessary to maintain a government semi-republican and semi-
monarchical. Each moiety must counterpoise and check the
other. If one principle possesses a supremacy over the other principle, and can remove out of its way all the obstacles which the
balancing principle may place in it, the consequences are
inevitable; because power can only be checked by power. Therefore an equal capacity in each moiety to maintain a government
half federal and half national, is as indispensable, as in the case of
a government half republican and half monarchical. If the state
governments individually, or a bare majority of the states, were
supreme, or had a negative over the acts of the federal government, that moiety would soon perish; and in like manner, if the
federal government should acquire the same powers over the
state governments, they must perish; just as a limited monarchy
would perish if one of its principles obtains a supremacy over the
other.

The Federalist

I have arrived at the most difficult portion of the contemporaneous construction of the constitution, urged for the purpose of obtaining its ratification; difficult, as ingenious ambiguities and contradictions are to be detected. A conscious inferiority to its accomplished authors in a capacity for investigation, except that which arises from equal integrity, renders the task truly alarming. These gentlemen believed that a supreme national government was best for the United States, and I believe that a genuine federal system is more likely to secure their liberty, prosperity, and happiness. Two of them had avowed their preference in the convention, and although they were defeated, yet the opinions by which their efforts had been excited, could not have been obliterated. How unfortunate it was, that these two chief authors of the Federalist were not divided between a federal and national system of government! Had this been the case, the question would have been discussed by the most eminent talents; and the publick might have been assisted by all the arguments on both sides, couched in the most elegant style.

The turbulence of a free government is perpetually contrasted with the repose of tyranny, by those who plead for power, and dread the untractableness of checks devised for its control. Men are apt to see very clearly, whatever they wish or fear; and often surrender the soundest principles to their imaginary apparitions. Tinctures of such impressions are discernible in the Federalist,

in suggestions of the disorderly and discordant proceedings of the
state governments, and in captivating pictures of the safety and
splendour to be expected from a supreme national government.
Its authors had a difficult task to perform, and they performed it
with an ability, which must excite our admiration, though it
may fail to reconcile contradictions. They laboured to gratify
both their own prepossessions and those of the states; and if their
success in effecting the ratification of the constitution, shall be
followed by the reinstatement of a rejected national government,
their ingenuity in proving that a federal system is both right and
wrong, good and bad, must excite our amazement. The difficulty of proving that the constitution had reserved a great portion of sovereign rights to the states, and yet tacitly subjected
them to some unexpressed supremacy, is now vastly increased
by the publication of the journal of the convention, disclosing
the proposal of a supreme national government, the thorough
consideration of it, and the complete expurgation from the constitution, both of its principles and phrases. An honest preference of this project, would be rather whetted than extinguished
by disappointment; and it was almost impossible, whilst the subject was yet fresh, that all the ideas by which it was impressed, and
all the phrases by which it was inculcated, should have been forgotten. It is even wonderful, that the struggle between a prepossession for the rejected supreme national government, and loyalty
to that which was adopted, should have terminated so honourably, and should have disclosed so few traces of a preference
recently riveted to the mind by its long and animated exertions.
The stray words and constructive supremacies, interwoven with
the constitution by the Federalist, look rather like the casual
over-flowings of an accumulated fund, than the effect of a criti-

cal examination into their consistency with the form of government adopted. A national and a federal form were the rivals for preference; and if the same terms and the same construction were applicable to both, the contest in the convention was frivolous, and the preference of the latter form unsubstantial. Hence, although many of the interpretations of the constitution comprised in the Federalist, are profound and correct, it does not follow, that interpolations of words used and of provisions proposed for establishing a national government, ought to countermine the constructions which are federal. I shall endeavour to demonstrate the inconsistency between them by quotations, distinguishing the writer by the initial letter of his name.

H. No. 9. "The proposed constitution, so far from implying an abolition of the state governments, makes them constituent parts of the *national* sovereignty, by allowing them a direct representation in the senate, and leaves in their possession certain exclusive and very important portions of sovereign power." The ambiguity of this sentence arises from the interpolation of the words national sovereignty, which are not in the constitution; from admitting that the powers not delegated were sovereign powers belonging to the governments of the states; and from making these governments constituent parts of a national sovereignty, in virtue of their representation in the senate; by which representation they become the subjects of the assumed national sovereignty. State sovereignty is lodged in the people of each state, but by supposing it to be lodged in their governments, and considering these governments as constituents of a national sovereignty in consequence of their representation in the senate, state rights are made to derive their security, not from the limitations and reservations of the federal compact, but from this representation of their governments, just as Englishmen derive theirs from their representation in parliament. Whatever may be the rights of Englishmen, representation invests the parliament with a supreme power over them; and whatever may be the rights of the political individuals called state governments, representation creates a *national sovereignty* over these also, according to this ingenious sentence.

By taking it for granted that the constitution has established a national sovereignty, the difficulty of proving it is avoided. The phrase "national sovereignty," is assumed in correspondence with that of the British parliament; and the state governments are turned into its constituents by the structure of the senate. Mr. Hamilton thus concedes to himself the essential principle of his plan for a government; knowing that if the concession should succeed, its consequences would certainly follow. A national sovereignty would remove most obstacles to his system, and to use his own sound language, "if it was once formed, it would maintain itself."

The most ingenious and conciliating ground upon which a national sovereignty is erected, is this of representation in the senate. It has an aspect of securing instead of abolishing the reserved rights of the states. This representation was not intended to create a sovereignty in Congress over the reserved rights of the states, but only as one check to secure a correct exercise of the delegated powers. The rights of the states were not reserved to the senate of the United States, but to the states themselves; and are not conveyed to an imaginary national government, upon the ground that their governments are represented in the senate. The journal of the convention shews that a national sovereignty, founded upon the principle of representation, was contemplated so long as the project for a national government prevailed; but it does not contain a solitary intimation, after that project was abandoned, that the representative character, either of the president, the senate, or the house of representatives, conferred sovereign or supreme powers on one or all of these departments, as had been contemplated before a federal system was adopted. If representation is necessarily attended by sovereignty or supremacy, the Congress under the confederation was indeed a sovereign body, but a very dull one, in not having made the discovery; and no limitations of power can be created by constitutions which resort to representation, if it inherently possesses the quality of turning agents into sovereigns.

Suppose it is admitted, as Mr. Hamilton seems to intimate, that the constitution has created two sovereignties, one of the federal and the other of the state governments. By dividing sovereignty into portions, and calling the portion of state governments exclusive, he states a very plain case. The owners of a loaf of bread divide it between two persons. The donation of one half, does not imply a right to eat up the other half. If the state governments possess exclusive sovereign powers, they cannot be deprived of this exclusiveness by their representation in the senate; and if that representation does not deprive them of their exclusive powers, it conveys nothing at all. It follows, that the powers of the federal government are derived from the constitution, and in no degree from representation. Under the constitution, it is a limited government; by inferring sovereignty from representation, it would become unlimited.

Those who deal most in paradox and superlatives, find the least truth. The consolidating school contends that we have two sovereignties; but that one is sovereign over the other; Mr. Hamil-

ton, that we have co-ordinate sovereignties, each invested with
exclusive powers, but that one is made superlative by the representation in the senate. That a *federal* senate should beget a *national*
sovereignty, if we have one, is a political curiosity. These superlative sovereignties, in all their forms, have been less friendly to
human happiness, than limited, divided, and balanced powers.
Lodged either in a monarch, an aristocracy, or a representative
body, they have an innate tendency towards tyranny. Lodged in
one government, they have disclosed combinations among its
members to extort from the people as much property as possible.
They are uniformly oppressive in a high degree, when the territory is extensive. Such imperfections of a superlative sovereignty, indicated our improvement of a system for checking it,
otherwise than by the agency of its own members, or of its own
will. By returning to a sovereignty consolidated in one government, we should revive all the evils of which a superlative
sovereignty has been productive, and surrender all the benefits
hitherto derived, from having superadded to the English mode of
restraining the excesses of sovereignty condensed in one government, the new remedy of assigning different powers to two.
The hostility of consolidated sovereignties to human happiness,
is frequently demonstrated by their recourse to paradoxical arguments, in order to defend their measures. They contend, that the
greater the revenue, the richer are the people; that frugality in the
government is an evil; in the people, a good; that local partialities are blessings; that monopolies and exclusive privileges are
general welfare; that a division of sovereignty will raise up a class
of wicked, intriguing, self-interested politicians, in the states;
and that human nature will be cleansed of these propensities by a
sovereignty consolidated in one government. But in proportion

as power becomes superlative, its ambition and avarice are inflamed; and our division of it between two governments, is one more attempt, in addition to those which have been unsuccessful, to assuage the inflammation, and diminish its malignity. The consolidating school rejects the experiment, however hopeful, and contends, that it degrades the federal government below the English standard. Such is the argument of limited kings, and such the motive by which they are stimulated to acquire the power enjoyed by absolute monarchs. The morbid suggestions of envy cause them to look with longing eyes upon a superiority of power; and it will not be contrary to human nature, if our statesmen should also contemplate the situation of English statesmen, as more desirable than their own, and should languish for an equal degree of exaltation.

H. No. 23. "If the circumstances of our country are such, as to demand a compound instead of a simple; a *confederate* instead of a *sole* government; the essential point which remains to be adjusted, will be to discriminate the objects, as far as it can be done, which shall appertain to the *different provinces or departments of power.* The government of the union must be empowered to pass all laws in relation to its powers. The local governments must possess all the authorities connected with the administration of justice between citizens of the same state. Not to confer in each case a degree of power commensurate to the end, would be to violate the most obvious rules of prudence and propriety."

Mr. Hamilton admits the distinction between a federal and a sole government, and allows that the constitution annexes to the different provinces or departments of power, state and federal, an authority to pass all laws commensurate to the exercise of the rights assigned to each. From this distinction, the existence of separate governments under the constitution, would apparently result; but this conclusion is defeated by the previous doctrine, that a national sovereignty is lodged in the federal government, by the instrumentality of state representation in the senate. We have two governments mutually invested with independent rights, and with authority to exercise these separate rights; and yet but one sovereignty. What are mutual rights, unattended by a mutual power to preserve those rights? Satraps subservient to a superior power. Is there not an obvious inconsistency between the admission of two distinct governments, constituting different provinces or departments of power, and the assertion, that one possesses a sovereignty or supremacy over the other? Under its kings, France was divided into provinces, each having separate rights, but the royal sovereignty reduced France into one consolidated government. Turkey contains many provinces, but all are subservient to one consolidated or superlative sovereignty. By allowing the separate existence of states, invested with distinct powers, but contending for a national sovereignty in the federal government, the United States are placed in the situation of the provinces of France and Turkey.

That this was not the intention of the constitution, is admitted by the hypothetical manner in which Mr. Hamilton introduces the subject. Under his prepossession in favour of a consolidated government, expressed in the convention, he observes, "if the circumstances of our country demand a confederate instead of a sole government." Whence arose the doubt, or what foundation existed for the contrariety, if the constitution had created a sole sovereignty? The doubt is evidently suggested by his own opinion, that the circumstances of our country did not forbid a sole government; the contrariety had been impressed by the debates in the convention, and was fixed by the principles of the constitution. The proposal and rejection of a sole government was felt; but the predilection for it was also felt; and the two sensations generated a profound attempt to reconcile these contradictions. To advance it, the local authorities are reduced to the judicial sphere of dispensing justice between citizens of the same state. A judicial department is always subservient and necessary to an absolute sovereignty, and by reducing the state governments to that sphere, their insinuated subordination to a national sovereignty, as being represented in a federal senate, is cautiously maintained. The next quotation will demonstrate the struggle between an inveterate opinion, candidly and honourably avowed by Mr. Hamilton in the convention, and the plain intention of the constitution.

H. No. 28. "In a confederacy, the people, without exaggeration, may be said to be intirely the masters of their own fate. Power being almost always the rival of power, the *general* government will at all times stand ready to check the usurpations of the state governments; and these will have the same dispositions towards the general government. The people, by throwing themselves into either scale, can make it preponderate. If their rights are invaded by either, they can make use of the other, as the instrument of redress. How wise it will be in them, by cherishing the union, to preserve to themselves an advantage which can never be too highly prized!"

"It may safely be received as an axiom in our political system, that the state governments will, in all possible contingencies, afford complete security against invasions of the publick liberty by the *national* authority. Projects of usurpation cannot be masked under pretences so likely to escape the penetration of select bodies of men, as of the people at large. The legislature will have better means of information; they can discover the danger at a distance; and possessing all the organs of civil power, and the confidence of the people, they can at once adopt a regular plan of opposition, in which they can combine all the resources of the community. They can readily communicate with each other in the different states; and unite their common forces for the protection of their common liberty. If the federal army should be able to quell the resistance in one state, the distant states would have it in their power to make head with fresh forces. The people are in a situation, through the medium of their state governments, to take measures for their own defence, with all the celerity, regularity, and system, of *independent nations.*"

But of what use is this eulogised capacity in state legislatures to discover usurpations, if they cannot constitutionally resist them; and how can they resist usurpations, if they are subjected by the constitution to a sovereignty or supremacy in the usurper? The people of each state are recognised as independent nations; and the state governments, not as judicial, but as political departments, intended to watch over the constitutional rights of these nations, and invested with a power to resist federal usurpations. They are recognised as possessing all the organs of power necessary to discharge the important duty of breaking the snares of tyranny, by which the people are frequently caught, for want of the means of discovering the danger, which these select bodies of men possess. It is even admitted that the state governments may form regular plans of opposition, and appeal to arms for the defence of their rights. But what becomes of this whole fabrick intended by the constitution to preserve the rights and liberty of the people, if the federal government is sovereign, or the federal court supreme? What becomes of the essential right in these independent nations to control their governments for the preservation of the union, if these governments cannot control a sovereignty or supremacy, usurped for the purpose of destroying the union by a consolidated national government? Of what value is the responsibility of state governments to the people, when it is liable to be rendered inefficient by a supremacy in a federal court? How can the people cherish or preserve the union, if its preservation depends on this court, and not on their state governments? What good can the people reap from the intelligence and foresight of their state governments, if the supreme mandate of this court can forbid them from seeing or resisting usurpations? Where lies the mutual check between the two governments, if a supreme power to expound the articles of the union, is thrown into the scale of one by construction? By this contrivance, the influence of the people over their state governments, urged as necessary for the preservation of their rights, both state and federal, is transferred from them to a federal court. The state governments may still "adopt regular plans of opposition." Opposition must therefore be constitutional. They may even oppose armies to armies. Why then may they not array laws against laws, and judgments against judgments? This is the very remedy contemplated by a system compounded of co-ordinate and divided powers, against wars with guns and bayonets. Whence arises the state right to resist usurpation, to form regular plans of opposition, and to watch over the liberty of the people by organised governments, except from the sovereignty and independence attached to the powers reserved, and the inherent mutual right of self-defence attached to each division of power, state and federal. But the two formidable words "national and general," still tingle in our ears, and protrude themselves against these concessions. I protest against them, because they are not in the constitution, although they have been drawn from the recess of the convention, borrowed from a rejected plan of government, introduced by the high authority of the Federalist, and accepted with avidity by the consolidating school. In contending that we have neither a national nor a general government, nor a national nor a federal sovereignty, nor a judicial supremacy, it is necessary to point out the inconsistency between allowing great political powers to the states, and rescinding them by these illegitimate expressions.

The Subject Continued

L et us proceed in our quotations, and the comparison between the positions which they advance.

H. No. 31. "The state governments, by their original constitutions, are invested with *complete sovereignty*. In what does our security consist against usurpations from that quarter? Doubtless in the manner of their formation, and in a due dependence of those who are to administer them upon the people."

H. No. 32. "Although I am of opinion that there would be no real danger of the consequences to the state governments, which seem to be apprehended from a power in the union to control them in the levies of money; because I am persuaded that the sense of the people, the extreme hazard of provoking the resentments of the state governments, and a conviction of the utility and justice of local administrations, for local purposes, would be a complete barrier against the oppressive use of such a power; yet I am willing to allow the justness of the reasoning, which requires that the individual states should possess an independent and uncontrollable authority to raise their own revenues for the supply of their own wants. And making this concession, I affirm that (with the exception of duties upon imports and exports) they would, under the plan of the convention, retain that authority in the most *absolute and unqualified* sense; and that an attempt on the part of the *national* government to abridge them in the exercise of it, would be a *violent* assumption of power, *unwarranted by any article or clause* of the constitution."

"An entire consolidation of the states into one complete *national sovereignty,* would imply an entire subordination of the parts; and whatever powers might remain to them, would be altogether dependent on the general will. But as the plan of the convention aims only at a partial union or consolidation, the state governments would clearly retain all the rights of sovereignty which they before had, and which were not by that, delegated *exclusively* to the United States."

"The power of imposing taxes on all articles, other than exports, is manifestly a concurrent and equal authority in the United States and individual states. In any other view it would be dangerous."

"It is not a possibility of *inconvenience* in the exercise of powers, but an immediate constitutional repugnancy, that can by implication alienate and extinguish a pre-existing right of sovereignty."

"The necessity of a concurrent jurisdiction in certain cases, results from the *division of sovereign power,* and the rule, that all authorities, of which the states are not explicitly divested in favour of the union, remain with them in full vigour, is not only a theoretical consequence of that division, but is clearly admitted by the whole tenour of the instrument which contains the articles of the proposed constitution."

H. No. 33. "The declarations authorizing the *national* legislature to make all laws which shall be necessary and proper for carrying into execution the foregoing powers, and all other powers vested by this constitution in the government of the United States, or in any officer thereof, and that the constitution and laws of the United States made in pursuance thereof, and the treaties made by their authority, shall be the supreme law of the land, is predicated upon the specifick powers, tantology, or redundancy, and perfectly harmless."

"Who is to judge of the *necessity and propriety* of the laws to be passed for executing the powers of the union? *The national government, under the control of the people.*"

"A law, by the very meaning of the term, includes supremacy. Laws not pursuant of the constitutional powers, are not the supreme laws of the land."

H. No. 34. "To argue upon abstract principles, that the co-ordinate authority cannot exist, would be to set up theory and supposition against fact and reality. However proper such reasonings might be to shew, that a thing ought not to exist, they are wholly to be rejected, when they are made use of to prove that it does not exist, contrary to the evidence of the fact itself. In the Roman republick, the legislative authority resided in two different legislative bodies, commitia centuriata, and the commitia tributia, as independent legislatures, each having power to annul or repeal the acts of the other; in each of which an opposite interest prevailed, the patrician, and plebeian. A man would have been regarded as frantick, who should have attempted to disprove their existence. These two legislatures co-existed for ages, and the Roman republick attained to the highest pinnacle of human greatness." He might have added, that when the two independent Roman legislatures ceased to exist, the splendour of the republick was obscured, and liberty was destroyed.

The principles I am advocating are forcibly sustained in these quotations. The original sovereignty of the states; the legitimate control over the state governments; the unconstitutionality of an attempt by the federal government to usurp or abridge state rights; their independent possession of all rights not delegated; the insufficiency of inconveniences to extinguish pre-existing sovereign rights; the necessity of concurrent powers, as arising from a division of power; and the incapacity of the declaratory clauses of the constitution, for extending the limited powers delegated; are all positively stated and plainly enforced.

Lest these plain principles should be evaded by subterfuges, or facts should be assaulted by suppositions, an example is happily introduced, illustrating the intention of the constitution, and placing its construction beyond the reach of uncertainty. However proper reasonings might be, to shew that co-ordinate legislative authorities ought not to exist, and though Mr. Hamilton was ardent in his antipathy towards them; yet he candidly admits that such reasonings ought wholly to be rejected, when made use of to prove that these co-ordinate legislatures do not exist, contrary to the evidence of the fact itself. He defines, by the example of the Roman co-ordinate legislatures, his idea of the state and federal legislatures under the constitution. They were co-equal, as to concurrent powers; and a man would have been considered as frantick, who should have attempted to disprove it. This phrenzy is stated as emblematical of that which should deny the existence of our co-equal and independent legislatures. Any inconvenience which may result from our constitutional co-equality of legislatures, is not sufficient to convert phrenzy into sound understanding. Each of the Roman legislatures often thought the other very inconvenient. Both legislated over the same objects, and exercised concurrent powers. Their collisions were therefore more frequent and inveterate than those to be expected from our co-ordinate legislatures, chiefly restricted to different spheres. The Roman legislatures were exasperated against each other by a real hostility of interests; ours, so long as each state is undisturbed in providing for its internal happiness, are bound together by a common interest. If the Roman republick was raised to the pinnacle of human greatness, by a political check so defective, what may be expected by the United States, from a purification of the principle, expelling its defects, and retaining its friendship for liberty?

But the fact which it would be phrenzy to deny, is yet denied; and the co-ordinateness of state and federal legislative authorities, emphatically contended for, is destroyed in the very mode unsuccessfully proposed in the convention, in the face of its rejection, of this positive vindication of the principle, and of the asserted constitutional constrution.

"Who is to judge of *the necessity and propriety* of the laws to be passed for executing the powers of the union? The *national* government, under the control of the people."

It will appear in the sequel, that Mr. Hamilton and Mr. Madison have answered this question differently. Mr. Hamilton's supremacy is bestowed on a *national* government under the control of the people; Mr. Madison's, upon a court, not under the control of the people. Each of these profound politicians sought for a supremacy conformable to his own opinion expressed in the convention. Mr. Hamilton has found one similar to that of the British parliament, and by endowing a national president, senate, and house of representatives, with it, has gotten back to his plan of government offered to the convention. Mr. Madison, adhering to his opinion, that the state governments should be preceptively retained, gives his supremacy to a court, upon the supposition that a court will preserve them. Mr. Hamilton controls his supremacy by the people, in imitation of the mode by which the British parliament is supposed to be controlled. Mr. Madison only controls his by the will and power of the supremacy itself. He rejects the suspicion which has suggested checks and divisions of sovereignty or supremacy, and bestows absolute power, unexposed to any control at all. The reader will discern which would be the best security for the rights and even the existence of the states; the opinion of the people, or the opinion of a court. The court swear, but state and federal legislative departments swear also; so do kings; yet this species of control has been sufficiently exploded as a security for liberty. When great men differ as to the residence of a national or federal supremacy, is it not presumable that it resides no where?

Mr. Hamilton asserts, that the "state governments, by their original constitutions, are invested with complete sovereignty. In what does our security consist against usurpations from that quarter? Doubtless in the manner of their formation, and in a due dependence of those who are to administer them upon the people." May I not have been mistaken in supposing that he intended to invest the federal government with a supremacy over state laws? If he is consistent, he denies any supremacy in one of our legislatures over the others, and asserts their co-equality. By uniting the extracts, we may discern whether they are repugnant or homogeneal. The federal government is to judge of the necessity and propriety of the laws to be past for executing the powers of the union; and the state governments are to judge of the necessity and propriety of the laws to be past for executing the powers reserved to the states, each under the control of the people. Thus only the interpretations of the constitution by Mr. Hamilton, can be made consistent, and thus a co-equal supremacy is attached to each sphere of legislation, subject to no control but that of the people.

Mr. Hamilton, in reference to the federal government, adds, "that a law, by the very meaning of the term, implies supremacy. Laws not pursuant of constitutional powers, are not the supreme law of the land." I accept the definition, but I deny its exclusive application to federal laws, and contend, that it co-extensively applies to state laws. It is admitted that unconstitutional laws are not supreme. From this admission it results, that the expression in the constitution, "shall be the supreme law of the land," is restricted by its limitations and reservation, and did not convey any species of supremacy to the governments, going beyond the powers delegated or those reserved. The supremacy allowed to legislation flows from, and does not exceed it. Therefore the laws of the states within the scope of their reserved powers, are equally supreme with those of the federal government within the scope of its delegated powers. The division of legislation cannot be sustained, unless the constitutional laws of each allotment are invested with legal supremacy. If the proposition, that unconstitutional laws are not the supreme law of the land, is true, its converse, that constitutional laws are the supreme law of the land, must be also true; and of course the constitutional laws of the states are equally supreme with those of the federal government.

Mr. Hamilton admits a concurrency of legislation in the state and federal governments, as to taxation; and that a violation of this concurrency by the federal government, would be manifestly unconstitutional. How can this doctrine consist with his position, "that the national government have a right to judge of the propriety and necessity of the laws for executing the powers of the union, under the control of the people only." Concurrency of power implies an equality in its exercise. So Mr. Hamilton expounds it. But then he creates a *national* government, and a *con-*

solidated nation, and invests this imaginary government under the control of this imaginary nation, with a supreme power over the co-equality he admits, by bestowing upon it an exclusive right to decide whether its own laws, and consequently whether the laws of the states, are necessary and proper, according to the articles of the constitution. Thus he destroys the admitted concurrency, and revives the identical supremacy in construing these articles, proposed in the convention for the establishment of a national government. By this assertion, he invests Congress and the supreme court with a right to violate the inviolable concurrent right of taxation, as was done in the bank case.

Yet he declares that the right of taxation would be dangerous in any other view, than as a *concurrent and equal authority* in the United States and the individual states. Why would it be dangerous? Because a supreme power in the federal government to construe the articles of the union, so as to defeat this concurrency, would suffice to destroy the state governments.

Mr. Hamilton invests the state *governments* with complete sovereignty. Why does he abandon our principle, that complete sovereignty resides only in the people of each state? The reasons are obvious. His prepossession in favour of the English form of government, induced him to deposit a complete sovereignty in governments. Therefore he proposed a national government in the convention, empowered, like the British parliament, to pass all *laws whatsover.* And the same object would be effected, if a national government assumed as established by the constitution, can pass *all laws which it may deem necessary and proper.* The British parliament do no more than pass laws which it deems necessary and proper, according to the British political system. Yet he admits unconstitutional laws to be void. How can their unconstitutionality be ascertained, except by uniting a concurrent right of construction with our concurrent right of legislation? In England, legislation is lodged in the king, lords, and commons, and each department has an independent concurrent power of deciding whether the law is conformable with the English political system. Here, legislation is a concurrent power, lodged in the state and federal departments, to which a concurrent power of construing our political system must also appertain, or this system must be destroyed, as that of England would be by a supreme power in one of its legislative departments to impose its own constructions upon the others. But this reasoning is provided against, first by investing the state governments with complete sovereignty, and then by transmitting all these sovereignties to the federal senate by representation. These ideas cannot be correct, if Mr. Hamilton is right in observing, that "our security against usurpations by the state governments, consists in their dependence upon the people." Upon what people? Certainly, the people of each state. In this place, we find that the state governments are to be controlled by the people; in another, that the national government, as he is pleased to denominate the federal government, is also controllable by the people; and in a third, that one government is controllable by the other. These controls refute the idea that either of these governments possess a complete sovereignty, or a supremacy over the other. The concurrency in the modes of control, sustain a concurrency of power to construe the articles of the union, and constitute the mutual check for which Mr. Hamilton contends, as the only means of inculcating that mutual moderation in the exercise of power, so indispensable for promoting the happiness of the people.

Mr. Hamilton affirms, that the individual states possess an *independent and uncontrollable* power to raise their own revenue for the supply of their own wants; and that an attempt on the part of the *national* government to abridge them in the exercise of it, would be a *violent assumption of power,* unwarranted by *any article of the constitution.* How came the states to possess this independent and uncontrollable power in the case of taxation? Undoubtedly as a portion of the sovereign power previously held by them. The illustration of state rights, by their right of taxation, includes all their other undelegated rights, as being also derived from state sovereignty. Neither the state right of taxation, nor any other reserved state right, is bestowed by the constitution. They all either flow from state sovereignty, or none of them are genuine. Therefore if the state right to tax, is independent and uncontrollable by the federal government or the supreme court, their other undelegated and reserved rights are also independent and uncontrollable. If an attempt on the part of the federal government to abridge the states in their right to tax, would be a violent assumption of power, an attempt to abridge them in the exercise of any other reserved right, must also be a violent assumption of power. And if an assumption of power over an undelegated and reserved state right "is unwarranted by any article or clause in the constitution," no construction can justify it. The mysterious supremacy supposed to be tacitly conveyed to the federal government (but in what way, the eminent men whose works we are considering, have not agreed) or Mr. Hamilton's vindication of state rights, must be given up, as utterly incompatible. The exemplification of the independent and uncontrollable character of state rights under the constitution, by the right to tax, embraces exclusive as well as concurrent rights, as all are derived from the original sovereignty of the states, and must live or die together.

H. No. 36. "As neither the federal nor state governments, in the objects of taxation, can control the other, each will have an obvious and sensible interest in reciprocal forbearance." Thus we are conducted to the precise end intended to be accomplished by the division of sovereignty, supremacy, or powers (all equivalent words), displaying its contrariety to a concentration of sovereignty, supremacy, or powers, in a national government. Moderation was not equally to be expected from these hostile principles; and moderation in the exercise of power was thought necessary to foster social happiness. "Reciprocal forbearance" was inculcated by the intire division of legislative powers; and not by the item of taxation alone; to compel the federal and state governments to travel kindly and sociably together. Their friendship, like that of individuals, could only be supported by their mutual independence in the exercise of their own rights, and if the plain arguments of Mr. Hamilton ought to have more weight than illicit words and dark allusions with which they are sparingly, and perhaps carelessly, sprinkled, they supply us with a conclusive construction of the constitution, namely, that federal and state legislatures are co-ordinate, co-equal, and independent, neither being controllable by the other; that only legal supremacy appertains to both; that their mutual independence was intended to inspire them with mutual moderation; and that if collisions occur which they cannot amicably settle, the control of the people over both, and not a dictatorial supremacy of one, or some portion of one, is an umpire.

The Subject Continued

M No. 39. "The constitution is to be founded on the assent and ratification of *the people of America,* given by deputies elected for the special purpose, not as individuals composing one intire nation, but as composing the *distinct and independent states,* to which they respectively belong. It is to be the assent and ratification of the several states, derived from the *supreme* authority of each state, the authority of the people themselves. The act therefore establishing the constitution, will not be a national, but a federal act.

"That it will be a federal, and not a national act, the act of the people, as forming so many independent states, not as forming one aggregate nation, is obvious, from the single consideration, that it is to result, neither from the decision of a majority of *the people of the union,* nor from that of a majority of states. It must result from the unanimous assent of the *several states that are parties* to it, differing no otherwise from their ordinary assent, than in its being expressed, not by the legislative authority, but by that of the people themselves. Were the people regarded in this transaction as forming one nation, the will of a majority of the whole people of the United States, would bind the minority, in the same manner as a majority of each state would bind the minority; and the will of the majority must be determined, either by a comparison of individual votes, or by considering the will of the majority of states, as evidence of the will of a majority of the people of the United States. Neither of these rules has been adopted. Each state, in ratifying the constitution, *is considered as a sovereign body,* independent of all others, and only to be bound by its own voluntary act. In this relation then, the new constitution will be a federal and not a national constitution.

"The next *relation* is, to the sources from which the ordinary powers of government are to be derived. The house of representatives will derive its powers from *the people of America,* and the people will be represented in the *same proportion, and on the same principle,* as they are in the legislature of each particular state. So far the government *is national and not federal.* The senate, on the other hand, will derive its powers from the states, as political and co-equal societies. So far the government is federal and not national. From this aspect of the government it appears to be of a mixed character, presenting at least as many federal as national features. The local or *municipal authorities,* form distinct and independent portions of the supremacy, no more subject, within their respective spheres, to the *general* authority, than the general authority is subject to them within its own sphere. In this relation then, the proposed government cannot be deemed a national one, since its *jurisdiction extends to certain limited objects only,* and leaves to the several states a residuary and *inviolable sovereignty over all other objects. It is true, that in controversies relating to the boundaries between the two jurisdictions, the tribunal which is ultimately to decide is to be established under the general government. The decision is to be impartially made, according to the rules of the constitution, and all the usual and most effectual precautions are to be taken to secure this impartiality.*"

M. No. 45. "The states will retain, under the proposed constitution, a very considerable portion of active sovereignty. The powers delegated by the proposed constitution to the federal government, are *few and defined*. Those which are to remain to the state governments, are numerous and indefinite. The former will be exercised principally on external objects, as war, peace, negotiation, and foreign commerce; with which last the power of taxation will for the most part be connected. The powers reserved to the several states will extend to all objects, which, in the ordinary course of affairs, concern the lives, liberties, and properties, of the people; and the internal order, improvement, and prosperity, of the state."

It is necessary to look back at the journal of the convention, before a critical examination of these extracts is attempted. The great difficulty which protracted its debates, was the struggle between the large and small states. On one hand, to obtain an intire influence for population by a national government; on the other, to preserve the moral equality of state sovereignties by a federal government. Virginia, Massachusetts, and Pennsylvania, then the three states containing the most people, though remote from each other, united upon that consideration. New-York, then intermediate between the large and small states, as to population, was divided. Other states, looking at their small population, and at their large unsettled territory, vacillated; and the gentlemen in favour of a consolidated national republick, or a limited monarchy, availed themselves of this unsettled disposition.

Alas! poor human nature; how short is its foresight, and how small is its prudence! Neither the map of Massachusetts, nor its impending division, was thought of. Virginia did not anticipate an exchange of situations with New-York. The western and southern expansions of territory rested in oblivion, and supplied reason with no deductions. Time has removed the obscurity, and disclosed how short-sighted were the motives which laboured to consolidate the states into a national government. Why should this project be revived, now that these motives are extinct? The film of a fluctuating census, which prevented patriotism from discerning the great difference between a federal and consolidated system of government, being removed, it can contemplate more justly the consequences of both. The time may come when a national government would talk of its eastern provinces. On the north, population meets with the white cliffs of snow and ice; on the west and south, its waves flow on. A contiguity of interests has abolished the ephemeral intrigues of states remote from each other, founded on population; and this temporary cement of state ambition has mouldered into dust. The apprehensions it once excited are effaced by the increase of states; and it is now demonstrated, that geographical combinations, founded in a similarity of interest, are the evils in future to be apprehended. Whether these will be best prevented by the military force of a national government, or by the milder means of faithfully leaving to each state the exclusive management of its local interests, is now the question. The southern aristocracy, inclined by pride to a national form of government, is already melted by the abolition of entails and primogeniture, into a democracy. These circumstances constitute a happy juncture for fixing the principles of the constitution by federal constructions, as the only security against geographical combinations, and the consequences of enabling ambition to wield the sceptre of a national government; and the time has arrived for rejecting opinions, suggested by a short-sighted computation of a temporary and fluctuating state population.

Yet consolidating projects are still vibrating in the souls of ambition and avarice; they seize upon the motives, now extinct,

which induced the deputies of large states, and aristocratical individuals, to contend for a supreme national government; and use
the terms and phrases which these motives suggested, in order
to overturn a federal system, because it is the strongest imaginable
barrier against usurpation and fraud. It is no longer an honest
estimate of population, nor the prejudices of a virtuous aristocracy, by which a national form of government and an unchecked
supremacy are advocated, but the heroes of the project are now
the evil spirits, which are constantly at the elbow of power. As
the deputies of the three large states were evidently influenced in
advocating a national form of government, by the object of
obtaining a preponderance for populousness, and no such preponderance being now attainable in consequence of the increase
of states, it is probable that the same men would not think now
as they did then; those excepted who preferred a consolidated
government, resembling the English system. This opinion is
therefore at present the solitary advocate for a national government, because no state can expect to obtain any preponderance
over the rest, in consequence of its population.

But the delusion was not extinguished when the Federalist
was written, and therefore Mr. Madison's construction of the
constitution was as likely to be influenced by it, as Mr. Hamilton's, in contending for a supremacy according to the British
model. It was no easy matter to discern a mode of re-instating
half a national government for a plain rejection of the whole;
but the same ingenuity which conceived a simultaneous sovereignty in the states, and an absolute federal legislative, executive,
and judicial supremacy, suggested a nice constructive dissection
of the constitution, so as to make two nations with the same
individuals.

Inexplicit as words may be, they are untoward instruments for proving contradictions. Mr. Madison asserts, "*that the assent and ratification of the people of America, is the foundation of the constitution,*" and "that the assent and ratification was not to be the act of individuals, as composing one nation, but of the *people of each distinct and independent state.*" The contradiction is explicit. The existence of an American people is conceded to the project for a national government, and the existence of a distinct sovereign people in each state is conceded to the constitution. Yet if there was no American people, the abstract idea of such a people, could not make a constitution or union for real state nations; and if there was really such a people, the municipal authorities, as he calls the states, could not make a constitution for them. It was necessary to premise the existence of an American people, to sustain the semi-national physiognomy ascribed to the federal government; and it was necessary to admit the distinct and separate sovereignties of the states, to find a sound ratification of the constitution.

An American nation, *able to make a national constitution,* is not to be found in the declaration of independence, in the confederation of 1777, in the constitution of 1787, or in its mode of ratification. And if no such nation existed, having the right to make a whole national government, can the idea of such a nation make half a national government? To form a national government, the state nations must first dissolve themselves, and these fragments must constitute themselves into one nation; but instead of any such dissolution, the contrary is established by the constitution, and the mode of its ratification. To obtain a semi-national government, Mr. Madison supposes "a people of America," as assenting to and ratifying the constitution, though he proves that both

acts were done by a people of each state; and asserts that the
house of representatives of the federal legislature, derives its powers from "a people of America." But if there never was, nor yet
is, such a people, able to make a national constitution, or to alter
that made by the states, how can there be such a people for this
house to represent? Had there been such a people, state conventions would only have been a mode for collecting their ratifications of the constitution, similar to that practised by states for
collecting the opinions of the counties into which state nations
are divided, when a majority decides for the nation, and a dissenting county cannot establish a distinct government for itself.
But "the constitution was to result from the *unanimous assent of
the several states that are parties to it,* expressed, *not by the legislative
authority, but by the people themselves.*" This language contains an
insinuation to sustain the ideas of an American people and a
national government, utterly groundless, although it has been
often repeated. No distinction between the legislatures and conventions of states, as organs for expressing the assent of the states
to their federal compacts, was meditated. Conventions were
recommended by the framers of the constitution, to avoid the
disinclination which the state legislatures might feel to part with
power, and not to recognise the existence of an American nation.
As a proof of this, the constitution may be altered by the assent of
state legislatures, because they represent the state nations who
assented to it. Had it been ratified by an American nation, the
legislatures of these state nations could not have altered it. The
extract exhibits a distinction by a mere tautology. The states, and
the people of the states (as Mr. Madison has ably proved in the
extracts) are expressions completely equivalent when applied to
the ratification of the constitution; and the antithesis between

them is therefore without foundation. If it was made by the people of a state, it was still a state ratification, as Mr. Madison has proved. If the states are parties to the constitution, the individuals of an American nation are not so. If it was established by the assent of states, however expressed, that assent cannot be turned into the assent of individuals, for the sake of creating a national government, by changing a federal, into a national act.

The fact was, that no assent to the constitution was expressed, or to be expressed, by individuals; and Mr. Madison intimates this erroneous idea by a figurative expression, so as ingeniously to convert the state organ, called a convention, into individuals composing an American nation. But state conventions are as distinguishable from an American people, in expressing the assent of the state to a federal union, as state legislatures are in expressing the same assent to its amendment; nor is there any difference between the character and effect of this assent, whether it was expressed by state representatives, called a legislature or a convention. The difference is contended for to give the constitution a national hue, contrary to its own verdict that there is none, pronounced in the mode of its amendment.

An argument of less weight, but not to be disregarded, is, that these conventions were called by the authority of the state legislatures. Being invested with the authority of the state, they had a right to command or prohibit the election of conventions, which they would not have possessed, had an American people existed. The convention which framed the constitution, did not presume to call conventions of an American people, nor did Congress usurp such an authority. No authority existed for calling a convention of an American people; none was even called by an usurped authority; and yet the consolidating project claims the benefit of three usurpations, neither of which was ever thought of. First, that a combination of individuals, calling itself an American people, had usurped an authority to make a constitution for sovereign and independent states. Secondly, that some body had usurped an authority to empower these individuals to elect conventions. And thirdly, that these conventions had usurped the character of representing an American people.

The constitution in a multitude of places refutes Mr. Madison's distinction between the states, and the people of the states, by considering them as the same bodies politick. Mr. Madison concurs with it in this idea. He observes, "in this transaction" (the establishment of the constitution), "each state is considered as a sovereign body, independent of all others, and only to be bound by its own voluntary act." This body was formed by the people of each state; the people of each state are therefore the same body as the state; the assent of the people of the states to the constitution, is precisely the same as the assent of the states distinctly, and equally disproves the existence of an American people. Mr. Madison adds, "in this relation then, the constitution will be a federal, and not a national act," intimating, that in some other relation, it was a national and not a federal constitution; and he proceeds to sustain this intimation by reviving the American people, both killed and resuscitated in the preceding extracts.

"The next *relation* is, to the *sources* from which *the ordinary powers of government* are to be derived. The house of representatives will derive its powers from the *people of America,* and the people will be represented in the same *proportion, and on the same principle,* as they are in the legislature of each particular state. So far the government is *national and not federal.* The senate, on the other hand, will derive its powers from the *states,* as political and co-equal *societies.* So far the government is federal and not national. From this aspect of the government, it appears to be of a mixed character, presenting at least as many federal as national features." So then the government is as much national as federal. To come at these wished-for national features, Mr. Madison distinguishes between a people and a state, and discards political associations by which individuals are made a people; forms one state or political society, calling it a people of America, of the same individuals, who had formed themselves into separate societies; founds the constitution upon the assent and ratification of this newly conceived people of America; yet asserts that it was exclusively ratified by distinct and independent sovereign states; and declares that the house of representatives will derive its powers from the people of America; but that the senate will derive its powers from the states, as co-equal societies. Words and facts unite in detecting these contradictions. States, and the people of each state, are synonymous words. No American people existed. A confederation of states was the only political association which could be called American, when the constitution was framed. It therefore could only be made and ratified by the existing political societies, and was so made and ratified. If no American nation then existed, or yet exists, to make or mend it, can the house of representatives have derived any powers from a people merely surreptitious? When the constitution is amended, does not this house derive its powers from the states? Can an ideal American people, from which it neither does or can derive any powers, infuse into it any political character? Can a political character be acquired without powers, or political powers without a source? Is it true, that the states are only represented in the senate? According to Mr. Hamilton, the state *governments* are represented in the senate.

According to Mr. Madison, the *people* of America are represented in the house of representatives. These governments, in the opinion of one writer, transfer their powers to the senate; and this American nation, in the opinion of the other, infuses its powers into the house of representatives; both by representation. Between the two, the states are not represented in either house of a federal legislature, created by them for executing a federal government, to which Mr. Madison says they are the only parties; and according to either, whether representation bestows the powers of the state governments on the senate, or whether it conveys the powers of an American nation, supposed to be supreme, to the house of representatives, an indefinite national government is introduced. Now I contend that no powers at all are conveyed to the federal government by election or representation, and that these are only means for selecting the persons by whom the powers vested in the federal government are to be exercised. If I am correct in supposing that the powers of the federal government are derived from the constitution, how can Mr. Madison be correct in asserting, that the powers of the house of representatives are derived from an American people?

Mr. Madison's oversight, in not discriminating between the instrumentality of election to convey powers in the different cases of a national government, or a federal union, must have arisen from his opinion in favour of the former; and nothing could be more happily contrived to advance that opinion, than a construction by which the unknown powers of an American people are conveyed to the house of representatives.

The constitution declares, "that all legislative powers herein granted, shall be vested in a *Congress of the United States,* which shall consist of a senate and house of representatives." Congress, according to the true political meaning of the term, is thus expressly defined to be a convention of states. It is neither a convention of state governments, nor of an American people. No legislative powers are given by the constitution to a Congress of state governments, nor to representatives of an American people; and no such Congress would have any more power than the Hartford convention. All legislative powers granted by the constitution are vested in a Congress of states, to consist of two houses. These houses or chambers are described by one title. How then can one be a federal, and the other a national representation? Can one branch of the legislature have only federal, and the other only national powers? Would it not be a usurpation in the senate to exercise national powers? Are not the legislative powers of both limited "to the powers granted by the constitution?" What then was the design or effect of Mr. Madison's distinction between the senate and the house of representatives? Was it to extend the legislative powers of a Congress of states, beyond those granted by the conventions of states? He has not said so; but commentators have seized upon this distinction between the two legislative branches of Congress, although the constitution makes none, to effect that purpose; and for any other, it is quite immaterial.

The constitution in fact refutes Mr. Madison's idea. "*Each state* shall have at least one *representative*. Each state shall *choose* a specified number of *representatives*. Each state shall *elect representatives* in the manner prescribed by its legislature. The *representation of each state* shall have one vote in choosing a president." No language could be more explicit for expressing the fact, that the house of representatives was a representation from each state, and not of an American nation.

The distinction between a state and a people, upon which Mr. Madison's idea seems to be founded, is contrary to the settled political idiom; and too feeble to defeat the plain words of the constitution. It has often been correctly said by the best writers, that there is no people where there is a despot. Not that there are no men, but no political society, defined by the term people. As a despot annihilates a people, so would a consolidated government annihilate the people of each state. Upon their rights, the supremacy of a despot, or any other supremacy, would have the same effect. To obtain an American nation, Mr. Madison confounds the words men and people, as if they were of the same political import; and as state representatives could only be elected by men, he makes this unavoidable act an instrument for the destruction of the rights of these men, obtained by their having constituted themselves into nations, or a people of each state; and transforms these men into an American people having no rights, upon no other grounds, than that they are men, live in America, and vote for the formation of one branch of a federal Congress.

The only justification of this transformation which he alleges, is, that these men will be represented in the same *proportion, and on the same principle,* as they are in the legislature of each particular state. I can neither accede to the facts nor the inference. As to the fact of proportion, it is defeated by the circumstance of counting a portion of slaves to apportion representation, and by the loss of any surplus of population beyond the quota adopted for fixing the number of state representatives; and as to the principle of state and federal representation, it is intirely different. State legislatures are a national representation, and as such invested with general powers. Upon this principle, the men composing a people or a state, are represented in state legislatures. But the men or people of each state are represented in Congress, upon the principle that it is a federal legislature, invested with limited, and not national or general powers. The first principle of representation invests state legislatures with a power to pass national laws for the government of actual states or nations; but the second does not invest Congress with a power to pass national laws for the government of an imaginary state or nation. If however the facts were true, they could not destroy the restrictions of the constitution.

The difference between a representation for special or for general purposes, is well understood, and has been practically settled in this country in many instances. The Congress under the confederation of 1777, was a representation for special purposes. Many representations of the people of each state have taken place, for the special purposes of enacting or amending state constitutions. And in conformity with the established difference between a representation for special or general purposes, the intire representation in Congress is only for the special purpose of exercising the delegated powers. Suppose a convention, representing a nation or people, for the special purpose of enacting or amending a constitution, should undertake to make roads and canals, or to exercise local and temporary powers, because it represented a people or a nation. Would the exercise of such powers be justifiable upon that ground? So, if it should be admitted that the house of representatives is a representation of an American people, it would not derive any national or general authority from that source, and is equally restricted to the special purposes for which it is convened, as any other representation for special purposes. If this argument is sound, it demonstrates the error of thrusting the words general and national into the constitution, and destroys all the inferences drawn by judges and statesmen, from that source, because, though very fertile, it is not constitutional.

The distinction between the senate and house of representatives, in order to obtain a government partly federal and partly national, seems to be untenable in another view. Mr. Madison asserts, as the foundation for it, "that the house of representatives derives its powers from the *people of America,* but that the senate derives its powers from the *states."* Where is the difference between these representations? The people include all the states, and the states include all the people. If representation conveys powers to either house, it conveys them to both. The representation of the states would convey the same powers to one, as the representation of the people of each state would to the other. Mr. Hamilton makes the state governments, and Mr. Madison the states themselves, the constituents of the senate. Either mode of conveying power would suffice to establish a national government. If the principle is true, that the house of representatives derives power from its imaginary constituents; an American people; the principle, that the senate derives power from its real constituents, must also be true, upon the ground that representation comprises the power of constituents. It is quite the same thing, whether one house can exercise the powers of the people, or the other, the powers of the states or of their governments, because either source of power would expose the whole treasury of state rights to defalcation, and effectually establish the national form of government advocated by both gentlemen. If the powers of the senate were federal, and those of the house of representatives national, by what authority could the latter exercise federal, or the former national powers? It would be a plain usurpation for either house to exercise powers, with which its constituents themselves were not invested. But if both houses derive the same powers from the same source, they may act concurrently in exercising them. It follows that the powers of both, must either be derived from the constitution, or from a representation, comprising all the powers to be concurrently exercised; that in either view, Mr. Madison's distinction is groundless, and that the government is either wholly federal or wholly national.

But ought the powers of the federal government to be defined by the mode of nominating its officers, or by the articles of the constitution? Can the means by which its powers are put into operation, change its character, or alter its principles? If the government was made federal by the constitution, can either of the modes for effecting a representation of the parties to this federal compact, destroy the principle of the compact itself? Yes, says Mr. Madison, it may be effected by "a relation to the sources from which the *ordinary powers of a government* are derived." The obscurity of this expression is admirably contrived for changing the federal system adopted, into the national system rejected. What are these ordinary powers of a government? Are they powers usually resulting from the establishment of a general government by a national representation? If so, then this relation would invest the federal government with the ordinary powers of a national government. If not, then this relation cannot invest it with any power at all. The fact is, that the federal government derives all its powers from the constitution, and none from its relation to the sources of ordinary power, whether they are conquest, usurpation, legitimacy, or representation. If this is true, then no relation can exist between the federal government, and the ordinary sources of power.

There are two plain relations established by the constitution; one, between Congress and the sovereign states by which it was created; the other, between Congress and the special powers with which it was invested. To substitute for these relations, one between a government and the ordinary powers conveyed by representation, is only an attempt to make a limited government the carver of its own powers, instead of deriving them from a federal compact; so as to convert state elections, intended as one means to enforce the compact, into an instrument for its destruction. If the words "national, general, and ordinary powers," convey no powers not delegated by the compact, they have no weight in the argument; if they do, the limitations of the constitution are quite indefinite and frivolous. Such is the new scheme of measuring the powers of the federal government by the ordinary powers of a national or general government, instead of measuring them by the intention and articles of the union. It is only the old artifice in a new dress, of using the people to destroy the rights of the people; for state rights are the rights of the people.

Is it true that the rights of the federal government ought to be measured by the rights of the people? Then indeed it would follow, that as all state rights are rights of the people, the whole would be transferred to the federal government, if it is a representation of an American nation, and if representation conveys to a government the rights of the people. But if the powers of the federal government are only emanations from the constitution, and are not derived from representation, these emanations really constitute the government, and it is not constituted by emanations from representation. The contrary hypothesis would destroy all the state rights of the people. It is as easy to use words which will include absolute power, as it is hard to discern the futility of

having limited the powers of the federal government. Mr. Madison avails himself of the facility by reviving the rejected words,
national and general; and he surmounts the difficulty, by drawing
powers from his assumed American people, as a higher authority than that which prescribed the limitations. These doctrines
have generated the difficulty of discerning a distinct line between
state and federal powers.

At this line Mr. Madison and his commentators split. He
asserts the existence of state sovereignties, invested with exclusive
independent powers; his commentators deny it. This event has
proved that the idea of a federal and also of a national government, acting upon the same men, was too fine to be practical, and
that a naked precept could not withstand an absolute supremacy.
Accordingly, constructions are already advanced conformable to
the proposed plan for a national government; proving that the
supreme negatives for which it contended, were justly considered
by its opponents as sufficient to destroy any rights preceptively
reserved to the states, but deprived of the power of defence. To
effect the same end, the commentators who still wish for a consolidated national government, have seized upon Mr. Madison's
doctrines, endowing the federal government with national powers, and also with a supreme negative over the laws and judgments of the states, for the purpose of destroying the state
sovereignties which he admits. They see, what every sound
understanding must also see, that spheres of exclusive state rights,
and their subjection to a national supremacy, are incompatible;
and between unavoidable alternatives, elect that which they prefer; adopting one half of Mr. Madison's theory, and rejecting the
other, as the two halves are incapable of reconciliation.

There is no choice offered to either party, but one between a
federal and a national government; and the only question to be

decided is, which of these forms has been established by the constitution. It must be admitted, that a national or general government, unable to punish thieves and murderers, or to regulate the descent and distribution of property, would be a political anomaly, never attempted, nor hitherto conceived even by Utopian historians. A government, unable to provide for social safety and happiness, could hardly be called a government. The only modes of surmounting this formidable objection, are either to absolve the federal government from all the restrictions of the constitution, or to admit that these great ends of society are provided for in the structure of the state governments.

One argument to prove that no part or parcel of a national government was contemplated by the constitution, seems to be incapable of refutation. The federal government cannot alter a county or incorporate a town. It cannot divide a state. And above all, it cannot obtain a pittance of land, without the consent of a state government. A national right of territory is positively recognised as residing in state nations, and not in an American nation. These recognitions affirm the existence of state nations, and deny the existence of an American nation. A nation without a territory, erratick tribes excepted, is a contradiction; and a national government, without a nation invested with territorial rights, is a castle in the air. A Congress composed of deputies from sovereign states, is invested with ten miles square to meet upon, just as towns or districts have been assigned in Europe, and anciently in Greece, for holding federal diets; but this Congress, like those diets, cannot exercise any power upon the lands composing the territory of each state nation, either by regulating inheritances, or cutting them into roads or canals, because it is not a representation of an American nation, invested with an American territory.

As territory, the necessary basis for a national government, belongs exclusively to state nations, the fact is an index directing us to the true intention of the constitution. It was intended to unite the energies of these state nations; to defend, and not to consolidate their territories, by creating an American nation, and a government deriving its powers from this supposed nation; and to prevent collisions with each other. For these federal ends, federal, and not national powers were created. If so, the government was intended to be wholly federal.

The formulary of electing one house of Congress, was either intended as one means for effecting the federal ends expressed, or for establishing a national or general government, not expressed. It could not be intended for effecting both objects, because the latter, if effected, would supersede the former. If this formulary can establish a national or general government, there would be no occasion at all for a federal government.

The mode of constituting the two houses of "a Congress of the United States," is accounted for, without ascribing to it a tacit design of exchanging an ostensible federal, for a recondite national government. It was the result of a compromise between the large and the small states. Suppose the small states had succeeded in obtaining an equal vote in the house of representatives with the large states, and the representatives had been elected by the people of each state, would this house have derived any powers from the supposition that it was chosen by the people of America? If not, the same credential cannot convey national or general powers, in consequence of a compromise, not intended to have this effect; but to give weight, both to population and the moral equality of state sovereignties, in the exercise of the federal powers created by the constitution. The mode of representation in either house of Congress, was not designed to enlarge or contract the powers given to the body composed of both, and had it been the same in the house of representatives as in the senate, the powers would not have thereby been altered. Had the states been considered as the election districts of an American people, Congress would have been empowered to provide against the inequalities of representation arising from a surplus population, and the absence of such a power is an exposition of the motive of the compromise between the large and small states, proving that it did not contemplate any annexation of national features to the federal government; any creation of an American people; or any restriction of state rights beyond the delegations of powers expressed in the constitution.

With the argument, "that the house of representatives is appointed by individuals," is combined the circumstance, "that the federal government acts upon individuals," to infer from the united force of both, that it is wholly or partly a national government. The old Congress acted upon individuals to a great extent in many cases, particularly in the government of an army, and in making peace or war; yet it was never imagined that its powers were enlarged by this circumstance so as to enable it to make roads and canals through the lands of the officers and soldiers, or deprive them of any rights, over which it was not invested with power; although these officers and soldiers individually assented to their constitution by inlisting or accepting commissions.

This auxiliary doctrine is the most plausible, inasmuch as the intire federal government acts directly upon individuals; whereas direct individual election extends only to one of its departments, unable to legislate alone. And yet it cannot sustain the inference of a national government, because it is impossible to imagine a form of government neither flowing from nor acting upon individuals. Every hereditary power originally flows from individuals, but wherever it does not exist, both positions are unexceptionably true. Neither fact therefore can furnish a perfect distinction between the nature or principles of different governments. Both are mere truisms applicable to all governments, amounting to the meagre logick, that government is government. If the powers of a government can be enlarged by such reasoning, all the inventions for restraining power are ineffectual, and all the securities for civil liberty are defeated. The right of self-government can no longer be vindicated by constitutions; and though it should be nominally conceded, it would be practically undermined by the doctrine, that as governments are created by and act upon individuals, they may disregard constitutional restrictions.

This new doctrine, by attempting to prove too much, proves nothing. The state governments proceed from and act upon individuals more extensively than the federal government. If these circumstances extend the constitutional powers of the latter, they would extend those of the former; and if they invest the federal government with legislative or judicial powers beyond those delegated, they must also invest the state governments with legislative and judicial powers, beyond those reserved.

Governments must flow from individuals to be free, and they must act upon individuals to have any effect. Both circumstances are necessary to constitute a government, good or bad. The difference between them does not lie in either, but in the restraints imposed upon an abuse of power. If these restraints are necessary to secure the rights of individuals, they are also necessary to

The Subject Continued 121

secure the rights of confederating states; and if the rights of individuals would be endangered or lost, by the despotick doctrine, that the power of a government is co-extensive with its actions; the rights of states would be endangered or lost under the same doctrine.

By the confederation of 1777, powers operating upon individuals were bestowed upon Congress; yet that instrument, far from creating a national government by such powers, or investing the federal government with any supremacy over the states, asserted their sovereignty and independence. It is true that the people of the states were the ultimate source of the powers conveyed to that Congress by the instrumentality of their agents, but by the same instrumentality, they are the ultimate source of the powers conveyed by the constitution, as they will be of powers conveyed by amendments through the agency of their state legislatures. The powers both of the former and present Congress, being both derived from the people, through the instrumentality of their agents, and mutually operating upon individuals, comprised both the circumstances from which a national government is now inferred; but had the inference been correct, it would have supplied every deficiency, and removed every defect of the old union, and rendered a new one unnecessary.

If the ends of both the old and the present union were federal, the degrees in which each flowed from and operated upon individuals, could not alter the federal character of either. By the articles of both, federal ends are explicitly avowed, and local ends explicitly renounced. The insufficiency of the first to effect the contemplated federal ends, and not its insufficiency to establish a national government, suggested the substitution of the second union. To remove this insufficiency, the imperfect mode of federal taxation was amended. But a right to tax, and the appropriation of taxes to federal objects, is nearly the same in both instruments. The first declared that "all charges of war, and all other expenses which shall be incurred for the *common defence and general welfare,* and allowed by the United States in Congress assembled, shall be defrayed out of a common treasury to be supplied by the several states, in proportion to the value of all lands and buildings, to be estimated in such mode as Congress shall from time to time direct and appoint. And that the taxes for paying that proportion shall be laid and levied by the state legislatures within the time agreed upon by Congress." By the existing union, Congress may tax, not indirectly but directly, "to pay the debts and provide for the *common defence and general welfare* of the United States." In both, federal and not national ends are expressed as objects of taxation, and in both the taxes would operate upon individuals. But no effectual security for a revenue existed in the first mode of taxation; and it furnishes an example, foretelling the effect of a naked precept for the security of state rights, coupled with a supreme power able to prevent their exercise. A federal supremacy can as easily defeat state rights preceptively reserved, as the state supremacies defeated the preceptive power of taxation delegated to the old Congress.

The power of taxation operates upon individuals more extensively than any other, yet we see that under both unions, Congress was invested with it for federal ends. The similitude of the powers granted by both, continues, in the cases of war, peace, embassies, treaties, commerce, piracies, coin, weights, and measures, post-offices, postage, appointing officers, governing the army and navy, and in others, comprising most of the powers granted to our present Congress; yet it was never imagined that these powers operating upon individuals constituted a national or supreme government, or abolished the sovereignties of the states. All the inferior powers over individuals, as plainly refer to federal ends, as the great power of taxation; and if the ends are federal, it cannot be inferred from the means necessary to effect them, that the government is national.

It was impossible to form a confederation of popular republicks, of which the people were not the source, and which could not act upon individuals. Let us suppose that thirteen monarchs should unite in a league for mutual defence, investing their delegates with limited powers over individuals, for the purpose of effecting their object. Would this confederation condense the thirteen monarchies into one? But if we add to the supposition that by this confederation of monarchs, their delegates were invested with a supreme negative over all the acts of those monarchs, and an exclusive right to construe their own powers, is it difficult to discover, that the monarchs would be deposed, and their monarchies melted up into one consolidated government? It will not be said that free and sovereign states occupy a political rank inferior to that of absolute monarchs.

The doctrines of Mr. Madison and his commentators, terminate in a syllogism. A government, the ordinary powers of which flow from the people of the several states, and operate upon individuals, is national; but no federal government can be formed which does not flow from this source, and will not operate upon individuals; therefore a federal government cannot exist in the United States. Is this hypothesis a sufficient security for the state rights of the people?

The Subject Continued

M r. Madison proceeds. "The local or *municipal* authorities form distinct and independent portions of the supremacy, *no more subject, within their respective spheres,* to the *general* authority, than the general authority is subject to them within its own sphere. In this relation, then, the proposed government cannot be deemed a national one, since its *jurisdiction extends to certain limited objects only,* and leaves to the several states a residuary and *inviolable sovereignty over all other objects. It is true, that in controversies relating to the boundaries between the two jurisdictions, the tribunal which is ultimately to decide, is to be established under the general government. The decision is to be impartially made, according to the rules of the constitution, and all the usual and most effectual precautions are taken to secure this impartiality."* That the state governments are subject and not subject to the federal government, is his result.

Mr. Hamilton also frequently and emphatically admits the sovereignty of the states, and he illustrates it by the concurrent power of taxation, supposing it to be perfectly unquestionable in the case of exclusive powers. Even in the weaker case, he asserts "that an attempt on the part of the national government to abridge the concurrent state power of taxation, would be a violent assumption of power, unwarranted by any article or clause of the constitution." But he adds, "Who is to judge of the necessity and propriety of the laws to be passed for exercising the powers of the union? *The national government, under the control of the people.*"

Even a humility, inspired by the deepest conviction of inferior talents, cannot be taxed with presumption, for differing in opinion from gentlemen at variance both with each other and with themselves; as no authorities, however respectable, can expect an assent to contradictions. Both have however extracted their respective supremacies from the same source; Mr. Madison from the supposition that the constitution established a *general* government; and Mr. Hamilton from the supposition that it had established a *national* government. From this equivalent supposition, they have drawn different inferences; one, that this general government may establish a *tribunal* to determine the extent of the rights reserved to the states; the other, that the *national* government itself may determine the extent of its own powers, under the control of the people. Both, by the interpolation of the word general or national into the constitution, violate the inviolable sovereignty bestowed by both on the states. Mr. Madison defeats the spherical relation of equality, from which he extracts the conclusions that "the government cannot be called a national one, and that its jurisdiction extends to certain limited objects *only,*" by calling it a *general* government, invested with a power to create a *tribunal* armed with unlimited jurisdiction. Do we find this power given by the constitution to the federal government?

I understand Mr. Madison to mean, that the federal judiciary is imperatively to settle controversies between two spheres, "neither of which is subject to the other, and both of which are independent and supreme," that is, although the whole of each is independent of the whole of the other, yet the whole of one is subjected to and dependent upon a part of the other.—And

Mr. Hamilton to say, that the whole of the national sphere, as he is pleased to entitle it, is invested with a power imperatively to determine the necessity and propriety of its own laws, under no control but that of the people. Propriety includes constitutionality. I discern no substantial difference between an exercise of ultimate supremacy by the federal government over the state spheres, or its bestowing the same supremacy upon a tribunal to be appointed by itself; but these contradictory constructions are accounted for by the journal of the convention. "It was moved by Mr. Randolph, seconded by Mr. Madison, that the jurisdiction of the judiciary should extend to questions which *involve the national peace and harmony;*" and Mr. Hamilton proposed "that a supreme legislature should have power to *pass all laws whatsoever.*" Both these propositions were made, considered, and rejected, and yet each commentator has discovered that his own is tacitly inserted in the constitution, by the instrumentality of first inserting in it the word "general or national."

But Mr. Madison's discovery is evidently more ingenious than Mr. Hamilton's. He supported propositions for investing a judiciary with a negative power over state laws, and with a jurisdiction in questions which might involve the national peace and harmony, both of which powers would be obtained by a power to settle the rights of independent spheres, unsubjected to any control.

Mr. Hamilton's plan for a government was adverse to this exorbitant judicial supremacy, because it was quite inconsistent with its model. No such judicial power existed in the English system of government. He therefore proposed a national legislature with a power to *pass all laws whatsoever,* in accordance with that system; and his construction "that the national government can judge of the necessity and propriety of the laws to be passed under no control but that of the people," gains this point contended for by him in the convention. He assumes the existence of a national government, and invests it with a power to pass all laws whatsoever, exactly as the plan proposed; for that also subjected the national legislature, as in England, to the control of election.

Mr. Hamilton prefers the control of the people over legislatures to the control of a court; Mr. Madison prefers the control of the court to the control of the people; but both reject the mutual check or control between the independent state and federal spheres, for which both had positively contended whilst construing the constitution. Which ought to have most weight, their constructions, mingled, or unmingled, with their prepossessions in the convention?

It was regretted that these eminent men were not opposed to each other, as to the great question, whether a federal or a national government was to be preferred; and their difference of opinion upon the important point of judicial supremacy, discloses the loss the publick has sustained from their having united in a preference for a national form of government. Mr. Hamilton having previously asserted that "a law, by the meaning of the term, includes supremacy, and that the national government was to judge of the necessity and propriety of laws," is called forth by Mr. Madison's construction transferring supremacy from his national government, and his control from the people, to the federal judiciary; and by a long and able argument, he energetically discloses his disapprobation of the novel idea.

In the numbers 47 and 48 of the Federalist, he examines the "meaning of the maxim, which requires a separation of the departments of government," and concludes his reasoning in the following words: "The conclusion which I am warranted in drawing from these observations, is, that a mere demarkation on parchment of the constitutional limits of the several departments, is not a sufficient guard against those *encroachments, which lead to a tyrannical concentration* of all the powers of government in the same hands."

In the numbers 49 and 50, Mr. Hamilton proves, that the supremacy of the people, alone, is not a sufficient security, to prevent these encroachments leading to tyranny; and that frequent appeals to them for the maintenance "of mere parchment demarkations of constitutional limits," would not only be exposed to many objections, but utterly insufficient to prevent these fatal encroachments.

In number 51, Mr. Hamilton explicitly states, and powerfully enforces, the true remedy to prevent them. He evidently considers Mr. Madison's remedy "of a parchment security for the state departments under a supremacy of the federal court," as visionary and unsubstantial. He examines the control of political departments by the people only, and also a concentration of power in one department, unsubjected to the control of another; and ably vindicates the remedy for the insufficiency of both to prevent tyranny. Having previously concluded "that mere demarkations in a constitution, are not sufficient to restrain the several departments within their legal limits, and that frequent appeals to the people would be neither a proper nor an effectual provision for that purpose," he proceeds to vindicate the only precaution commensurate to the end.

H. No. 51. "To what expedient then, shall we finally resort for maintaining in practice the *necessary* partition of power among the several departments as laid down in the constitution? The only answer that can be given is, that as all these exterior provisions are found to be inadequate, the defect must be supplied, by so contriving the interior structure of the government, as that its several constituent parts may, *by their mutual relations, be the means of keeping each other in their proper places.*

"In order to lay a due foundation for that separate and distinct exercise of the different powers of government, which, to a certain extent, is admitted on all hands, to be *essential to the preservation of liberty, it is evident that each department should have a will of its own.*

The permanent tenure by which appointments are held in the judicial department, *must soon destroy all sense of dependence,* though they should have even been conferred by the people."

"The great security against a gradual concentration of the several powers in the same department, consists in giving to those who administer each department, the necessary constitutional means and personal motives to *resist encroachments* of the others. The provision for defence must in this, as in all other cases, be made *commensurate* to the danger of attack. Ambition must be made to counteract ambition."

"This policy of supplying, by opposite and rival interests, the defect of better motives, might be traced through the whole system of human affairs."

"There are two considerations particularly applicable to the *federal system* of America, which place it in a very interesting point of view. First: In a single republick, all the power surrendered by the people, is submitted to the administration of a *single government.* In the compound republick of America, the power surrendered by the people, is first divided between *two dis-*

tinct governments, and the portion allotted to each subdivided among distinct and separate departments. Hence a double security arises to the *rights of the people. The different governments will control each other, at the same time that each will be controlled by itself.* Secondly: It is of great importance in a republick, not only to guard the society against the oppression of its rulers, but to guard one part of the society against the oppression of the other part. If a majority be united by a common interest, the rights of a minority will be insecure. A method of providing against this evil, will be exemplified in the federal republick of the United States. The society will be broken into so many different parts, that the rights of individuals or of the minority, will be in little danger from interested combinations of the majority. In a society, under the forms of which the stronger faction can readily unite and oppress the weaker, anarchy may as truly be said to reign, as in a state of nature, where the weaker individual is not secured against the violence of the stronger."

H. No. 52. "The federal legislature will not only be restrained by its dependence on the people, as other legislative bodies are, but it will be moreover watched and *controlled* by the several *collateral* legislatures, which other legislative bodies are not."

Mr. Hamilton's construction of the constitution may be thus condensed: "Mere preceptive paper declarations are insufficient to restrain political departments within constitutional limits. The supremacy of the people, alone, is also insufficient. A concentration of power is a tyranny. A judicial department retains no sense of dependence, even upon the people. Ours is a federal system. The partition of power between the state and federal departments, is necessary, and can only be maintained by an independent will of its own in each, admitted on all hands to be

essential for the preservation of liberty. The great security against
a gradual concentration of power, is, that each possesses constitutional means to resist encroachments of the other. The provision for this end places the system of America in an interesting
point of view. It does not constitute a single government, but two
distinct governments with separate powers. Each can control
the other, whilst each is controlled by its own internal construction. This system exemplifies an important security against the
oppression of rulers, and secures a minority of states against the
oppression of a majority of states. The federal legislature will be
watched and controlled both by the people and the collateral
legislatures, which other legislative bodies are not. *Hence a double
security arises to the rights of the people.* If a faction of states could
unite and oppress a weaker faction of states, anarchy would reign;
just as in a state of nature, weak individuals are exposed to the
violence of the strong."

Such is Mr. Hamilton's construction of the constitution, when
he forgets his imaginary national government, and the supremacy
with which he invests it, under the control of the people only.
Mr. Madison's is extremely different. Instead of the collateral governments controlling each other, and both being controlled by
the people, he concentrates an absolute power of control over
both, in the supreme federal court. The contrariety between the
two constructions, and of each commentator with himself, seems
palpable. Mr. Hamilton, having drawn a picture of our system of
government, in lines so beautiful and strong, expunges it by a single dash of his pen, wherein he asserts, that the national government may exclusively decide upon the necessity, propriety, or
constitutionality, of its laws, under the control of the people
only. Immediately before this assertion, he had forcibly urged a

construction of the constitution, in reference to the concurrent right of taxation in the state and federal governments, inconsistent with it. "An attempt on the part of the national government, to abridge the former in the exercise of it, would be a *violent assumption of power, unwarranted by any article or clause of the constitution.*" The selection of a concurrent power, to illustrate his assertion, that the state and federal governments had a mutual constitutional right to prevent the aggressions of either upon the sphere of the other, was the strongest mode of enforcing it; because if a concurrent power could not be abridged, the abridgement of an exclusive power, such as making roads and canals, would be still more violent and unconstitutional. His two propositions amount to this. The national government cannot abridge a concurrent nor an exclusive power, but it may abridge both, by a supreme power to decide exclusively upon the constitutionality of its own laws. Mr. Hamilton has ably proved, that the solitary control of the people was insufficient for the preservation of liberty; and that the additional mutual control of the two governments, was essential to prevent a tyrannical concentration of power in one; yet his dictum surrenders this essential control. It must either exist or not. If it does not exist, no effectual or constitutional mode of resisting federal encroachments remains in the states, separately, and a majority may usurp any powers whatsoever, over a minority of states, by the concurrence of a majority of the people; the assertions that the people alone are insufficient to control political departments, and that such departments must mutually control each other, are both revoked; and the federal, is converted into the national form of government proposed by Mr. Hamilton. If the mutual control exists, Mr. Hamilton's dictum is destroyed; if it does not exist, his able vindication of it, and his double security for the rights of the people, are overthrown. Either way, a contradiction is manifest. Mr. Hamilton perplexes the argument, by changing the epithet of the government from federal to national. The *federal* government cannot, he says, abridge a concurrent power constitutionally; but the *national* government is the exclusive judge of its own laws, under the control of the people only. From this variation of words, we discern a struggle between his prepossessions, and a fidelity to the constitution. The contrariety between the national government proposed, and the federal government adopted, required the use of the words and phrases employed in the convention to describe the former for the purpose of supplanting the latter; but this recourse to words not expressed in the constitution, far from reconciling, illustrates the contradiction.

Mr. Hamilton might have stated an opinion, both true and consistent, by saying, that the federal and state governments might mutually decide upon the constitutionality or propriety of their own laws, and check the encroachments of each other, under the control of the people. Hence only a double security arises to the rights of the people. But upon what ground is the control of the people resorted to, to effect his deprecated concentration of power in the federal government, and rejected, as a restraint upon state encroachments? Applied to both, it becomes a mutual auxiliary of the mutual control between these departments, and constitutes a security against a pernicious concentration of power in either. Admitting that the people are an effectual control upon political departments, which however Mr. Hamilton denies, it would follow that they might at least be as much depended on, to prevent the state governments from violating the constitution, as to prevent a geographical majority in

Congress, from defrauding a geographical minority. By forget-
ing that the principle of popular supremacy is the true justification of the mutual and co-ordinate control between the federal
and state departments for which he contends; and by assuming
the exclusive sufficiency of this principle in reference to the
federal department, after having denied it, Mr. Hamilton destroys
one half of the principle itself, and the whole of the mutual control between the two departments.

With great humility I conceive, that the disagreements of
Mr. Madison with himself, are at least equal to those of
Mr. Hamilton. Mr. Madison derives his national government
from the form of electing the house of representatives by the
people of the states; but having obtained it from the relation
between the people and this house, he severs the relationship;
creates in its place a dubious and distant relation between an
American nation and a federal judiciary; and transfers the
national power supposed to have been generated by election
and representation, to a court having little or no relationship with
either. Mr. Hamilton having also assumed a national government from the forms of election and the principle of representation, adheres to the relationship between them, and does not
destroy it by transferring the supremacy he makes it produce, to
the federal court. By lodging his supremacy in an American
nation, popular control, however defective, retains some value,
and might possibly be exerted by the people to preserve their
state rights. Mr. Hamilton only destroys what he has stated as
the strongest of his two controls for preventing a tyrannical concentration of power; namely, that between collateral political
departments; but Mr. Madison rejects both this mutual control,
and also the supremacy of the people.

Let us advert to Mr. Madison's construction of the constitution. "The *local or municipal authorities,* form distinct or independent portions of the supremacy, no more subject, within their respective spheres, to the *general authority,* than the general authority is subject to them, within its own sphere. In this *relation* then, the proposed government cannot be deemed a national one, since its *jurisdiction* extends to certain limited objects only, and leaves to the several states *a residuary and inviolable sovereignty over all other objects.*" Though the phrases, local or municipal authorities and general authority, are not in the constitution, and are ingeniously equivocal, they must mean the state and federal governments; and of course the construction assigns an inviolable sovereignty to the rights of the states. The word sphere is happily chosen for embracing all the parts of which each great department of our political system is compounded. It therefore comprises the state and federal judiciaries, as well as the state and federal legislatures and executives. If the respective spheres are sovereign and independent of each other, the parts of which these spheres are compounded, must also be sovereign and independent of each other. No species of sovereignty or independence could exist in the state spheres, if each part of them was subject to the supreme negative of a correspondent part of the federal sphere. These spheres are each composed of legislative, executive, and judicial parts. If one part of the federal sphere possessed a supreme negative over the acts of all parts of the state spheres, the sovereignty and independence allowed to the latter, would be as completely destroyed, as if the intire state spheres were thus subjected to the intire federal sphere. If the judicial part of the state sphere was thus subjected to the judicial part of the federal sphere, it would destroy the residuary and inviolable sovereignty, both judicial and legislative, allowed to the state spheres. In either view, the states would cease to possess the portion of independence, supremacy, or sovereignty, conceded to them by Mr. Madison. It was attempted in the convention, to subject all the parts of state spheres to the control of the correspondent parts of a national government; to give a national executive a supremacy over state executives, a national legislature a supremacy over state legislatures, and a national judiciary a supremacy over state judiciaries. Had these proposals succeeded, Mr. Madison could not have allowed an inviolable sovereignty to the state spheres, because a subjection of all their parts to the relative parts of a national government, would have been a subjection of one whole to the other whole. The titles national and general, gratuitously bestowed on the federal government, must either bestow on each of its parts a supreme power over the correspondent parts of the state governments, or upon none. If a supreme power over the state spheres is exclusively held by the federal judiciary, it proves that these titles are inapplicable to the other parts of the federal sphere. It would be infinitely more dangerous and less republican to invest a few men not controllable by the people, with a supreme power over the uncontrollable sovereignties allowed to the states, than to have divided this supremacy, as was proposed, among the departments of a national government, exposed to the control of each other, and of the people; as Congress cannot revive a state law annulled by the federal court. If the words national and general are as applicable to Congress and the president, as to the federal court, they cannot be used to create a national or general judiciary, and not a national or general legislature and executive. If they are applicable to all three of these departments, they establish Mr. Hamilton's system of government proposed in the convention; if to the judiciary only, they establish a form of government, national, as it regards a power in a court fixed for life, and not national, as it regards the representatives of the people or the states.

I cannot discern the remotest consistency between Mr. Madison's sovereignty of states, and the supremacy of a federal judiciary. The federal government cannot be both a hemisphere and the whole of a system. Mr. Madison says, "in this relation," meaning the mutual independency and supremacy of the state and federal governments, "the proposed government cannot be called a national one, because its *jurisdiction* extends to certain limited objects only, and leaves to the several states a residuary and inviolable sovereignty over all other objects." Mr. Madison extracts his federal character of the government, from the co-equal, coordinate, and independent relation between the state and federal departments. Take away this relation, and no vestige of a federal government would remain. The relation is destroyed, if a portion of the federal department possesses a supreme power over the state departments. The doctrine amounts in this. The whole federal sphere possesses no supremacy or sovereignty or power over the state spheres, but a part of the federal sphere does possess power or supremacy or sovereignty over the state spheres. As if to exclude the federal judiciary from being the part to be thus endowed, Mr. Madison states that the independent relation between the spheres by which a federal form of government is constituted, arises from the circumstance "that federal *jurisdiction* extends to certain limited *objects only*, leaving to the several states a residuary and inviolable *jurisdiction over all other objects.*" How can any inviolable sovereign state jurisdiction exist, if it is subject to a federal or national judicial supremacy?

Mr. Madison affirms the construction of independent state sovereignties as explicitly as words would allow. "The states will retain, under the proposed constitution, a very considerable portion of active," not passive, "sovereignty. The powers delegated by the proposed constitution to the *federal* government, are *few and defined*. Those which are to remain to the states, are *numerous and indefinite*. The former will be exercised principally on *external* objects, as war, peace, negotiation, and *foreign* commerce; with which last, the power of taxation will for the most part be connected. The powers reserved to the several states will extend to all objects, which in the ordinary course of affairs, *concern the lives, liberties, and properties of the people;* and the *internal order, improvement, and prosperity of the state."* The gentlemen who approve of concentrating power in the federal department, which Mr. Hamilton thought would be tyrannical, have resorted to the great extent of its powers, as the ground for giving it national or general supremacy. But how can powers few and defined, be better entitled to the epithets general or national, than powers, numerous and indefinite? There seems to be no sound reason, why a department established for external objects, should have tacitly received a supremacy over internal objects. Is the class of powers reserved to secure the lives, liberties, and properties of the people, and the internal order, improvement, and prosperity of the states, less important than the class of delegated powers? How can the state governments fulfil these great duties, if they are controllable by the federal judiciary? Are these duties assigned to the federal judiciary or to the state governments by the constitution? To the state governments, according to the constructions both of Mr. Hamilton and of Mr. Madison; who have repeatedly asserted the sovereignty and independence of the states as to the great class of reserved rights or duties; and that its violation would be violent, arbitrary, tyrannical, and unconstitutional; and yet one has said that this violation may be committed by the federal judiciary; and the other, by his imaginary general government. But how can a government be called general, which is not entrusted with the great duties enumerated by Mr. Madison, as exclusively assigned to the state governments? Under colour of these dicta, the delegated power to regulate *foreign* commerce, and the undelegated power to create corporations, have been exercised by the federal government to affect very materially the properties of the people, and the internal prosperity of the states, although these objects are enumerated among those reserved to the sovereignty of the states.

Mr. Madison considered the powers of the federal government as capable of being counted, as there was no other means of discovering that they were few and defined; and he subjoins to a general enumeration of reserved and delegated powers, the generick distinction of internal and external. Mr. Hamilton illustrates the independence of the reserved and delegated powers upon each other, by the concurrent power of taxation, as the weakest example he could select. These commentators agree, that the reserved powers are sovereign, supreme, independent, exclusive, controlling, applicable to the lives, liberties, and properties of the people, and the internal order, improvement, and prosperity of the states; that they cannot be abridged without violence and usurpation; that liberty cannot exist unless political departments are so contrived as to control each other; and that a concentration of power in one is tyranny. But having asserted the existence, the nature, and the usefulness of the powers reserved to the states, each has settled the great question, as to who shall count them, by a different dictum without examination, according to his own wishes. They agree that the division of powers into two classes, delegated and reserved, and the independency of each class upon the other, is unquestionable, and that the only difficulty is, who shall keep the tally. Mr. Hamilton says, that a general government must count both classes; Mr. Madison, that it can count neither, and that the important office of measurer, devolves on some other tribunal. In the common affairs of life, the fancy of securing distributive justice by making a receiver the measurer to himself, or by allowing him to appoint a measurer subject to his own control, never entered into the head of a moralist. The politician who adopts the same system of ethicks, ought to prove that men are more disposed to measure powers to themselves with justice and moderation, than grain or money. If few and numerous powers go into partnership, with a right in the smaller stock to cut out notches from the larger tally and add them to its own, it would not require much divination to foretel how the trade would end.

The Subject Concluded

A supreme, general, or national government, has been inferred from three sources, and deposited in two places. It has been inferred from the election of the house of representatives, from the magnitude of the powers delegated to the federal government, and from the supremacy of the federal court; but it is sometimes deposited in this court, and at others in a federal government. Those who contend for the latter doctrine, connive at the claim of the judiciary, well knowing that it is a powerful instrument for effecting their object of introducing a consolidated national government. Being merely the executive instrument of legislation, it is better calculated to extend than to control the powers of a legislative department, on which it is dependent. The claim of the judiciary, therefore, to settle the rights of the federal and state departments, merits a section appropriated to the construction of Mr. Madison, from which it has originated.

"The local or municipal authorities form distinct or independent portions of the *supremacy,* no more subject in their *jurisdiction* to the *general authority,* than the general authority is to them." What does Mr. Madison mean by the word authority? Does it include both the state and federal judicial authorities? If so, he asserts that the jurisdiction of each is supreme and independent of the other. Or, does the word general, include the federal judiciary? If so, he asserts that the state judiciaries possess a jurisdiction no

more subject to the federal judiciary, than this is to them. In the face of this dilemma, Mr. Madison proceeds. "It is true that in controversies relating to the *boundaries between the two jurisdictions,* the *tribunal* which is ultimately to decide, is to be established under the general government." This construction simply asserts, "that the state jurisdiction is no more subject to the federal jurisdiction, than the federal jurisdiction is subject to the state jurisdiction; and that the state jurisdiction is subject to the federal jurisdiction." An equivalent inference from the general position, that neither of these authorities was subject to the other, would have made the doctrine complete; namely, that the federal authority was subject to the state authorities; and it would have contained more truth. The ambiguities of the words used by Mr. Madison, will shed much light on his conclusion. What is meant by the words general government? Is general equivalent to national? Either term includes the house of representatives in Congress; and as Mr. Madison deduces his national government from the mode in which that house is elected, it would be evidently incorrect to exclude it from his general authority. If it constitutes a portion of this general authority, and if a general authority has the power of appointing a tribunal to settle the boundaries of state and federal jurisdiction, the house of representatives ought to participate in its exercise. But that house does not participate in the appointment of the federal judges, and therefore these judges do not seem to constitute the tribunal contemplated by Mr. Madison. If the word tribunal means the supreme court, then the president and senate confer on a few men a power, supposed to be within the gift of the general authority only. As the word tribunal does not designate this court, the words used imply, that the tribunal for deciding controversies between the federal and state governments, as to the extent of their mutual powers, is to be established by the federal government; and this would be less objectionable than the selection of these supreme censors by the president and senate, because the house of representatives would participate in its establishment, under the influence of the people. The word under means, by or subordinate to, the general government. If this objection is answered by asserting, that Congress may extend or contract the constitutional jurisdiction of the federal court; the formidable doctrine, that it can alter the constitution by laws, presents itself; furnishing the consolidating inference, that it can also extend or contract the powers of the legislative and executive federal departments. Whatever Congress can do by its agent, is a power in itself. If it can confer a legal concentrated supremacy on the judicial department, it can enable this department to extend its own powers or contract those of the states, and create a concentrated supremacy in itself. Congress might suppress a refractory majority by additions of new men to the tribunal, as kings of England have managed a more numerous body of aristocratical noblemen, by making new peers; or it might by impeachment remove a firm patriot, and terrify others, as has been often practised. Suppose a constitutional article had been proposed in Mr. Madison's words: "The general government shall establish a tribunal to decide the limits between the delegated and reserved powers." Would it have been acceded to? It was proposed in the convention to effect this end, by investing a national government with a negative over state acts; and the proposition was rejected. Could it have been intended to empower such a government to effect by an agent, that which it was not allowed to do itself? Or was not such a power either in

itself or its agent, superseded by the mode prescribed for altering the constitution?

"It is true that in controversies relating to the boundaries
between the two jurisdictions, the tribunal which is ultimately to
decide, is to be established under the general government." These
words irresistibly imply, that the tribunal to decide was to be
distinct from the parties litigant for jurisdiction. There could be
no controversy of the kind, if one party could dictate to the
other. In that case, submission and not controversy must ensue.
Could Mr. Madison have intended to say, that in controversies
between the state and federal judiciaries for jurisdiction, the general government might make either of the parties the judge of
its own cause? Or did he mean, that it might establish an impartial tribunal to decide between them?

"The decision is to be *impartially* made, according to the rules
of the constitution, and all the *usual and most effectual precautions*
are taken to secure this impartiality." Parties litigant always claim
under the same law, as federal and state judiciaries contending for
jurisdiction, claim under the same constitution; but it was never
before inferred from thence, that a party deciding in his own case
would construe a law or a constitution impartially. To secure this
impartiality, however, Mr. Madison says, that all the usual and
most effectual precautions are taken, by the constitution, and thus
he recognises the federal judiciary as the tribunal intended.
Where are we to find these precautions, which have had the
rare effect of compelling a party to decide impartially in his own
case? Or is it usual to invest a judicial department with a supreme
power of regulating the boundaries between independent legislative departments? It would be difficult to discover a single
instance, either in laws or constitutions, or in the theoretical

reveries of political writers, wherein the most distant idea was entertained of effecting impartiality in either case. We must therefore search in vain for "usual and most effectual precautions to secure impartiality," in cases never before contemplated, namely, those of a party empowered to try his own cause, and that of a judicial department empowered to exercise the supremacy of regulating political powers between independent legislative departments. To assume the sufficiency of the usual precautions to secure judicial impartiality, in the exercise of the usual judicial power, as a proof that they will secure judicial impartiality, in the exercise of these unusual judicial powers, is utterly inconclusive. The mutual control of political departments, both in theory and practice, has hitherto been considered as the usual and most effectual precaution, for keeping them within the spheres prescribed by constitutions; and as the most essential security for liberty; nor do I recollect that this security has ever before been abandoned in pursuit of judicial impartiality. Mr. Hamilton considers this control as an axiom, and as the only effectual security for a good form of government; vindicates the republican supremacy of the people over the controlling departments; and rejects a political supremacy of judges, as utterly inconsistent with it. So far his construction is true to his creed, and he only cripples, though he does not quite kill it, by changing the federal government from a department, into a general government; yet he retains the supremacy of the people. But Mr. Madison obliterates the whole axiom, and the supremacy of the people; and confides intirely in judicial impartiality for a free form of government. Yet it has been experimentally established, in every instance of a supreme control of one political department over the others, whether it is itself elected by the people or not, that the nature of the government is overturned. A supremacy of the British house of commons, though elected by the people, would not tolerate any control by the other departments; and those who admire that form of government, are careful to maintain a mutual power in its departments to control each other, as the only means by which it can be preserved. Those who admire our federal system, may therefore read in the book of experience, that it cannot exist, unless a mutual power of control between the state and federal departments is effectually maintained and exercised, under the supremacy of the people. To exchange this best security against ambitious usurpations, for the untried novelty of exalting a single court into a supreme political power, upon the ground that its integrity in exercising it is secured by certain usual precautions, is a hazardous experiment; because, if political integrity could be obtained by these precautions, they have not been ever thought of as imparting political wisdom to a court, which is quite distinguishable from the legal knowledge considered as the recommendation to office.

To ascertain the force of this reasoning, let us consider what are "the usual and most effectual precautions to secure judicial impartiality." The judicial system of this country has been modelled in imitation of the British, and by borrowing their precautions, we have demonstrated an intention of effecting the same end which theirs contemplated. Tenure for life, fixed salaries, and impeachment, are both their means and ours. The end of the British precautions, was to obtain judicial impartiality in the distribution of justice between individuals, and not in a distribution of powers between political departments. Had the latter new and extraordinary end been contemplated by the establish-

ment of a British judiciary, new and extraordinary precautions
would have been invented, for preventing political partialities or
errors, infinitely more dangerous than any frauds which could be
committed in relation to individuals. And had our constitution
contemplated an extension of judicial power to an object so
superior, it would not have been contented with precautions
contrived for securing distributive justice to individuals. For this
end, judicial tenure for life, fixed salaries, and impeachment, were
deemed sufficient. These might prevent any undue influence, and
remove the temptations of bribery. But these precautions were
not intended to change the federal government into a judicial
aristocracy. Impeachments were not to be tried by a party to
the controversy, but by a power which could not be involved in
the suits or questions to be decided; and which might, by increasing salaries or exerting influence, regenerate a national government, rejected by the constitution. Although these usual
precautions might be sufficient for the attainment of judicial
impartiality between individuals, yet a supreme power of distributing rights to political departments, would have an effect
precisely the reverse, if one of these departments could exclusively appoint, pay, influence, and try, the judges. Fear, hope,
undue influence, and money, would convert all these usual precautions into instruments for soliciting partial political decisions, instead of being means to prevent them. If the solicitations
of ambition, the invariable appurtenance of enormous power,
could be resisted, yet the government would be moulded by the
opinions of a few men, and not by the publick judgment. Were
these usual precautions designed to induce the supreme court
to make a good government? To imagine that the convention
intended, by copying the British precautions for securing justice

to individuals, to invest a single court with a power to regulate
the rights of the federal and state departments, would charge it
with a degree of simplicity, which the character of the members
does not justify, as tenure for life is at least as well calculated to
produce political partialities, as to prevent partialities between
individuals. Suppose the court, or Congress, or a popular and
powerful individual, should prefer a national government or a
limited monarchy to our federal system, is it not obvious that an
exclusive power of appointing, paying, advancing, and trying,
the judges, united with a tenure for life, will be means of advancing, rather than of preventing the design? May not a power in the
federal government be generated by a confederacy between
Congress and its court, equivalent to the power of the British
government, often exercised in altering its form and principles?

The constitution acquits the convention of a design to confer
this moulding power on the federal government, by containing
provisions both for securing an impartial dispensation of justice
to individuals, and also an impartial dispensation of constitutional
alterations to the United States. Instead of confounding the two
ends, it contemplates the attainment of one, by the usual precautions for securing judicial impartiality; and the attainment of
the other, by so bestowing the moulding power, that even a
majority of states cannot transform our federal into a national
government. Is there no difference between these new and extraordinary precautions, provided for the new and extraordinary
object of securing a federal form of government; and the usual
precautions for securing judicial impartiality in the usual dispensation of justice between individuals? Could the latter have
been intended to secure judicial impartiality in the dispensation
of powers between the state and federal governments, when a

very different tribunal is positively invested exclusively with this jurisdiction? Could a majority of one man, in a court consisting of six or seven men, have been invested with a moulding power, only intrusted to three-fourths of the states, under the control of the people? It is impossible that the framers of the constitution had the same confidence in a court not influenced by the people, as in three-fourths of the states, for the purpose of moulding anew state and federal powers; upon the ground, that the usual precautions were taken to secure judicial impartiality in the distribution of justice between individuals; because it cannot be imagined that they thought a majority of one judge, was equivalent to a majority of three-fourths of the states, to which the power of re-moulding the rights of the federal and state departments, is jealously confined.

Has this enormous absurdity been committed undesignedly in defining the jurisdiction of the federal judiciary, so as to invest three-fourths of the states and the supreme court, with a concurrent right of dispensing powers to the state and federal governments? Had this intention existed, it would have appeared in the article prescribing the modes of amending the constitution. It would have declared, that the constitution might be amended by three-fourths of the state legislatures, or of state conventions, or by a majority of the supreme court. Whilst one alternative is expressed, the absence of another amounts to its rejection. But it is said, that the judges cannot alter or amend the constitution, and are to decide impartially between the state and federal governments, in a contest for power, which impartiality will be secured by the usual precautions we have considered. If the state and federal governments should differ in its construction, they may refer to the tribunal able to remove the ambiguity, but the court has no power to appeal to this referee. The opinion of the court cannot remove the ambiguity, unless that opinion shall operate as an amendment, and supersede the opinion of one or both of the parties. Suppose the constructive opinion of the court shall be erroneous; it must either have the effect of altering the constitution, or be void as not proceeding from the authority empowered to alter it. Why is there no provision in the constitution to provide for an event not only possible but certain? Because an erroneous construction by the court could not alter the constitution. Both Mr. Madison and Mr. Hamilton have provided for the case of adverse constructions of the constitution by the state and federal departments, in admitting their mutual independence, and mutual right to control each other, as the genuine principle applicable to co-ordinate political departments; but the erroneous constructions of the court would be liable to no such check, and the constitution, for want of it, would be divested of the best security for its preservation.

Neither the declaration of independence, nor the confederation of 1777, referred to a judicial department for their preservation, and the constitution refers to the states for this purpose. These three constitutional acts unite in establishing the principle, that the guardianship of each belonged to the people as organized into states, and they have never surrendered a power, essential for the preservation of their liberty, to a chamber of men inducted, like bishops, for life, by executive selection. If the king of England had a power to appoint a tribunal to settle the rights of the regal, aristocratical, and republican departments, it would be equivalent to a power in the federal department, to appoint a tribunal for settling the rights of the federal and state departments. Any mode, direct or indirect, by which the people of the states are deprived of this power, will destroy the basis upon which the validity of both departments rests; and this basis must be the master-key for unlocking the meaning of its subordinate regulations, or these subordinate regulations will become pick-locks, for stealing the treasure of liberty, the master-key was intended to secure. Unless it can control constructive thefts, its efficacy is lost. In searching for the intention of any article of the constitution, we must either sustain or surrender the foundation of our liberty, and remember that good principles are not as corruptible as great men.

With these preliminary observations unforgotten, I will endeavour to discover the meaning of the constitution in relation to the federal judiciary, and to prove that the appellate jurisdiction given by law to the supreme court, was deduced by Congress from the Federalist, and by its elegant authors, from their personal opinions, disclosed by their propositions made in the convention. The three first articles are devoted to its legislative, executive, and judicial departments, defining and limiting the powers of each. It will not be contended, that all or either of these departments were intended to be exonerated, or that one or two could exonerate another from the duty of confining themselves within the powers delegated to each. Neither article empowers the department which it creates, to confer an additional power upon an associate, nor to extend the powers bestowed by its peculiar article. The special legislative modifications provided for, do not create a new constituent principle. In the legislative article, no power can be found, enabling Congress to confer any species of supremacy upon the federal judiciary over the state judiciaries, or to bestow upon the former an appellate jurisdiction extending to the latter. Congress is empowered "to constitute tribunals *inferior* to the *supreme* court," demonstrating the true relation between the words "supreme and inferior," repeated in the judicial article; and evidently excluding the idea, that Congress could make state courts inferior to the supreme federal court, any more than it could make state legislatures inferior to the federal legislature. The states derived their judicial, as well as their legislative and executive powers, from state sovereignty. All the arguments extracted from the supposed inconveniences likely to be produced by the clashing of state and federal judicial powers, in order to justify an appellate supremacy in the latter, apply with more force to the justification of a supreme controlling power in the federal legislature and executive, over the state legislatures and executives; and if federal laws can confer a supreme power on one of its departments over the correspondent state department, they may confer a similar supremacy upon all. The construction deduced from supposed inconveniences, would establish the national government proposed and rejected in the convention. That project did not contemplate the immediate destruction of the state governments, but only their subordination to a complete national government. Let us consider whether this proposed subordination was revived by the constitution, or whether Congress can revive it by law, in favour of the supreme federal court, and thereby make the reserved sovereign rights of the states dependent upon the will of the federal government; since, if they cannot be protected by the state judiciaries, they will evidently be divested of all protection, except that which may arise from the deprecated recourse to war.

This construction given to the third article, is to be suspected, as abolishing in fact the state sovereign powers reserved, attempted to be abrogated by the proposition for a national government; but happily its words are too consistent with the principle of a division of powers between the federal and state governments, and too literally adverse to the rejected project for a consolidated national government, to have contemplated the idea of destroying this principle, with all the good effects it is capable of producing. State rights can no more exist than federal, without free and independent departments for exercising and preserving them.

The third article begins with a provision for the exercise of the legislative power "to constitute tribunals *inferior* to the *supreme* court," by declaring that "the judicial power of the *United States* shall be vested in *one supreme* court, and in such *inferior* courts, as the Congress may from time to time *ordain and establish.*" The whole legislative power given to Congress is to be executed by *ordaining and establishing supreme and inferior federal courts.* Does this empower Congress to ordain, that superior state courts shall be inferior to federal courts? The supremacy and inferiority to be derived from federal legislation, are both limited to the judicial power of the *United States.* Were state courts contemplated as constituting any portion of the judicial power of the United States? If not, then as the third article throughout refers to "the judicial power of the United States" only, it is not by a single word extended to the state judiciaries, though the gentlemen in favour of a national government may think that this ought to have been the case. The article proceeds to demonstrate its meaning, by declaring that these supreme and inferior judges, invested with the judicial power of the United States, "both of the *supreme* and *inferior* courts, shall hold their offices during *good behaviour,* and receive salaries not to be *diminished.*" All the judges in rela-

tion to whom Congress could legislate, were to be reached by
these provisions; but they did not include state judges, whose
tenures and salaries Congress could not fix. Congress was not
invested with any legislative power over state courts, since their
legislative power is confined to judges embraced by these two
federal provisions. The supremacy expressed can therefore refer
only to the inferior courts or judges described in the same section, as reached by the two provisions annexed to their offices,
and not to state courts, or judges, to whom these provisions did
not extend. The projects for a national form of government in
the convention, confirm the construction dictated by the words.
One of these contemplated an abolition of the state governments; the other, an adoption of state legislatures, executives,
and judiciaries, as subordinate parts of a national government.
The latter contemplated a supremacy of national departments,
legislative, executive, and judicial, over the correspondent state
departments. Instead of this proposed national government, the
constitution established a federal government, invested, not with
supreme, but with limited powers; and the consolidating words
used to describe both projects, were rejected in the deed. There
would have been a manifest absurdity in coupling a supreme
national judiciary with a legislature not national, as it would not
have corresponded, either with the national government proposed, or the federal government adopted. Such a supreme judicial power, might have extended or diminished state powers,
against the will of Congress and the president, and these powers
would have lost the protection, designed by the Virginia plan
for a national government, to be derived from its proposed general supremacy. By an exclusive judicial supremacy, federal, as well
as state powers, would have been made subordinate to judicial

power. Therefore, when the projects for a national form of government were given up, the supremacy contemplated by them, for national legislative, executive, and judicial departments, was relinquished, and no supremacy over the powers reserved to the states, was incongruously given to a judicial department, exclusively of the other two.

The perseverance of the gentlemen in favour of a national government, proves that the subject was thoroughly considered; and the solemn preference of the federal form, demonstrates that no construction, by which that preference will be frustrated, can be just. Its basis was state sovereignty; compatible with a federal limited government, but incompatible with a supreme national government. Hence state sovereignty was denied by the gentlemen who proposed a national government. This sovereignty is the foundation of all the powers reserved to the states. Unless they are sustained by it, they are baseless. State legislative, executive, and judicial powers, must all or none flow from this source. All are necessary to sustain the state republican governments. Subject either to a master, and the others become subject to the same master. If the state judicial power, as flowing from state sovereignty, is not independent, state legislative and executive power, cannot be independent, because all rest upon the same foundation; and because, if a supreme federal judiciary can control state courts, it can also control state legislatures and executives. Thus a federal form of government would be rejected, though it was established, and a national government would be established, though it was rejected.

The second section of the article we are considering, begins with the following words: "The judicial power shall *extend*." The word extend, far from meaning supremacy, implies the reverse.

The distinction is expressed in the first article. The legislation of Congress is not *extended* to the ten miles square, but made supreme over that district, in order to abolish a state concurrency of power within it. The powers of Congress are extended to specified objects, but as these extensions did not imply supremacy, the powers bestowed are concurrent, except when attended by positive prohibitions upon the states. As the word exclusive is used when exclusiveness was intended, and as the extension of federal legislative power to specified objects, was not considered as conveying a supreme power, but as establishing concurrent powers in the state and federal governments, flowing to the states from their original sovereignties, and to Congress from delegations; so an extension of judicial power by delegations also, only created a concurrent state and federal jurisdiction in the cases, as to which it is not prohibited, arising under the constitution. No legislative, executive, or judicial power, is given to the states, for enabling them to exercise their reserved rights, because they were derived from their anterior sovereignty. From this source, and the special delegations, arose many cases of a concurrency in state and federal legislation, such as that of taxation, and this concurrency would have extended to all the delegated powers, except for the prohibitions of the tenth section of the first article. Those in relation to war, troops, and imports and exports, would have been useless, except that the states, in virtue of their sovereignty, would have retained an absolute power as to these objects, had no such prohibitions been inserted in the constitution. They might have declared war, raised armies, and imposed duties, though Congress might have done it also, upon the same ground that both the state and federal governments may tax. Now if an extension of some sovereign powers of the states to Congress, did not, without a special prohibition, take from the states their right to exercise the same powers, the constitution itself furnishes us with a construction of the judicial article. As the extension of legislative federal power to taxation, did not destroy the sovereign power of the states to tax, nor invest Congress with a supreme power to annul state laws for that purpose; so the extension of the federal judicial power to cases in law and equity arising under the federal constitution and laws, did not deprive the states of the inherent attribute of sovereignty to dispense justice to their people in these eases, nor expose their decisions in cases of law and equity, to be annulled by the federal judiciary. A concurrency of jurisdiction arose from the extension of judicial federal power, upon the same principles which produced a concurrency of legislation between the federal and state governments. Original sovereignties were not in either case surrendered to a delegated participation. It is owing to a concurrency of jurisdiction in the federal and state governments, that the judges of both are required to take an oath to support the constitution; and this concurrency is distinctly admitted by the federal judges, in revising state judgments, and affirming them, if right; whereas, if the state courts had no jurisdiction in cases of law and equity arising under the federal constitution and laws, all their judgments would have been coram non judice, and void. Their jurisdiction is thus admitted, and the only question is, whether Congress can empower the federal court to annul it.

If the concurrent powers of the states were not destroyed by delegations, and if the exclusive or supreme powers of the federal government, did not flow from these extensions, but from positive prohibitions; wherever no such prohibitions exist, the sov-

ereign powers of the states remain; and these comprise the right
of trying all suits in law and equity whatsoever. The prohibitions
are acknowledgments of this position, and even contain a construction of themselves, by which it is vindicated. The prohibition upon the states to engage in war, is void in cases of invasion
or imminent danger. In these cases, the sovereignty of the states is
absolved from the prohibition, and is not absorbed by the delegated power to declare war. It was not therefore absorbed by a
delegated power to try law-suits.

The constitution creates federal legislative, executive, and judicial departments; and such departments also are established by
state sovereignties. Are these departments concurrent or exclusive
rights, or does their extension to the federal government create
a supremacy in the departments delegated, over the departments
reserved? In either view, we discern the only imaginable distinction between a federal and a consolidated national government, and behold the identical question which long divided the
convention. The abolition of these state departments, or their
subordination to a national government, was contended for. Our
alternative is yet the same under the construction of the constitution subsequently advanced, as it was in the convention. We
must either vindicate the concurrency of powers, except where
the positive prohibitions intervene, or accept of the proposed
subordination.

The federal judicial power is extended to all "cases in law and
equity arising under this constitution, the laws of the United
States, and treaties." If the judicial power of the states, in virtue
of their sovereignty, extends also to these cases, we have only to
enquire, whether the constitution invests the federal judicial
power with a coercing supremacy over itself, or whether this

concurrency establishes a mutual independency, as in the case of federal and state legislative powers. Towards the solution of the question, we must determine, whether the enumeration of federal judicial powers, is not a limitation and restriction, like the enumeration of federal legislative powers. Congress is empowered to "make all laws necessary and proper for carrying into execution the *powers vested* by the constitution in the government of the United States." The federal judicial power is extended only "to all cases in law and equity arising under the constitution." The analogy between these expressions is considerable. Neither conveys a power to alter the terms of the compact between the states. Both must therefore have been intended as respectively prohibiting the federal legislative and judicial departments from effecting this end, either by laws or judgments. Otherwise Congress, by laws, or the federal courts, by judgments, might alter the constitution. The constitutional mode of amendment subverts this construction. It prohibits us from supposing that a concurrent power of amendment, was lodged in Congress, the supreme court, and three-fourths of the states. A power in any department of the federal government to amend, would have defeated the precaution of requiring three-fourths of the states to effect an alteration. If such a power is not given, how can its exercise be prevented, or does our federal system contain no principle of self-preservation? Suppose Congress should alter the constitution by laws, and the federal courts should execute them. Can the usurpation be prevented by any other principle, than a concurrent power in the state and federal governments to construe and preserve the constitution; or are unconstitutional federal laws void, and unconstitutional federal judgments binding? Can any other principle sustain the mode of amending the constitution, and the mutual check between the federal and state departments, so highly praised by the Federalist? If Congress, or the supreme court, can annul state laws or judgments, to what species of government are those of the states to be assigned?

Thus we are conducted to the restriction contained in the words "cases in law and equity." Their true meaning must be preserved, or the plain intention of the constitution destroyed. A power to try cases in law and equity, has never been understood to comprise a power of common legislation, and much less the higher power of altering constitutions or forms of government. The English judiciary try cases in law and equity, but this does not comprise a power to alter the rights of the English political departments. These are the guardians of their own rights, not to be altered except by a concurrence of all. The state governments are also the guardians of their own rights, not to be altered except by a concurrence of three-fourths. The senate of the United States is a precaution for preventing evasions of this concurrence, which would be defeated, if the supreme court could acquire a power of controlling the state governments, because the senate cannot revise judgments or decrees in cases of law and equity.

Controversies may arise under the constitution between political departments, in relation to their powers; between the legislative and treaty-making departments; between the senate and the house of representatives; between the president and the senate; or between the state and federal departments; but they would not be cases in law and equity, nor is any power to decide them given to the federal judiciary. One species of controversy relates to the form of government; the other flows from its operation. The power by which a government is formed or altered, is not the power by which the law-suits of individuals are tried; and therefore a power to try suits in law and equity, was never supposed to comprise the former power.

Among the cases to which the federal jurisdiction is extended, not one is to be found recognising a power to decide controversies between any of these political departments. It is inconceivable that a jurisdiction, transcending beyond comparison the jurisdiction cautiously specified, should have been tacitly given without any specification. In two cases only, the federal courts have received an exclusive jurisdiction, arising from the circumstance that these were cases created by the constitution, and not comprised by the anterior state sovereignties; in all other cases the states have a concurrent jurisdiction, because they were. Any other parties may institute suits in the state courts, and upon the same principle, an ambassador or consul fleeing from punishment for a criminal act, would be surrendered to the justice of the state tribunals.

The second section of the third article, resorted to as an extension of federal judicial power, into a supremacy over state judicial power, is in these words:"In all cases affecting ambassadors, other publick ministers, and consuls, and those in which a state shall be a party, the supreme court shall have *original* jurisdiction."In all the other cases *before mentioned,* the supreme court shall have appellate jurisdiction, both as to *law and fact,* with such exceptions, and under such regulations, as the Congress shall make." The words "original and appellate," both refer to the federal courts, and are used for dividing the federal judicial power previously defined, between these courts; and not for the purpose of extending that power to a supremacy over state judicial power, and thereby defeating its specified limitation. They are a consequence of the legislative power "to constitute tribunals inferior

to the supreme court." This inferiority could only be effected
by appeals from the inferior federal courts, to the supreme federal
court. As Congress could not constitute state courts, these were
not the inferior courts to which its legislative power is extended,
and therefore the appellate jurisdiction is limited from the inferior courts which Congress could constitute. And as the word
original created no new judicial power, so the word appellate
gave none. Both the words are expressly restricted to the judicial powers previously bestowed, by repeating that portion of
them to which the original jurisdiction of the supreme court is
extended, and including the rest by the words "in all other cases
before mentioned." No language could more positively have
excluded the idea, that this second section created any additional judicial federal power. And therefore, as the judicial power
previously defined and expressly referred to by this second section, does not give to the federal courts any power to try cases
in law and equity arising under state constitutions and laws; nor
controversies between political departments; nor the least power,
original or appellate, over the state courts; the second section
can give no such powers, because it is restricted by its reference
to the first. The appellate jurisdiction from the inferior federal
courts to the supreme federal court, provided for, was to extend
both to "law and fact, with such exceptions and under such regulations, as the Congress shall make." Could the words "law and
fact," have been intended to refer to political controversies
between the state and federal governments? What idea would
be conveyed by a power to try the constitution, according to
law and fact? These appeals were to be tried by such law and
fact as Congress might establish, or regulate. Had therefore an
appellate jurisdiction from the state courts been given to the

supreme federal court, a power in Congress to regulate the law and fact by which they were to be tried, would have comprised a federal legislative power to regulate the proceedings in the state courts themselves. In empowering Congress to regulate these appeals, a power of regulating the modes of proceeding prescribed by state governments to state courts, could not have been contemplated, because these are various; and though it was proper that the federal government should regulate the trials in federal courts, both as to law and fact, such a power in relation to state courts, would have produced infinite confusion, provoked litigation, and must have terminated in a national government. But as supremacy means, and appellate implies, dominion, the commentators have said, that this clause invests the supreme federal court with dominion over the state courts.

The constitution is susceptible of three distinct characters, which will shed much light on its construction. It ought to be considered as a compact, an organization of a government limited by the compact, and as a law in relation to individuals. Its essential stipulation as a compact, is the division of power between the state and federal governments. This feature is impressed upon it in the strongest lines, by the guarantee of a republican form of government to every state, and the reservation of undelegated powers. Can a government be called republican, or even be any government, if its powers may be taken away by another government, or if it is responsible, not to the people, but to a few judges, who are themselves responsible to another government? The argument used in the convention, now again advanced, that the states are subordinate corporations, is refuted by the constitution itself in its guarantee and reservation. Who are the guardians of the compact, the guarantee, and

the reservation; the people of each state, or the supreme federal
court? Is this court a state, a republican form of government for
every state, and the receptacle of the reservation? Even a criminal
is to be tried by his peers. Suppose the guarantee to convey a
power, instead of imposing a duty, the state forms of government fall under the jurisdiction of the United States, and cannot be regulated by a jurisdiction to try suits in law and equity.
If the guarantee is only a duty, the state governments, to be
republican, must be regulated by the people of each state. How
can they be republican, if they may be tried, their laws and judgments annulled, and their powers abridged, by a court, which is
neither their peer, their master, nor their guarantee? To abridge
the powers of state governments, is equivalent to the suppression of state legislatures. The constitution, in accordance with its
character as a compact, composes a jury consisting of three-
fourths of the contracting parties, for its own trial, because they
were compeers; and neither subjected itself as a compact, nor
these compeers and mutual guarantees, to the power of a few
men only enabled to try cases in law and equity.

By organizing a federal government to execute, the constitution did not intend to alter the compact. Its organick, was
intended to be subservient to its contracting character, and not to
be exalted above it. The departments and officers of the federal
government were a skeleton, intended as the residence of one
soul of the compact, and the departments and officers of the state
governments were considered as the residence of the other soul.
The federal soul might have been infused into a different piece of
mechanism. I have therefore objected to Mr. Madison's idea,
that the house of representatives, one part of the mechanism or
skeleton, contrived as a receptacle for the principles of the com-

pact, can alter those principles on account of the mode in which this limb is moulded. The president, senate, and house of representatives, all limbs of a federal mechanism, are somewhat formed after monarchical, aristocratical, and republican models, but this does not alter the principles of the compact, nor change the soul of the skeleton from federal to national, any more than the mode of making the presidential limb, can make our government a monarchy.

The third article of the constitution is both organick and legal. Organick, in establishing a federal judiciary; legal, in creating several new individual legal rights; but its legal character, to be discerned in this and other articles, is addressed to all individuals, and of course to all tribunals. The mechanism of a supreme and inferior courts, does no more create a supreme national judicial power, than the mechanism of Congress can create a supreme national legislative power. None of these wheels or pullies were intended to destroy the state governments, or their republican forms, or the reservation by which only life is infused into those forms. Hence the mechanism of the federal courts into supreme and inferior, was only intended as an auxiliary towards enforcing the legal character of the constitution, and not as an instrument for altering its organick, or its contracting characters. The constitution, as a law, would produce cases in law and equity. To such cases only, and not to the principles of the compact, nor to the mechanism of our system, the judicial power of the United States is extended. The state courts may also try cases in law and equity, but this gives them no power to alter the mechanism or principles of constitutions, or to determine the controversies of political departments. Authorities might be cited in great number, to prove that such powers have never been considered as annexed to a jurisdiction in cases of law and equity, but only a federal and state construction is adduced. Congress have given to the courts of Columbia a power to try *all cases in law and equity.* Do these words convey a power to regulate the political departments or principles by which the district is governed? The states gave to the federal courts the same power. Do the same words convey a power to regulate the political departments or principles by which the states are governed, and not those by which Columbia is governed? The state of Ohio gave a jurisdiction to one *supreme* court and *inferior* courts, in *cases of law and equity.* Did this create a jurisdiction able to regulate the powers of political departments, created by its constitution?

In order to elude the difference between the contracting and organick characters of the constitution, and to make the latter destroy the former, it has been said, that the federal is a perfect government, and not a political department; and therefore that a comparison between our political checks and those of England is not correct, or at least can only be applied to the departments of the federal government. These being, organically, legislative, executive, and judicial, their concurrence is supposed to constitute a supremacy like that of the British parliament, invested with a right to remove every obstruction out of its way; and an army sufficient to execute its pleasure, is then all that is necessary to perfect a national system of government. If this doctrine is insufficient to awaken the states, they will soon sleep forever. But the assumption on which it is founded is not true. Neither the federal nor state are perfect governments, both being only invested as distinct and checking political departments, with limited portions or dividends of civil and political power. If a political mechanism, resembling that of the British perfect government, and invested, not with any power, like that, to alter the constitution, but only with limited legislative, executive, and judicial powers, is sufficient to control both the principles of our compact and the organical mode for giving them efficacy; as the organization of both the state and federal governments equally resemble the British mechanism; both would possess all the powers of a perfect government. But our division of power operates upon this mechanism, and converts it into a mode of establishing collateral and balancing departments, similar to the division of rights and powers between the king, lords, and commons, of England. The king to preserve his prerogatives, the lords to preserve their privileges, and the commons to preserve their rights, do not resort to triers of law and fact. If the lords originate a money bill, the commons do not sue them at law or in equity. Nor do I discern, how the state department could, by such a suit, preserve its reserved rights. The federal court may be the aggressor, or possibly take sides with the federal legislative or executive power, if either of these should be the aggressor. Of all defendants, a political department, in trying its competitors, and deciding its own misdeeds, is the least likely to do justice. If the federal judiciary is a political department for the preservation of delegated powers, the state judiciaries are also political departments for the preservation of the reserved powers. But as no tribunal could ever be found able or willing to do justice between contending political and balancing departments, without subverting a division of power indispensable for the preservation of civil liberty, such departments have necessarily and invariably been considered as the guardians of their own rights, because the end could only be effected by their clashing with and controlling each other.

The legal feature of the constitution, in relation to judges, is expressed in the sixth article. "The constitution is the *supreme law* of the land, and the judges in *every state* are to be bound thereby." Can the judgments of the federal court be a supreme law over this supreme law? Is there no difference between the supremacy of a federal court over inferior federal courts, and the supremacy of the constitution over all courts? The supremacy of the constitution is a guarantee of the independent powers within their respective spheres, allowed by the Federalist to the state and federal governments. A supremacy in the court might abridge or alter these spheres. The state judges are bound by the constitution and by an oath to obey the supremacy of the constitution, and not even required to obey the supremacy of a federal court. Why are all the departments of the state and federal governments equally bound to obey the supremacy of the constitution? Because the state and federal governments were considered as checking or balancing departments. Had either been considered as subordinate to a supremacy in the other, it would have been tyrannical to require it by an oath to support the supremacy of the constitution, and also to break that oath by yielding to the usurped supremacy of the other. The oath requires loyalty to state and federal powers; judgments might require disloyalty to both. The answer to this dilemma is, that as the federal, in its mechanism, is a perfect government, because it somewhat resembles the British, the states are bound to consider whatever it does as constitutional; and that therefore the oath, though taken in fact to support the constitution, virtually binds the swearer to support both the laws of the federal government, and the judgments of its supreme court. But since the state governments, by their organization, and by the guarantee,

are considered as perfect governments also in relation to their
reserved powers, I do not see why the federal government is
not, by the same virtual interpretation of the oath, bound to support state laws and judgments. Is it not as obvious, by endowing
the federal government or either of its departments with this virtual supremacy over the state governments, deduced, not from
the principles of the compact, but from the form of its organization, that a consolidated national government and a destruction
of the state governments, would ensue; as that by endowing the
state governments upon the same grounds, with an unexpressed
supremacy over the federal government, a dissolution of the
union would be the consequence? The fact is, that both are perfect governments in relation to their respective powers, subject in
one case to three-fourths of the states, and in the other, to the
people of each state; and that neither this species of perfection,
nor the mechanism of either, invests one with any species of
supremacy over the other.

The arguments in confirmation of this construction of the
constitution, are abundant. Criminal prosecutions are allowed not
to be comprised by the words "cases in law and equity," because
these words refer to civil suits between individuals, and not to the
reserved powers of the states. This meaning equally excludes a
jurisdiction over the reserved powers themselves, as over the state
jurisdiction in criminal cases. The criminal state jurisdiction is
held to be independent, as a consequence of state sovereignty;
and would it not be absurd to admit, that an effect of a reserved
power is independent of the delegated powers, but that the
power itself from which the effect flows, is subordinate to and
dependent upon them? If the supremacy of the constitution cov-
ers the effect, it must cover the power. The supremacy of the

court only lifts it above the inferior federal courts, and not above the supremacy of the constitution. If the latter does not lift state powers themselves above the supremacy of the court, no effects of these powers can be beyond its reach.

Judicial and constitutional powers are made distinct for a stronger reason, than judicial and legislative. One species of monopoly would only endanger private justice; the other would destroy publick liberty. The limitation to cases arising under the federal constitution and laws, excludes cases arising under state constitutions and laws. An extension of the federal jurisdiction to a few specified cases of the latter description, excludes all not specified. The federal judges are not required to swear that they would support state constitutions and laws, because they had no jurisdiction over them. State and federal legislative powers cannot be independent of each other, if state and federal judicial powers are not. If Congress can extend judicial federal powers, and the supreme federal court can extend legislative federal powers, the constitution is not susceptible of the federal constructions given to it by Mr. Madison and Mr. Hamilton.

If the preceding argument is sound, the law of Congress declaring that the "supreme court shall have appellate jurisdiction from the courts of the several states; and that it may issue writs of error to revise, reverse, or affirm, judgments or decrees of the state courts," is precisely as unconstitutional, as state laws for bestowing an appellate jurisdiction from the decisions of the federal courts, upon the supreme courts of the states. No power is given to either legislature to pass such laws, nor an appeal from either judiciary to the other allowed, any more than from a legislative state or federal department to the other. The appellate jurisdiction given by the federal law, is unsubjected to limitation, and the writ of error is extended to every case which may call in question the sovereign, independent, and reserved rights of the states. Does the limited power of Congress "to constitute tribunals inferior to the supreme court," enable it to endow the judicial power of the United States with this mighty accession of jurisdiction, or with any jurisdiction at all? Congress is to create the courts, but the constitution created the jurisdiction; and its extension by law was only an extract from the monarchical or national tumour, which became so large in the convention.

The federal legislative and judicial powers are both plainly intended to be limited by the constitution, and any mode by which this limitation can be evaded, must destroy our federal system, or be destroyed by it. If Congress can give a judicial supremacy to a federal court, the federal legislative power must be itself supreme, and may extend its bounty to the executive also. This construction makes it the design of the constitution to introduce a limited monarchy or a consolidated national government, as proposed in the convention, disguised in the habiliments of a federal government, falsified by the misnomer of a union, and restrained by ropes of sand, or ineffectual precepts.

Even the law for giving to the supreme federal court an appeallate jurisdiction over the state courts, justifies this view of the subject. Why was it passed? Because the third article of the constitution gave no such jurisdiction to the supreme federal court. Because it was an exercise of that plenitude of power, said to be inherent to a perfect government, modelled with some resemblance to the British form. And because it was a precedent in favour of the capacity of construction, for turning war into roads, and commerce into canals. As Congress could make courts, it could pass any laws in relation to courts, state and federal, their jurisdiction, supremacy, or subordination; and by one profound effort, enlarge its own power, make a great progress towards the introduction of a consolidated government, and establish a mode of construing the constitution, by which that design might with ease and certainty be effected. And thus the mutual control between the state and federal departments, is in the road to ruin, although even Mr. Hamilton allows it to be the most excellent feature of our system of government, and that a concentration of power is on the other hand the most infallible evidence of tyranny.

The judicial power of the United States is extended to all cases in law and equity arising under the constitution, *the laws of the United States,* and treaties, without discrimination, demonstrating that these cases were of the same nature, whether they arose under the constitution or under laws; and as the latter must either be confined to private law-suits, or Congress must have a power of regulating the political powers of the state and federal governments by laws, it follows that the former were confined to the same cases. Therefore, as political controversies between the two governments were not considered as embraced by "cases in law and equity," and it being deemed necessary for the purpose of preserving amity between states, and effecting several federal objects, to extend the jurisdiction of the federal court to a few political cases, not reached by the jurisdiction to settle private rights comprised in the phrase "cases in law and equity," a specification of these few cases became necessary. As this jurisdiction did not extend to the sovereign or reserved rights of the states, and as it was necessary that some tribunal should exist, to preserve amity between the separate states, the federal judiciary is invested with a power of settling "controversies between states." This special jurisdiction, extending only to a distinct sovereign right of the states, is both an expression of the limited meaning annexed to the words "cases in law and equity," and also a positive exclusion from the jurisdiction of the federal court, of all other sovereign powers reserved to the states. Among the controversies of a political nature, not reached by the words "cases in law and equity," were such as might arise between the federal and state departments, as well as such as might arise between two states. By extending the jurisdiction of the supreme court to the latter controversies only, the former are excluded, because the federal court was considered as an impartial tribunal for deciding controversies between two state governments, but not for deciding controversies between the state and federal governments.

The specification of controversies between two states, interprets the word supreme, and the phrase "cases in law and equity," as insufficient to include such controversies; and if controversies between two states were not embraced by them, this word and phrase could not embrace controversies between the federal and state departments. Such would be the construction of the constitution, even if we could not perceive the reasons for extending the jurisdiction of a federal court to controversies between two states, and excluding it from any jurisdiction over controversies between the state and federal governments. But the reasons are obvious. A jurisdiction of the federal court in controversies between two states, could neither alter, extend, nor diminish, the political powers of the litigant states. Whichever might gain the cause, would not thereby transfer to itself the local rights of the other. But a jurisdiction of the federal court to settle controversies between the federal and state governments, in relation to their respective constitutional rights, might transfer power claimed by one party to the other; and would also supersede the essential principle, that the jurisdiction for distributing and regulating the powers of these departments, belongs exclusively to the people of the states, acting by their representatives. And moreover, all the benefits resulting from their mutual control, would by such a jurisdiction have been sacrificed at the shrine of the usual precautions for securing judicial impartiality.

Controversies between states, could not reach the sovereignty and independence of a state, and would also be rare. Those of a territorial nature, were few in number, and would soon cease. Pecuniary controversies between states were unknown and unexpected. The greater probability of controversies between the federal and state departments, would not have been over-looked, whilst some few between states were subjected to the jurisdiction of the federal judiciary. The convention must therefore have considered them as provided for by the division of powers between these departments, their mutual right of self-defence, and the mode prescribed for altering the constitution.

Neither of the enumerated cases of extraordinary jurisdiction contain the slightest insinuation, that they comprised a power to regulate or alter the division of powers made by the constitution. Even the jurisdiction of the federal courts over individuals, is limited; otherwise it would not have been necessary to extend it to the two specified cases of individual controversies between citizens of different states, or claiming lands under grants of different states. The limitation of federal jurisdiction over individuals, can only result from a supremacy of state jurisdiction over the same individuals. A supremacy over state jurisdiction in the fed-

eral court, would destroy the limitation acknowledged by specifying two cases to which it should extend; and also the
supremacy of state jurisdiction, as to those individual rights specified or not specified. This specification proves, that the words
"arising under the constitution," in the judicial section, and the
declaratory words of the sixth article, did not confer on the federal court any supremacy of jurisdiction over any cases belonging
exclusively or concurrently to state jurisdiction. Every right, civil
and political, is delegated or reserved under the constitution;
and if the words "cases in law and equity," united with special
extensions of jurisdiction, not comprised by them, are not limitations of federal jurisdiction, it would reach every right, civil and
political; and we should have the apparition of a judicial national
government, coupled with a federal legislative and executive
government.

I admit that the gentlemen who are for concentrating power
in the federal government, are not chargeable with the intention of creating this political monster, but to acquit them of an
intention so manifestly inconsistent with the universal relation
between legislative and judicial power, we must believe that they
consider the federal, as the very national government proposed in
the convention.

In No. 80, of the Federalist, Mr. Hamilton observes, "If there
are any such things as political axioms, the propriety of the judicial power of a government being co-extensive with its legislative, may be ranked among the number." To sustain the axiom,
the rights of legislating and judging must be co-extensive. To
whatever objects the right of judging can be extended, to the
same objects the right of legislating can go; and if the federal
judiciary may by judgments regulate the powers of the state and

federal governments, the federal legislature may by laws regulate the same powers. If it is true, that judicial power emanates from legislative, the converse of the proposition would be false. Both axioms would be destroyed if there was no judiciary to execute laws, or no laws to be executed. As the judicial flows from the legislative power, it would be an inversion of political order, to deduce legislative from judicial power. To avoid an absurdity without example, and in hostility with political axioms, if it can be established that the federal judiciary can regulate the rights of the states by its judgments, it must follow, that the federal legislature may regulate the same rights by its laws. And accordingly the supreme court declares that the federal government may remove all obstacles out of its way. Thus an unlimited national government is ingrafted upon a federal stock, by first cutting away the state branches with the pruning-knife of judicial supremacy.

In this view of the subject, it is unnecessary to estimate the power of the legislative department to influence the judicial, because no such influence will be needed to introduce a supreme national government; since, whenever the federal court shall determine that its jurisdiction extends to the regulation of state powers, federal legislation must extend as far; and a partnership between federal departments for the acquisition of power at the expense of the states, will be cemented by a common interest as strong, as that by which partners for the acquisition of money are invariably caused to act in concert.

Mr. Hamilton's axiom establishes a mutual right of control in the state and federal judiciaries, because if the state and federal legislatures can neither extend nor contract the powers delegated and reserved, and if "the judicial power of a government is only co-extensive with the legislative," it follows, that judicial power can neither extend nor contract the powers delegated and reserved, any more than legislative. If the state and federal legislatures may check each other, so may the state and federal judiciaries. The mutual control of the collateral legislatures, would be rendered abortive, unattended by a mutual control of the collateral judiciaries, which must execute the laws of their respective legislatures, or these laws would not operate. It is admitted on all hands, that judges, state and federal, ought not to execute an unconstitutional law. This doctrine is founded upon the supremacy of the constitution over laws, and is the source of the mutual control between all political departments. The axiom declares that the judicial power of a government is co-extensive with the legislative. The legislature cannot enforce unconstitutional laws. If judicial power can pronounce and enforce unconstitutional judgments, it would exceed legislative beyond computation. The same supremacy of the constitution, and the same reasoning which justifies judicial power in its refusal to obey an unconstitutional law, justifies also a state judiciary in refusing to obey an unconstitutional federal judgment; and there is no mode by which unconstitutional laws and judgments can be prevented, except the mutual control between the state and federal departments contended for by Mr. Hamilton, which cannot exist unless it extends to the spherical judiciaries as well as to the spherical legislatures.

Mr. Hamilton, it will be remembered, admits the existence of concurrent powers in the federal and state governments, illustrated by the mutual right to tax; and asserts that an abridgment of the state share of this concurrent power, would be a violent usurpation. Wherefore? Because a concurrent right of construing

the constitution attends concurrent powers. The same concurrent power of construction attends the delegated and reserved
rights, and is precisely of the same force in giving jurisdiction to
the state courts over the reserved rights, as in giving jurisdiction
to the federal courts, respecting the delegated rights. The reservation to the states equally includes their legislative, executive,
and judicial powers, and if the last are subordinate to the will of
federal power, so are the former. The concurrency of construction is as strongly annexed to one division as to the other, and it
cannot be invaded either by the federal legislature or the federal
court, according to Mr. Hamilton, without a violent usurpation,
because powers under the constitution could be neither concurrent nor exclusive between political departments, without a
concurrent right to construe the constitution. If the state and
federal departments have distinct and independent legislative
powers; and if it is an axiom, that the judicial power of a government is only co-extensive with the legislative; it follows, that
the state and federal judiciaries, must also have distinct and independent jurisdictions, whether we admit the general rule by
which both these judiciaries are circumscribed by the respective
legislatures to which they are annexed, or estimate the restrictions imposed upon them by the constitution.

Mr. Hamilton, in controverting Mr. Madison's idea, that the
federal judiciary had a power to decide controversies between
the federal and state departments, observes, No. 78, "I agree that
there is no liberty, if the power of judging be not separated from
the legislative and executive powers." Without estimating the
consequences of our legislatures, state and federal, having exercised judicial powers to a great extent, it may suffice to recollect, that this maxim was suggested by the oppressions which

the kings of England were enabled to inflict upon the people, and the conquests they made within the territories of other political departments, by the aid of their judicial power. It is true, that since the English judges have been manumitted from the influence of one political department, they have polished, by their precedents, the Gothick roughness of the common law; but as this constructive power was subordinate to legislative will, it was not that which Mr. Hamilton considered as inconsistent with liberty. A power in one department to exercise the powers of another, constituted the evil reprobated by the maxim. It cannot be aggravated beyond a federal judicial power to supervise the acts of state legislatures, executives, and judiciaries. This would confound departments which must be separated to preserve liberty, according to Mr. Hamilton. If the control of election is insufficient to prevent legislatures from wasting the money of the people, by an exercise of judicial powers, a power of altering the constitution, by judges without control, would certainly waste their liberties. Pecuniary taxation, intrusted only to temporary representatives, is sometimes oppressive; but a right to tax the powers of one department to increase those of another; or a right to transfer powers from another department to itself; has, I believe, invariably produced despotism. It is as tyrannical, that a court, by precedents, should make laws and constitutions, as that a legislature should render judgments. The English judges corrupted the English laws by precedents, whilst they were dependent on the monarchical department. Would not the federal judges corrupt our constitution, if invested with a power to alter it by precedents? They would thus acquire power for themselves, as well as for the departments on which they are dependent; whereas, the English judges only gained power for the king by their partial decisions. Does the consequence of exposing a judicial power to the influence of a political department, in England, invite us to revive it here?

It seems to me that Mr. Madison has departed from the essential principle of a division of power for enforcing the integrity of political departments, by estimating erroneously the usual precautions for securing judicial integrity. These were never intended nor used as a sufficient substitute for a division of power between political departments, or to enable a judiciary either to extend the powers of a political department, or enlarge its own jurisdiction. Derangements of powers between political departments, can only be prevented by investing them with a mutual power of controlling each other. This principle, in virtue of which the federal courts disobey an unconstitutional federal law, also empowers the state courts to disobey an unconstitutional federal judgment. Impeachment, one of the usual precautions to enforce judicial fidelity to a government which inflicts the punishment, is not designed to produce judicial impartiality in regulating the powers of another government, or of political departments; and under our system, would be a precaution, not for securing fidelity to state rights, but for extending federal powers at their expense. An authority, superior to the authority of Congress, established the supremacy of the constitution; and therefore, if a law of Congress is unconstitutional, it is void, as being treason against this authority. The same authority reserved the state rights, including those of a judicial nature; and if under its protection, the judicial federal department is bound to disobey an unconstitutional law of the federal legislative department, the state departments cannot obey an unconstitutional federal judgment, without also betraying the constitution. If the mutual control is imperfect, and sometimes inconvenient, so are all other precautions for the preservation of liberty. As mankind can only select the best, its imperfection is not a good reason for its abandonment. If the application of the supreme authority of the constitution to the judgments of the federal court, may sometimes be inconvenient, so may the application of the same principle to the laws of Congress. If the federal court may avail itself of inconveniences to crush the principle, as it regards state rights, Congress may use the same argument to crush it, as a justification of the judicial department in disobeying unconstitutional laws. If a mutual controlling power results from the supremacy of the constitution, between state and federal legislatures, the same supremacy establishes a mutual controlling power between state and federal judiciaries. Why should the federal judiciary be absolved from constitutional loyalty, to be enforced by the state judicial department, and the state and federal legislatures be held to it by the mutual check? If it is safe to transfer, by construction, the supremacy of the constitution, to an inferior authority, representation had stronger claims to a preference, than a tenure for life. The authority which created the supremacy of the constitution, refused to invest the federal legislative, judicial, or executive departments, with a negative over state laws or judgments, and relied upon the mutual control of political departments, eulogised by the Federalist, for its preservation. The principle is allowed to be good, as applicable to unconstitutional laws, and said to be bad, as applicable to unconstitutional judgments.

The supreme court was not intrusted with the trial of impeachments, as was proposed in the convention, because its judgments might deprive individuals of a few political rights; but it is contended that it possesses, constructively, a power to try impeachments of whole states, and to deprive them of political rights, infinitely more important. It was not allowed to disqualify an individual to hold a federal office, one political right, but it is said to be tacitly authorized to deprive all the individuals of the United States, of reserved constitutional rights without any restriction. It was not intrusted with a power to deprive the descendants of a guilty individual of any political rights whatsoever; but, say the consolidators, it may deprive all the descendants of the present generation of political rights, by its precedents. Does this latitudinarian power correspond with the reasons which caused the power of trying impeachments to be withheld from the supreme court? The usual precaution of impeachment was retained by the federal government, to secure fidelity to itself, and not to secure fidelity to state rights. Can we infer from a want of confidence sufficient to intrust the supreme court with the trial of federal officers, a confidence sufficient to intrust it with the enormous political power of trying whole states? If a power in the court to circumscribe the political rights of individuals, might have nurtured ambitious designs, would not a power to circumscribe state rights be a thousand-fold more dangerous? To confound legislative and judicial power in the same body of men, creates a tyranny, which both makes the law and applies the sword; and to enable a single court to cut off state rights by a supreme power of construing the constitution, would confound the power of creating a constitution, with the power of construing laws, and render these rights as precarious, as human heads are, under an absolute monarchy.

The process prescribed by the constitution, in the case of impeachment, suggests several weighty arguments. As impeachment was an engine, capable of being used for political purposes, great care was taken lest it might be abused from ambitious motives. These precautions forbid us to imagine, that the supreme court was empowered to arraign and try states upon the accusation of an individual, and to deprive them of political rights, so as to effect political innovations not exposed to the control of the senate. How can the cautions used in the case of impeachment, imply a subversion of the constitutional security for the existence of a federal form of government? The idea of extending the power of the supreme court, because impeachment is a usual precaution to secure impartiality, presents us with a political caricature. The political right of an individual to hold an office, cannot be called in question except by the representatives of the people of the states; but the political rights of the states may be called in question by an individual. The senate cannot deprive an individual, though condemned, of any state right, but the federal court may deprive all the people of many state rights. The federal check is preserved to secure one federal right to an individual, and abandoned as a security for all the federal rights of the people. A concurrence of two-thirds of the senate is required to deprive an individual of one federal right, but a majority of the court may deprive the states of all reserved rights. Thus we are led to compare a power in the federal court to decide controversies between the state and federal governments, with the security for a federal form of government, contemplated in the formation of the senate.

Mr. Madison admits that the senate was intended as a security to the states, against a concentration of power in a representation of numbers, contended for in the convention; and that the object of the compromise was to prevent constructive innovations dictated by the interest of large or small states. But if the

supreme court can abridge state rights, the object of this compromise is defeated. Neither the house of representatives can
maintain the rights of the people of the states, nor the senate
the rights of their governments. Impeachment is no remedy
against a judicial predilection for a national form of government, because the right of accusation is exclusively lodged in
the department, considered by Mr. Madison as bottomed upon
that principle, and tending towards that form. The senate was
modelled with a design to control this consolidating tendency;
but if the house of representatives should be influenced by the
pride of populousness, like many members of the convention,
to prefer a national to a federal government, it would not
impeach the judges for fostering its design by constructions of
the laws and the constitution; and the rights of the states might
be gradually abridged by the supreme court, without being
exposed to the control of the senate, though that body was modelled for the special purpose of controlling such abridgments.
Had the laws for establishing a bank and a lottery, contained
clauses prohibiting the states from taxing the stock or excluding
the tickets, these abridgments of state rights might have been
expunged by the senate; but the court, by constructively inflict-
ing them, has evaded the senatorial control over consolidating
laws; and by virtue of this supremacy assumed over state powers, the same species of evasion may be extended to a multitude
of cases, for the purpose of introducing a national form of government. Even if the house of representatives should magnanimously impeach the judges for extending its own powers, the
remedy would not reach the case of an honest opinion, though
unconstitutional. The constitution provides against the contemplated case of an honest opinion in favour of a national govern-

ment, demonstrated in the convention, by the counterpoise of an honest opinion in favour of a federal government, organized in the senate; and never intended to refer this great question to the honest opinion of the supreme court.

It will not be contended that the usual precaution of impeachment against partiality, was designed to prevent the judges from giving honest opinions, any more than the members of the senate and house of representatives, who are liable to be impeached; but this liability was not considered as affecting, in the slightest degree, the contemplated propensities of the two houses for a national and federal government. Impeachment, therefore, was not considered as a precaution against a propensity in the supreme court towards a national form of government; and if such a propensity should be attended by a judicial supremacy over state powers, it would effectually defeat the balance between national and federal propensities established by the constitution. A majority of the senate can reject consolidating laws, but two-thirds can only convict in cases of impeachment. If this remedy had reached consolidating judgments or precedents, it would not have been equivalent to that provided against consolidation by the constitution, because above one-third of the members of the senate might come from large states, and entertain consolidating opinions injurious to the small states. The difference between crime and opinion dictated the remedies against judicial partiality and political propensity. In the case of crime, the remedy might be safely restricted to two-thirds of the senate, but the contemplated inclination of a majority of the house of representatives towards a national government, was only to be restrained by a majority of the senate. Had this check been limited to two-thirds of the senate, it would have been ineffica-

cious, and therefore it cannot be imagined that the supreme
court were invested with a supreme power of indulging a consolidating inclination, without being exposed to any control,
except that of two-thirds of the senate, even if its movements in
that direction could be reached by an impeachment. The political error to be guarded against, was that of abridging the rights of
the states. Is a majority of the senate, or a majority of the supreme
court, the remedy provided against the anticipated disposition
of the house of representatives to fall into it?

The process of impeachment is not confined to judges, but
extends to the president, senators, and representatives. Does this
usual precaution invest them all with additional political powers? It reaches bribery in every case; and there is no difference
between the usual precautions in the case of the judges, and of
these other officers, except that the latter are exposed to a peri-
odical accountableness, and the former are not. May the president, senate, and house of representatives, constitutionally abridge
the rights of the states, because, as they are liable to be impeached
and convicted by two-thirds of the senate for criminal acts, it is
to be presumed that they will decide impartially the controversies between the federal and state governments? Such an inference is equally deducible from the process of impeachment, for
extending the powers of these departments, as for extending the
jurisdiction of the supreme court. The idea, that an exposure
to punishment, confers an enormous political power, amounts to
the idea, that a man who is liable to be hanged for treason, ought
to be considered as a monarch.

If this reasoning is correct, it proves that the words "cases in
law and equity," before noticed, does not include political
attempts to introduce a national form of government, because

the senate is one constitutional remedy provided to defeat them. Cases in law and equity arise both under the powers reserved to the states, and under those delegated to the federal government, but the mutual right to try these cases, implies no right to try and modify the powers themselves.

The delegations, reservations, and prohibitions of the constitution, combined with the rejection of powers proposed in the convention, constitute a mass of evidence, more coherent and irrefragable for ascertaining the principles of our political system, than can be exhibited by any other country; and if it cannot resist the arts of construction, constitutions are feeble obstacles to ambition, and ineffectual barriers against tyranny. Delegations are limitations; reservations are repetitions of these limitations; prohibitions expound the extent of reservations; and rejections of powers proposed in the convention, are constructions forbiding their assumption. This mass of evidence stands opposed to those constructions which are labouring to invest the federal government with powers to abridge the state right of taxation; to control states by a power to legislate for ten miles square; to expend the money belonging to the United States without control; to enrich a local capitalist interest at the expense of the people; to create corporations for abridging state rights; to make roads and canals; and finally to empower the supreme court to exercise a complete negative power over state laws and judgments, and an affirmative power as to federal laws. Without going into the wide field of argument, opened to our view by testimony so full and perfect, I shall select only such parts of it as seem particularly applicable to the question discussed in this section.

Powers neither delegated nor prohibited, are reserved to the states. A general negative power over state laws and judgments, is not delegated to the federal government. This was proposed in the convention and rejected. The supremacy of the states, legislative and judicial, in reference to their reserved powers, is not delegated to the federal government. By prohibiting to the states portions of their supremacy, the existence of those portions not prohibited, is acknowledged; and these remained to be exercised, according to their previous nature. The tenth section of the first article of the constitution, prohibits to the states the exercise of specified, supreme, or sovereign powers; but a long catalogue of such powers remained unprohibited. The powers of engaging in war, raising armies, and making treaties, are among those prohibited to the states. These prohibitions of sovereign powers, are acknowledgements of the inherent supremacy and sovereignty of the states, except for which, the prohibitions would have been idle and useless; and had they been omitted, the same concurrency of power to engage in war, make treaties, and raise armies, would have existed in the state and federal governments, as does exist in the case of taxation; as flowing from the sovereignty of the states. The powers of the states to punish crimes, regulate property, and impose taxes, not being given to them by the constitution, must either be usurpations, or be justified by their sovereignty and supremacy. If they are legitimate offsprings, then the sovereignty, from which they proceed, is reserved to the states, as necessary to give them birth, is not delegated to the federal government, and may be exercised in every case not prohibited.

For many years, previous, during, and subsequent, to the revolutionary war, it was the general opinion, that the provinces and the states ought to provide for their internal happiness in their own way; and millions have expended blood or treasure in defence of this opinion. The constitutions of all the states, the declaration of independence, and the confederation of 1777, concur in asserting the sovereignty of each state. According to the sound rule which advises us to consider old laws in construing a new one, the long standing publick opinion, and the solemn documents by which it has been frequently expressed, ought to be considered, in construing the existing confederation. By adverting to principles previously established, we are enabled to understand its limitations, prohibitions, and reservations, because all of them flow from and were modelled in reference to subsisting institutions. But instead of seeking for truth with these lights, we are advised to find it in the mystical doctrines: that we have several sovereignties, and but one sovereignty; that the states have independent local powers, and that these powers are dependent on some federal department; and that the residence of a supreme power, is a problem too obscure to be solved by eminent politicians, some contending that it is in a general government, and others in the supreme federal court. A curious consequence of this mystical mode of construction is, that the states, if willing to serve, cannot discover their master. Must they obey two masters? It is the duty of man to believe in mysteries revealed by inspiration, though beyond his comprehension, but he is not bound to believe in mysteries revealed by political prepossessions, and comprising contradictions.

The ninth and tenth sections of the first article of the constitution, are prohibitory; one upon the federal government, the other upon the states. These prohibitions are positive in several cases. For example: the United States are forbidden to grant titles, the states to coin money, and both to tax exports. In these and other prohibitions, the judicial power is incompetent to compel a compliance with the constitution, and no distinction is made between the federal and state governments, as to the mode in which prohibitions imposed upon both are to be enforced. It can therefore only be done by the influence of state nations, by the correlative check, and by the provision for supervising the constitution. The equal ground upon which the two governments are placed, as to these mutual prohibitions, proves that their mutual powers were intended to be independent; and that the constitution, though mandatory to both, did not endow either with a general supremacy over the other. If their respective powers within their assigned spheres are independent of each other, the parts of each political machine are uncontrollable by either intire machine, or by a component part of either; otherwise the spherical system, contended for even by the Federalist, cannot exist.

The negative given to Congress by the tenth section, over specified state acts, is an exception to the general principle of a mutual independence, quite sufficient to remove the obscurity into which mysteriarchs have endeavoured to plunge the constitution. "No state shall, *without the consent of Congress,* lay any impost or duties on imports or exports, *except what may be absolutely necessary for executing its inspection laws.* No state shall, *without the consent of Congress,* lay any duty on tonnage, keep troops or ships of war *in time of peace,* enter into any agreement or compact with another state, or with a foreign power, or engage in war, *unless actually invaded, or in such imminent danger as will not admit of delay.*" These limited negatives, prove that no general negative was intended to be given, either to Congress or the federal court, over state sovereign powers not prohibited. A prohibition upon some, demonstrates that the exercise of others was not prohibited. A special supremacy to Congress, demonstrates that no general supremacy was given to the federal court. The special supremacy was exposed to the federal control of the senate; the general supremacy assumed by the court, would elude that provision. The special supremacy reserves to the states their sovereign powers to tax exports for the execution of their inspection laws, to keep troops or ships in time of war, when invaded, or in danger, without the consent of Congress, and to enter into foreign compacts with it. These reservations would be swallowed up, with all other powers reserved to the states by the general supremacy assumed. Suppose Congress should consent, and the court should dissent. Is a state or the court to judge, whether peace or war, invasion or danger, may exist? The court was considered as incompetent to prevent the exercise of these sovereign state rights, because it was invested with no supremacy over the state powers reserved. If it was not contemplated as possessing a supreme power over state rights, to be exercised with the consent of Congress, it could not have been considered as empowered to control state rights, not prohibited, and for the exercise of which no such consent was required. A jurisdiction to try suits in law and equity, was evidently not considered as reaching the sovereign state rights specified in the tenth section, therefore it was not considered as reaching the sovereign powers reserved to the states, without being subjected to any prohibition. Reservations in grants are exceptions, and the special reservations to the states, annexed to the prohibitions of the tenth section, like the general reservation of the amendment, are exclusions of federal power from a supremacy. They reserved nothing to the federal court, because it had no previous supremacy over state rights, and could only operate in favour of the state sovereignties previously existing; and the limited negative given to

Congress, modifying some state sovereign powers, reserved, proves that no negative was designed to be attached to others.

There are two classes of prohibited powers, referring to the two governments. To enforce these mutual prohibitions, no censorial or supreme authority is created. Was this an oversight, or a necessary consequence of a division of power and a federal system? The mutual prohibitions, the federal system, and a division of power, would all have been defeated by a supremacy in either class over the other. These ends were only attainable by a principle able to reach them all. Whether that principle is the mutual check, or the power of the people, or both, it excludes the idea of a supreme power in one class of prohibitions, or in one class of limited rights over the other. The word government would be inapplicable to a political institution, which was subservient to the will of a supremacy in another government.

If the consent of Congress to the exercise of a few specified state powers, proves that no federal consent was necessary to the exercise of unprohibited state powers; it follows that a judicial federal consent to the exercise of the latter powers was not intended, because a concurrence of both governments in the allowed modifications, could not have been considered as subordinate to any such judicial consent, constructively superadded. The limitation of judicial power, state and federal, to their respective spheres, is the source of the duty, common to both, by which they are justified in disobeying unconstitutional laws brought before them in private trials; but neither can, like a council of censors, proclaim an unconstitutional law to be void, because neither is invested with a power to control the rights of sovereignty, or settle the controversies of political departments. Both state and federal judiciaries wandering into each other's territories, are fugitives from their own spheres, or hostile invaders, and ought to be arrested by the sphere attached, as the only means for preventing the conquest of the constitution by the assaults of ambition, or the stratagems of avarice. If state or federal legislative departments should attempt such eccentricities, resistance would be a duty imposed by the authority of the constitution, and the most solemn of obligations; yet the assumed supremacy of the federal court is founded upon the whimsical idea, that the state judiciaries are bound to disobey state laws, trespassing upon the federal sphere, and to obey federal judgments trespassing upon the state sphere. Upon this idea, a judicial supremacy is assumed, unexampled in the history of nations, except in the Jewish experiment, from which, though aided by Urim and Thummim, the people took refuge under a monarchy.

I cannot discern any reconciliation between Mr. Madison's assertions, that the constitution established a government partly federal, and partly national; and that it also invested a court with supreme power. Mr. Hamilton, by giving supreme power to a federal government, adheres to his preference of the English system. Mr. Madison gives no supremacy to either portion of his government, nor to both portions united. How are his federal and national features to preserve themselves, if they are both subjected to a supremacy of judges? Is the supreme court partly national and partly federal? He finds these features in the house of representatives and the senate, but the court represents neither the people nor the states. He uses representation to define the nature of the government, and rejects representation as the basis of power. Imagine a government compounded of monarchical and republican principles, and that a few judges should be invested with a supreme power to regulate both these princi-

ples, so that they could neither control each other, nor preserve
themselves. Would the government be, in reality, partly monarchical and partly republican? Supremacy is an attribute of government, and subordination an attribute of a judicial department.
Mr. Madison exchanges these attributes. He asserts that we have
a government partly national and partly federal, in consequence
of popular and state representation. But he reasons forcibly to
prove, that this government possesses no inexplicit supreme
power, that its powers are not augmented by its national feature,
and that these powers are limited by the delegations expressed.
If the national feature gives no additional power to Congress,
how can it extend the jurisdiction of the court? If the constitution had established a national government, its attribute,
supremacy, must have been attached to it; and accordingly, whilst
that species of government was in contemplation, it was proposed to invest it with a supremacy or negative over the acts of
the states, as essential to its existence. Had this form of government succeeded, could the supreme court, though vested with a
jurisdiction in the very words of the constitution, have exercised a constructive supremacy over the national supremacy
expressed? The supremacy of the states, expressed by the declaration of independence and the state constitutions, and reserved
by the federal constitution, is no more liable to be taken away
by a constructive supremacy, than an expressed supremacy of a
national government. In both cases, supremacy follows national
power, and does not belong to judicial. If the constitution establishes a government partly national, the quota of supremacy correspondent to the quota of national power, must also reside with
the power from which it emanates. Judicial power is created to
preserve, and not to destroy or usurp the supremacy of a national

government, and impeachment enforces its subordination. If judicial power does not imply political supremacy, and if national power does, then as the state governments are in fact national, and the federal government not so, the whole portion of supremacy of which our system admits, resides in the former; and the latter is excluded from any share of it, as not being a national, but a limited government. If both governments have national features, then each possesses the share of supremacy attached to these features; and judicial power cannot possess any supremacy over the supremacy of either, unless it possesses a sovereignty obliterating the national features of both. What national features can exist in either, under a supremacy of a few judges? If a single court can carve a supremacy for itself, from a constitution dividing all the high political powers between the state and federal governments, and not investing the court with a single national feature, it may take away the essential attribute which determines a government to be national. And if, as Mr. Madison asserts, the federal government has no more supremacy over the national features of the state governments, than the state governments have over the national features of the federal government, I cannot conceive any authority in the court to obliterate the national features of either. The same judicial supremacy which destroys Mr. Madison's national feature, destroys also his federal feature found in the senate. And thus both of Mr. Madison's features, national and federal, are made subordinate to a power having neither.

The idea of a national supremacy over the states, long kept alive in the convention, seems to have made so strong an impression on the minds of Mr. Madison and Mr. Hamilton, that they could not believe it was dead; and like the two aldermen in Don

Quixote, they have set out separately in search of the ass, but with better success; for in lieu of the one lost, they have found two. Lo, says Mr. Hamilton, the ass still lives on yonder mountain, called a national or general government, although the mountain itself is not to be found in our political map. The ass indeed lives, says Mr. Madison, but he was snugly concealed in a vale of the expunged mountain, called its judiciary. It is contrary to political order and relationship, replies the first gentleman, that supremacy should reside in a vale. There cannot be two asses; and the other asserts, that he should be placed in the vale, as the only means of re-establishing his rejected consolidating system. The commentators upon these authorities are divided. One party contends, that the constitution tacitly established a national or general government, and tacitly impregnated it with supremacy, according to Mr. Hamilton; another, that it only established half a national government, and tacitly also endowed the judicial department with supremacy, according to Mr. Madison; and a third, that the ass was only an embryo, never born, but smothered by the common consent of thirteen midwives, expressed both by their deputies and themselves. This party also believes, that a concentrated political supremacy, would find it harder to effect a uniformity of geographical interests in the United States, than the pope and his cardinals did to effect a uniformity of religious opinions in Europe; and that the attempt would produce several very determined sects of political protestants.

There are some principles necessary for the existence of the political system of the United States. One of these is, the supremacy, both of the state and federal constitutions, over the repositories of power created by their articles. Another, that this is a limited supremacy in both cases, subject in one, to the supremacy of the people in each state, and in the other, to the supremacy of three-fourths of the states. And a third, that no power created by these constitutions, can violate their articles, or evade the supremacies to which the constitutions are themselves subject. From these principles it results, that neither laws nor judgments are valid, which do not conform to constitutions; and that a mutual control of political departments, is the only mode of enforcing this doctrine, necessary to sustain both the supremacy of constitutions, and of those who make them. The federal judges do not take an oath to obey the state constitutions, because, as they derive no jurisdiction from them, there is no privity between the rights and powers which they establish, and these judges. If the federal courts could abridge these rights and powers, it would defeat the principle of the supremacy of the people of each state, over their constitutions. This would vitally destroy the federal compact, supposed to exist between republicks, because the states would not be republicks, if their constitutions were made subordinate to the will or the power of a court, instead of being only subordinate to the will or power of the people. But, though the federal judiciary, as having no privity with state constitutions, and no power to render a judgment resulting from their articles, take no oath to regard them, the case is different as to the state judges. They were in many cases obliged to render judgments conformable to the articles of the federal constitution, by which a privity was created between it and them, requiring this solemn security for obedience. The state judges in this view compose one portion of the judiciary, entitled to construe the articles of the federal constitution, as independently as the other portion. As state constitutions are subject to the supremacy of the people of each state, and the federal constitution to three-fourths of the states, neither are subject to laws or judgments state or federal, or to a consolidated American nation. A supremacy in a federal court to construe the articles of the declaration of independence, and of the federal and state constitutions, united with a power to enforce its constructions, would as effectually destroy the supremacy of the people, and of three-fourths of the states, as the same species of supreme power in state legislatures would destroy the supremacy of state constitutions, and of the people of each state.

If the constitution of a state should be so altered, as to bestow on the legislature a supreme power of construing its articles, and excluding the judiciary from the right or the duty of disobeying unconstitutional laws; or if the constitution of the United States should invest the federal judiciary with the same supreme power as to the construction of the federal constitution; the principles, necessary for the existence of our political system, would be abolished, and both the federal and state governments would substantially be reinstated, according to the English policy, by which the government itself can modify its own powers. A question somewhat similar to that now agitated here, has often occurred in England. Neither the king, the lords, or the commons, have been exempt from ambition, and the judges have been sometimes impeached and punished for the assistance they have yielded to an aspiring department; because the destruction of a mutual control between political departments, was considered as an inexcusable crime against a principle necessary for the preservation of liberty. But here, an exaltation of the federal political department, over the state political department, by judicial assistance, would be an act aggravated beyond the similar experiments made in England; because it would moreover destroy the supremacy of the people and of three-fourths of the states, considered and established as a higher security for liberty, than the counterpoise of collateral political departments in England. If the federal judiciary shall acquire such a supremacy over the articles of the constitution, over the departments created or recognised by delegations and reservations, and over the sources from which these powers flow, its judgments will be both laws and constitutions, like the acts of the British government.

There are three kinds of supremacy. A per capita supremacy, a hereditary supremacy, and a supremacy in the government. The evidences of a per capita supremacy in this country, are state constitutions, the declaration of independence, the two federal unions, and the mode of altering the last. These concur in bestowing a per capita supremacy on the people of each state; and both the federal and state constitutions were created by conventions representing the state per capita supremacies. These affirmative proofs establish the negative conclusion, that a per capita supremacy does not exist in an American nation. They demonstrate a necessary alliance between the sovereignty of the states, and a per capita supremacy of the people; and that the latter, without this alliance, cannot exist, in relation either to the federal or state constitutions. The negative conclusion, that no supremacy of an American nation exists, is therefore as evident, as that no hereditary supremacy exists. One is as much a fraud of ambition here, as the other is of royalty in Europe. Thus the difficulty is concentrated in the question, whether a supremacy resides in the government. Let us wave the per capita supremacy of the people of each state, and also the supremacy of three-fourths of the states, and admit that it does. We must yet find a government, before we can find its attribute supremacy. Do we find one or two governments in our political system? If one only, then we may have but one supremacy, according to the old opinion, that supremacy appertained to governments; if we find two, then, according to the same opinion, we must also find two supremacies. If these two governments are invested with distinct powers, they must also, in pursuance of the same doctrine, be invested with distinct supremacies. The federal court is neither a per capita, hereditary, nor governmental supremacy, and therefore it cannot claim this attribute either under the old or the new tariff of power. At most, according to the old idea, "that supremacy resides in a government," it can only participate in so much of it as appertains to the federal government, allowing it to be comprised by that term as one of its political members; as it would be utterly inconsistent with the European doctrine to imagine, that more supremacy appertained to a portion of the government, than to the whole. But the federal court constitutes no portion of the state governments, and therefore it cannot participate in any supremacy appertaining to them, though it should be admited that it may participate in the supremacy appertaining to the federal government. We thus discern in another view the question, whether the supremacy proposed in the convention for a *national* government, was given to a *federal* government; or whether a supremacy over the powers reserved to the states, appertained to the powers delegated to the federal government. If a per capita representation in one branch of Congress, or the powers delegated to the federal government, invests that government with a supremacy over its own powers, and those reserved to the states, it is undoubtedly the duty of the federal court to enforce and not to control this supremacy. The federal government is, or is not, invested with a supremacy over state rights. If it is, the court cannot constitutionally control the exercise of this supremacy; if it is not, the court cannot control constitutionally the state supremacy in exercising the reserved rights. If it is, it may enact positive or constructive alterations of both state and federal powers; if it is not, the state authorities can resist such alterations, both positive and constructive. Both are equally exposed to the mutual control, residing in the respective supremacies of each government. If neither a national per capita supremacy, nor a supremacy in a majority of states, nor a supremacy in a concurrence of all the federal departments, can alter the powers and principles of the state and federal governments; it follows that no supremacy in one of the departments of either government can do the same thing. All these apocryphal supremacies were proposed in the convention, under the shelter of the word national; and though neither this word, nor these its consequences, are to be found in the constitution, both the word and its progeny were resumed in the Federalist, and have since supplied a foundation for the project of a consolidated supreme government to stand upon.

To compute the force of these arguments, we must look back to the journal of the convention, where we shall find the source of the supreme political jurisdiction, bestowed by Mr. Madison on the federal court. June 8th, Mr. Pinckney moved "to strike out of the plan for a *national* government, the negative proposed to be given to the *national* legislature over state laws, which, in the opinion of the national legislature, should contravene *the articles of the union,* or any treaties subsisting under the authority of the union," and to insert, "to negative all laws which to them shall appear improper." This motion was seconded by Mr. Madison, and rejected; only Massachusetts, Pennsylvania, and Virginia, then

the three most populous states, having voted for it. The gentlemen in favour of a national government, having been defeated in
this attempt, Mr. Randolph, on the 13th of the same month,
moved that the jurisdiction of the *national* judiciary shall extend
"to questions which involve the *national* peace and harmony."
This motion was also seconded by Mr. Madison, and carried.
This proposition exactly comprises the jurisdiction given by
Congress to the federal judiciary, but it was excluded in settling
the jurisdiction of a *federal* judiciary, though it was sustained
whilst a *national* judiciary was contemplated. These several propositions are evidently the seeds from which have germinated Mr.
Madison's construction; parts of the court law, as it is called,
passed many years ago by Congress; and the subsequent extensions of its own jurisdiction by the supreme court. A preference
for a national form of government dictated the effort to give a
national legislature the power "to negative all laws which to them
should appear improper." This having failed, because it was
inconsistent with the idea of a federal legislature, an attempt
was made to establish a *national* judiciary, with a jurisdiction "in
all questions which involved the national peace and harmony."
A *national power* was the object, however unfit a court to decide
cases in law and equity might be for exercising it. At length the
ideas, both of a national legislature, and a national judiciary, were
abandoned in the convention, and with them perished the host
of supremacies and negatives proposed as necessary and proper
for a national government. The controversy between a federal
and a national form of government, could not have lasted for
months, if they had been the same. Yet Mr. Madison, under a
decided preference for some supreme national power, has constructively bestowed it upon the supreme court; and the court,

under the influence of the same preference, has received the supremacies and negatives, proposed to be given to a national legislature, as well as those proposed to be given to a national judiciary. Accordingly, it assumes "a power to negative state laws contravening the articles of the union, and a power to negative state laws, which to them may appear improper," both of which powers were proposed to be given to a national legislature; and also "a power to settle all questions which may involve the national peace and harmony," proposed for a national judiciary; thus making itself heir to two propositions for the establishment of a national legislature, and to one for the establishment of a national judiciary, though neither a national legislature, a national judiciary, nor either of the three propositions, are contained in the constitution. Congress seems to have a much better right than the court, to inherit the power of a negative over such state laws as might contravene the articles of the union, because it was proposed to be given to a national legislature; and neither the national nor federal parties in the convention, ever appear to have conceived the idea of investing a court, whether national or federal, with a political power so unusual and enormous.

Sovereignty

The reader has perceived that the question concerning state powers, is condensed in the word sovereignty, and therefore any new ideas upon the subject, if to be found, would not be unedifying. A will to enact, and a power to execute, constitute its essence. Take away either, and it expires. The state governments and the federal government, are the monuments by which state sovereignty, attended with these attributes, is demonstrated. But as the consolidating school will not see it, I will endeavour further to establish its existence, in order to prevent these beautiful examples of political science from falling into ruin.

The constitution, like the declaration of independence, was framed by deputies from the "states of New-Hampshire," &c. and at the threshold of the transaction, we discern a positive admission of the existence of separate states invested with separate sovereignties. This admission expounds the phrase "We, the people of the United States," which co-operates with the separate powers given to their deputies in the convention, and is distinctly repeated by the words "do ordain and establish this constitution for *the United States of America.*" Had the sovereignty of each state been wholly abandoned, and the people of all been considered as constituting one nation, the idea would have been expressed in different language. Suppose that Fredonia had been assumed as an appellation comprising the territories of all the states, and that a consolidated nation had been contemplated by the convention, would it have framed, ordained, and established, a constitution by states for states, or by the Fredonians for Fredonia. The appellation adopted by the declaration of independence, was, "The United States of America." The first confederation declares, that the style of this confederacy shall be, "The United States of America." And the union of 1787, ordains and establishes the constitution for "The United States of America." The three instruments, by adhering to the same style, co-extensively affirmed the separate sovereignties of these states. It was a style proper to describe a confederacy of independent states, and improper for describing a consolidated nation. If neither the declaration of independence nor the confederation of 1777, created an American nation, or a concentrated sovereignty, by this style, the conclusion is inevitable, that the constitution was not intended to produce such consequences by the same style. The word America is used to designate the quarter of the globe in which the recited states were established, and not to designate a nation of Americans. A league or union of the kingdoms of Europe for limited objects, distinctly reciting the name of each kingdom, would not have created a consolidated nation of Europeans. Suppose in such a union, the phrase, "We, the people of the united kingdoms of Europe," had been used, would it have destroyed the several sovereignties uniting for special purposes, and have consolidated them into one kingdom? Had these kingdoms conferred upon their federal representatives limited powers, and reserved all the powers not conferred, would they have had no remedy, had their federal representatives assumed the supreme power of abridging the powers reserved, and extending those conferred? If the word state does not intrinsically imply

sovereign power, there was no word which we could use better
calculated for that purpose. Will the words empire or kingdom
be considered as of higher authority, because they may exclude
a people as a political association, which the word state may
comprise?

This construction bestows the same meaning upon the same
words in our three constituent or elemental instruments, and
exhibits the reason why the whole language of the constitution
is affianced to the idea of a league between sovereign states, and
hostile to that of a consolidated nation. There are many states in
America, but no state of America, nor any people of an American state. A constitution for America or Americans, would therefore have been similar to a constitution for Utopia or Utopians.

Hence the constitution is declared to be made for the "United
States of America," that is, for certain states enumerated by their
names, established upon that portion of the earth's surface, called
America. Though no people or nation of America existed, considering these words as defining a political association, states did
exist in America, each constituted by a people. By these political
individual entities, called states, the constitution was framed; by
these individual entities it was ratified; and by these entities it
can only be altered. It was made by them and for them, and not
by or for a nation of Americans. The people of each state, or
each state as constituted by a people, conveyed to a federal
authority, organized by states, a portion of state sovereign powers,
and retained another portion. In this division, all the details of the
constitution are comprised, one dividend consisting of the special powers conferred upon a federal government, and the other,
of the powers reserved by the states which conferred these special powers. The deputation and reservation are both bottomed

upon the sovereignty of the states, and must both fall or both stand with that principle. If each state, or the people of each state, did not possess a separate sovereignty, they had no right to convey or retain powers. If they had a right both to convey and to retain powers, it could only be in virtue of state sovereignty. Admitting the utmost which can be asked, and more than ought to be conceded, by supposing that these sovereignties, in conveying limited powers to the federal government, conveyed also a portion of sovereignty, it must also be allowed, that by retaining powers, they retained also a portion of sovereignty. If sovereignty was attached to the ceded powers, it was also attached to the powers not ceded, because all or none of the powers of the states must have proceeded from this principle. In this observation, no use is made of the power reserved to the states to amend the federal form of government, by which a positive sovereignty is retained to the states over that government, subversive of the doctrine, that the constitution bestows a sovereignty upon it over the states. But a delegation of limited powers, being an act of sovereignty, could not be a renunciation of the sovereignty attached to the powers not delegated. A power to resume the limited delegation, was the strongest expression of sovereignty, and rejects the idea, that the delegated authority may positively or constructively subject the sovereign power to its own will; that no sovereignty may destroy an actual sovereignty. By this power of amendment, the states may re-establish the confederation of 1777, and thus unquestionably revive their separate sovereignties said to be extinct; because they are positively asserted by that confederation. If it is not absurd, it is yet a new idea, that a dead sovereignty contains an inherent power to revive itself whenever it pleases.

The mode of making amendments to the constitution, expresses its true construction, and rejects the doctrine, that an American people created a federal government. Their ratification is to be the act of states. It is the same with that of the confederation, which asserted the sovereignties of the states, in concomitancy with this mode of ratification, with only two differences. By the first confederation, the ratification was to be the act of state legislatures, and unanimous; by the constitution, the ratification of alterations is to be the act of "state conventions, or legislatures by three-fourths." The last difference extended the power of the states, by removing the obstacle of unanimity, and was not intended to diminish it. State legislatures and conventions are united, as equivalent state organs. Thus the constitution construes the phrase, "We, the people of the United States," and refutes the doctrine of an American people, as the source of federal powers; because, had these powers been derived from that source, it would have referred to the same source for their modification, and not to state legislatures. It declares that both state legislatures and state conventions, are representations of state sovereignties, equally competent to express their will. The same opinion is expressed by declaring that "the ratification of the conventions of nine states, shall be sufficient for its establishment between the ratifying states." Of the two equivalent modes of ratification, it selects one for that special occasion, not because it substantially differed from the other, and was not an expression of state will, but because it was apprehended that a considerable transfer of powers from the state governments to a federal government, might produce an opposition from men in the exercise of these powers, although when experience should have ascertained the benefits of the innovation, and time should have cured the wounds of individual ambition, a further adherence to one equivalent mode in preference to the other, might be unnecessary and inconvenient to the states. The equivalency of the modes is obvious, as state legislatures are empowered to revoke the act of state conventions, by which the residence of state sovereignties in these legislatures is considered as the same as its residence in state conventions, upon no other ground, than that both constituted a representation of the state, and not a representation of an unassociated people.

An adherence to our original principle of state sovereignty is demonstrated both by the confederation and constitution. Unanimity was necessary to put the first, and a concurrence of nine states to put the second, into operation. The operation of the first, when ratified, was to extend to all the states, and the operation of the second, "to the states ratifying only." Both consequences are deduced from state sovereignty, by which one state could defeat a union predicated upon unanimity, and four states might have refused to unite with nine. The latter circumstance displays the peculiar propriety of ordaining and establishing the constitution "for the United States of America." The refusing states, though states of America, did not constitute a portion of an American nation; and their right of refusal resulted from their acknowledged sovereignty and independence. "The United States of America" would have consisted of nine states only, had four refused to accede to the union; and therefore thirteen states could not have been contemplated by the constitution, as having been consolidated into one people. Hence it adheres to the idea of a league, by a style able to describe "the United States of America," had they consisted but of nine, and avoids a style applicable only to one nation or people consisting of thirteen states. By acknowledging the sovereignty of the refusing, it admits the sovereignty of the concurring states. Assent or dissent, was equally an evidence of it. The limitation of federal powers by assent, establishes the principle from which the assent flowed. There could be no sound assent, nor any sound limitation, unless one was given, and the other imposed, by a competent authority; and no authority is competent to the establishment of a government, except it is sovereign. The same authority could only possess the right of rejecting the constitution. Had it been the act of an American nation or people, a state would have possessed no such right. The judicial sages have allowed the federal to be a limited government, but how can it be limited if the state sovereignties by which it was limited, do not exist, and if the state powers reserved, which define the limitation, are subject to its control?

Having proved that state sovereignties were established by the declaration of independence; that their existence was asserted by the confederation of 1777; that they are recognised by the constitution of 1787, in the modes of its formation, ratification, and amendment; that this constitution employs the same words to describe the United States, used by the two preceding instruments; that the word state implies a sovereign community; that each state contained an associated people; that an American people never existed; that the constitution was ordained and established, for such states situated in America, as might accede to a union; that its limited powers was a partial and voluntary endowment of state sovereignties, to be exercised by a Congress of the states which should unite; that the word Congress implies a deputation from sovereignties, and was so expounded by the confederation; and that a reservation of sovereign powers cannot be executed without sovereignty; the reader will consider, whether all these principles, essential for the preservation both of the federal and state governments, were intended to be destroyed by the details of the constitution. The attempt to lose twenty-four states, in order to find a consolidated nation, or a judicial sovereignty, reverses the mode of reasoning hitherto admitted to be correct, by deducing principles from effects, and not effects from principles. But in construing the constitution, we shall never come at truth, if we suffer its details, intended to be subservient to established political principles, to deny their allegiance, and rebel against their sovereigns. A will to act, and a power to execute, constitutes sovereignty. The state governments, says the Federalist, are no more dependent on the federal government, in the exercise of their reserved powers, than the federal government is on them, in the exercise of its delegated powers.

The treaty between his Britannick majesty and the *United States of America,* acknowledges "the said United States, viz. New-Hampshire, Massachusetts-Bay, Rhode-Island and Providence Plantations, Connecticut, New-York, New-Jersey, Pennsylvania, Delaware, Maryland, Virginia, North-Carolina, South-Carolina, and Georgia, to be free, *sovereign,* and independent states; as such he treats with them, and relinquishes all claim to their government and territorial rights." This king acknowledges, individually, the sovereignty of the states; he relinquishes to them, individually, his territorial rights; three eminent envoys demanded this acknowledgment and relinquishment, as appertaining, individually, to the states; a Congress of the United States ratified the act and the doctrine; the treaty was then unanimously hailed, and is still generally considered, as a consummation of right, justice, and liberty; but now it is said that the states are corporations, subordinate bodies politick, and not sovereign. By the admirers of royal sovereignty, the treaty ought to be considered as valid; by those who confide in authority, it ought to be considered as authentick; by such as respect our revolutionary patriots, it ought to be venerated; and by honest expositors of the constitution, it will be allowed to afford conclusive proof, that the phrase "United States of America," used both in the treaty and the constitution, implied the existence, and not the abrogation, of state sovereignty. Consolidators, suprematists, and conquerors, however, will all equally disregard any instrument, however solemn and explicit, by which ambition and avarice will be restrained, and the happiness of mankind improved.

One of the People

It has appeared that a respectable party in favour of a monarchical or national form of government, existed in the United States, from the commencement of the revolutionary question, down to the meeting of the convention, and that it predominated for a time in this body. Whether the monarchical branch of it still subsists, must be left to the fact, that it is constantly perceivable in large territories, and generally in small; so that we may conclude, that this imperishable alloy is incorporated with human nature. It being on record that a majority of the convention was in favour of a supreme national government, though we should admit that the portion of this majority, which then preferred the monarchical form, has emigrated, to a man, into the portion which preferred a republican form of national government, because the people were not ripe for monarchy; yet it may be safely concluded, that this emigration has not destroyed the predilection for a supreme national government in one or the other of these forms, then entertained by many eminent men, whose talents insured to them a great share of the power to be obtained. The allurements of anticipated power, can hardly be greater than those of restricted power in possession, united with a consciousness of integrity; and if a prospect of power generated a wish for some national form of government, it would be rather inflamed than extinguished by a limited acquisition. This natural inclination suggested the division of power between the federal and state departments, their mutual independence, and all the precautions in the structure of the state and federal governments, for the preservation of civil liberty.

But if all these facts are insufficient to prove that the influence of power prospective or possessed, will generate a longing after a form of government which will increase it; others ascertain, that the party to be expected from this natural cause, universally operating, does yet exist, and will probably exist forever. Exclusive of the encroachments of the federal government upon the rights of the states, many pamphlets and essays have appeared, for the purpose of proving that a supreme national government was, or ought to have been, established by the constitution. These demonstrate, that an active, intelligent, and numerous party, similar to that formed in the convention by the junction of the two parties in favour of a government, either monarchical or national, is still in operation; and to the doctrines of this party, the people must apply the most mature consideration, if they wish to understand a subject upon which their liberty depends.

The first proof of this fact to which I shall recur, is a pamphlet by "One of the People," in South-Carolina. If the author neither possesses nor anticipates power; if he is too old for office, and beyond the reach of that species of ambition and avarice which feeds upon nations; if he is dead to fame and alive to moral rectitude; we shall have to examine arguments urged by a spirit of moderation and veracity. But if he is young, and burning with hope, which raises before his eyes all the allurements of wealth and power; we must expect the vehemence and vituperation, inspired by personal interest or corrupted by zeal. By the word people, used in contrariety to the word government, we mean that numerous portion of society, which neither possesses nor has a prospect of obtaining offices; and if the writer of this pamphlet really belongs to this class, his signature is a fair solicitation for popular confidence, by the strong argument of a perfect similarity between this class and himself in point of interest; but if not, the signature is a good reason for distrust. Being ignorant of the fact, this observation is not made for the purpose of weakening his arguments, but merely to remove the prepossession which the signature supplicates, and bespeak an unprejudiced consideration of the opinions he advances.

Extracts from "National and state rights considered, by one of the people." Pages 1 and 2. "The *general* government is as truly the government of the *whole* people, as the state government is of a part of the people. The constitution, in the language of its preamble, was ordained and established by the people of the United States. The moment the people met in convention, all the elements of political power returned to them, to receive a new modification and distribution, by their sovereign will. What security then, did the convention, or in other words, "the people of the United States," provide, to restrain their functionaries from usurping powers not delegated, and from abusing those with which they are really invested? Was it by the discordant clamours and lawless resistance of the state rulers, that they intended to insure domestick tranquillity, and form a more perfect union? No, the constitution will tell you what is the real security they provided. It is the responsibility of the officers of the general government to themselves, the people. The states, as political bodies, have no original, inherent rights." Does this string of coarse assertions, bottomed upon the ingenious though erroneous distinctions in the Federalist, which its authors would have viewed with derision, contain a solitary truth, or even a plausible suggestion?

Has the federal government the same powers over all the people of the states, as the state governments possess over the people of each state? Was the constitution established by each state, that is, a people of each state, or by a consolidated American nation? Did the meeting of state conventions possess all the elements of political power, to be modified or distributed by the sovereign will of an American nation, or did these conventions possess only the naked right of adopting or rejecting the constitution? Did an American nation meet in a convention and invest the federal government with powers, to be exercised under no other control, but the responsibility of its officers to this nation? Can such a nation diminish or extend the powers of the federal government, and if not, must not the substantial control over its usurpations, reside where the power of doing both resides? Does the federal government derive its powers from the federal compact, or from a convention of a consolidated nation? Does the constitution consider state rulers as discordant, clamorous, and lawless, or recognise them as securities for social order, and supporters of civil liberty? And have the states no original, inherent rights?

By these assertions, the dogmas of the consolidating school are stated without being complicated by ingenuity, and the federal system is overturned, without any apparent consideration. The very title of the pamphlet settles every difficulty, assumes the existence of a national government, and buries in its capacity, both the rights of the states and the limitations of the constitution. "National and state rights" is used as a phrase equivalent to "sovereign and corporate rights," and therefore, though the consideration of both is promised, the promise is not fulfilled as to either; and the title of the pamphlet comprises the whole argument for

its conclusion, "that the states, as political bodies, have no original, inherent rights." The reservation of these nothings, being
only a fraud to procure the ratification of the constitution, their
consideration was precipitately promised, and unavoidably abandoned. The author, however, ought at least to have informed us
how these no political rights have managed to create, sustain, or
exercise, the whole mass of political rights existing in the United
States.

Let us add a few other arguments to those before advanced
upon a point which really includes the whole question. Under
what authority have the several cessions of territory been made
by particular states? One, I believe, has been made by Georgia,
since the establishment of the federal constitution. A cession of
territory is a very plain act of sovereignty. If the states had no
original or inherent political rights, these cessions are void; if
the cessions are good, the assertion is false.

Upon what principle has the constitution declared, that no
new state shall be formed within the jurisdiction of another state,
nor by uniting two states or parts of states, without the consent
of the legislatures of the states concerned, and of Congress?
Undoubtedly for combining a sovereign and a federal consent, to
effect an act, by which both the sovereign and the federal interest might be affected. If a territorial dismemberment cannot take
place, except by the consent of the state possessed of the territorial sovereignty, no dismemberment of any other rights possessed by the same sovereignty can take place, except by its
consent also; and the federal government or the federal court,
might claim a power to regulate the territories of the states, upon
as strong ground as they claim a power to regulate the other
sovereign rights of the states, not ceded but reserved, like the sov-

ereign right of territory. In short, by what tenure does the federal government hold the ten miles square, and the sites for forts, arsenals, and other federal buildings, if the states are not invested with sovereignty?

The doctrine "that the constitution has established a supreme national government, and that the states are only corporations having no inherent and original rights," would reach and destroy the state sovereign right of territory, if it can reach and destroy any other sovereign right reserved by the states. But sovereignties and corporations are very easily distinguished. Sovereignty is distinctly seen in the rights to create a political society, to form leagues, to cede territory, to punish crimes, and to regulate property. Are corporations defined by such powers? As states and corporations have no resemblance in their origin or powers, a violent zeal for a consolidated government, can only mistake one for the other; just as some hidden light within makes us see strange sights without. The term corporation, implies a derivation from a sovereign power, and the term state, a sovereignty. One is associated with the idea of dependence, and the other, of independence. Common sense never thought of proclaiming to the world the sovereignty and independence of thirteen corporations. What a figure would they have cut with such a declaration to prepare the way for a treaty with France? Corporations are the creatures and subjects, and also proofs of sovereignty. Hence the states, being sovereign, can empower their governments to create counties and corporations, as objects like individuals for sovereign power to act upon; and corporations or counties being subjects, cannot create other corporations and counties, constitute a state, cede territory, regulate property, or pass laws for punishing crimes. The rights of towns, counties, or corporations, were not reserved, because they were subjects of sovereignties, whose rights were reserved. Whence did the reserved rights originate? Had they originated from an American nation, they would have been given and not reserved; and they must have been enumerated, like the rights given to the federal government. As the reserved rights were not given by an American nation, the states, as corporations, can have none. To find receptacles for the reservation, we must find rights; and if we can find rights, as they were not derived from the sovereignty of an American nation, we must find some other sovereignty having power to create them. We are therefore reduced to the alternative of admitting the sovereignties of the states, or allowing that the states are incorporated subjects of an imaginary American nation, and liable to be modified or abolished in virtue of its sovereignty.

A corporate character implies a derivation from, and subjection to, some sovereignty; and a power to modify or abolish this corporate character, designates the exact place where the sovereignty resides. The federal government is derived from, and may be modified or abolished by the states; and its corporate character is its only tenure, good only on account of the validity of the sovereignties by which it was bestowed. The style of the constitution, however hackneyed by construction, admits the fact explicitly. It is not "We, the people of the united corporations of New-Hampshire," &c. Could corporations, having no political powers, both create and retain the right of altering or resuming political powers? If not, the gift and limitation of federal powers, united with an actual exercise of the sovereign power of resuming and modifying them, point both to a sovereign and a corporate character. If we should admit that the sovereignty thus exercised, is spurious, its issue must also be spurious; and if we contend for the legitimacy of the issue, the parental competency to produce it, must be admitted.

These observations are alone sufficient to refute the positions assumed in the convention, and revived by one of the people, as the only basis for a supreme national government, contended for and denied by the parties for and against it. The first party assumed the ground work of one of the people, "that on the meeting of the convention, all the elements of political power returned to the people, to receive a new modification and distribution by their sovereign will." That which had never been possessed, could not be returned. Did a consolidated American nation ever possess all the elements, or any elements, of political power? A few gentlemen made a nation, only that they might make a consolidated government, either of a monarchical or national complexion. The federal party denied that any of the elements of political power were dissolved by the meeting of the convention; asserted that the meeting itself flowed from existing political power; and that its proceedings must be exposed to the ratification and future alteration of this state political power, thus recognised as existing. It was a strange dissolution of political elements, which no body perceived; and as credible, as if we were told that an eclipse of the sun had produced total darkness for several months, though we were all daily enjoying its light and warmth. If all the elements of political power ceased on the meeting of the convention, those only can exist, which were revived by the constitution. But it does not revive, and only reserves, state rights. Powers which were dead, could not be reserved. If the convention had not framed a constitution, or the states had not ratified it, would no elements of political power have existed?

The meeting of the state conventions must have been peculiarly inauspicious, and provokingly irksome, under this doctrine. All the elements of political power were gone. Whither? To these conventions? No. They could only ratify or reject the constitution. To that or to this dissolution of political power, their alternative was confined. They could not revive any of these elements, not revived by that federal instrument. Had the conventions of states been equivalent to the convention of a consolidated nation, or a representation of an American people, they might have modified political power without restriction; but as they were only state organs for expressing a state opinion, acceding to or rejecting a federal compact between states, they had no power, if they were so inclined, to change the existing political elements into a national government, republican or monarchical. As these conventions did not receive all the elements of political power, but were limited to a single act, they were not the representatives of an American nation, and thence arises a complete refutation of the construction which supposes that the words "We, the people of the United States," had any reference to a consolidated nation; since the convention of such a people would have constituted an unrestricted element of political power. The truth is, that the idea of a consolidated nation crept out of the convention, where it was invented before the state conventions were even mentioned, and settled itself in the minds of those gentlemen who still have in view one or the other of the forms of government it was started to produce. But if it is not too late to revive it, after the rejection of these forms, and after the establishment of a federal government, founded upon the co-equal sovereignties of the states, the constitution is rotten at its base, and the superstructure must be forever tottering.

Let one of the gentlemen who advocated the project for a national government, expound the object. Mr. Morris, in opposition to a federal compact, observed "that a government by compact, was no government at all." This was true, if the states were corporations, because under that character, they could form no government, federal or national. Compact and power are the different elements of forms of government, and one principle is opposed to the other. This profound politician rejects compact, because he knew that the rival principle must prevail, if a national government was established; since power only, and that of the highest degree, could govern a consolidated nation spread over an immense surface. Compact being nothing, power, which is something, comes out naturally as the basis of the national government he preferred, and the way is smoothed for playing this deadly engine upon the state governments, and all the rights of the people, each and every one of which are founded in compact.

"Discordant clamours and lawless resistance." Words constantly applied by tyranny to the people, and by every political department, to another, which it wishes to suppress. It is remarkable that mobs and tyrants are supplied by forms of government resting upon power, and not upon compact, with arguments exactly of the same weight. Without mobs, tyrants will oppress; without tyrants, mobs will disorganize; both, therefore, are necessary in governments resting upon power, as a sort of mutual check. No remedy exists in most countries against sedition, but despotism, nor against despotism, but sedition. Therefore both with equal propriety assert, that they commit their respective atrocities for the sake of an ultimate good. Such is the ground occupied by the advocates for a national supremacy in a federal government. It is necessary to suppress "the discordant clamours and lawless resistance of the state rulers." When this is effected by substituting power for compact, the same argument will be applied to the people with infinitely more plausibility. The discordant clamours and lawless resistance of a populace, will be better reasoning for adding link after link to power, to suppress the rights of the people, than it is for suppressing the rights of the states. If the state governments ought to lose their rights because they may be discordant, clamorous, and lawless, it follows very clearly that the people ought to lose their's for the same reason. But this foreign mode of reasoning was necessary to establish a foreign principle of government, which the constitution endeavoured to shun, by substituting for the eternal collisions between a populace and a despotism, the mediatorial check of state governments; and by establishing a division of power for the purpose of preventing its accumulation, by which discordant clamours and lawless resistance are invariably provoked. As it is a political axiom, that great concentrated power begets popular commotion, and that popular commotion begets great concentrated power, the constitution relied upon a sounder check to prevent both, in the state governments. There cannot be a more direct advance towards monarchy, than the dissolution of the orderly and organized control of the state governments, and an exclusive dependence upon the control of the people; because the very first popular commotion excited by an oppressive or partial law, would furnish a pretext for its introduction. To talk, therefore, of an American people, as sufficiently able and willing to act in concert, so as to furnish a security against the effects of a supreme concentrated power, and to render the mutual control of the state and federal departments unnecessary for the preservation of liberty, to my mind conveys the idea of great ignorance or of great ambition.

The artifice of destroying the rights of the people, under the mask of vindicating them, is as old as government itself. If the people of the United States should constitute themselves into one nation, the question would still occur, which was the best mode for preserving liberty, that of dividing or concentrating the powers of government? The election would lie, in fact, between a disorderly and lawless resistance of mobs, and the orderly and constitutional resistance of state governments. Suppose a majority on one side of the United States, to oppress a minority on the other. Would this probable and meditated evil be best controlled by mobs or state governments? The Federalist eulogises the latter mode of control, as the distinguishing superiority of our system for preserving the rights of the people. A sufficient mode of preventing geographical districts from being oppressed, must be found in all extensive countries, or they will be oppressed. Is it better to intrust this indispensable office to mobs or self-constituted combinations, than to organized departments? Which will act with most knowledge, discretion, legality, and effect, in maintaining the rights of the people, mobs or state governments? In a country so extensive as the United States, we must have one or the other, to countervail the propensity of great concentrated power to oppress, from ambition, avarice, or local ignorance; and the state governments exposed to the control of the people in each state, and to the power of three-fourths of the states to amend the constitution, is infinitely preferable to insurrections, exposed only to the control of physical force.

I have reserved an argument to face the undisguised doctrine of One of the People, that a power in the state governments to sustain state rights, is a diminution of their liberty; and the same argument, if it is just, will overturn the whole mass of more complicated assertions, advanced to establish a concentrated supremacy. Let us again select the state territorial right, from the rest of the reserved rights. Can Congress, the supreme court, or a concurrence of the whole federal government, abridge the territorial rights of the states without their consent? Why not? Because these rights are vested in the people of each state, of which they are not to be divested, without the consent of their state representatives. Suppose that an abridgment of state territory should be attempted by all or either of these self-constituted supremacies, would the state governments have no mode of defending the territorial rights of the people, and be constitutionally compellable to suffer their loss? What remedy can they have, except the power arising from the mutual obligation of the state and federal governments, to defend the rights of the people intrusted to each, against the encroachments of the other. Why is this an obligation common to both governments? Because the rights of both, being also rights of the people, comprising their whole moral security for civil liberty, it would be treachery to the people, should either surrender the rights intrusted to it for their benefit. If it is true that a state government has a constitutional right, and is bound by its duty to the people, to resist an abridgment of a territorial state right without its consent, by either of the supposed supremacies, it must also be true, that it has a constitutional right and is bound to resist similar abridgments of all other rights of the people, intrusted to it by the constitution. The power given to the state governments to participate in certain specified federal rights, with the consent of Congress; and the power given to the federal government to participate in the specified territorial state rights, with the consent of the state legislatures; unite in demonstrating that no supremacy existed in either government, over the rights of the people intrusted to the other, even by the mutual consent of the federal and a state government, except in the cases specified. The territorial and other state rights, are reserved to the people of each state, upon the ground of the primitive and inherent sovereignty of each state; and powers being delegated to the federal government upon the same ground, it could not abridge the territories of a state, because the idea was interdicted by the sovereignty of a state. By the very same principle every other abridgment by either government of the delegated or reserved rights, is interdicted. If state sovereignty is able to secure the territorial rights of the states, it is able to secure all the other reserved rights; and if the federal government possesses no supremacy by which it can abridge this right without the consent of the state, it cannot abridge a right as to which no consent is permitted. If such a supremacy could have abridged the territorial right of a state, why was the consent of the state legislature required? The requisition of this consent acknowledges state supremacy over state rights reserved, and opens the way to an argument in my view conclusive. Why were the state governments allowed to consent to an abridgment of the territorial right of the people of each state, and not allowed to consent to any abridgment of the other rights reserved to the people of each state? Because the people, convinced that the undiminished preservation of the other reserved rights was necessary to secure their liberties, did not choose even to intrust their representatives with a power of abridging them. From this supremacy of the people in each state, arises a construction of the constitution, universally, I believe, admitted to be correct, namely, that no state government can cede the reserved rights of the people to the federal government, and that the federal government cannot cede the federal rights of the people to a state government, because it would defeat the division of power made by the people of each state, for the very purpose of preserving their rights and liberties; and a jealousy lest this should be effected, dictated, in a great degree, the mode of amending the constitution, as necessary to preserve both the delegated and reserved rights of the people. If state consent cannot justify the federal government in exercising powers reserved to the states, nor federal consent justify a state government in exercising exclusive federal powers, there cannot be the least reason to suppose that either government can violate this division of powers by its own consent. That which a concurrence of both is not allowed to effect, cannot be effected by the will of one. If not, then there cannot exist any mode by which the state and federal rights of the people can be preserved, except the mutual control and independency of the state and federal departments. This mutual control is the most essential of the rights of the people, but of no efficacy, if either sphere, even by the consent of the other, and much less without such consent, can derange the division. The division of power cannot be constitutionally surrendered by either department, because it is a right belonging not to itself, but to the people. Let the people look abroad, and contemplate the situation of the rights of the people, unsupported by a division of power between political departments comprising a mutual control; and they will discern that the rights of the people in the whole world, have shrunk to nothing in the hands of every species of concentrated or consolidated government. In England they are betrayed to a king, and a monied aristocracy. Should our state governments betray the reserved rights of the people to the power and influence of the federal department, they will commit the same treachery committed by the house of commons, acknowledged to be fatal to the rights of the English people. In France, we behold the rights of the people daily perishing under the solitary protection of one elected legislative branch. Such a protection in both countries, has even been unable to prevent the departments of one supreme government from uniting in a conspiracy for suppressing the rights of the people. It does not even save the freedom of the press. This right has been assailed here by a sedition law, preparatory to the establishment of a supreme consolidated government, when it was attempted to force this country into the European alliance against the rights of the people, by a war with France. Spain, Portugal, and South-America, are yet floating in the storms of revolution. These nations, and all those more completely enslaved, have never established a division of power bearing any resemblance to that between the state and federal governments; and under this system, the rights of the people in the United States are infinitely more substantial, than in any other country. Has this fact no connexion with the system under which these rights enjoy an exclusive superiority? Will they be increased by resting them on one house of representatives, as in France and England, or on one court, installed for life, of which there is no example. If they owe their security and superiority in any measure to the system under which they have so singularly flourished, the declamatory exclamations, that the responsibility of federal officers to an American people is sufficient to preserve them, must be counted among those flatteries for deluding the people into a confidence, by which their rights will be reduced to the same state with such rights in the rest of the world.

But before we can know how to secure the rights of the people, it is necessary to know what those rights are. As the people of all the states never associated themselves into one nation, and as the political rights of the people must be derived from such associations, they rest wholly upon their state communities. By destroying or impairing the foundation of these rights, the rights themselves must be endangered. Among them, the right of election, retained by the people as the first security for all their rights intrusted both to the federal and state governments, becomes ineffectual for preserving those intrusted to the latter governments, if the federal government or the supreme court, can destroy its effect. Election may dictate the preservation of the reserved rights of the people, under an opinion that when they were reserved, the mode by which they were to be preserved, was also reserved; but a judicial or federal supremacy may dictate their destruction or abridgment. If state representatives adhere to the opinion of the only people to whom state rights belong, it is only necessary to call them discordant, clamorous, and lawless, to deprive the people themselves of rights, which they declared by the division and reservation of powers, to be essential for the preservation of their liberty. Of what value is state representation, if the reserved right of state election is deprived of its efficacy by federal supremacy? It is in form a supremacy over the state governments, but in fact, a supremacy over rights reserved to the people of each state.

A compensation for the loss of the contemplated efficacy of state election, is offered to the people in the election of one legislative branch of the federal government, as sufficient for restraining federal officers "from usurping powers not delegated, and from abusing those with which they are really invested." The people have retained the power of securing both their federal and reserved rights, by election, to be separately applied to each class, in different modes. State election was not retained by them to control the delegated powers, nor federal election to control the reserved powers. How then can one species of election compensate for the loss of the other, or answer the purposes of both? How can the people preserve their reserved rights by federal election, if their federal representatives have no power to regulate those rights? The popular right of election was divided, together with the delegated and reserved powers, relatively to both classes. When applied to the first class, it is not applied to the reserved powers; and when applied to the second, it is not applied to federal powers; therefore federal election cannot convey reserved powers, nor state election federal powers. If the efficacy of state election is destroyed by federal election, the people will lose their reserved, and retain only their federal, right of election; and their reserved rights will not enjoy any security at all from election. The mode proposed for getting over this difficulty is, to transform federal election into national election, that it may reach both classes of rights, state and federal; under the pretence of compensating the people for actual rights resulting from their actual state associations, by a supremacy collected from a spurious national election. But this contrivance would vitally derange the principle of representation, because federal election is modified for effecting federal purposes, or securing a proper exercise of the delegated powers only; and state election for purposes wholly different. A deputation modelled to fit one end, cannot possibly fit a different end.

Federal election is by no means modified upon principles calculated to establish a general government able to regulate the
affairs of a consolidated nation, and prevent fatal geographical
partialities or errors. The hypothesis of a general government, and
the supremacy deduced from it, is therefore false, upon the principle of representation itself, referred to in its defence, for want of
such a responsibility in federal officers to the people, as would
be necessary to create a national government thoroughly republican, like the national state governments. Is it true, that the officers of the federal government are completely responsible to
the people? If not, did the people intend to confide in a falsehood for the preservation of their rights and liberties? If the
people are to be moulded into a consolidated nation, they ought
to have an opportunity of providing, that any supremacy with
which they might intrust their national government, should be
quite responsible to themselves, according to our republican
principles. In fact, the imperfect responsibility of the federal officers to the people, dictated the necessity of securing their
reserved rights by a sounder responsibility. No responsibility to
the people can be found in a political supremacy of the federal
court; on the contrary, its essential character of a tenure for life,
would defeat that responsibility, in its most important intention,
that of enforcing a loyalty to the rights of the people, in construing the constitution. The responsibility of Congress to the
people, though far exceeding that of the supreme court, is far
more imperfect than that of the national state governments. The
influence of the people extends only to the house of representatives, and the senate is exposed to the influence of "the discordant, clamorous, and lawless resistance of state rulers." The
house of representatives alone, is inert, and the influence which

reaches it is not that of a consolidated people, but of separate states; and therefore a responsibility was contrived for the federal government, to prevent a majority of people inhabiting a minority of states, from oppressing a majority of states. How can it be contended that the constitution relied upon a responsibility to an American people for its faithful observance, when it abounds with precautions to prevent a majority from using its influence to destroy the moral equality of the states? It is at least strange doctrine to states, which can never use population as a passport to geographical power.

The electors of the president are appointed as these discordant, clamorous, and lawless state rulers shall direct; so as to secure, wisely and properly, in my opinion, a state influence over this officer; and if no choice is made, he is elected by states in the house of representatives. Far from being responsible to the people, considered as a consolidated nation, he is made responsible to them considered as state nations. The mode of his election is federal, and not national, because the constitution intended to establish a federal and not a national government. If the states should ever part with this federal feature of the constitution, it will be a great and probably a conclusive stride towards a consolidated, and perhaps a monarchical government.

Even the house of representatives is neither a national representation, nor exposed to a national influence. The exclusive influence of each state over its own members, was so inevitable, that the large states contended for the mode by which it is appointed to extend their own power, by means of the responsibility of the members to their own states; and it is both false in fact, and fallacious in theory, that this house was ever considered in the convention, or could be made, a national representation. To

check the infallible influence of the great states by their greater
number of votes, the small states obtained the representation in
the senate; and the expectations of both are realized by experience. The representatives of no states feel any responsibility to the
people of other states, nor have the people of one state any influence over the representatives of another. The influence over this
house is therefore state or federal, and its responsibility to a consolidated nation quite chimerical. A foresight of this dictated its
appointment by states, and excluded fragments of state population from representation, because the representation, both in theory and fact, would be state and not national. The contemplated
responsibility of the representatives of each state to the independent nations by which they were elected, was a federal and
not a national feature of the constitution. They may be elected by
a general state national ticket. Their responsibility to their own
states is real; to an American nation, imaginary. By catching at the
shadow, the substance would be lost. A real and a nominal
responsibility plead for the preference, as securities for the state
rights reserved to the people. The responsibility of the house of
representatives to the separate state nations, is sufficient to preserve the federal rights of these nations, but wholly insufficient,
and therefore never relied upon, to preserve their separate and
dissimilar reserved rights; the nominal responsibility assails the
real responsibility with opprobrious epithets, to destroy the real
friends and sincere defenders of the reserved rights of the people,
and introduce a national government. One of the People quarrels
like the natives of Hindostan, who stigmatise the object of hatred
by disparaging his nearest relatives, in order to render him contemptible. In like manner he labours to destroy the state rights
of the people, and a federal form of government founded in a

republican equality of states, by calumniating their best friends, the state governments.

The doctrine of One of the People displays the difference between Mr. Hamilton's and Mr. Madison's plans of government, and adopts the former. Mr. Hamilton was for "establishing a general and national government completely supreme, annihilating state distinctions and state operations, and giving a national legislature unlimited power to pass all laws whatsoever, and to appoint courts in every state, so as to make the state governments unnecessary to it." Mr. Madison was for "retaining the state governments and operations, but subjecting them to a supremacy or negative in federal officers, legislative, executive, and judicial." Mr. Hamilton confessed that both plans "were very remote from the idea of the people." One of the People contends, in fact, that Mr. Hamilton's plan was adopted; that the constitution established a national government; that it abolished the discordant, clamorous, and lawless state governments; and that they were not relied upon to insure domestic tranquillity or a more perfect union, nor to defend and preserve the rights reserved to the people; so that these rights, being unprotected by the states, have no defenders at all.

To re-instate Mr. Hamilton's rejected system, he brings forward the hackneyed quotation from the preamble of the constitution, to prove that the United States were consolidated into one nation. If this was even true, it would not follow that we must have a consolidated supreme national government. A nation may establish whatever balancing political departments it thinks necessary for preserving the rights of the people; and the constitution, in reserving a great mass of rights and powers to the people of each state, without the exercise of which civil government could not go on, acknowledges and uses the instruments by which only these indispensable rights and powers can be exercised. To the reasons before urged to prove the fallacy of this argument for introducing a national government, I shall subjoin others, apparently new and strong. "Treason against the *United States,* shall consist only in levying war against them, or in adhering to their enemies." In this clause of the constitution, the word "people" is dropt, and the words "United States" used to define the nature of the government. I have selected the case of treason to illustrate the argument, for reasons which will appear as we proceed, but the reader will be pleased to recollect, that throughout the constitution the word people is never associated with the words United States, except in the first line of the preamble. We have a Congress, a president, and a judicial power of the United States, but no such departments of the *people* of the United States. Even in the preamble itself, the constitution is established, not for the *people* of the United States, but "for the United States of America." The reconciliation of these different phrases seems to be easy. That used in the first line of the preamble refers to the ratification of the constitution, and that used in the last line, and throughout the constitution, to the character of the government. The ratification was to be the act of the people of the states, by conventions, but the government was to be a confederation of United States, and not a consolidated or a national government of the people inhabiting all these states. The form, therefore, of the ratification, could not alter the nature of the compact, nor reflect upon federal rulers the least power or supremacy whatever. "The president, and *all the civil officers of the United States,* shall be removed from office by impeachment." The article reaches representatives and senators.

Both are contemplated as equally officers of a federal, and neither as officers of a national government, or officers of an aggregate nation. They are to be tried by a federal tribunal. Had any of them been national officers, they would have been tried by some national tribunal. The case of treason suggests several important observations. It is divided into two classes, high and petit. The first class comprises crimes against sovereignty, and their punishment is an appendage of sovereign power. State governments exercise the right of defining and punishing these crimes, because they represent state sovereignty, and corporations can do neither, because they are not sovereign. Indictments are drawn in the name of the commonwealth, or of the people of the state, and conclude "against the peace and dignity of the commonwealth, or of the state associated people, or of the state, or against the peace, government, and dignity of the state," for these varieties are used in state constitutions, expressing the social sovereignty, by which traitors and other criminals are brought to justice. Why was it necessary to invest the federal government with a power to punish only a species of treason defined by the constitution? Because it was not a national government, and therefore had no power to define or punish any crime whatsoever, committed against sovereign power. Why was it allowed to punish only a few specified crimes? Because they were injurious to the federal union of states, and the state sovereignties were competent to the punishment of all crimes against the peace and dignity of the state, or injurious to individuals. Treason might have been committed formerly, by words or writings, intended to subvert a government. It may be well for One of the People, that federal treason was not extended to such attempts for subverting our federal form of government. If the old art of finding constructive treasons had remained, he might perhaps have himself become a precedent to some future logician, for finding a constructive national government. Suppose an indictment for federal treason should be brought in the name of the *people* of America, and conclude against their peace and dignity. Would it not be an error sufficient to arrest the judgment? Or suppose an indictment for state treason should be instituted in the name of the corporation of South-Carolina, and conclude against the peace and dignity of the said corporation. Would not the error be equally fatal? Why would both these indictments be erroneous? Because no American people or nation existed, and because South-Carolina is not a corporation. I do not know how federal indictments are drawn for punishing crimes, the punishment of which is not delegated to the federal government. As to treason, they must conclude against the peace and dignity of the United States. As to those committed against individuals or corporations, I should be glad to see an indictment concluding against the peace and dignity of the people of America, as a basis for federal jurisdiction. It might settle the jurisdiction of the federal judiciary, both original and appellate; for if the supposed national sovereignty can bestow jurisdiction in one case, it may do so in the other.

Let us return to One of the People. P. 3. "As long as we (the people,) continue the officers of the *general* government in office, their acts are ours; as their business is of greater importance than yours, (the business of the state governments,) we of course select the most intelligent men to perform it, and your attempt to control them is therefore peculiarly unbecoming and arrogant." This would be awful, and not very modest language, in the mouths of any rulers whatsoever; but suppose Congress should adopt it,

and say, "our importance and superior intelligence makes it peculiarly arrogant for any state government to attempt to control us."
The supreme judges may also declare that, being as important
and intelligent as the members of Congress, they are entitled to
the same implicit obedience. The pretensions of the president,
under this new rule for dividing power, may be still better. Such
a constellation would soon establish Mr. Hamilton's system of
government, if it would be peculiarly unbecoming and arrogant
to control any of its doings, and presently add irresistible power
to its other brilliances. But if this splendid being is really a fiction,
this rule for dividing power between the federal and state departments, though compounded of good words, is so very imperfect, that the claim for veneration seems to be nearly as arrogant
as any other idolatry ever forged to obtain power and money. Is
it true that the officers of the federal government carry with
them a greater mass of intelligence than they leave among the
officers of the state governments; that their business is more
important to the happiness of the people, than the business of the
state officers; or that any people, state or national, invested them
with a power to abridge their reserved state rights? Which class
of officers may be able to do the people most harm, is another
question; but ought Milton's poetical decoration of the devil to
entitle this powerful being to implicit obedience, and convict
his less dangerous adversaries of arrogance for withstanding his
machinations? The chief distinction of state officers, like that of
beneficent angels, consists in a power to do much good, and but
little evil; by which they are indicated as a happy expedient for
controlling the excesses of tremendous power. If the constitution
had contained an article in the precise words of One of the People, would it have been what it is, or would it have been rati-

fied? If not, can any act of the state governments be more arrogant, than an attempt, by an individual, to impose such an article upon the people? If charges of unimportance, ignorance, and arrogance, can confer power, where would it stop, or how can it be limited? How arrogant might it be for an humble magistrate to vindicate the rights of the people against a member of Congress? The important functions of a president, selected for his intelligence, would render it highly unbecoming and arrogant for a member of Congress to resist his usurpations. No weaker political department could defend its constitutional rights against a stronger, without being chargeable with arrogance. And if this doctrine is true, all divisions and limitations of power, for the preservation of civil liberty, are absurd. Every usurpation implies power, and every resistance to power is said to be arrogant.

P. 3. "The assumption of state authorities will appear still more glaring and unwarrantable, when we reflect, that whatever is assumed as a state right, pertains equally to every state in the union, separately and individually." The defence of individual rights is unwarrantable, because they are separate and individual; all social rights are individual, therefore none can be withheld from power. What are state authorities, if they cannot be assumed, because the same authorities pertain to other states? This doctrine gets rid of the states according to Mr. Hamilton's principles, and concentrates the right of governing in power, according to Mr. Morris's. The author's insinuations that the states have some powers, mean nothing, if their individuality makes it unwarrantable to assume them. It was of course unnecessary to make any distinction between state rights and state usurpations, or between federal rights and federal usurpations, because individual rights are naturally subject to concentrated power, and power

244 NEW VIEWS OF THE CONSTITUTION

is concentrated in a national or general government. Accordingly he disencumbers himself of these inquiries as frivolous.

P. 5. "Ambitious men of inferior talents, finding they have no hope to be distinguished in the councils of the *national* government, naturally wish to increase the power and consequence of the state governments, the theatres in which they expect to acquire distinction." If an argument may be balanced, it weighs nothing. Ambitious men of superior talents, naturally wish to increase the powers of the federal government, for the sake of increasing their own power and distinction. The last argument is the heaviest, if the liberties of mankind are exposed to most danger from ambitious men of superior talents. The division of power between the state and federal governments, was designed to control the achievements of both the wholesale and retail dealers in the wares of ambition, and why the men of great capital should be relieved from the competition of the state pedlars, except for the purpose of increasing their profits, at the expense of their customers, is not perceivable.

P. 6. "But I will offer some additional views, tending to shew that the fears that the general government will prostrate the state sovereignties, are wholly unfounded." After having asserted that the states had no original political rights, so that it was impossible for the general government, if there is one, to prostrate what was never erected, it is a great condescension to prove; what! that the said general government *cannot* prostrate the state sovereignties. By no means. This would overthrow the author's whole doctrine. His conciliating humour therefore is exerted, only to prove that the general government *will not* prostrate the state sovereignties. And these are his arguments to prove that it has a right, but not a disposition, to do so.

P. 6. "The powers of the state governments constitute precisely that class of political powers that has the least attractions for ambition. They establish the rules of property, and fix and define the rights of persons."

P. 7. "Ambition holds a loftier career. The states are excluded from all the pride, pomp, and circumstance of glorious war. When, therefore, we consider the nature of ambition, when we reflect that it is desirous of performing those actions only which history records with her brightest and most enduring colours, and nations behold with the highest admiration, the folly of the apprehension that the general government will subvert the state governments, is most strikingly apparent."

"Upon the discretion of Congress in laying and collecting taxes, and in raising and supporting armies, there are no restrictions except those imposed by nature. Congress may draw from the people (of the states too,) the utmost farthing that can be spared from their suffering families, to fill the national coffers; and call out the last man that can be spared from raising the necessaries of life, to fill the national armies, and fight the battles of ambitious rulers. These tremendous engines are harmless to the people, and will not be depredators upon the more peaceful, inefficient, and unattractive powers of the state governments. We are called upon to believe that our federal rulers will use with moderation the very power by which ambitious men have, in all ages, built up the movements of their own aggrandizement; and yet that these rulers will consummate their ambitious purposes, and subvert our liberties, by the paltry and petit larceny process of pilfering little fragments from the temple of sovereignty. It is not in the course of ambition to descend, for in its proper motion it ascends. Abstractedly considered, power has no

allurements. It is only desirable from its imposing associations."
Such is the author's political theory, and he adduces the following proofs of its goodness.

P. 8. "Congress possess absolute power over the ten miles
square, yet they neglect its police, and seem willing to abdicate
the government."

P. 9. "The state governments delegate portions of their power
to city and county corporations. Great-Britain, though despotick
over the colonies, did not usurp their domestick regulations.
Despotick monarchs disburden themselves from the cares of local
government, as in Persia and Turkey, by delegating these functions to royal satraps; and in Russia, many provinces have scarcely
been visited by a ray of imperial power, and manage their own
internal concerns in their own way."

P. 10. "From these examples it is apparent, that if governments
are fond of power, they are fond of ease."

We can only oppose to the torrid temperature of these political opinions, the cold dulness of common sense. Do the sparks
of ambition really produce etherial and not terrestrial confla-
grations? If state powers have the least attraction for ambition,
how happens it that those who exercise these humble powers are
most likely to be ambitious? Mankind have hitherto believed,
that great power begets arrogance and ambition, and it was this
opinion which dictated the divisions and limitations established
by the constitution. But if it is true that the general government
will be ambitious, and that therefore it will pursue a loftier career
than that of usurpation, or that great power will prevent ambition
and arrogance; then the remedy for removing the ambition and
arrogance of state rulers, and for preventing them from usurping federal powers, is to give these rulers more power. Whether

this will inspire them with the idea of making lofty careers, or with an etherial ambition only, to obtain the admiration of nations, it will constitute the same security for the federal government against the encroachments of the state governments, urged as sufficient to secure the state governments against those of the federal government.

The powers of the states extend only to life, property, and the rights of persons, but ambition holds a loftier career. I thought that ambition fledged itself with feathers plucked from other birds; and that it could not ascend without lubricating its wings with oil squeezed from the rump of society; that it never confined itself, like the phoenix, to aerial flights, but descended to the earth in search of food; that war, the instrument of ambitious rulers, might reach life, liberty, and property; and that the lofty career of Julius Cæsar required men and money, for the purpose of subjecting all social interests to its control. If the only object of ambition is to provide matter for the eloquence of historians, it has been unfortunate in not being able, by the brilliancy of its actions, to dazzle them against the heinousness of its crimes. The durable colours in which these are recorded, were not intended to inspire us with an admiration of a tyrant, but of the historian; and if we bestow our applause upon the wrong object, the end of history is defeated. Instead of teaching us to resist the inexhaustible frauds and oppressions of concentrated power, perpetrated by its progeny, arrogance, ambition, and avarice, history would only teach us to behold its vices "with the highest admiration."

The tremendous powers of glorious war and unlimited taxation, to fight the battles or fill the pockets of ambitious or avaricious rulers, have suggested political divisions and checks.

Concentrated power has other affections, nearly as pernicious to human happiness as its love of war and taxation. It loves implicit obedience, and partisans purchased at the expense of the people. On the contrary, it hates whatever obstructs the gratification of these passions. If we have married Congress to men and money, and to several other rich wives, why should we endow it with an unlimited polygamy, by allowing it to take away the plain housewives of the states; and break the tenth commandment, in order to establish a political seraglio for satisfying the lusts of ambition? Truly, because the concubinage of power is exposed "to no restrictions except those imposed by the laws of nature; because, though tremendous, it will be harmless to the people, and will not become a depredator upon the peaceful, inefficient, and unattractive rights of the state governments, since power only inspires a love of glory; because our federal rulers will use with moderation the powers by which ambitious men have, in all ages, built up the monuments of their aggrandizement; because they will never pilfer fragments from the temple of liberty; because ambition will ascend and not descend; and because, abstractedly considered, "power has no allurements." But the author has not informed us what is to be done, if this glorious ambition should not prevent federal rulers from usurping the state rights of the people. Are the powers of these rulers exposed to no restrictions? Tremendous power, restrained only by the natural moderation of ambition, is a very new plan for a constitution. I imagined that our army and treasury were not a natural, but a conventional army and treasury, created "for the defence and welfare" of the confederated states, and not to establish a tremendous unlimited natural power. If they are used to fight the battles or fill the pockets of federal rulers, and the states should say to Congress, "You have perverted the powers of raising men and money from the objects specified by the constitution," and Congress should answer, "True, but our power is exposed to no restrictions, except those imposed by the laws of nature," would the sufficiency of the answer be admitted? If the new phrase, "imposed by the laws of nature," is a parody of "national government," it well expounds the design of the project for introducing that system.

Besides the restriction of the powers of the purse and the sword to federal objects, others abound in the constitution. Of this nature are the restrictions of taxation, as to its modes; the concurrency of taxation; by which the states may also draw the last farthing from the people; comprising a mutual check; the division of the power of the sword in its great reservoir of the militia; the right of the states to raise fleets and armies in time of war; and the division of powers into delegated and reserved, not intended to be abrogated by the powers to tax and to raise armies. The resources of the constitution for enforcing these restrictions, are, state election of one branch of a federal legislature by the people, of another, by state legislatures, of a third, in a federal mode, and the natural state right of self-preservation. Congress are also restricted to three cases in calling out the militia, neither of which extends to fighting the battles of ambitious rulers; it cannot order them out of the United States; nor can it raise regular armies by compulsion. Finally, the sovereignty of the states is a barrier against the tremendous natural power contended for. "Ambitious men will not pilfer fragments from state sovereignties." This admits their existence, and the question is, whether they constitute a temple of liberty, which ambition is only prohibited from pilfering by its natural moderation.

Tremendous powers are said to be harmless, and sufficiently restrained by the laws of nature; state powers to be peaceful, inefficient, and unattractive, but too arrogant to be restrained by these same laws; and federal rulers to be too ambitious to be guilty of petit larceny pilferings from the temple of state sovereignties. But may they not be inclined to commit grand larceny. The project of sweeping off all these sovereignties by the supremacy contended for, does not remove this apprehension. The doctrine of One of the People does indeed soar far above the petit larceny of pilfering fragments from the temple of state sovereignties, and magnanimously leaves not a fragment standing. It is a Gengis Khan in political conquest. Ambition uses any means, great or small, to effect its ends. Like a balloon, it even sometimes employs vapour to raise itself. The happy contrast between grand and petit larceny, furnishes the argument in favour of ambition. It is made to say, "I am too high-minded to be content with pilferings from the temple of state sovereignty, but I will nobly carry off the intire temple, by proving that the states have no original rights, and that I hold the purse and the sword subject to no restrictions but those of the laws of my nature." As no moral edifice is more splendid than the temple of liberty, ambition in all ages aspires to the fame of pulling it down, and whether it succeeds by piece-meal, or by a single exploit, by the sublimity of grand larceny, or the cunning of petit larcenies, has never been very material to the people, however its own fame may be graduated by an achievement which must owe its splendour to its superlative atrocity.

These comfortable securities against the consequences of tremendous concentrated power, are founded upon the fine idea, "that power, abstractedly considered, has no allurements, and is only desirable from its imposing associations," or that power ought to be gazed at abstractedly from man, or man abstractedly from his passions and qualities. By not associating man's qualities with power, it becomes a metaphysical thing, incapable of doing harm; or by stripping a man of his qualities, he may be converted in an idea as sublime as you please. To consider power abstractedly from its associations, or man abstractedly from his qualities, may be a sublimated mode of reasoning, highly agreeable to the aspiring sons of ambition, and yet quite unintelligible to the humble admirers of common sense. Let us reduce this reasoning in favour of a supreme consolidated government to the form of a constitutional article. "The powers of the purse and the sword herein delegated, are subject to no restrictions, except those imposed by the laws of nature. They may therefore be used to fight the battles of ambitious rulers, or to destroy the rights reserved to the states. But though tremendous, they must be harmless to the people and the state governments, because, although in all ages ambitious rulers have used them for their own aggrandizement, yet our rulers will use them with moderation, since ambition is too sentimental to commit petit larcenies, and ascends to elevated crimes to obtain admiration, and since power, having no allurements, requires no restrictions."

Such are the principles necessary to introduce a supreme national government; but are these the principles of the constitution? That is one continued lecture against the doctrine, that liberty will be secured by a confidence in concentrated power. Instead of relying upon this speculation, in all ages so unsuccessful, the constitution circumvolves power with restrictions, and moderates it by divisions. But One of the People judiciously overlooks these restrictions and divisions, because they subvert

his theory, and substitutes for them several metaphysical pretti-
nesses, by which he thinks it may be defended.

"Congress is tired of its absolute power over ten miles square,
and neglects its police." This unfortunate piece of imaginary evidence is another hypothesis to sustain the previous hypothesis,
that power, abstractedly considered, has no allurements, and is
therefore more inclined to contract than to extend itself. The
reasoning is again abstracted from the facts. Congress still hold,
and by the help of the court, has stretched this little power to an
indefinite size, to foster the "paltry and petit larceny object of pilfering" the states by a lottery. It is an instance to shew that ambition and avarice are not uniformly superior to little means; but
it is a bad one to prove an aversion to power, as it is made the
most of, and as indeed Congress could not relinquish this, any
more than another delegated power. If the neglect of the police
of the ten miles square, is a fact, though the members of Congress
see and inhabit it near half the year, it does not recommend a
national supremacy in that body. This has happened, not from
want of knowledge, but from want of interest in the concerns
of the district. How then can Congress become a good legislative
body for states which they never see, and in the concerns of
which most of its members have no interest? Thus the reference
to the ten miles square recoils in every view with some force
against the project for a national government. Even the existence
of this district decides the question, because it would have been
unnecessary for the constitution to have bestowed a supreme
jurisdiction upon Congress over the ten miles, if the federal government possessed a supreme jurisdiction over state rights; nor
was there any meaning in the establishment of this district, if
the constitution had established the general or national government now contended for.

Sensible of the incapacity of Congress for exercising the powers of a consolidated government, so as to preserve the liberty and advance the prosperity of the people of each state, the author endeavours to evade the objection, by observing, "that the state governments delegate portions of their power to city and county corporations," inferring, that Congress may remove the objection, by also delegating portions of its power to the state governments. This construction of the constitution derives the powers of the state governments from Congress, and not from the people. It is necessary to sustain the federal supremacy contended for, but it is as visibly contrary to the most explicit meaning of the constitution. A supreme national government would be exactly as incapable of regulating with justice, and impartiality, and fellow-feeling, the local interests of the states, by deputies, as of governing them directly. The comparison between a responsibility of these interests to the people of each state, or to the supremacy of a national government, therefore still remains. Will internal commotions and local oppressions be prevented or provoked by depriving the people of a right essential to their liberty and happiness?

More unfortunate still is the next evidence adduced to prove, that state rights have nothing to apprehend from a concentrated supremacy. "Great-Britain, though despotick over the colonies, did not usurp their domestick regulation," and therefore the federal government, though despotick over the states, will not usurp theirs. Had the fabulous river of the Pagan hell caused men to remember what had not, as well as to forget what had happened, One of the People ought to have administered to his readers copious draughts of this miraculous stream, to enable them to remember that Great-Britain did not usurp the regulation of colonial domestick affairs, and to forget that the colonies went to war with her for having done so; as both facts are necessary to prove the superiority of a concentrated supremacy over our federal system.

But most unfortunate is the proof of the harmless nature of a concentrated supremacy, in the examples of Persia, Turkey, and Russia. If local interests may possibly feel the rays of a concentrated supremacy, yet as "it is apparent, from these examples that governments are fond of ease," it follows, "that many provinces will scarcely be visited by them, and may manage their own internal affairs in their own way." But the rays of a concentrated supremacy happen to be armies, fleets, satraps, and a multitude of officers. England, Persia, Turkey, and Russia, send forth such rays in abundance, and do not hoard them up in a cave, as old Neptune did his storms, for the occasional amusement of mankind. They are admitted to be bad things, and a right in provinces to manage their local affairs in their own way, is admitted to be a good thing; and we are advised to turn loose the bad things, because the good thing will be obtained by means of the laziness or love of ease in the bad things, as a new political check for the security of civil liberty preferable to our constitutional restrictions.

Are mankind yet to learn, that concentrated power has never yet been made virtuous by its love of ease, nor forgotten provinces having money, through its idleness? that it becomes suspicious, restless, and oppressive, in proportion to its extension, and multiplies armies, satraps, and officers, for its security? Every great country, subjected to an undivided sovereignty, must sooner or later be divided into military commanderies, and crowded with officers. If a consolidated sovereignty will neglect distant provinces, it is unfit for the management of local interests.

Its rays will operate differently upon these interests, in proportion to their distance or proximity. If they are good things, the distant provinces will suffer injustice for want of their share; if bad, the provinces within their reach will be partially oppressed. It was the intention of our federal system to prevent the partialities and inequalities of concentrated power, whether they proceed from its laziness, or avarice, or ambition, or ignorance, or capriciousness, or want of sympathy.

But "the authority of Washington, Madison, and Hamilton, proves that the danger to the union proceeds from the centrifugal tendencies of the states." The weight of authority depends upon known, and not upon unknown opinions; yet One of the People claims for himself the respect due to these eminent men, without even endeavouring to ascertain their opinions. He takes it for granted that our federal system, in their judgment, was exclusively endangered by a centrifugal, and perfectly safe against a centripetal tendency. The latter, however, was the object of apprehension which obstructed the ratification of the constitution, and to remove this apprehension was the end of two of these gentlemen in writing the Federalist. Did the three unanimously subscribe to the doctrines advanced by One of the People; or did two of them express positive opinions as to the sufficiency of the constitution to prevent the apprehended centripetal tendency? Constitutional restrictions, and a division of spheres, were as necessary to prevent the state planets from being absorbed by a vortex, as to prevent them from wandering into some other system. The delegated powers were therefore given to one sphere, to prevent a centrifugal, and the reserved powers retained for the other, to prevent a centripetal tendency. Let us look again at a few of the doctrines of One of the People, in defence of which he claims the authority of these three eminent men.

"State rulers are discordant, clamorous, and lawless. The states have no original rights. Their attempts to control officers of the general government, are unbecoming and arrogant. Ambition is only desirous of performing admirable actions. Congress are under no restrictions in drawing men and money from the people, except those imposed by the laws of nature. Ambition will not descend to petty larcenies for subverting liberty. Power has no allurements. Governments love ease. The supremacy of Great-Britain did not usurp the domestick regulation of her colonies. Despotick monarchs do not send the rays of power into distant provinces, which therefore manage their internal concerns in their own way." When did these three gentlemen express such opinions as these?

It is difficult, but not impossible, to ascertain the political opinions of Washington. He fought faithfully and gloriously for many years, under the authority of the states, against a national supremacy claiming local powers. He suppressed a plot for establishing a national government. He recognised state sovereignties and the division of powers between the state and federal governments, in his letter as president of the convention. And he introduced the important custom of confining the presidency to two terms, as a precaution against a centripetal tendency. As he was not a political writer, we can only deduce his opinions from his actions.

Mr. Hamilton approved of a national government like the English form, and Mr. Madison of a national government, excluding the monarchical and aristocratical features preferred by Mr. Hamilton. To which of these opinions does One of the

People mean to subscribe? Is he a monarchical, a consolidating, or a federal republican? Mr. Hamilton, in the convention, was the first, Mr. Madison, the second; both their plans failed; and the constitution, to personify it, is the third. Three different principles cannot be one principle. A federal republican cannot approve of the destruction of federal and state rights, by either of the forms of national government rejected in the convention. Mr. Madison and Mr. Hamilton differed in the construction of the constitution, as to an important point. Which authority is recommended? But they concurred in a multitude of constructions, at violent enmity with the string of doctrines just quoted. Let us again look at their opinions, for the sake of comparison.

"The state and federal governments are mutual checks upon each other. Each is independent of the other. The state governments will afford complete security against invasions of liberty by the federal government. These cannot so likely escape the penetration of select bodies of men as of the people at large. The state legislatures will have better means of information, and can adopt a regular plan of opposition. They can unite with their common forces for their own defence, with all the celerity, regularity, and system, of independent nations. The state governments, by their original constitutions, are invested with complete sovereignty. They possess an independent and uncontrollable authority, and all the rights of sovereignty, not *exclusively* delegated to the United States. From the division of sovereign power, all the rights of which the states are not explicitly divested, remain with them in full vigour, according to the whole tenour of the constitution. The constitution was a federal and not a national act. The states retain under it a very considerable portion of active sovereignty. The state and federal governments will control each other. The federal legislature will not only be restrained by its dependence on the people, but will moreover be watched and controlled by the several collateral legislatures." It would be necessary to copy the greater part of the Federalist, to collect all its constructions adverse to the doctrines of One of the People. Do these few prove that, in the opinion of its authors, the states have no political, original, or inherent rights, or justify the centripetal doctrines of One of the People? Against an apprehension that such attempts might be made, these, and many other arguments were urged in the Federalist. Authorities cannot justify opinions which they contradict. One of the People should tell us whether he quotes the authority of these gentlemen in the convention or in the Federalist; their opinions about government in general, or as to the nature and principles of that established by the constitution. Different opinions, in reference to different objects, cannot be fairly blended so as to make up one authority. If he says he refers to the opinions of these gentlemen in the convention, he must admit that he is aiming at a supreme national government; and he must also say whether he prefers, with one, a monarchical, or with the other, a republican form, for this national government. If he refers to their authority in the Federalist, he must admit that it establishes constructions of the constitution utterly inconsistent with their range of opinion expressed as to government in general, whilst they were unrestricted by the federal principles adopted.

Why was the authority of Mr. Jefferson over-looked? Its exclusion is an acknowledgment, that his difference of opinion with two of the gentlemen referred to, was real, and not fabulous. In accounting for this omission, several weighty considerations present themselves. The political principles of Mr. Jefferson and Mr. Hamilton, being thoroughly opposed to each other, these gentlemen could not be united as one authority. An honest contrariety of opinion between a federal and a national government, and not an unprincipled difference, originally created the great parties in the United States; and the several attempts to assign their origin to other causes, were only expedients to conceal from the people the true principles by which they were actuated. This contrariety in principles, arranged Mr. Jefferson and Mr. Hamilton as the leaders of opposite parties, and either would have been instantly displaced, if he had changed his principles. The fact was so notorious, that foreign governments and foreign politicians took sides with one or the other, as they were influenced by republican or monarchical principles. This could not have happened, had our parties been created by the frivolous views to which they have been assigned, in order to shun the republican prepossessions of the people, indicated by the popularity of Mr. Jefferson, and get past them towards the monarchical opinions entertained by Mr. Hamilton. Thus the only reason which could have excluded Mr. Jefferson, and selected Mr. Hamilton, as an authority, becomes visible. The different opinions of these gentlemen have still their disciples, and some of us would refer to Mr. Jefferson as an authority, for the same reason that One of the People refers to Mr. Hamilton. The warfare is still between republican and consolidating principles, and therefore a champion of one policy could not be made the champion of the other. Had Mr. Jefferson avowed the same principles avowed by Mr. Hamilton in the convention, he would have been praised and quoted by the same principles which praise and quote Mr. Hamilton. The political principles of these gentlemen, and not their private characters, provoked the slanders, and excited the applauses, which they have suffered or received.

Why was the venerable John Adams not referred to as an authority? In all those qualifications which merit respect, he was at least equal to Mr. Hamilton, and in learning, his superior. Was it because he had openly and honourably avowed a predilection, secretly avowed by Mr. Hamilton in the convention, and lest the publick opinion might not yet be ripe for adopting his candour by claiming the benefit of his authority? He left his principles to seek for advocates by their strength, and never availed himself of meretricious partisans, purchased by funding, banking, and offices; and working with construction, invective, and declamation, instead of a candid integrity. Was his authority rejected, because his defence of the state constitutions admitted and asserted the sovereignties of the states? or was it rejected because he was too patriotick to use the indirect mode of advancing his principles by uniting with European monarchs, and involving his country in a war with France? A pamphlet written by Mr. Hamilton, suggested by this squeamishness in Mr. Adams (as it was considered is said, by its effects in South-Carolina, to have prevented Mr. Adams's re-election to the presidency. In point of patriotism, this step suggests a comparison between Mr. Adams and Mr. Hamilton; in point of political wisdom, between Mr. Hamilton and Mr. Jefferson. Mr. Adams would not involve his country in a war, as a mode of advancing his political opinions; and Mr. Jefferson never committed the indiscretion of defeating his great end of fixing republican principles in the publick mind, by provoking divisions upon points of minor importance. Mr. Hamilton undermined his own party, from a thorough-going zeal for his monarchical dogmas, which disregarded the means for advancing them. Was it this distinction between the modes of attaining the same end, which awakened

a congeniality with Mr. Hamilton, and an aversion to Mr. Adams?
To whichever of these causes, the exclusion of one, and the adoption of the other, as an authority, are attributed, the true principles by which One of the People is actuated, are displayed.

A deep conviction of inferiority to each of the eminent men
quoted, excludes the idea of a competition with either for publick confidence, and only admits a hope that the humiliating
acknowledgment may not weaken the principles in which those
great characters concurred. If their concurrence in asserting state
sovereignty and independence, will not outweigh a discrepance
between Mr. Madison and Mr. Hamilton, it will surely suffice to
restore liberty to reason; and the authority of Mr. Jefferson
thrown into the scale, ought at least to produce a counterpoise
in this mode of argument. It would be well if another false
weight could be as easily balanced. By not having thoroughly
discharged the meconium with which we were born, it generated an English fever, which was nearly fatal in the revolutionary struggle. It produced a plot at its termination. It preyed
inwardly on some political vitals, after the plot was suppressed.
It disclosed its malignity to republican principles in the convention. And now, weary of our refrigerating federal system,
it breaks out in the guise of a national government, invested
with a supreme concentrated authority. The patients afflicted
with this disease have all along rejected the prescriptions of
Mr. Jefferson.

The next example adduced to prove that the rights of the
states are subordinate to a national supremacy, is that of the Hartford convention.

P. 12. "Who that feels any interest in the glory of his country,
does not wish the story of the Hartford convention blotted for-

ever from her annals? Who that regards her permanent happiness, would not deprecate the recurrence of such another infamous association, as the greatest calamity that could befal her? And do we not see, almost passing before us, in this tranquil period of peace, an example of state insubordination, less glaring, but more alarming, than that to which I have just alluded?" It was impossible to select a happier example for displaying the principles of One of the People, than this of the Hartford convention; a body of men having "no inherent original political rights," as he asserts to be the case with the state governments. Yet it was not strong enough to furnish a comparison quite satisfactory. That was only an infamous association; but state insubordination is even more alarming, and therefore deserves a harsher epithet. Let us suppose that the Hartford convention had resolved "that state rulers are discordant, clamorous, and lawless; that the states had no original rights; that the state governments had no political rights, except the right of obedience; that their attempts to control officers of the general government are unbecoming and arrogant; that they were worse than infamous; that they would be aggravated if made in time of peace, and more alarming than such attempts made by the Hartford convention in time of war; that ambition is only desirous of performing admirable actions; that Congress are under no restrictions in drawing men and money from the people, except those imposed by the laws of nature; that ambition will not descend to petty larcenies for subverting liberty; that power has no allurements; that the supremacy of Great-Britain did not usurp the domestick regulation of her colonies; that despotick monarchs do not send the rays of power into some provinces, which therefore manage their internal concerns in their own way; and that subordination to the federal government, instead of rights, was reserved by the constitution to the state governments." Would this convention, in asserting that such were the true principles of the constitution, have acted with no presumption, and drawn upon themselves no odium? Had they thus anticipated One of the People, it might have furnished him either with a precedent or an admonition. As it is, a parallel between the Hartford convention and his consolidating doctrines, seems to be infinitely more proper, than one between this convention and the state governments. Its apparent intention was to destroy a federal government by centrifugal means; his, to destroy it by centripetal means; and it would require great casuistical skill to assign more censure to the design of the convention, than to his. Either project would have a tendency to enthrone the author's king "anarchy to wave his horrid sceptre over the broken altars of this happy union." The states are the altars of our federal union; break them down, and there is no union. A national government would swallow up both federal and state rights, and the whole would more probably disgorge a civil war, than either. If the success of the suspected design of the Hartford convention to impair or destroy federal powers, would have overturned the constitution, the avowed design to impair or destroy state powers by consolidating constructions, if successful, will also overturn it. The Hartford convention might be used as a good temporary warming-pan, but it is too late, after it is cold, to frighten the state governments out of their rights by beating a larum upon it, and by the noise to make them settle in the hive of consolidation.

The constitution does not say that the state governments are subordinate to the federal government; and Mr. Madison and Mr. Hamilton repeatedly deny that they are so. It does not say that these governments cannot preserve the reserved rights of the people, intrusted to their care, without committing an atrocity against a supremacy so mysterious that we know not where to find it, and more alarming and reprehensible, than the design ascribed to the Hartford convention. Most, if not all the state governments have asserted a controlling power, by attempts to check the federal government, without suspecting themselves to have been guilty of an infamous degree of arrogance. If the distinguishing feature in the constitution, preferring intelligence, weight, dignity, and an orderly resistance, to popular commotions, is lost, it will possess no superiority over the British system of government. Like that, it may be easily corrupted by a coalescence between the sympathies of ambition and avarice, collected to one centre. Some governments theoretically acknowledge the sovereignty of the people, but hang such of them as question the despotism of the government; so the consolidating school theoretically acknowledges the state rights of the people, but calls their vindication, by the only departments able to preserve them, an infamous and alarming crime. A short parody of the language applied to the states through the medium of the Hartford convention, may both qualify the censure, and illustrate the utility of state influence. Who that feels any interest in the liberty and glory of his country, does not wish the sedition law blotted from her annals? and who that regards her permanent happiness, would not deprecate the recurrence of such another act of legislation (I reject the word infamous) as a great calamity? Would it be more absurd to infer, from the passage of this law, that federal powers ought to be abolished, than to infer from the story of the Hartford convention, that state powers ought to be abolished?

Attempts to bring a government into contempt, by writing or speaking, have been punishable by all sovereignties. Such laws exist in England, and were rigorously executed during the administration of the last Pitt. Our federal sedition law punished Lyon for circulating, and Callender for writing, with that intention. A man in New-Jersey was punished for speaking irreverently of the president; and had this law then existed, the members of the Hartford convention might have been arraigned under it. If the sovereignty of South-Carolina has a law for punishing attempts by writing to render its government contemptible, the assertions "that it is ignorant, arrogant, more infamous, and as lawless, as the Hartford convention," can hardly avoid its lash.

I object to the invective mode of reasoning, though not punishable judicially, as neither calculated to disclose truth, nor to ascertain principles. It is only a repetition of the old fraud of conjuring up spectres and manufacturing miracles, to conceal imposture. The consolidating school reduces its arguments to a single syllogism: "The union is our first political blessing; the preservation of state rights will destroy the union; therefore, state rights ought to be destroyed." If this is reasoning, any addition to it is superfluous; if it is a burlesque upon the understanding of the people, it is something worse than declamatory. By reforming the syllogism, though nothing is proved, the question is left where it was. The federal republicans say, "The union is our first political blessing; it can only be preserved by preserving state rights; therefore, these rights ought to be preserved." If one side substitutes assertion for reasoning, and seizes upon the settled affection of the people for the union, to create a relish for invective; and the other proposes for their consideration the essential principle of dividing and balancing powers, as adopted by the constitution, for preserving both the union and the liberties of the people; which discloses most love for the union, or merits most distrust as to its design?

P. 16. "Suppose a state legislature should pass a law, forbidding the execution of a constitutional law of Congress. In all governments there should be a supreme power." Suppositions, like syllogisms, may prove nothing, when they may be reserved with as much force as they are urged. Suppose Congress should pass a law prohibiting the execution of a constitutional state law, or forbidding the execution of a constitutional judgment, state or federal. Or, suppose the federal court should forbid the execution of a constitutional law passed by Congress. All these suppositions only prove, that every division and balance of power must be subject to collisions, and this is no reason why they should be destroyed, or that they are unnecessary for sustaining a free form of government. If such collisions are good reasons for justifying a concentrated power, then the principle which asserts that its division alone can preserve civil liberty, is false. This supposition places the question on its true ground, namely, which is the best principle for the preservation of the rights of the people; the concentration of power in the federal department, or its division between the federal and state departments? The latter principle is founded on the supposition, that all good governments must contain collateral, balancing, and controlling departments. The constitution, by dividing powers, and declaring itself to be supreme, prohibits either the federal or state governments from usurping that character; and the powers assigned to each, to be held under its supremacy, express a prohibition against an assumption of supremacy by either over the other. It establishes a mutual and collateral tenure and fealty in both, under its own authority; and not a tenure or fealty of one, under the authority of its co-partner. When we hear the state governments reprobated in contumelious language, decried into subordinate corporations, the original rights of the people denied, and the supremacy of the constitution transferred to the federal government, although we may allow to declamation such accomplishments as may be consistent with a license so excessive, it is impossible to perceive any respect for those principles which suggested the resistance to British supremacy, and dictated the limitation and reservation established by the supremacy of the constitution. Whether there is courage or arrogance in undermining the authority of the people, exercised in the declaration of independence, the establishment of state governments, and spread upon the face of the constitution, both by dividing powers and declaring its supremacy, may depend upon success; but in that event it will soon become perfectly plain, that the attempt corresponds more intimately with the propositions in the convention to establish a monarchical or republican national government, including a suppression of state rights, and with the principles of tories and anglo-statesmen, than with those of the sages who effected our revolution, or of the people who recognised the sovereignty of the states in every act by which political power has been delegated or reserved, and by making these sovereignties the foundation of both the federal and state governments.

But no constitution, founded in the principle of dividing, limitting, balancing, and controlling power, could suffice to put an end to the natural enmity between this principle and that of concentrating power, which has appeared in all nations, under all forms of government. Accordingly their eternal warfare subsists here, as in other countries. The whole-blooded republican federalists, take one side, and the whole-blooded monarchists and consolidators, the other. A half-breed, speculating about a government half federal and half national, entertained an idea, that by splitting both the hostile principles, and gluing the two halves together by a watery precept, the moieties of these natural enemies might be changed into artificial friends. This project being too metaphysical for practical use, left the controversy undecided, and only excited the efforts of each moiety to get back to its natural associate. The didactick party do not perceive that a precept to the federal government not to invade the reserved rights of the states, is exactly equivalent to the precept solemnly preached to the states by the first confederation, requiring them to supply the federal government with money; and that if one precept could get no money, the other would secure no rights. Therefore, the natural enmity of the contrary principles, has compelled these wavering individuals to vacillate between the other two parties in pursuit of attainable ends. Those who wish for the preservation of state rights, incline towards the federal republican party, and those who wish for a national government, either monarchical or republican, incline towards the doctrine of a supremacy in the federal government over the state rights of the people. So far the two substantial parties are guided by opinion. But the struggle is never conducted upon this fair ground. That class in society which is actuated by avarice or ambition, universally becomes a zealous ally of the concentrating party, and carries with it a great accession of talents. This disadvantage was surmounted in Mr. Jefferson's election to the presidency, by the rare occurrence of a balance in mental capacity between the advocates of hostile principles, and victory of course followed the better cause; and that result affords an anticipation of what will happen, whenever the same struggle is carried on by a fair appeal to the publick understanding. The impossibility of preserving their state rights by a dormant precept, coupled with a supremacy always awake and active, will enable every impartial man of good understanding, to discriminate between the two principles of dividing and concentrating power, and to subscribe to one or the other, since, as in the convention, they will produce conflicting political parties. There the concentrating system was painted by a pencil dipped in the exigencies of the revolutionary war, with which the states were unjustly charged; now, it is painted by a pencil dipped in the hopes of avarice and ambition. Both have drawn caricatures, for the purpose of disguising truth; one, by hiding a beautiful object under hideous figures; the other, by hiding a hideous object under beautiful figures. One fair inference suggested by the contest between the federal and consolidating principles, is, that the people should require from all candidates for representation, both state and federal, an explicit avowal of their preference, that suffrages may answer the purpose they are intended to obtain.

We are in fact involved in the very struggle now going on in France. In that country, as in this, there are two parties; one labouring to sustain, and the other to destroy, the charter, retaining to the people a portion of liberty by an imperfect division of power; one for receding to the old regime, the other for keeping the ground gained by the new; one for a mutual check between political departments, the other for re-establishing the supremacy of the king. So here, the struggle is between the mutual check of the state and federal departments, and the absolute supremacy of the latter. The motives which invigorate the combatants are not to be distinguished. They are illustrated by the union of the deputies from South-Carolina in the convention, with Massachusetts, Pennsylvania, and Virginia, in favour of a supreme national government, exhibiting the curious spectacle of a symphony between the pride of aristocracy and the pride of population. The deputies of South-Carolina were willing to surrender her moral equality, but this disposition flowed from the high-toned political opinions of a predominating aristocracy, and not from a calculation of advancing her power upon the basis of her population. It is still more curious, after this aristocracy has been melting for thirty-five years; after Virginia has seen the error of sacrificing the sound principle of a division of powers between the federal and state governments, for mischievous speculations founded upon a fluctuating population; after Massachussetts has felt it; when Pennsylvania would advocate the republican equality and independence of state sovereignties; and when the comparative population of South-Carolina has diminished that a single individual of the state should be willing to overwhelm the right which gives her importance as a member of the union, in the ocean of a consolidated national government.

Whatever may be the merit of the vituperations against the state governments, the object for which this pamphlet has been exhibited, is certainly accomplished. It is used as an evidence to our rulers, state and federal, that a project for introducing a supreme consolidated national government, is actively in operation, and will draw their attention to a design so momentous. The design is proclaimed by its principles, and impressed by its examples. It is proved by the reference to the supremacies of Great-Britain, Persia, Turkey, and Russia, as symbolical of the supremacy contended for. It is proved by contending that the concentrated power constructively claimed, though it will embrace the supremacy which its types possess, will not interfere with state rights, because it will either be too ambitious or too idle to do so; and it is proved by the comparison between the states and the ten miles square, for the sake of inferring that the neglect of the district by the supreme power of Congress over it, promises a neglect of the states by a similar power, and is a sufficient surety, that they may still manage their local affairs in their own way.

Other Consolidating Doctrines

The newspapers have also abounded with opinions in favour of a supreme national government, and though it is probable that several ingenious writers will be surprised to find themselves identified with the doctrines of One of the People, they must discern, upon reflection, that their separate constructions of particular words and phrases extracted from the constitution, unchastened by the tenour and intention of the whole instrument, inevitably lead to the same conclusion. I shall notice a few, to prove further that a consolidating project exists, and to illustrate the incorrectness of this mode of construction. It has been said that the single word constitution contains innate powers, and implies sovereignty or supremacy in the federal government. Johnson expounds confederacy by the word union, and the constitution expounds itself by the same word. It is an instrument for uniting any nine of specified states, and not for constituting a government for a consolidated nation. Its provisions are so many recognitions of its federal character. If the word implies sovereignty or supremacy, it also conveys these attributes to the government of each state, and destroys the sovereignty of the people. Both the state and federal governments having been created by instruments thus denominated, whatever powers the word can convey, would be received by both, and the equality of the inferences would of course have the effect of a counterpoise between them. If it conveys an implied power sufficient to release the federal government from restrictions, the same implied power must release the state governments from them. Congress is compellable by state legislatures to call a convention, and every alteration of the constitution must be ratified by three-fourths of the states. If the word constitution had implied a national government, not a convention of states, but a national convention would have been provided for; and amendments would have been final, and not liable to be rejected by a minority of states. The force annexed to the word constitution, is borrowed from the word national, which is not in the instrument; but the difference between a national constitution, to be made and altered by a nation, and a federal constitution, made by a convention of states, ratified by conventions of states, and only capable of being altered by three-fourths of the states, proves that this supposed invisibility is like those which induced Charles the First, rather to part with his head, than with his political prepossessions.

The ideas that we have not an aggregate nation, and yet that we have a national government, reverse political order, and subvert national authority. An aggregate nation did not make a constitution, but the word constitution is supposed to have made an aggregate nation; states enter into a federal compact, and a federal compact creates a national government. The house of representatives derives no power from a consolidated nation, if the word constitution did not create one, and the whole process for effecting and sustaining the union of states, plainly denies the existence of an American nation. In fact, this house, though elected by the people of each state, only receives limited powers from the constitution itself. The modes of designating the individuals by whom federal powers were to be exercised, extend both to the state and federal governments. If the mode of designating state individuals and state governments to exercise some federal powers, was not intended to create a national government, a mode of designating the members of the house of representatives to exercise other federal powers, could not have been intended to produce a consequence so unexpected. It would be as correct to infer a national government from the fact, that the constitution has given federal powers to the state governments, as from the fact, that it has given federal powers to Congress. It is said to have created a nation, by delegating a limited power over individuals. If delegated powers, restricted to specified objects, can make a nation, the articles of war for giving very extensive powers over individuals, would consolidate an army into a nation, and it has often made itself formidable by usurping supreme power. If we relinquish the rigid federal character of the constitution, and admit that the government may be made national, either by the word constitution, by the mode of appointing its officers, or by the limited powers with which these officers and the state governments are intrusted for its execution, arguments may be drawn from the same sources, to prove that our government is of any kind, which a political party may think necessary for advancing its designs, or gratifying its prepossessions. The doctrine, that limited can create unlimited powers, and even make a nation, is as able to establish a monarchy, as a national government of any other complexion. All our elections are in different degrees federal, as state governments are to exercise sundry important federal functions, and the representative character of these state federal functionaries, would be as good an argument for converting the federal into a national government, as the representative character of any others.

Many expressions in the constitution prove that its name did not imply a national government, nor convey any power. Under such a construction, its whole tenour would be absurd, and all its limitations useless. "The president shall, from time to time, give to Congress information as to the *state of the union.*" Why not as to the state of the nation? Because there was no nation, the state of which was subjected to the legislative power of Congress. Thirteen political individuals, being sensible that a mutual interest invited them to unite for special purposes, long acted in concord without any positive compact; and discerning the mutual benefits resulting from this tacit alliance, at length entered into a written one. This, as a first experiment, having proved defective, was exchanged for another more perfect. To effect its object, the president, as the officer best informed of foreign relations, is required to communicate his knowledge to Congress, concerning the interest delegated to their care; and not concerning the interests of a consolidated nation, because no such community existed. The individual states are named, both in the title and body of the constitution, as parties to the union, showing that the word constitution was used to describe a union of states, and not a union of individual men; and this intention is demonstrated by the circumstance, that those states only which should accede to the compact were to be bound by it, because in a constitution formed by individual men composing one nation, a minority cannot reject it, and remain disunited from the majority.

Many different words have been used to express a compact between independent states, such as Helvetic body, diet, and holy alliance. The Swiss association was entered into by "united cantons," and the Dutch by "united provinces." These precedents of federal compacts between sovereign states, use the word

united, in the sense in which it is used by the constitution; and
the words cantons and provinces less conclusively convey the
idea of independent sovereignties able to form a league, than
the word states. Yet it was never contended that these cantons
or provinces were subordinate to a tacit supremacy in their federal governments, emanating from the mode in which their
deputies were appointed, or from the limited powers over individuals, with which they were invested. On the contrary, sundry
rights were reserved by the Swiss cantons and Dutch provinces,
beyond the control of their federal governments; such as different religions, a right to form partial leagues with each other,
and the powers of local government, in the case of the cantons;
and a power in one province to defeat a treaty, in the case of the
Dutch. Under such trammels these federal compacts flourished
more than the neighbouring consolidated governments, and
therefore it is probable that our more perfect federal compact
will experience still greater prosperity, from a better distribution
of local and federal powers, if the division is not defeated by a
concentrating supremacy.

The guarantee of a republican form of government by all the
states to each state, has also been supposed to confer some indis-
tinct and unlimited national supremacy upon the federal government; but this guarantee itself affords arguments subversive
of the inference. It expresses a particular duty, and cannot therefore convey powers, especially such as would defeat the end it
expresses. It was intended to secure the independence of each
state, and not to subject each to a majority of all. Like a mutual
territorial guarantee between several kingdoms, it imposes an
obligation, but does not invest the parties to the guarantee with a
power of diminishing the territory, or other rights of one king-

dom.The word republican includes a right in the people of each state to form their own government; and reserves whatever other rights may be necessary to the exercise of this cardinal right. The right of the people in each state to create, and to influence their government, is the essential principle of a republican form of government, and therefore the guarantee could not have been intended as a means for destroying the essence of a republican form of government, by subjecting the people of every state to the arbitrary will of a federal majority, or to a majority of the supreme court. The word republican includes both the rights of the states and those of the people. The states united to preserve their republican equality among themselves, and also the individual republican rights of the people. Can it be a question what these are, when it is considered that the people of each state created a government, that conventions of each state ratified the constitution framed by a convention of states, and that this constitution can only be amended by states? These acts define the meaning of the word republican, in respect both in the people and the states; but all these definitions would be defeated, if the guarantee can be made to invest the federal government or the federal court with a supremacy over these state and popular rights, necessary to create and maintain a republican form of government. Self government is its end, and this can only be effected by a complete capacity in the people, through the instrumentality of election, both to form and to influence a government; but a supremacy over this capacity, destroys that, without which the species of republican government intended by the constitution, cannot exist. How can the states, or the people of the states, be said to possess the right of self-government, if either the forms of state governments or the reserved local powers, are subjected to a supremacy constituting no portion of the people of the states, nor exposed to their control? When the right of self-government is superseded, no republican rights will remain, because all proceed from it, and the guarantee would have no republican form of government to secure.

The terms of the guarantee in other views demolish the doctrines of a union between individuals constituting an American nation, and of recondite powers in the word constitution. "The United States shall guarantee to *every state in this union.*" Thus it is positively asserted, that our union is a union of states, and not of individuals, and that it is a guarantee by states to states, and not of an American nation to states. The sovereignty of states is necessary, both to undertake and to require the fulfilment of the guarantee. Corporations could do neither. Had the attempt in the convention to establish a national government succeeded, the recognition contained in the mutual guarantee, that the union was a union of independent states, could not have been consistently introduced into the constitution.

This guarantee ought to be considered in another very important light. Is the supreme court of the United States invested with a power of supervising and enforcing it? The question must be answered affirmatively, if this court can abridge or measure the rights of the states. A republican form of state government can only be constituted by rights. Are these rights guaranteed to the states by each other, or by the federal court? Had Mr. Madison and Mr. Hamilton adverted to this guarantee, when they were discussing the question, whether the court or Congress possessed the supremacy contended for, over the state governments, it would have furnished them with some lights towards its decision. As it is a guarantee by states to states, Mr. Madison must have proved that the court, and Mr. Hamilton that Congress, was the United States, to have invested either with a power of abridging (if a guarantee possesses this power) these republican rights. It seems to be a plain matter of fact, whether the court, or Congress, or the states themselves, are considered by the constitution as the guardian of state rights. It contains two positive stipulations for the preservation of state rights, or a republican form of government; their reservation, and a guarantee of this reservation. Neither Congress nor the federal judiciary is mentioned in either. Had the powers of either department embraced a right to regulate the division of power between the federal and state governments, this could not have happened. To counteract the ambition of usurpation, and the ingenuity of construction, the positive division of power is protected by the solemn compact of a mutual guarantee between the states themselves. This compact extends to all the rights, only to be secured by a republican form of government, and includes constructive alterations of the constitution, by which these rights may be abridged, without the concurrence of the parties to the guarantee. The federal judiciary does not contract with each state to preserve its republican form of government; and if it obtains a power to regulate those rights by which this form is constituted, it may destroy the republican forms of state governments, without violating an engagement. This consideration discloses the wide difference between the guarantee expressed, and the constructive guarantee usurped. The first does not comprise a power of taking from the states their republican rights; the other does. The federal court, by seizing upon the guarantee, and transforming it from a duty to preserve the republican rights of the states, into a power of abridging them, has claimed a supremacy over this compact,

without being even a party to it. The supremacy claimed for
Congress, is also extracted from the guarantee usurped by the
court, by confounding the words United States and Congress,
as of the same import. But the constitution plainly distinguishes
between them. The United States, and not Congress, are invested
with the powers of appointing the members of the three great
departments of the federal government, and of amending the
constitution. Specified powers are given to each federal department, repeatedly distinguishing between them all and the United
States, the donors. The members of Congress are to be paid out
of a treasury of the United States. Had this treasury been a property and not a trust in Congress, there would have been no occasion for adding this item to the other demands, to which the
property of the United States was subjected, because it was not
the property of Congress. The citizens of each state shall be citizens in the several states, excluding the idea that Congress, as
being the United States, might grant this mutual citizenship;
and acknowledging state sovereignties by acknowledging state
citizenship. A criminal fleeing from justice shall be removed to
the state having jurisdiction of the crime. If Congress or the
court are to be considered as the United States, yet the exclusive jurisdiction of each state is here acknowledged. Treason
against the United States is specified by the act of the states, and
its punishment only intrusted to Congress. Can Congress, as
being the United States, extend or abridge this crime? If not, it
cannot extend any other delegated power, or abridge any
reserved power upon the same ground. But a majority of the
United States themselves can do neither, and a majority of Congress, even if it is the United States, can have no greater power
than a majority of the states. Neither of these majorities were

invested by the guarantee with a power of transforming our federal system into a supreme consolidated government; and no
powers or duties assigned to the United States, were intended
to have the effect of enabling either a majority of states or of
Congress, to subvert the rights of the states, which the guarantee was intended to prevent.

The prohibitions upon the states, and the powers delegated
to the federal government, comprise the intire mass of materials
from which a subordination of the former, and a supremacy of
the latter, are attempted to be extracted. For this purpose, the
prohibitions have been considered as proofs of inferiority, stated
to exemplify a general subordination; and the delegated powers
as proofs, stated to exemplify a general supremacy. Thus, restrictions are converted into enlargements, and exceptions into a general rule. By this inverted mode of reasoning, the veto of
Congress is extended immeasurably beyond the cases to which it
is limited. Suppose the powers reserved to the state governments
had been defined and limited, like those delegated to the federal
government. As both governments are subjected to prohibitions,
neither could have advanced a plea for supremacy, which the
other could not have alleged. And is not such the fact, since
reserved powers are at least equal to delegated powers? How does
the federal government endeavour to prove its supremacy? By
delegations and prohibitions. Have not the state governments the
same proofs? Both governments are fiduciaries, and their delegations and prohibitions proceed from the same authority. Not
the weight of a trust, but the authority of the donor, decides the
power of the trustee; and a great trust derives no right from its
size, to usurp a small one. Therefore distinct delegations and prohibitions could not have been considered as investing one class of

these delegations and prohibitions with a supremacy over the other, but as exceptions to the general principle of state sovereignty, which remained unimpaired, so far as these exceptions did not extend. The question must be decided by one of these modes of reasoning; and the delegations and prohibitions quoted as selections most favourable to the doctrine of a federal supremacy, will suffice to prove whether one class of special delegations and prohibitions possesses a supremacy over the other, or whether one distinct trustee is impliedly subordinate to another, each being subjected to limitations and prohibitions, imposed by the same authority. The Congress under the first confederation was invested with great trusts, but their magnitude did not absorb powers not delegated.

There must have been some general principle, to which these special delegations, reservations, and prohibitions, referred, because if none existed, and the constitution had created a supreme power, able to prohibit the states from exercising rights not prohibited, and to allow the federal government to exercise rights not delegated, both delegations and prohibitions would have been useless and absurd; and therefore the existence of such a principle can alone make either substantial. A previous principle must be admitted, to sustain both exceptions and delegations. None can be found, except a sovereignty able to bestow power, and to impose limitations. To evade an argument so conclusive, recourse is had, first to the acknowledged sovereignty of the people, and secondly to a fabulous consolidated American nation; and the fable is made to supplant the fact. The fact is, that the people and the states are one and the same; but the fable supposes that the states are distinguishable from the people, not to sustain, but to destroy the principle, to which all our delega-

tions, reservations, and prohibitions of power, refer. When we
speak of Pennsylvanians or Virginians, it would be absurd, if these
people had not constituted themselves into states. The state of
Pennsylvania means the people of Pennsylvania. The constitution, by reserving powers to the states or to the people, recognises
the words states and people, as perfectly equivalent, and does
not intend to express the absurd idea, that either A or B shall
exercise powers, without defining which shall do so. The word
or, is used to connect repetitions, and not to express a contrariety. Admitting the latter to be the idea intended to be expressed,
yet the states, whatever they may be, may exercise the same powers with the people. That they are, however, the same with the
people, results from the recollection that the state governments
are not the states. They are instruments used by the states or the
people, for exercising the powers reserved to them. The ingenuity of dividing states from the people, consists in this. A sovereignty of the people may be acknowledged as resting in an
American nation, to which the delegations, reservations, and prohibitions, of the constitution, have no reference, as all are exceptions referring to state sovereignties, and none of course can
operate as exceptions to the fabulous national sovereignty. If,
therefore, the federal government can acquire a sovereignty over
the sovereignties referred to by the constitution, as being the representative of a great fabulous nation, none of these delegations,
reservations, and prohibitions, can balance, check, or control its
power. And in this way an acknowledgment of the sovereignty of
the people is made to destroy their sovereignty, by subverting
the original principle to which the delegations, reservations,
and prohibitions of the constitution refer.

Why are the states prohibited from taxing imports and
exports? Because it was a right included by the established prin-

ciple of state sovereignty, which right the states consented to relinquish. Why was the consent of Congress required to state laws in relation to duties, keeping troops in time of peace, or entering into compacts? Because these also were rights included in the principle of state sovereignty, subjected to a limited federal control. Had a national sovereignty existed, that would have possessed a general control over the state sovereignties, of which these subordinate sovereignties could not deprive it, by limited exceptions in favour of a federal department. Two of these sovereign state rights, of the highest order, those of keeping armies and engaging in war under certain circumstances, are retained by the states, for the purpose of self-defence. The consent of Congress to particular state acts would not have been required, if a federal or national supremacy over any other state acts existed; and the sovereign state right of self-defence, would not have been retained by subordinate corporations. The specification of particular cases, in which the consent of Congress is required, admits an independent power in state legislation, as in those cases in which the consent of Congress is not required. The concurrent powers of the state and federal governments, to tax, and to defend themselves, are happily contrived for sustaining the mutual independence and control between these primary divisions of power; and if one could impose on the other a subordination in either of these powers, it would very soon absorb all the rest. If it is admitted that the federal government possesses no supremacy over the two reserved state rights of taxation and self-defence, it follows that all other reserved state rights are held independently of any federal supremacy. If these two rights are incidents of an original state sovereignty, all the other reserved rights must originate from the same source. The states have retained a right to defend themselves, if invaded by a federal army, because the constitution was not to be construed by force, but by the mutual control, and if that failed, by three-fourths of the states themselves.

These two rights of taxation and self-defence, without which the other reserved rights are nothing, are assailed by precedents and supremacy. Not the consent of the federal court, but the consent of Congress, is required in a few specified cases relating to these rights, leaving their exercise in all other cases, unexposed to any federal dissent. The supreme court, however, claims a veto upon state laws, whether subjected or unsubjected to the veto of Congress; and assumes both the special veto exclusively intrusted to Congress, and also a general veto, withheld even from the representatives of the states. By constructively substituting the general veto proposed in the convention, for the special veto bestowed by the constitution, it is substituting a national for a federal government. Congress could not say that state laws for taxing banks or prohibiting lotteries, were void for want of its consent; but the court steps in and extends the limited veto of Congress to every state law which may obstruct a federal law, although no such veto is bestowed upon Congress. The consent of Congress to state laws prohibiting banks or lotteries, is not required by the constitution, but is required by the court. Had Congress, in its bank and lottery laws, declared that the states might tax or prohibit these internal projects, the court could have had no ground for nullifying them; and as no such consent is required by the constitution, its being gives or withheld cannot alter the right of the state, or the jurisdiction of the court. Some state right to legislate independently of a federal veto, evidently results from the specification of cases to which this veto should extend; but according to precedents, there is no such right. The constitution declares that the consent of Congress shall only be necessary, to give validity to a few specified state laws, and that the republican forms of state governments shall be guaranteed by the states themselves. The precedents assert, that the dissent of the court may defeat any state laws, and that the court may control the republican rights of the states. These powers, exposed to no limitation, and capable of being perpetually increased by precedents, are not given to the federal government, and are deduced from constructions inconsistent both with the prohibitions and guarantee. They are extracted from a new species of political regeneration, supposed to have sanctified the federal, but not the state judicial power, against sin, and to endow it with the supremacy due to perfection. But however respectable may be the claim of virtue to absolute power, yet as it is not inheritable, the existing great qualities of the court, though united to the patriotism of Congress, will not remove the objections to a supreme concentrated government. Congress, by extending the jurisdiction of the court, and the court by extending the legislative power of Congress, might rapidly effect a revolution, without the consent of the authority by which the constitution was established. It is impossible to believe that the states intended, by the limitations and prohibitions of the constitution, to invest the whole or any portion of the federal government, with an unlimited veto over their laws, or an exclusive guarantee of their republican forms of government; and we must either convict them of stupidity or gross inconsistencies, to find the constructive consolidated government, which the legislative and judicial federal supremacies contended for, would infallibly establish. These arguments apply to all other limitations and prohibitions of the constitution, as well as to those quoted. As to all we must admit that legislative and judicial power are correlatives, and that the latter cannot outrun its ally in the race for power; or that the constitution, whilst cautiously prescribing limits to the federal legislature, intended that the federal judiciary should be unrestrained. If the limitations imposed upon the federal legislature do not extend to the federal judiciary, the federal would cease to be a limited government, because one department may dissolve the restrictions imposed upon the other, against which its dependency and subordination would be no security. If the judicial veto does not stop where the legislative veto stops, the federal cannot be a limited government. Was the legislative federal veto limited, to bestow an unlimited veto upon the court, or to secure to the states some independent right of legislation? Was the guarantee intended to preserve republican governments, or to create a judicial sovereignty? These questions must be answered in one way by those who believe that the delegations, reservations, prohibitions, and guarantee, all imply a general principle; that this principle can be no other than state sovereignty and independence; and that all the attributes of this principle remain, except those expressly prohibited to the states. It is said that they have been surrendered to the finer principle, that judicial power is a political mint, which coins human nature without any alloy.

It has been most strenuously contended, by all those who affect to consider the union as an association of individuals, that independent state rights are incompatible with it. This is both true, and an avowal of the design to establish a supreme consolidated government. But if the union is an association of states, and not of individuals, it is also true that the destruction of these rights by a constructive or a fabulous supremacy, would be also incompatible with a federal government. The word union is used like the word infidelity, by the disciples of a consolidated national form of government. Infidelity, as an object of general abhorrence, is often alleged by one creed or dogma against another, not for the sake of finding truth, but for that of using a publick prepossession to hide error, ambition, avarice, or pride. It vociferates, "Your faith is not my faith, and therefore you are an infidel." Thus the consolidating says to the federal doctrine, "Your union is not my union, and therefore you mean to destroy the union;" using the general enmity against its subversion, as religious politicians use the word infidelity. But if the union is a compact of states, and not of a consolidated American nation, our love for it must be an ally, not of a national, but of a federal form of government.

Hitherto my efforts have been chiefly directed towards the principles by which the constitution ought to be construed, and to the establishment of the fact, that from the commencement of our revolution, down to this day, a succession of eminent men have uniformly disapproved of the union of states, and endeavoured to introduce a consolidated government, invested with supreme power. Whether these efforts have failed or succeeded, is submitted to the reader.

A Federal and National Form
of Government Compared

T he great question, whether a federal or a national system of government will best secure the liberty and happiness of the people, remains to be more fully considered; and though it must be referred to the better understandings which abound in our country, yet a few observations will be hazarded as to this point, in addition to those unavoidably mingled with the subjects we have passed over.

Liberty and power are adverse pleaders, and the arguments or temptations offered by both, have never failed to make proselytes. Between the tyranny of concentrated power, and of unbridled licentiousness, is a space filled with materials for computing the effects produced by controlling both extremes, and estimating the chances for promoting human liberty and happiness. It seems to be nature's law, that every species of concentrated sovereignty over extensive territories, whether monarchical, aristocratical, democratical, or mixed, must be despotick. In no case has a concentrated power over great territories been sustained, except by mercenary armies; and wherever power is thus sustained, despotism is the consequence. It was in accordance with this natural law, that Catharine of Russia published her manifesto, affording the following extracts: "The sovereign of the Russian empire is absolute; for no other than an authority concentrated in his person alone, can adequately operate through the extent of so large an empire. An extensive empire presupposes an unlimited power in the person who governs it. The celerity of decision in matters that are brought from distant places, must compensate the tardiness that arises from that remoteness. Any other government would not only be prejudicial to Russia, but even at length be the cause of its total ruin. Another reason is, because it is better to obey the laws under one ruler, than to conform to the will of many. The object and end of an unlimited government, is to direct the actions of mankind to the glory of the citizen, of the state, and of the sovereign. This glory in such states, bursts forth in such great actions as are able, in the very same proportion, to promote the happiness of the subjects, as liberty itself." Catharine insists on the necessity of a concentrated supremacy over extensive territories, and uses the arguments of our consolidating politicians, not forgetting to urge that ambition, from its love of glory, is equal to liberty. She asserts, in concurrence with history, that absolute power is necessary to govern an extensive territory. Between this conclusion, dictated by the laws of nature, and a territorial division of powers, lies our alternative. The geography of our country and the character of our people, unite to demonstrate that the ignorance and partiality of a concentrated form of government, can only be enforced by armies; and the peculiar ability of the states to resist, promises that resistance would be violent; so that a national government must either be precarious or despotick. By dividing power between the federal and state governments, local partialities and oppressions, the common causes of revolution, are obliterated from our system.

This division is contrived, not only for avoiding such domestick evils, but also for securing the United States against foreign aggression. For the attainment of both ends, it was equally necessary to bestow certain powers on a federal government, and reserve others to the state governments. The two intentions point forcibly towards a genuine construction of the constitution, and the theory is defended by the only principle capable of securing civil liberty. Communities possessed of sufficient knowledge to discriminate between liberty and slavery, have uniformly laboured to invest governments with a portion of power sufficient to secure social happiness, but insufficient for its destruction. The United States understood the discrimination, and in the formation of the federal government endeavoured, by limitations and prohibitions, to reserve and secure as many of their individual rights as might be retained without defeating the end of providing for their common interest. The two principles of a division or a concentration of power, are the adversaries contending for preference. Every government must be of one or the other description. An absolute supremacy in one, belongs to the concentrating principle, like an absolute supremacy in one man. Hence it has happened that an aristocratical or representative body of men, exercising supreme power, has been as tyrannical, or more so, than a single despot. The United States saw that any geographical interest, if invested with supremacy by the establishment of a consolidated national government, would oppress some other geographical interest; and made a new effort to avoid this natural malignity of a concentrated supreme power, though lodged in the representatives of the people. The ingenious effort of the English form of government, extended only to the contrary interests of classes of men, and has no reference to the contrary local interests of states. However sufficient it might be for effecting the end meditated, it would be insufficient for effecting an end totally different. States cannot mingle like men,

nor change their climates, as men do their principles, to reap
the partialities of a concentrated supremacy. If, therefore, the
English system had so far prevented a concentrated supremacy,
arising from a coalescence of king, lords, and commons, as to
secure equal justice to individual men, it does not follow that a
concentrated supremacy in the federal government would prevent a coalescence between geographical representatives, and
secure equal justice to individual states. The case of Ireland
demonstrates that representation and supremacy united, will not
administer geographical justice. Accident sometimes directs us
to valuable discoveries; but though our division into states,
induced us to consider the hostile principles of power concentrated or divided, in a geographical light, yet our decision was
rather the result of an improvement in political knowledge,
matured by reflection and experience, than casual. The disquisi-
tions produced in resisting the supremacy of the British parliament, had shed volumes of light upon the subject; the people had
imbibed convictions from critical examinations of history and
of moral rights; and a profound consideration was bestowed
upon the rival principles in the convention. If it is yet doubtful
which is best, it cannot be denied that the people have constantly
considered them as distinct, and unexceptionably expressed their
preference. To deprive them of their choice by construction,
would be the same species of dexterity by which the elements
of the eucharist are endeavoured to be transubtantiated into
substances totally different.

It is as impossible that politicians can extend the intellectual
powers of men beyond their natural limits, as that priests can turn
bread and wine into flesh and blood. The incapacity of one mind
for securing the liberty and happiness of an extensive country,

dictates the wisdom of dividing power; and the same natural incapacity in the representatives of one state to provide for the local good government of another, more forcibly dictated the internal independency of each. A division of mechanical labour is so highly valuable, that even a pin can be better made by many workmen than by one. In like manner it is at length happily discovered, that a division of intellectual labours is equally necessary for the construction of the most perfect form of government. It would have been more preposterous to expect that the representatives of Massachusetts could provide for the prosperity of Louisiana, than that we might get to the moon in a balloon. The human mind can only act judiciously within the scope of its intelligence. Accordingly, those powers only are intrusted to the federal government, as to which the intelligence and interest of the states are the same; and those are withheld, as to which the similarity between the intelligence and interest of the states fail. A uniformity in the operation of federal laws throughout the states, is required to prevent these wise precautions from being defeated. This uniformity illustrates the independency of local rights, because if these were liable to be regulated by federal laws, great inequalities would have ensued. The interest of one state is embraced by the intellectual powers of representatives chosen by counties, because the counties have a common interest, just as the intellectual powers of members of Congress will reach the common interests of the United States; but there would be no difference between requiring the county representatives of Virginia to regulate the local affairs of Massachusetts, and requiring the representatives from Virginia in Congress, to do the same thing. Why would the first mode of governing Massachusetts be tyrannical and absurd? Because neither the sympathies nor intellectual powers of a resident in Virginia; are adequate to the local government of Massachusetts. Are they rendered more adequate if he is chosen by the whole state, or by a district of it, instead of being chosen by a county? Will the mode of appointment revoke the laws of nature? A conviction that this could not happen, suggested the division of powers between the state and federal governments, as being a preference of knowledge to ignorance. To expect from ignorance or an adverse interest, the fruits of knowledge and a common interest, would have been unnatural. Calamities or blessings are their respective consequences. Our system, therefore, draws upon federal knowledge and sympathy for federal prosperity, and upon state knowledge and sympathy for local prosperity. By reversing its draughts in either case, they would either be protested, or paid in very bad paper.

Against this beautiful theory, an appetite for power in all ages, urges the same objection. It uniformly asserts that divisions of power obstruct, paralyze, or defeat, the splendid actions to be expected from a concentrated supremacy. Before this argument can have any force, it ought to be settled, whether the achievements of concentrated power are good or bad things; since, according to the determination of this fact, the argument becomes an objection to the principle of dividing power, or its recommendation. Will this principle defeat most good or bad measures? Its value should be ascertained, not by a partial exhibition of the good measures it may have obstructed, but by its general tendency to prevent oppression. The fact, that mankind have suffered the sorest evils from a supreme concentrated power, is undoubtedly well established; and it is equally a fact, that no remedy against these universal calamities, has ever been suggested, except divisions of power. All writers in favour of a free government, have opposed this, as a good principle, against concentrated power, as a bad one; and although exceptions to its good effects do occasionally occur, as well as exceptions to the bad effects of a concentrated power, yet these exceptions do not constitute the general character of either principle.

The evil effects resulting from a division of a large country into baronial, or other personal sovereignties, cannot be justly urged as objections to our state sovereignties, because the former were only divisions of territory, subjected to the bad principle of a concentrated political power, and not moral divisions of power itself. Personal ambition and avarice were still the supremacy by which each division was governed. When the baronial supremacies of France were swallowed up by a monarchical supremacy, though the people of the whole country were consolidated into one nation, tyranny and oppression still remained; because it was only a transition from one species of concentrated power to another, neither being exposed to a sufficient moral limitation or control. Germany still suffers under concentrated powers of both descriptions. In Britain, the division into departments has a reference to classes of men only, as in France formerly, and in Germany, to territorial lines, and therefore it has not prevented the establishment of a supreme concentrated power, nor removed its malevolence to human happiness. In all these countries, liberty is of course dealt out to the people by mercenary armies. Ireland, though represented in both houses of the British congress, is a standing memorial of the fate to be expected by geographical sections from a concentrated supremacy lodged in men, the majority of whom are ignorant of local wants, and not participating in local evils.

The antiquated doctrine of the divinity of kings was the only remedy able to shield concentrated power against the resentments inspired by its tyranny, until standing armies were thought of, because mankind had discovered no medium between the dissolution of society, and investing despotism with a sacred supremacy. Tyrants were thought better than savages. The supposed necessity for one of these extremities, generated the nice question, how far the evil of tyranny should be endured, before the remedies of insurrection or assassination were applied. Representation was the first attempt to get rid of this alternative; but it has been rendered an incomplete remedy, by coupling it with a supreme concentrated power. The United States dissolved this infectious association, by uniting a division of state and federal powers with representation, as a mode of enforcing upon governors the admirable discovery of constitutional laws. These, intrusted to a concentrated power, have uniformly became a dead letter; but a reasonable hope was inspired that they might experience a better fate, under the mutual control against their violation, deposited in the state and federal governments, so confidently relied upon by the Federalist. The intervention of the state governments between the people and the federal government, seemed to be a better security against the effects of a concentrated power, than the boasted intervention of a king between lords and commons, and less capable of a nefarious coalescence to gratify a mutual passion for money and power.

But concentrated power is ever active and ingenious in repairing its defeats, and inventing new expedients for the gratification of its propensities. When its divinity was exploded, it resorted to armies, as an effectual mode of destroying the control of election. The United States, sensible that it would proceed in the use of its customary expedient, should it be established, would not establish it at all, and it now discloses its hatred against the division of power invented to keep it down, as it formerly did against the detection of its usurped divinity. It proposes that we should renounce our progress in political science, recede by the road of construction, dissolve our new and soundest division of power, and revive a concentrated supremacy, which will ultimately maintain itself by a standing army. It would be better and cheaper for the people to restore to concentrated power its ancient supremacy, sustained by the doctrine of its divinity, than to establish a concentrated supremacy, sustained by the new expedient of standing armies. The representation in Congress being extremely deficient in the two qualities of local knowledge and sympathy, a federal concentrated supremacy, instead of sustaining our constitutional laws, must itself be sustained by force; and this force would certainly be applied to the compulsory exercise of every power it might covet. The revival of the divinity of concentrated power may delay a recourse to mercenary armies, so long as a court of law and equity can persuade those who hold the purse and the sword, that it is better entitled to this high distinction than themselves; but this reprieve would be of very short duration.

Let us now turn our eyes towards the state sovereignties, and consider whether they are like baronial, or other concentrated supremacies, universally hostile to liberty. State governments are confined to local objects, as the powers of an individual as to his own domicil. They are excluded from declaring war, from keeping armies in time of peace, and from entering into foreign treaties or internal confederacies. They are restrained both by the principle of division, and by their responsibility to the people. They are checked by the federal government, as the federal government is by them. They are controllable by three-fourths of the states. The principles of division and control are applied extensively to the state governments, whereas they are not applied at all, or ineffectually applied, to the concentrated baronial, monarchical, or mixed governments of Europe. This difference accounts for the exclusive blessings we have reaped from our modes of dividing and controlling power. If we should exchange them for a concentrated supremacy in the federal government, the internal divisions of the state governments would be rendered useless, and state elections for controlling state departments, would dwindle into an idle ceremony. The European supremacies possess no principles sufficient to secure the liberty and happiness of the people, and are naturally guided by the worst passions; the states have united, not to awaken these bad passions by creating a concentrated supremacy, but to secure the liberty and happiness of the people, or the most holy interests of mankind. Are the people of each state, or a supreme power in Congress, or a federal court, best qualified to judge of and to foster their local interests?

The objection, that the state governments may obstruct federal measures, unless they are subordinate to some federal supremacy, is only equivalent to the objection, that the federal government may obstruct state measures, unless it is subordinate to a state supremacy. Neither objection affects the argument, if the constitution intended to confide both state and federal measures to a representation of a mutual and common interest in each separate case. Such objections are urged against all divisions of power. Limited kings complain that their measures are obstructed by the departments created to obstruct them. Reason, compact, and a common interest, and not a supreme power, are the only resources for settling such collisions, compatible with a division of power. These umpires have inspired the king, lords, and commons, of Britain, with a mutual moderation towards each other. If the preservation of the rights of free states and free men, cannot inspire the state and federal governments with mutual moderation, it will unfortunately prove that the children of mammon are wiser than the children of liberty. If the common interest of the states to preserve the federal government, will not be regarded, a government by force must succeed, and all our social improvements founded upon a common interest, will be lost. But have not the states as strong and better motives for nourishing their federal, as well as local prosperity, than the king, lords, and commons of England have for nourishing their concentrated supremacy? What checks against tyranny can be devised, if those founded in a common interest are unsuccessful? and can they be unsuccessful, except by exchanging them for a concentrated supremacy?

Society, well constructed, must be compounded of restraint and freedom, and this was carefully attended to in framing our union. The states are restrained from doing some things, and left free to do others; and the federal government was made free to do some things, but restrained from doing others. This arrangement cannot be violated, without making one department a slave or an usurper. A division of political rights between the people and a government, can only preserve individual liberty. In like manner the liberty of the states cannot exist, except by a division of rights between these political individuals and the federal government. The rights of whole states may at least be as necessary to the happiness of mankind, as the rights of an individual. Freedom without restraint, or restraint without freedom, is either anarchy or despotism. The states did not design to avoid both, by placing around their necks a halter, called a national or a judicial supremacy, capable of being tightened or relaxed; or used to inflict upon them the suffocation proposed in the convention. A concentrated power destroys the counterpoise between freedom and restraint, and never fails to become the executioner of human happiness. The constitution, with consummate wisdom, has effected this counterpoise, and also provided against foreign and state collisions, without sacrificing state prosperity. It did not design to embitter the best fruits of government, by tacitly creating a concentrated supremacy.

Though mathematical certainty may not be attainable by the science of politicks, because the human mind cannot be delineated by a diagram, yet much truth may be found in the solutions of historical facts. These prove that every body of men invested with supreme power, whether collected together by the single principle of representation, or by the mixed principles of monarchy, aristocracy, and demoracy, is influenced by a secret or an avowed spirit of avarice and ambition. They demonstrate the propensity of men to combine for bad as well as good ends. In our federal combination, the difficulty was to give efficacy to the good, and to expel the bad motives, leading men to combine or unite. Various divisions and balances of power had been previously tried, but all of them had been ineffectual for producing both ends. The English experiment, though fraught with useful hints, had demonstrated a necessity for further efforts. We availed ourselves of its hints, and were warned by its insufficiency to produce a mild and just government, to reject its monarchy and aristocracy, and also its concentration of supreme power in men assembled at one place; because they would be induced by the bad propensities of human nature, to combine for bad purposes. Instead of this English supremacy, which was unable to prevent such combinations, and has fed avarice and ambition at the expense of the people, the constitution most wisely availed itself of the good motives which induce men to combine, by making the interest of the states the basis of the union of states, and the interest of individuals the basis of state rights; by dividing instead of concentrating supremacy. By reinstating a concentrated supremacy, we should exchange the natural propensity of the states to combine for their common benefit, for a natural propensity to combine, from the motives of avarice and ambition; and the constant succession of these ravenous combinations, would probably be more mischievous to the people, than the less changeable combination produced by the supremacy of the king, lords, and commons of England. The representation in Congress would be better calculated to awaken than to suppress the bad motives of combination, if it should obtain supreme power. An imperfect local knowledge and interest, and a new supremacy every two years, would then expose it to more temptations than the British parliament can resist, because our local sympathies lie wider apart than in England; and would suggest the maxim of making hay whilst the sun shines; which can only be rendered innocent, by withholding from Congress a supreme power to gather any crop at all from local rights. In England, combinations between privileged orders were to be guarded against; here, geographical combinations were far more dangerous. If in England, representation, united with a concentrated supremacy, though assisted by a sympathy infinitely more perfect, fosters instead of checking wicked combinations, what would be the effects of our representation in Congress, uncontrolled by state rights, and urged by local interests to perpetrate geographical partialities? Success in obtaining local advantages would

be considered as an evidence of patriotism by state representatives in Congress, and approved by their constituents; but it
would be considered as fraudulent, and resisted as tyrannical, by
the injured states. The malignity of a concentrated power to a
free and fair government, being greater here than in England, it
required better controls than have been there ineffectual; more
especially as it would destroy our happy union. Geographical
partialities would excite more indignation, than the patronage
of individual and corporate interests, involved in a national mass,
prevented from acting in great combinations by an inextricable
complication, and uncombined by distinct geographical circumstances. Oppressed or plundered states would do what Ireland is
unable to do. If the national government proposed in the convention had succeeded, it could not have oblitered the local
interests established by nature; and these would have remained
as a pledge for a revolution. Even under the limitations of the
constitution, local prejudices and partialities have been disclosed
in Congress, and these occurrences have excited local resentments. A supreme power in the federal government over state
rights, would accumulate local aggressions and dissatisfactions,
until they would be insurmountable by laws and judgments,
and be only conquerable by an irresistible mercenary army. A
national government, though established by popular consent,
could only be sustained in this mode; established by construction, the reservation of state rights would leave no other mode
for enforcing its supremacy. The impossibility of sustaining a consolidated national government by any other means, suggested the
constitutional effort to dissever the causes which would disunite
or enslave the states, from those which would unite and leave
them free. Separate geographical interests were the dissolvents

to be apprehended; a common or mutual interest the only cement to be relied upon. The elements hostile to union were rejected, and only those used which promised strength and duration. The principle of civil liberty, that men should be left to provide for their own happiness in their own way, as far as a good social compact would permit, suggested the reservation of state rights; and the union was bottomed upon those interests of the states which were mutual or common, that the same principle might secure the affection of the states for the federal government, which secures the affection of the people for their state governments. Infringements of this principle in relation to individuals, are indications of approaching despotism; in relation to the states, they equally foretel their subjugation. If the constitution pursued it, no construction by which it is defeated can be correct. To sustain this reasoning, I will quote two authorities, valuable, as proceeding from eminent men, but more valuable for the truths they inculcate:

Yates's notes, p. 190. "Mr. Madison observed, that the great danger to our federal government, is the great northern and southern interests of the continent being opposed to each other. Look at the votes in Congress, and most of them stand divided by the geography of the country, not according to the size of the states." This just observation has become more impressive, by the addition of a powerful western interest to the two then so formidable, and the objections to a national government are already nearly doubled by the increase of states. The danger to the union is most truly stated to reside in geographical interests, and it is as truly stated, that a Congress will be divided by the geography of the country. It being more impossible now than at that time to consolidate these geographical interests under a national government, or to divest Congress of geographical partialities, or to inspire it with a degree of knowledge adequate to just local regulations, there seems to be no remedy against this formidable geographical danger, but to let it alone. If a northern, southern, and western interest, are not opposed to each other in Congress, by investing it with a supreme power over state rights, they cannot endanger the union; but if either can acquire local advantages from a national supremacy, it will aggravate the geographical danger apprehended by Mr. Madison, a perpetual warfare of intrigues will ensue, and a dissolution of the union will result. To prevent this calamity, our political system is compounded of two unions, one of local state interests, and the other of common federal interests. The reservation of powers to one, was a prohibition to the other, intended to avoid geographical collisions; and the expressed prohibitions upon the states were intended, not to take away the local rights reserved, nor to give to the federal government a power to exercise geographical partialities, but to prevent the states from assuming the regulation of the common interests intrusted to the care of a federal government. The two unions were respectively allotted to the care of governments which could feel and understand them, and made independent of each other to prevent geographical combinations of some states in Congress from making local laws for others. All the states were subjected to three-fourths of the whole, as a complete security against the geographical partialities of a majority; and this inevitable geographical temper in Congress, was also subjected to uniformity in the effect of federal laws, practicable in relation to federal, but impracticable in relation to local interests. Can any other system be more happily contrived to avoid the danger to which the union is exposed by the geographical dissimilarities between the three great divisions of the United States, established by nature and fostered by habit?

Yates's notes, p. 200. "Judge Ellsworth observed, I am asked by my honourable friend from Massachusetts, whether by entering into a national government, I will not equally participate in national security? I confess I should; but I want domestick happiness, as well as general security. A general government will never grant me this, as it cannot know my wants, or relieve my distress." This, though a short, is a lucid commentary on our political system, by an eminent member of the convention, excluding the idea of a national or general government, assigning the reason for that exclusion, and drawing a line between federal and state powers, by the incapacity of a general government to provide for the first object of human solicitude, namely, domestick happiness. The division of local from federal interests, was a fine idea for excluding geographical collisions, for effecting a lasting amity between federal interests, and for shielding the people against a concentrated supremacy, ignorant of their wants, and incapable of providing for their happiness.

It is repeatedly urged, that the division of powers between the federal and state governments, will neither secure a mutual spirit of moderation, nor control the ambition of either department. If not, what will? The objection only propounds the question of preference between a federal and a national government, or between divided and concentrated power, in a new form, and endeavours to defeat the best political principle, by charging it with imperfection. In estimating this objection, we ought to consider that both these governments have, in a vast majority of instances, adhered to the constitution, and acted with moderation; and that both, in cases comparatively few, have exceeded their powers. Mutual moderation is therefore the general effect of our system, and occasional excess an inconsiderable exception. What produces the general effect but our division of powers, the moral co-equality of the states, and a congeniality in the state and federal governments with the powers assigned to each? Ought this general effect to be surrendered, because it is exposed to exceptions? It is an axiom, that the means must be commensurate to the end. If the moderation of power is the end, is its concentration, or its division, the best mode of effecting this end? But collision occurs when power is moderated by division. This is not a vice, but the very virtue in the principle of dividing power, which gives it all its efficacy and all its value; and the absence of collision from a concentrated supremacy, is exactly the vice which engenders all its oppressions. The authors of the Federalist earnestly and frequently impressed the mutual control between the federal and state governments, as the chief recommendation of the constitution. Without collision, this control could not have any operation. Let us contrast this remedy against oppression, with the project for putting an end both to this admired control and the collisions it produces, by converting Congress or the supreme court into a council of censors, able by laws and judgments to abrogate state laws, and to create constitutional laws. Either censorial supremacy will put an end to the division of power, with all its controlling and moderating effects, so highly praised and so ably defended by the Federalist.

We have seen a censorial experiment in Pennsylvania, under a notion that it was a good mode of preserving and improving a constitution. Though the Pennsylvanian college of censors was invested with less power than is claimed by the supreme court; though the individuals composing it were also selected on account of their eminent talents and integrity; and though it could neither commit geographical frauds, nor distribute powers partially between two departments designed to control each other; yet party spirit and personal prepossessions appeared in this concentrated power, unbalanced and uncontrolled by another department; and two years sufficed to sicken Pennsylvania of her concentrated censorial supremacy. All the vices by which her supreme college was infected, will follow human nature into the supreme court. And moreover the state sympathy of the judicial supremacy, would be infinitely less perfect than that of the Pennsylvanian college; it would be under no state control in modelling the rights of the people like the Pennsylvanian censors; and inextinguishable geographical feelings would reach the court as well as Congress in the exercise of local supremacy. If a supreme censorial power over state laws and the constitution is given to Congress, the vices which rendered the Pennsylvanian censors intolerable, will be attended by a supernumerary host of mercenary allies. Party spirit, geographical interests, and personal views, will constitute the college. Such hungry guardians of state rights, and usurping controllers of federal power, will mangle the constitution by any constructions for which they may have occasion. When Congress was divided into two parties, called federal and republican, only theoretically sectarian, and not geographically united, each had its own fashion of construing the constitution. The fluctuating constructions of money-hunting parties would be worse guardians for state rights, or for securing the purity of the constitution, than honest zealots. But now that these honest zealots no longer balance each other, a federal college of censors, either legislative or judicial, would be exposed to no check in deciding whether federal powers ought to be increased or controlled. When the parties were nearly equal, and contending for the favour of the people, though contradictory constitutional constructions were produced, such excesses were avoided as would expose one party to publick censure, and risque the loss of power. Whilst this check remained, the better check of co-ordinate departments was not so necessary as it is at present. Besides, so far as these parties were influenced by speculative opinions in relation to the principles of government, they were expositors of the constitution, infinitely more honest than the geographical parties which a federal supremacy must produce. A speculative opinion may be upright; a geographical interest, opposed to another, is always a knave. The trivial geography of a president, sufficiently demonstrates, that Congress would be a bad guardian of state rights, even with the assistance of its federal court.

The variety in the local laws of the states, is a necessary consequence of the variety in their circumstances. An intimate knowledge of these laws, and also of the facts by which they were dictated, could alone provide for state prosperity. The censorial college of Pennsylvania possessed this knowledge; yet as it was a species of concentrated power, unexposed to any wholesome restraint by the principle of division, it speedily became intolerable. Neither the members of Congress, nor of the supreme court, can possibly possess that intimate knowledge of state laws or circumstances necessary to enable them to provide adequately for the wants of the states. If their codes are exposed to be garbled by federal ignorance and partiality, the intellectual and sympathetick capacity of the states to provide for their local exigencies, would be of little or no use. It would be exactly reduced to the same situation as the intellectual and sympathetick capacity of Pennsylvania would have been, had its censorial college been composed of men from South-Carolina, selected by the people of the latter state. Local laws or judgments, passed or rendered by Congress or the supreme court, are exposed to the same objections, and would terminate in the same consequences.

Love and respect for a form of government can only be inspired by duration, and fixed by habit; and fluctuations in constitutional laws, produced by forensick constructions, constitute a national calamity of inexpressible magnitude, by depriving them of the love and respect arising from stability. To secure stability, slow and difficult modes of altering the constitution were prescribed, and the momentous power was exclusively confided to the best talents of the country. But talents were not absolutely trusted, and precautions of great importance were added, with no other intention but that of preventing the rights of the states from being absorbed by the federal government. The constitution was not turned afloat to be carried hither and thither by the winds and waves of forensick and geographical constructions; of prepossession, avarice, and ambition; without the concurrence in making amendments required to give it stability. To these winds and waves, a censorial supremacy in Congress or the court, or in both united, would be so constantly exposed, that in floating about it would certainly be wrecked upon consolidation and monarchy, the Scylla and Charybdis by which it is beset. Such a supremacy would be exposed to far more pestilential defects than those by which the censorial college of Pennsylvania was rendered intolerable. This Pennsylvanian supremacy could neither increase its own power, nor feed its own ambition, nor extend its own patronage.

The censorial supremacy exercised by the federal court, has been proposed to be transferred to the federal senate, by investing that body with a supervision of political judgments; but this would be an exchange of the mutual control between the state and federal governments, and of the mode prescribed for amending the constitution, for the very principle which the court is labouring to establish, namely, that of a national supremacy in the federal government, able to alter the constitution by construction, without the concurrence of three-fourths of the states.

The constitution is accused of wanting precision in its division of powers between the state and federal governments; and I shall attempt to defend it against a charge intended to deprive it of its federal principle, to make way for a consolidated government. Every body admits, that it does not invest either the people of the United States collectively, nor the people of any one state, nor the government of a state, nor the government of the United States, nor any one department of the federal government, with a power to alter its stipulations. Let these acknowledged truths be the guides of our reasoning, and the tests of its correctness. The censorial power established by the constitution, embraces and exhausts the whole right of altering it. The supreme censorial power of construction contended for, is not recognised in defining the right of alteration. The proposition to invest the senate with a power to supervise the political judgments of the court, is an admission that the judicial federal department may alter the constitution by such judgments, and against this evil the remedy proposed is to transfer from the judicial department to the federal senatorial department, the same supreme right of alteration. But both the admission and the remedy are equally contrary to the constitutional definition of the right of alteration, equally an acknowledgment of a supreme concentrated power, and equally an obliteration of the division between state and federal powers.

If neither of the enumerated departments can alter the constitution, the chief difficulty of my course of reasoning is removed, and the arguments by which it is assailed, are surmounted. The word constitution can no longer be construed to contain recondite powers, to be drawn from it by departments having no power to alter it. We have used it to express the formation of both the state and federal governments; but not with a design that it should furnish a pretext for altering the form or principles of either, without the sanction required in each case. If the word gives no authority to any department of state governments to alter state constitutions, without the consent of the people, it can give no authority to any federal department to alter the federal constitution, without the consent of three-fourths of the states. Though we have obtained this undeniable truth, it is said to be inert, for want of means to give it efficacy. The union is admitted to be constituted of state and federal powers, but it is contended that the constitution has been inexplicit in dividing them. An apprehension of difficulty from this circumstance, caused the supremacy over the constitution to be deposited in three-fourths of the states, and not in a majority of Congress, nor in a majority of the supreme court. Even a majority of the states themselves was not intrusted with this power. But other precautions were necessary to prevent the state or federal department from altering the constitution by construction. Among these, the chief must be a principle applicable to both departments, or it could not have any effect. Neither can alter the constitution. What principle can enforce this truth, except that of a co-equal right of construction, and of self-preservation? If no department throughout our whole system can, by any unconstitutional act, legislative or judicial, deprive a citizen of a constitutional right, it would be strange if either the federal or state governments could be thus deprived of constitutional rights. Modes are resorted to for securing the rights of individuals. As to the rights of these departments, they are first secured by their co-equality. Neither or both can construe the constitution. Neither or both can alter it by construction. Neither or both can exercise the power of usurping a right belonging to the other. Neither or both can defend its own rights. The constitution gives no supremacy to either of these departments over the other. But the constitution, aware that this mutual right of self-defence against unconstitutional construction, might produce collisions, has provided a remedy to act in concert with the mutual check, as well devised for securing state and federal constitutional rights, as any which has ever been devised for securing the rights of individuals. If these departments should differ as to the extent of their respective rights, the remedy provided is not that one should exercise dominion over the other. On the contrary, the constitution contains a different, and probably the best remedy, which could have been devised, both to restrain and give effect to the salutary mutual check between the state and federal departments. Two-thirds of Congress may appeal from an erroneous state construction, and propose an amendment for controlling it, to the tribunal invested with the right of decision. Why was this right of appeal limited to two-thirds of Congress, if a majority was invested with a supreme power of construction, or if the same majority could appeal to the federal court? Can a majority evade this limitation, with or without the aid of its court? Two-thirds were required to prevent hasty and frivolous appeals, and to preserve the rights of the states against party majorities and geographical prepossessions. If two-thirds will

not appeal against a state law, it is an admission of its constitutionality, by the constitutional mode established for deciding
the question. If this specified mode is defeated by transferring the
supremacy of construction from two-thirds of Congress and
three-fourths of the states, to a majority of Congress and a
majority of the court, one of these majorities would be invested
with a power of deciding collisions between the state and federal governments, although neither is invested with a right even
to propose an alteration of the powers given to either department by the constitution. The precision in the mode of amendment, is the remedy provided against any want of precision, in
the division of powers, which the licentiousness of construction
might lay hold of. The security against unconstitutional or inconvenient state acts, is deposited in two-thirds of Congress and
three-fourths of the states, as a provision for settling collisions
between the state and federal governments amicably, and for
avoiding the more dangerous conflicts which a supremacy of
geographical majorities would produce, if invested with a
supremacy liable to geographical fluctuations. In this provision
the constitution discloses an eminent superiority over every
other division of power which has hitherto been invented. The
mutuality of the check alone can settle collisions between the
English political departments; here, the constitution has established a mode by which either the federal or state governments
can refer their settlement to a regular tribunal, so as to obviate
any inconvenience arising from a division of power, and also to
preserve the mutual check between collateral political departments. The difference between the two resources is disclosed by
the consideration, that our tribunal for settling such collisions, is
deeply interested to preserve a free form of government, and that

each English department is deeply influenced to get as much power as it can from its rivals. Is there no difference between an appeal by two-thirds of Congress to the tribunal invested exclusively with the power of altering the constitution, in order to settle any difficulties as to the extent of reserved or delegated powers, and an appeal by a majority of Congress to a majority of the supreme court for the same purpose? Suppose one English department could settle its own collisions with the others. It would reduce that government to the form now proposed for us, by expunging from the constitution both its provision for settling such collisions, and also the mutual check between independent political departments. The state and federal departments are essential portions of our form of government. These were intended to be preserved by their mutual independence, and by the special remedy to meet collisions, which we have just considered, and not by a supremacy in one department over the other. That would establish a concentrated sovereignty in the federal government, as absolute as a supremacy of the king of England over the lords and commons. If the constitution had invested the federal department with this supremacy, it would not have provided a mode for deciding collisions, because these could not have arisen between supremacy and subordination; but this mode was suggested by a foresight, that collisions would be produced by the counterpoise and mutual check, without which its division of powers would be nominal and ineffectual.

The necessity for a substantial division of state and federal powers, constituted the chief tenet of our political creed, when the constitution was adopted; and it is probable that a great majority of the people are still adverse to the recent heresy of a concentrated supreme power in the federal government, because divisions of power have been conclusively proved to comprise the only mode of maintaining a free government by the verdict of experience, declaring that the people have never been able to fathom the depths of ambition, or to detect the designs of affected patriotism, whilst they are controllable. Engaged in their private affairs, they have neither time nor information for unraveling intrigues, or detecting artifices. It is true that their interest invites them to applaud patriotism, but it is also true that they are easily misled by ingenious projects, and deceived by specious professions. Hypocrisy can assume the garb of honesty, and ambition can embellish itself with ostentation, whilst both are meditating an embezzlement of publick rights. The people can never act with concert against these, their natural enemies, unless roused from the lethargy of inattention by sentinels able to discover the secret approaches of the foe, and of a character annexing weight to their notifications. Where can such political sentinels be found, except in a division of power between co-ordinate departments? If the favour of God does not suffice to prevent wickedness, will popular favour alone ensure political virtue, when it may be stolen? The theft may be more easily perpetrated in the United States than in other countries, by inlisting geographical interests as accomplices. Even where these powerful associates do not exist, and under republicks, as at Athens, the people have been used like the figures upon a chessboard, merely to decide the fortune of political gamblers; but where these can play with geographical interests and prepossessions, an augmentation of the danger requires peculiar precautions. That chiefly relied upon by the constitution, and singularly distinguishable from other divisions of power, which have been unsuccessful under more manageable circumstances, is the mutual check between the state and federal governments; and if this is lost, the subjugation of the people to some despotick form of government, will be more probable here, than in countries where equivalent auxiliaries for political vice do not exist. At Rome, the division of power between the people and the senate, terminated in a despotism. In France, its division between the people and their representatives, steeped the hands of representation in blood, and obliterated national liberty. And in England, a concentrated supremacy is dealing out oppression to Ireland. In these instances, the want of some division of power, able and interested to excite the attention of the people to usurpations and frauds, has exposed them to be harassed into languor and moulded into servility. Had experience determined that the people alone can prevent the introduction of an oppressive government, constitutions providing for them the auxiliaries of divisions and checks of power, would have been useless; and it must have been admitted that a concentrated power was a complete security for liberty. But as this postulate, far from being a truism, is only a flattery to induce the people to become the instruments of their own subjugation, it is still the basis upon which ambition commences its superstructures.

In fact, a supremacy in one man, or in one body of men, is the very circumstance which has led mankind through a long course of calamities, to the introduction of checks and balances, not as adversaries to the natural sovereignty of the people, but as its best allies. The history of England discloses the throes and anguish of society under the concentrated power of a king, of a king and his barons, of a house of commons, to which the supremacy of Cromwell was preferred, and of a king, lords, and commons, corrupted by a monopoly of power, and coalesced by a sympathy for themselves adverse to the liberty of the people. This last fortuitous medley, into which the English nation were rather justled by rugged circumstances than conducted by reason, retains the vices of a concentrated power. The people of England took refuge from a concentrated representative supremacy, to a Stuart. The people of France fled from a concentrated representative supremacy, into the arms of a military despot. When James the Second was expelled for usurping a supreme power over the other English departments, the experience that kings, lords, and commons, could combine to oppress the people, suggested a lecture to restrain them from doing so, called a declaration of rights, which serves no other purposes but to acknowledge the probability of such nefarious conduct in political departments, when gathered together, and to demonstrate the feebleness of a didactick parchment for securing the liberty of the people against a concentrated supremacy. When the revolution changed our dependent provinces into free and independent states, we were to consider whether a supreme national government, compounded of balancing departments according to the English model, though attended by a declaration of state rights, would suffice to secure the sovereignty, happiness, and liberty of the people, or whether powers should be divided between a federal and state governments, as a better mode of effecting these great objects. The representation in the house of commons had not prevented the bad effects of a concentrated supremacy. The geography of the United States rendered it impossible that a Congress should be as well qualified to exercise a national supremacy as the English parliament; and our heterogeneous local interests could not be governed by a concentrated power, except by melting them up together in the crucible of despotism. Such a project, with only half our present extent of territory, was but little less chimerical, than one for coercing a whole continent into a consolidated government, from an expectation that geographical lines could be obliterated by representation. It was even then foreseen that a Congress would have its geography and climates, like the surface of the United States. To avoid a concentrated supremacy, and also geographical collisions in or out of Congress, the expedient of conforming to the laws of nature, was preferred to a war with them. The division of local and federal interests united each allotment of powers with the strongest natural motive for their preservation. It was the interest of each state to manage its local affairs in its own way, and it was the interest of all the states to manage their common affairs by a mutual concert. Thus both interests were made to harmonise with both objects; they were not violated in either case; and a common interest was used as the cement both of local and federal powers.

To suppose that the state governments, operating within limited territorial lines, either would or could defeat our federal prosperity, and yet that a national government, operating without any limitation, would not or could not commit local partialities, is in theory a contradiction. A common federal interest prevents a state from attempting the first mischief; all the allurements of supreme power, would invite a national government to commit the second. That these can get into a federal Congress, has been practically proved, upon occasions both important and frivolous. Ought they to be multiplied by changing a federal into a national Congress? The geographical question about unsettled lands, was so managed as to get them from some states and leave them to others. The funding and banking questions were decided by geographical motives. The sedition law was intended to operate geographically. The controversy for the presidency discloses geographical feelings, both in Congress and the states. The Missouri question displayed a more formidable geographical spirit in Congress, than has ever appeared in a state government. The usurped supremacy over a federal treasury, has cost the people many millions. These and other facts prove, that a national supremacy would be only a perpetual lottery for distributing blanks and prizes to states and individuals, by the will of a geographical majority; and that excessive corruption and the keenest resentment would probably be produced by these geographical benefits and injuries. The result of the practical testimony is, that local interests, if left at home, will never hurt the federal union; but that, if assembled in Congress, they will produce a government influenced by fraud, which must end in tyranny, or destroy the union. An exercise of local powers by Congress and the supreme court, has already interrupted our federal harmony; and it is obvious, that the division of powers between the state and federal governments, must have been the true source of that share of prosperity which we have hitherto enjoyed.

The expedient for counteracting the evils likely to ensue from the dissimilarity between geographical interests, was to leave the lines between the states, and the local interests which these lines embraced, undisturbed, instead of collecting them into one intriguing arena. The more numerous are state governments, the less able will one be to usurp federal powers. Each will be controlled by the others in such attempts. But if a supreme power over state local rights should be concentrated in Congress, an injudicious or fraudulent exercise of it would be the consequence, and provoke pernicious geographical combinations. Congress would become an assembly of geographical envoys, perpetually exposed to the same difficulties which made it so hard for the state deputies to frame a federal constitution. If a large state was divided into two counties, a legislature composed of representatives from each, would exhibit a scene of geographical contentions. A concentrated supremacy in Congress would substantially divide the United States into three great counties, northern, southern, and western; and their representatives would be influenced by geographical circumstances and habits, tenfold stronger than those which would produce pernicious collisions between the two supposed dividends of one state. There existed no remedy against an evil so certain, but to divert a majority of Congress of a power to exercise local partialities.

The force of this argument depends upon the fact, whether the name, Congress, can wring out of human nature its acknowledged qualities. But is not human nature liable to a geographical mensuration? If it receives impressions from locality, its geography may be almost as distinctly ascertained, as that of the earth. The geography of human nature sticks to a man like his skin, or travels with him like his shadow. Will he be flayed of this adhesive integument, by calling him a member of Congress? The sages who have formed and improved our system of government, sensible that the man and his geography could never be separated, have used this quality of human nature so as to make it a friend, and not an enemy to the union. They saw its efficacy to unite the provinces against England, and wisely inferred that it would also unite the states in reference to other countries, and they availed themselves of the geography of the mind, both to effect the union and also to prevent a disunion. They did not depend upon its force in one case, and go to war with it is another, but they conformed to it in both, by using it as the instrument for securing the states against foreign nations, and also as the instrument for expelling the evils which would be produced by a concentrated power at home.

To prevent local interests from going to war with each other, they are incarcerated within the lines of a state, and if they should be let loose through the avenue of Congress, and the postern of the supreme court, the soundest security for the union of the states and the liberty of the people, will be lost. Local interests, instead of being confined within the boundary of each state, will go to war with each other in Congress, the causes of their hostility, intended to be removed by the union, will be revived, victories will be gained and defeats suffered, and both will generate new battles. Repulsion and attraction, arising from the difference and similitude of geographical interests, would create combinations to commit local injuries or obtain local advantages by the laws of Congress; conflicts between states, intended to be prevented, would be excited, and multiplied; and a national supremacy over state rights would either produce a mass of fragments as materials for some new form of government, or require the almighty power of despotism to enforce its fraudulent awards. Against this host of evils, the constitution provides, by using the geographical interest of the United States to unite them against the geographical interest of other countries, and by leaving the internal geographical interest of each state undisturbed, that it may not destroy our internal tranquillity.

We must not forget that the people of every state are freemen, and that their local interests can never be subjected to a partial or incompetent government, without depriving them of their highest distinction, by the strongest mode of coercion. To avoid an extremity, odious to liberty, a line was marked out by the eighth and tenth sections of the first article of the constitution; one section defining all that Congress can do, and the other all that the states cannot do, so far as the question under consideration is affected. To unite the states against foreign aggression was visibly the chief intention of the first section, and to prevent conflicts between the geographical interests of the states, that of the second. If a double specification by delegations and prohibitions positively expressed, cannot draw a distinct line between political departments, it is true, as ambition uniformly contends, that no such line can ever be drawn; and this mode of securing human liberty must be given up as impracticable. But the twelfth amendment, by referring to both these sections, supposes that they had drawn a plain line between state and federal powers. Those not delegated by the eighth, nor prohibited by the tenth, are reserved to the states. Yet it is said that this line may be obscured and obliterated by verbal constructions and arbitrary inferences, so as to beget the contentions between the state and federal governments it was designed to prevent. But as our federal union would be lost by losing the line, its discovery would be worth all the efforts of those who believe that the liberty and happiness of the people depend upon the preservation of the federal system established by the constitution.

Every sound argument must comprise a beginning, continuity, and conclusion. Its beginning should establish a plain and true principle, sufficient to support its reasoning, and justify its conclusion, which will be unavoidable, unless its premises are false. The states which established the union had assumed sovereignty and independence; they solemnly asserted both, by their first confederation; and the existing federal constitution, in its commencement, ratification, and structure, recognises these rights. These are the premises able to sustain or explode the federal supremacy contended for. If they are true, every construction at enmity with them must be false.

The territorial lines between the states are acknowledged by these three solemn instruments. Why was this done? For the plain reason, that these territorial lines were intended to define the compass and range of the political rights assumed and reserved by the states. Territorial lines between states answer no other purpose; they would be useless and absurd, except to ascertain the extent of their sovereignty and independence. When the moral or political rights within any geographical space are brought under one supremacy, no internal territorial lines are necessary, because they would imply neither independence nor sovereignty; and though old names may remain from habit, they would not be definitions of political rights. The geographical lines of Ireland, before her consolidation with England, served to define the boundary of her political rights; but when these were lost by that consolidation, they became, politically speaking, quite nominal. The United States, instead of consolidating themselves into one political or geographical mass, retained their territorial lines for the very purpose of defining the boundaries of reserved political rights. This demonstrated an intention of dividing powers between the federal and state governments, because the territorial boundaries of each state were necessary to ascertain the extent of the reserved powers. The federal government, if these principles are true, can have no authority over the rights reserved to be exercised by a sovereignty and independence, recognised as existing within territorial state lines, because it would be inconsistent with them. It is manifest that some state rights were intended to be placed exclusively under the guardianship of these principles, and that a visible territorial line was admitted to exist between state and federal powers; we have therefore only to find the sovereign, independent, political reservations, of which territorial lines were a definition.

The constitution availed itself of pre-existing political sovereignties, and the powerful qualities of human nature, in creating a system of government to be enforced, not by the penalties of power, but by the sympathies of a common interest; and therefore it assigned federal powers to a federal sympathy, and local powers to a local sympathy. To find the line between them, we have only to consider upon which sympathy the measure proposed will operate. This substratum of the system is violated, either by using a federal sympathy to regulate state interests, or one local state sympathy to regulate federal interests. These sympathies, undisturbed, will move quietly along, like rivers, each in its own channel; and though they may be occasionally ruffled, no danger is to be apprehended so long as their channels are unobstructed. But as a river, stopped by a land slip, or the disruption of a mountain, becomes turbulent, and finally cuts out a new channel for itself, so if state sympathy is disturbed by the gradual encroachments of federal power, or overwhelmed by a national supremacy, it will become turbulent, and find a vent in some unforeseen direction.

It is a fact that a national supremacy was proposed and rejected in the convention. An inference, that a refusal of supremacy to the whole government established, was a gift of it to a part; that a denial of it to elected representatives indicated an intention of bestowing it on a few men appointed by and responsible to the government from which it is withheld; contradicts this fact, because the states could not have intended partly to reserve, and entirely to destroy, their local sovereignties. If no supremacy is given by the line between state and federal powers, the line is found. The respective sympathies cannot be gotten at, nor any state or federal powers placed under their guardianship, unless an usurped supremacy is put out of their way. Their importance for preserving the union, might be demonstrated by a multitude of cases. Why did the Missouri question produce discontent? Because it violated state or local sympathies. Why have the bank and lottery laws (moralities of the same complexion, and exposed to the same construction) caused state opposition? Because they are trespasses upon state sympathies. And why are internal improvements by Congress unconstitutional? Because, being of a local nature, they violate the division between local and federal interests, established by the constitution. The competence of either sympathy in almost every case, to determine fairly, constitutes a plain line between them. One cannot decide justly for the other. The constitutional qualification and disqualification of both arises from its perfect interest and sympathy with the measure, or from the absence of this security for justice. By this light the line of division between state and federal powers is easily found; without it, construction may wander wheresoever it listeth.

No words have produced more declamation and fraud, than confidence and distrust. Factions, mobs, and governments, often call themselves the people, to obtain a confidence intended to be abused. But both distrust and confidence must be graduated by the moral scale of similarities and dissimilarities between sympathy and interest, to be correct. The provinces, contending with

England, reposed a just confidence in Congress, dictated by this similarity. But in controversies between the states and the federal government, when the question is, whether the latter possesses a supreme power over the rights of the former, the case is very different. A party existed in the provinces, willing to allow a supremacy to the British parliament, unsustained by a mutual sympathy and common interest. Was it guided by the best principles for preserving civil liberty? The answer decides the question, whether the people of the United States will enjoy most liberty by applying the principle of a mutual sympathy and common interest to both their federal and local affairs, or by sacrificing it to a federal or national supremacy. Confidence is not the shadow of every form of government, because it is an effect of a common sympathy and interest, not of power. So far as this ligament bound the states together, federal powers were delegated by the states, and at the point where it failed, a line was drawn upon the same ground which dictated our controversy with England, on each side of which lay the motives, sufficient to carry confidence both to the federal and state governments, so long as they kept within their limits.

Let us illustrate this reasoning by the powers apparently most adverse to it, those of war and commerce. Used to alter our system of government, like the attempted war with France, or to effect local pecuniary ends, as Indian wars might be, or to gratify avaricious or ambitious combinations, the war power, though literally pursued, would be really abused; and an abuse of power cannot be a just construction of the constitution.

The power of regulating commerce was given to the federal government for two purposes; to prevent foreign nations from obtaining unjust advantages over the United States, and to prevent one state from making another tributary to itself. The latter purpose is defeated by using this power to make some states tributary to others, and still more glaringly by making the people of all the states tributary to a pecuniary aristocracy. The Federalist urges "the injustice of the maritime states in levying contributions from the interior states, *by means of commercial regulations,*" as a forcible reason for the union, and a justification of the delegated power to regulate commerce. It was not made a concurrent power, like other modes of taxation, lest some states might use it to inflict a tribute upon others, and the duties are not appropriated by the constitution to produce local or individual wealth, but to the equal benefit of the whole union. If their partial appropriation was considered as unjust previously to the constitution, how can a construction, by which the injustice is revived, be correct, or consistent with the division of powers into local and federal? The Federalist emphatically observes, "that the opportunities which some states possessed of rendering others tributary to them, by commercial regulations, would be impatiently submitted to by the tributary states, and be a cause of war and standing armies." Did the constitution design to suppress this cause of war and standing armies, or only to transfer it from some states to a different geographical combination, or to a capitalist combination? Used for either purpose, it would revive the deprecated evils, and probably dissolve the union; used fairly, it is excellently contrived to abolish local frauds, and to preserve it. Is there any difference between one state making another tributary to itself by means of commercial regulations, and a capitalist or geographical combination obtaining from particular states a tribute by the same means, except in the magnitude of the imposition, and the aggravation of the danger? Must not a remedy for evils be misconstrued, if the evils are magnified and the remedy defeated? The construction would moreover change our federal system into an aristocracy of states or of capitalists, interested to commit frauds. Has it ever been proved, that some republicks will govern others justly? As a geographical interest influences its representatives in Congress, should it have a power of regulating commerce, not for the purposes of preventing injustice, external and internal, but to make some states tribu-tary to others, or to a capitalist combination, one great inten-tion of the constitution is defeated, and the federal government converted into an engine for committing the partialities it was designed to prevent. Used to create a capitalist interest, it would produce the consequence of subjecting the people of all the states to those oppressions which have been produced in England in the same mode. As to this power, as might be the case with the war power, the constitution is verbally complied with, and substantially violated. A proposition made in the convention, to invest the federal government with a power "to establish rewards and immunities for the promotion of agriculture, commerce, and manufacturers," was rejected, and this rejection as forcibly forbids a construction to come at the rejected power, as the rejection of the proposed national government forbids its introduction by construction. Will it be said that Congress may promote manu-factures by rewards, but not agriculture? A power in the federal government to grant rewards and immunities for the promo-tion of agriculture, commerce, and manufactures, would have embraced local interests to an extent quite sufficient to create a national government, and therefore when that was rejected, this proposition of course was also rejected. If a verbal compliance with the constitution, by which its essential division of powers is destroyed, would amount to its violation, constructions, unsustained by its letter, having the same effect, are deprived even of this sophistry, unless abuses of good powers have a right to make bad governments.

Our history, short as it is, proves that this constructive supremacy has been highly injurious to the states, and seems to have decided the preference between a genuine federal government, and a national government in disguise. The assumption of state debts, and the abandonment of paper money, pretended to reimburse the people for the latter injury, by entailing upon them a pecuniary aristocracy; banking, besides cramming the idle child of legislation with more money, contains most of the furniture of Pandora's box; bounties to capitalists, under the rejected proposition to give rewards for the promotion of manufactures, constitute a large annual tribute imposed upon labour for their benefit; a lottery, evinced by the diminutiveness of the fraud, the contempt of geographical and personal avarice for the division of powers; the pension law is of a sufficient size to prove that these motives can make heavy as well as light obliterations of this plain federal principle; a single road evinces the capacity of local powers in Congress for squandering the money of the United States; and the supremacy of the federal court is another apple of discord thrown among the states, sufficient of itself to obliterate all the best principles of the constitution. Local powers, not enumerated among those delegated, and most of them even rejected, have been already drawn from the inexhaustible store-house, construction, so as to inflict an annual tribute on the states, (chiefly paid by about two-thirds of them,) of more than ten millions. The people of a few states are deluded into an opinion, that they receive it, whereas it is received as in England by the capitalist aristocracy. The profit of agricultural capital is reduced to three per centum, and that of pecuniary, enhanced up to ten or twenty. Does not this fact decide who pays and who receives the tribute? The acquisition of other interests, even in those states where the pecuniary aristocracy resides, is like that which would be derived from the establishment among them of a tribe of archbishops endowed with enormous salaries drawn from the United States; they would contribute towards the payment, though these bishops might not be able to influence the government, or to effect a constant increase of their salaries. Land and pecuniary speculators may effect a combination, of which the majority of every state must be the victim. These effects are notable proofs of what is to be expected from constructive evasions of the division of power by a geographical Congress. They would have been avoided by an adherence of the federal government to federal objects. That government was not instituted to distribute wealth between the cities and the country; between inland and maritime people; between states thinly and thickly peopled; between the rich and the poor; and between the several interests of society. Did the constitution intend to invest it with these powers? The notion of some western states, that its exercise of such powers may be beneficial to them, is the same as if the South-American Spaniards should give the product of their mines to England, to make her a great pecuniary capitalist, with the crafty intention of enriching themselves. A policy so strange can only be accounted for by the interest of combinations; because it never fails to introduce a pecuniary aristocracy, which impoverishes nations by prodigality, and replenishes treasuries by oppression. The annual bounty given to monied men, by protecting duties alone, would suffice to pay the president, members of Congress, and judges, thirty times as much as they now receive; but the whole income drawn from the people by the federal assumption of local powers, would pay sixty presidents, eighteen thousand members of Congress, and above four hundred supreme judges. Is it not a humiliating illustration of the human understanding, that it should have been led to pay sixty times more to make a government bad, than what is sufficient to make it good, for the purpose of substituting avaricious combinations for the states, as pillars of a federal government? Such pillars in England have proved but a bad foundation for liberty, although every man is within fifteen miles of water-carriage, and manufactures are brought to perfection. The success of our pecuniary aristocracy in taxing the people with the expense of a navy to protect commerce, and also with prohibitions upon commerce, to enrich itself, shews that its influence can even reconcile contradictions, to come at money. The supremacy of construction is in fact as arbitrary and oppressive as the supremacy of legitimacy; with equal facility it can oppose ridicule, contempt, or a bayonet, to reasoning; and it can also as effectually demonstrate the truth of Mr. Hamilton's position, "that a national government will maintain itself." By investing one of its armies with a monopoly of a species of ammunition not less powerful than the ancient Greek fire, and arming the other with more harmless military weapons, its campaigns against liberty will be crowned with success, and it will finally disclose a very plain difference between the delegated and reserved powers, and also the reasons why the distinction was made by the convention.

But, as has been said of ambition, it may be said of the system for creating pecuniary capital by laws, "that it has no allurements, except from its imposing associations," and is therefore innocent; or that it will be controlled by the federal departments, because one of them is elected by the people, so that our liberty and property will be secured by its natural moderation, or by this check upon its natural rapacity. In England, the same species of concentrated power has proved insufficient to protect the people against the imposing associations of pecuniary capital created by laws. But it is urged, that its failure arises from the imperfect mode in which the English balancing departments are constituted, and we have therefore been compelled to consider whether a sympathetick combination of our federal departments, assembled like the English at one place, converted by construction into a national government, and coalesced by the same motives, has chastened a concentrated power of the vices experienced in England. Agriculture constitutes the chief employment or interest of a vast majority of electors in the United States, yet election has not shielded them against the oppressions of a concentrated supremacy. It has raised the profit of pecuniary capital far beyond the profit to be made by agriculture, and effected its impoverishment by seducing capital from its improvement, by an enormous deduction from its income, and by a system of legislative partiality to pecuniary capital. The high profit bestowed by laws, is paid by the low profit earned by labour, whilst the receivers retain all the benefit of their own labour co-extensively with other people, and their legal income is exposed to no deduction by the expense of taxation and tools. These legal enhancements of the profit of pecuniary capital, instead of contributing towards a good government, constitute the very policy by which mankind are oppressed. Yet it has been pursued to a great extent by an assumed supremacy, liberated from control by a supremacy of construction. As the internal

checks of the federal government have proved insufficient to prevent this enslaving policy, it seems to follow, that the division of
powers between the federal and state governments, is necessary
to prevent the evils which a concentrated national government is
ever prone to inflict. And as no legislative power to introduce it,
nor any judicial power to enforce it, is given to Congress, a line
between the delegated and reserved powers for preventing a consolidated national government seems to be visible. Although
Congress has assumed a judicial power, in cases where the
United States are a party, expressly assigned to the federal judiciary, to be tried by a jury, according to the ninth amendment,
and gratuitously reimbursed the loss, by a liberal donation of
jurisdiction over the state judiciaries, so as to complicate two
important divisions of power, neither ought to be considered as
obliterated. Collisions between departments cannot legitimately
destroy constitutional divisions of power. As judiciaries are the
executives of legislatures, their subordinate office does not
empower them to defeat a division of powers between the legislatures themselves, because judgments may clash, if these legislatures cannot defeat it, because laws may clash. A judicial revision
would be the same as a legislative, and a contrariety between
laws, as sound an argument for a federal supremacy, as a contrariety between judgments. But this contrariety was not considered
in either case as a good reason for establishing a supreme national
government. It is not by the difficulty of finding the line between
federal and state powers, that it is attempted to be obliterated, but
by objections against finding it, urged for the purpose of changing our federal into a national government. It is said to be better
that banks, lotteries, and other local laws, should be forced upon
the states, than that one visible division of powers should exist.

We look for the line by the light of consolidating prepossessions, and of the spurious words, national, supreme, and inconvenient. These glimmerings are used to make us believe, that
federal powers, said by Mr. Madison to be few and distinct, are
countless and indefinite; and what is more extraordinary, the
adjectives, national and supreme, are exclusively appropriated to
one division of power, so as to deprive the other of its substantive
character, bestowed by a line common to both. It is lost in words,
because they are susceptible of fluctuating hues, to elude a comparison of acts with the plain division of powers. This would
constitute an unambiguous line between federal and state powers. A good translator adheres to the spirit of his author; a bad
expositor of the constitution rejects its spirit and principles.

One very plain principle will suffice to restrain the licentiousness of construction. A constructive power must be of the
same nature or sui generis with the power from which it is
deduced, or an usurpation. If the maternal power is exclusive or
concurrent, the constructive offspring must also be exclusive
or concurrent. Therefore, an exclusive supremacy cannot be
inferred from a power made concurrent by the constitution.
Suppose the creation, prohibition, and taxation of banks and
lotteries, to be concurrent and not exclusive powers in the state
and federal governments, neither can constitutionally extract
from this concurrency an exclusive power to control the other in
its exercise. A concurrent power to impose other taxes stands on
the same ground. A concurrency of power in many cases results
from delegation and reservation, and an exclusiveness of power
from limitation and prohibition. When powers given to the federal government are prohibited to the states, they are exclusive;
when powers given to the same government are not prohibited

to the states, they are concurrent; and powers not given to the federal government, constitute the exclusive powers of the state governments. If it is conceded that Congress may create, prohibit, and tax banks or lotteries, and exercise other powers not delegated, yet it does not follow that it can add new prohibitions upon the states, by preventing them from exercising these concurrent powers; or that the federal court can extract an exclusive supremacy for itself, from a concurrent federal power. Such a doctrine would convert all the concurrent powers of the states into subordinate powers, and all the concurrent powers of the federal government into exclusive powers. It is true, as is urged in its defence, that it would bestow more efficacy upon the delegated powers, but it is as true, that it would destroy the efficacy of the reserved powers. Without a concurrency of efficacy, no concurrency of power could exist, and therefore one efficacy was not invested with an authority to prohibit the other. A testator bequeaths several carriages to a special, and his horses to a residuary legatee, but the special legatee contends that he has a right to the horses also, because it will be convenient to him, and that they are naturally attracted by the splendour of the carriages. Such is the case of assumed supremacy. But if neither Congress nor the federal court can increase the prohibitions of the constitution in relation to powers, concurrent or exclusive, to render them more or less convenient or efficacious, the difficulty vanishes, and the line of division is found.

On the contrary, should either the federal or state governments assume an exclusive supremacy over the concurrent powers of the other, neither would be a limited government, a confusion between local and federal powers would ensue, and the wholesome distinction between local and federal interest or sympathy would be expunged. If the federal government should acquire an exclusive supremacy, it becomes effectively a national government. The position advanced by the federal court, "that a power to create involves a power to destroy," to defend this exclusive supremacy in the federal government, subverts it. The federal government cannot create any exclusive or concurrent state power, therefore it cannot destroy any. It cannot create states by dividing them, therefore it cannot destroy them. A state may create banks, roads, or lotteries, therefore it may destroy them. The states created the federal government, therefore they may destroy it. If it is possible to foresee how far statemen and pre-possession can go, this maxim would disclose it. A power can only destroy that which it can create. It results, that as the federal government cannot create either state laws or judgments, it cannot destroy either. Yet the maxim is advanced as a proof that it may destroy both. The rejection of the proposal in the con-vention to invest the federal government with a power to create banks, amounts to an internal construction of the constitution by itself, yet as the power prohibited by rejection was assumed, it was unavoidably assigned to the class of concurrent powers. This left a mutual right to destroy, attached to the mutual right to create. Congress assume an undelegated power, and the court, to make it more efficacious and convenient, step in, abolish the state pow-ers to create or prohibit banking, and to tax pecuniary stock, and thus extend the assumed power of Congress to create or destroy banks, into an exclusive supremacy, able to destroy state rights which it cannot create. Such philological machines can turn out any kind of work, and make any thing or nothing of the constitution. By its constructive prowess the federal government can invest itself with a local power expressly withheld, and of course with local powers not withheld; then it may subject the state concurrency to a federal concurrency, and increase without limitation the special prohibitions imposed upon the states by the constitution, so as to subject all state acts, both negative and affirmative, to federal supremacy; and a consolidated national government is made in the Laputa mode of making books. The federal government first endows itself with a concurrency in the exercise of exclusive state powers, then converts the usurped concurrency into supremacy, and the states are finally swallowed by a sovereign concentrated government.

The constitution establishes three classes of powers; two being exclusive, and one concurrent; and to find the line of division, we have only to discover whether a state or federal act conforms to its classification, and not whether the exercise of one power is inconvenient to another. The exclusive powers of the federal government are so precisely defined by the prohibitions upon the states, that they have neither been questioned nor usurped. But the exclusive powers of the states being only secured by an indefinite reservation, are first hunted down into the class of concurrent powers, and then fettered with a federal supremacy. Federal legislation kindly extends federal jurisdiction, and federal jurisdiction acknowledges the favour by extending federal legislation to state exclusive powers; and the polite reciprocation establishes a supremacy which finishes the obliteration of the divisional line established by the constitution. By discovering the mode in which the line will be destroyed, we discover the line itself. Its existence is copiously proved by the respectable authors of the Federalist, but under the influence of a preference for a national form of government, they pasted over it a federal supremacy, without concurring in the constructive acquisition, because they did not concur as to the form of national government to be preferred. From constructions, dictated by prepossession, contradictory in themselves, and hostile to each other, the difficulty of discovering the line plainly drawn between exclusive and concurrent powers has originated. Party confidence in eminent men, caused party interpretations of the same instrument, and weakened the constitutional classification of power vindicated by both. The line is demonstrated by their constructions asserting the classification and independence of powers, but obliterated by subjecting state powers previously said to be sovereign and independent, to a supremacy in Congress, or in the supreme court, or in a national government, by two gentlemen who advocated propositions for a supreme concentrated power. The present advocates for the same form of government, reject their plain line, and adopt the obliterations intended to regenerate one of the national forms of governments. If these great men had stopt with their definition of the line, and forborne to annex to it obliterating assertions, no difficulty or defect in the constitution on this score would have been discovered. These assertions were originally suggested, and are still used to defeat a federal system; and the real question is, not where the federal line runs, but whether it shall be expunged?

The case of slavery helps to illustrate the federal line, and to refute the doctrine of a national supremacy. A federal compact, and not an American nation, caused slaves to be counted in adjusting a federal representation. A national representation would not have been in any degree deduced from slaves. Independent of other circumstances, slavery demonstrated the necessity of a line between state and federal powers. An usurped federal supremacy could as easily get over it in this case, as in those of banks, lotteries, and an appellate jurisdiction; and there would be less difficulty in proving that slavery, abstracted from local circumstances, is prejudicial to the welfare of the United States, than that banks, lotteries, and the appellate jurisdiction, will advance it. The states, ignorant of facts, might be enchanted with the theory of converting black slaves into good patriots, whilst the states experimentally qualified to judge, might know that the idea was visionary. Every other local interest to which a general sympathy does not extend, was provided for by the division of power, which provided for the case of slavery. All or none of the powers reserved to the states, must be embraced by the federal supremacy contended for. The English introduced slavery to get money from the provinces, by their capacity for making tobacco; the capitalists use it also to get money from some states, by their incapacity to become manufacturers, which England had also in view from her monopoly through the pretext of commercial regulations. Both used it to extract an enormous tribute from a local misfortune. A federal division of power was designed to prevent such frauds of a concentrated supremacy, and not to fleece local incapacities to enrich superior industry.

The second article of the constitution, by explicitly asserting the federal character of the house of representatives, definitively excludes a national character from the federal government, and abolishes intirely a place of residence for the supreme authority, by which the reserved powers of the states are assailed. "In choosing the president, the votes shall be taken by *states, the representatives of each state* having one." Was the constitution mistaken in expounding itself; and is Mr. Madison's construction, which has been made the basis of consolidating inferences, "that this house is a national representation," more correct than the constitution in calling it a representation of states? It describes all its branches as federal. The house of representatives is repeatedly recognised by the mode of its formation, and positively in this quotation, as a representation of states. The senate is allowed to be so. And the president is either to be chosen by electors to be appointed as the states shall direct, or by the representatives of these states in Congress. Thus the federal character of the union seems to have been as plainly established, and the proposed national character as plainly rejected, as could have been effected by words. But how seldom can words remove prepossessions. A "judicial power of the *United States*," though thus also recognised as federal, is considered as national, as able to assume or to receive from Congress a new species of national supremacy, and as invested with a power to impair or destroy the federal character, repeatedly avowed by the constitution itself.

The president is made responsible to the states in the modes of his election and trial, as a security for state rights, against his geographical propensities. The incongruity of annexing a national president to a federal Congress, would almost have been equal to that of associating a federal Congress with a national court. It would have been highly objectionable to choose a president by a national, and to try him by a federal principle. A loyalty to federal interests and to state rights, were the two objects designed to be effected in the structure of the federal government. Its legislative and executive departments were constructed upon federal and not national principles with that intention. If the supreme federal court is to be considered as a political department, any more than the inferior federal courts, consistency required that it should be federal as well as the other departments. It would have been as absurd to invest it with a national supremacy, and to try it by a federal senate, as to have done the same thing in the case of the president. Liberty is often the victim of executive power. A national election of this department has universally inflamed its ambition and favoured its usurpations, as in the cases of Cæsar and Bonaparte. Therefore the constitution wisely subjected it to organized states, as constituting a control more vigilant and powerful than disunited individuals. The provision is indispensable, if the preservation of state rights is necessary to secure the liberty and prosperity of the people. A national mode of electing the president, would destroy the state or federal influence over federal executive power, and like supremacy annexed to a general government according to Mr. Hamilton, or to a supreme national court, according to Mr. Madison, would infallibly change the federal into a national government. Ambition could more easily corrupt individuals than state governments, and seduce them into a consolidated government. A tendency towards an aristocracy of states, a national government, or a monarchy, was guarded against by the federal system in various modes, one of which was to subject the geographical partialities of a legislative majority to the control of a federal president. By converting a federal into a national president, he would be influenced by a national majority, and a great security against a consolidated government would be defeated. Mr. Hamilton, sensible of this, in number sixty-eight of the Federalist, assumes a very obvious misconstruction of the constitution, as an advance towards the form of government he preferred, by observing, that it has "referred the election of the president, in the first instance, to the immediate act of the *people of America.*" On the contrary, "the electors of the president are to be appointed *as the legislature of each state shall direct,*" for the purpose of impressing upon him a federal loyalty, and creating a check apprehended from a consolidating influence in the house of representatives, arising from a different mode of election. It is wonderful to discern a concord between the consolidating Mr. Hamilton, and the jealous federalism of the small states. He wanted a national president towards effecting his avowed object. Is it a better policy which contends for a president to be elected by a majority of states? The constitution supposed that a federal president would be more likely to sustain the federal system and the rights of the states. It knew that a glare of character would more easily deceive the multitude than the state legislatures, and that a species of popularity so easily obtained, much oftener bestowed repentance than liberty on the people. Mr. Hamilton, with other profound politicians, knowing that the dazzling phantom of a perfidious popularity, frequently becomes a real plague, eulogises the provision against its visitation by the intelligent control of the state governments; but he strives to reconcile this conviction with his other conviction in favour of a limited monarchy, and therefore he says that the president is to be elected by the people of America. Great use is made by the consolidating doctrine, of the injury which this imaginary people sustains, if the election is made by states in the house of representatives. The senate is exposed to the same objection; and if it is sufficient to prove that a national is preferable to a federal president, it proves also that we ought to have a national senate. The objection therefore terminates in the preference between a national and a federal form of government.

If the federal form is best, it is of little importance whether it shall be mortally wounded by misconstructions, by amendments, or by habitual evasions of the constitution, so as to come at its

competitor by the help of a national president; and even his election by states in the house of representatives, though exposed to
great objections, would be exposed to fewer than an election by
an American people, because the former being federal, bad as it
may be, is a better control of executive power. It is exposed to still
fewer than the extra-constitutional habit of virtually electing
the president by a majority of the members of Congress. This has
nothing federal in it; if it contains any principle, it is of a national
complexion; it swallows up the small states; and the states, both
large and small, are thus seduced to surrender their federal influence over the executive department, to a combination of men
divested of all responsibility. If a president is elected by the house
of representatives, each state would know how its deputies voted,
and this knowledge would be some security for their patriotism; but when virtually elected by a caucus of Congress-men,
the absence of this knowledge is an additional solicitation, and a
powerful security for corruption against detection. By the first
mode, a little man from a small state may be made of great value;
by the second, a great man from a great state may be made thirty-
fold more valuable. The first mode is undoubtedly federal; the
second is not even national. It may be called a mode of making
presidents by making bargains, and the most extraordinary circumstance attending it is, that an American nation, or a union
of states, should be induced to believe, that by obeying an edict,
contrived originally by a secret combination between a few men,
they are electing a president. According to the constitution, the
number of electors is fixed by a ratio compounded of the number of states, and the number of people in each state, counting a
portion of the slaves, and excluding the idea of an American
nation; but their character is made federal by the mode of elec-

tion. Perhaps no better principle could have been contrived for uniting states and individuals in one interest. Numbers are chiefly regarded in fixing each state's quota of electors; but the small states are reimbursed, and the large ones secured, by the power reserved to the states of maintaining their federal rights, by a federal influence over the president. The common interest of all is combined and united to act for the common security. A virtual election by a caucus, and a formal election by the house of representatives, are both prejudicial to the common interest provided for by the primary mode of election, because the first deprives all the states, great and small, but especially the small, of all influence in the election, and the second deprives the large states of the proportion of electors assigned to population. If the compromise between these principles is preferable to either in its extremity, the proposition to amend the constitution for giving efficacy to that compromise, is preferable to a struggle between the small and large states to defeat it; the first class, by getting the election into the house of representatives; the other, by placing it under the control of a caucus. If the small states should succeed, it would place the executive department under the influence of a majority of states containing a minority of people, a kind of aristocracy; if the large, it would expose all the states to the secret intrigues of monarchical or consolidating factions. Should the federal principle of electing the federal executive, be exchanged for a national principle, by dividing all the states into districts, it will both subvert every vestige of a federal influence over him, and also foster the habit of designating the man by a self-constituted caucus, which would be thus delivered from the control deposited in the state legislatures to prevent the introduction of a national executive. Besides, an election by the electors is exposed to less danger from corruption, than an election by a caucus or the house of representatives, and this is another reason why it would be better to perfect the preferable constitutional mode, than to defeat it, either by a caucus, or by an election in the house of representatives, or by converting all the states into districts, so as to destroy a federal influence over the president of the United States, by making him a president of the people of America, according to Mr. Hamilton's policy.

This gentleman speaks of the "*concurrent* jurisdiction between the *national* and state courts." He says, "that the judicial is beyond comparison the weakest of the three departments of power; that impeachments will control it; that the judges would never hazard the resentment of the body intrusted with it, as this body would punish their presumption by degrading them from their stations; that the word supreme refers to the *federal* tribunals inferior to the supreme court; that the federal courts have an appellate jurisdiction from the state courts; that the *national legislature* may modify federal jurisdiction; that it is inherent in the nature of sovereignty not to be amenable to the suit of an individual without its consent; and that the states do not lose any of their rights by a change in the form of their civil government." Are not the collisions between these assertions equal to any which can be expected from our division of power? How can state and federal jurisdiction be concurrent, without being independent? How can federal jurisdiction be a competent guardian of state rights, if it is feeble, controllable by impeachment, and liable to be modified by a national legislature? Whence did it derive an appellate jurisdiction over state courts, if the supremacy of its highest tribunal refers to the inferior federal courts? How can Congress have a right, derived from his assumption of a *national legislature,* to modify judicial federal powers, and no right to modify federal legislative and executive powers? How can it be inherent in the nature of sovereignty not to be amenable to the suit of an individual without its consent, and that the state political rights should also be liable to be abridged by suits between individuals, without even a capacity in the states to defend themselves before the assumed sovereignty over their rights? And how can the states lose none of their rights by a change in their civil government, if they may be made amenable to a supreme federal tribunal? It is neither difficult to discern nor to account for these contradictions. The constitution was construed by two souls, one impressed with the force of its principles and language, the other by a prepossession in favour of a national form of government. Of course we find in the Federalist the dictates of both a national legislature, a national president chosen by the people of America, and a national judiciary, are all said to have been created by the constitution. Even that is said to have been the national act of this American people, by subsequent commentators. And lest these gentlemen should be led astray by the constructions of the federal soul from the design of the national soul, the concluding page of the Federalist solemnly declares, "that the constitution would be the act of a whole people, that it comprises a general national government, and that a nation, without a national government, is an awful spectacle." Such is the source of the difficulty in finding the line drawn by the constitution between federal and state powers. It has been by degrees made fainter with patches of national or consolidating colours. If the states should be induced to part with their federal influence over the president, and to take from their legislatures the power of investigating his loyalty to their rights, by an amendment or a habit, they will finish its obliteration, by adding a national executive to a national legislature and judiciary, proposed in the convention, rejected by the constitution, and revived in the Federalist. Under these modifications, would the constitution retain its great principle of referring state exigencies to state sympathy, and federal exigencies to federal sympathy, or could our system be denominated federal?

If the desired line is found, we come to the true question, namely, which is best for the United States, a federal or a supreme national government; or which will best secure their strength, wealth, and liberty? The difference between the strength, wealth, and liberty of a government, and of a people, first presents itself. Wherever a government possesses too much of these, the people have too little. Restraints upon a government alone beget liberty, and liberty alone begets that high degree of national strength, able to withstand both foreign aggression and domestick usurpation. Like Mahomet's tree of Paradise, it bears the best fruits in most abundance, and among them national strength and individual happiness. Is it enthusiasm or sober reason, which believes that a division of power begets liberty; that liberty animates the people to defend their country; that it extorts admiration from nations compelled both to applaud and to envy; and that it brings wealth and comfort by invigorating industry? Can the artifices for destroying our division of powers, be better than these benefits, both splendid and substantial? These artifices contend that liberty will be secured by a responsibility of a supreme national government, or of some of its departments, to the people, without a division of powers between the state and national governments; and flatter our vanity by asserting, that the exercise of state powers is founded in arrogance, and inconsistent with the rights of man; but if the experience of the whole world has demonstrated that despotism cannot be prevented by any other expedient, this, like other flatteries, is intended as a seduction to defraud the people of their most valuable property. This truism, peculiarly applicable to the territories of the United States, suggested the division of power between the state and federal governments, not to impair, but to secure the liberty of the people; because it his never been safe in the keeping of any concentrated government over a consolidated territory of equal extent. Its brilliant effects were predicted by history, and have been demonstrated by experience. The lustre of Greece appeared under a very imperfect confederation, and vanished when her independent states were melted into consolidation. Even the embers of her federal liberty, were an over-match for the mighty consolidated Persian empire, whilst her independent states, reduced to a consolidation, became an easy prey to the ambition of the Romans, and the tyranny of the Turks. The strength of the Romans diminished, and their glory began to fade, when the collateral legislative power of the senate and the people was exchanged for consolidation. Venice and Genoa have been entombed in consolidation. Holland, strong and flourishing whilst its seven little provinces were more loosely united than our great states, is reaping the harvest of consolidation, and no longer a star in the galaxy of nations. Switzerland has been made stronger and happier, by a confederation weaker and more imperfect than ours, than could have been expected from a consolidated government, and enjoys more liberty and comfort upon a sterile soil, than the great consolidated fertile contiguous countries. England lost thirteen provinces by attempting to establish a concentrated supremacy. The power of liberty, in its paroxysms, is a proof of its capacities in sobriety. The love of liberty in France proved too strong for great combinations of concentrated powers, and when it was smothered by Bonaparte's imitation of their forms of government, his concentrated power became unable to resist them. Thirty millions of people remained, but the impulse was gone.

The reader anticipates me, and has already seen the blaze of that elevated beacon, which enlightens the world and directs it to truth. A mutual sympathy and common interest, caused thirteen disunited provinces, under innumerable disadvantages, to be successful against a mightier concentrated power. The same principle conducted our federal government with honour and reputation through another unequal war with the same consolidated government. The vigour of mind and perseverance of exertion it begets, has twice memorably displayed its superiority over the concentrating principle, within our own view. Philosophers assert its wisdom, and tyrants fear its prowess; and our prosperity under its influence, upon an inferior soil, has exceeded that of all contemporary consolidated nations, and outstripped the records of history in the circle of ages.

Does this accumulation of facts contain no truth, and convey no admonition? To me, it seems that our union, founded in the division of powers between the state and federal governments, and annexing a genuine sympathy to each department, is the strongest government hitherto discovered for securing all the benefits which have induced mankind to construct political societies. It opposes activity to torpor, a common interest to monopoly, and a union of nations to a mercenary army. Bad passions, however, prefer a concentrated supremacy, because it affords them more room, and subjects them to less restraint.

If all the people of the United States were assembled to pass local laws, they would now be arrayed in three parties, each inclined to obtain advantages over the others. The venom scattered by a contest for offices, would be aggravated a thousand fold by a contest for geographical advantages. These parties will shortly be reduced to two, the geographical ins and outs of a concentrated supremacy. An absolute monarchy might become preferable to the nefarious struggles which will ensue, because the geographical interest of a king would be merged in power, and the avarice of one man could be more easily gratified than the avarice of a multitude. A power of local legislation in Congress, would create logicians, guided by inextinguishable geographical inducements. This source of partiality, oppression, and disunion, is dried up, by dividing local and federal interests. It will be made to flow in copious streams, by enabling local interests in Congress to make other local interests subservient to their passions; and also create a new fountain, at which ambitious and avaricious men may satisfy their thirst; and thus exchange our homogeneous union of power and sympathy, for the European heterogeneous union of power and antipathy, which produces either resistance or oppression. If a brotherhood between power and sympathy constitutes our strength, our renown, our industry, our wealth, our local justice, and our liberty, a dissolution of this moral association, by riving it asunder with a concentrated supremacy, may be computed by a very moderate capacity. It is universally agreed, that this association, so friendly to human happiness, has never been brought as near to perfection by any form of government, as by ours. By what can this opinion be justified, except by our division of powers between the state and federal governments? If the makebate construction should be able to drive into the constitution the anomaly of subjecting state powers to an unsympathizing federal majority, legislative or judicial, our government, from being the best, might become the worst in the world; because one nation is the most inexorable of all tyrants over another; and state nations, by their representatives in Congress, would become the tyrants over other state nations, by being able to oppress them for their own emolument. I know not whether this, or that of an absolute monarch, would be the worst species of tyranny.

An absolute concentrated power was resorted to in Europe, to prevent baronial wars, and a division of power was resorted to here, to prevent state wars. By the European expedient, baronial wars were prevented, and the oppressions of a supreme concentrated power obtained. Barons might be easily melted into a consolidated nation, but the latitude and local interests of the states are not susceptible of a similar fusion. Feudal lords do not, like geography, exist forever. As local interests could not be abolished, like barons, an attempt to subject them to a concentrated supremacy, composed chiefly, not of friends, but of rivals for money, might rather provoke than suppress state wars. To prevent both these, and European oppressions arising from a concentration of power, the happy expedient of an affiance between local interest and local power, and between federal interest and federal power, was adopted. As local interests could not be annihilated like feudal barons, and as the members of Congress could not be divested of local partiality, no other expedient, hitherto discovered, was sufficient to effect the meditated ends. To prevent some states from being made tributary to others by commercial regulations, was one, and it was not intended, in removing this injustice, to revive it in an aggravated degree, by enabling a geo-

graphical majority to oppress a geographical minority in a multitude of modes, without the least check of the fraud from an
apprehension of counter-regulations, or the kindness of contiguity, which might have moderated it between two states. It was not
intended to create a family of knaves to get rid of one, as would
have been the case, if local ignorance, local prepossessions, and
geographical rapacity, all more inveterate in Congress than
between adjoining states, had been invested with a power of
legislating for countries which they never see, for customs which
they never practise, and for interests which they never feel, except
when they are to be shorn.

However the causes of political oppression may be diversified
by circumstances, violations of geographical interests are so egre-
giously adverse to moral rectitude and human happiness, as not
to admit of a reconciliation with either. The long-standing contest between monarchy, aristocracy, and democracy, excited
struggles, without producing any permanent advantage to
mankind, by offering prizes to bad passions, and over-looking a
truth, essential to their happiness, upon which our federal system is founded. These three principles were supposed to cover
every species of government, because it was taken for granted
that every species must possess supreme power, and therefore it
only remained to determine by which of these rival principles
supremacy might be most safely exercised. Absolute power was
the golden apple contended for by three idols, each of which
purchased votaries by promises and bribes. The idols, separately
exploded, have combined for the purpose of retaining more
securely the coveted dominion, and constituted a triumvirate
which promised little and performed less. The United States
withdrew their adoration from these spurious deities, separately

or united, and extracted a political system from geographical indications and moral qualities, imprinted by the Creator on the face of the earth and the heart of man. These happily impressed upon them the uncontroverted truth, that the people are more honestly wedded to their own happiness, than a supreme power in any form. They have therefore vindicated the sovereignty of the people. From this primary truth, they extracted another, equally undeniable, namely, that the people of a state love themselves and understand their own interest, better than any other people can possibly do; and upon this consideration, exactly as sound as the wide distinction between a monarch and a nation, they have established a political system, by which each state is enabled to exercise its exclusive knowledge, and gratify its own self-love. Local regulations, made by a majority of states, or by decisions of the supreme court, are only metaphysical satraps, despatched by despotism into provinces, for the usual purpose of gathering money; as in the cases of assuming state debts, banks, protecting duties, internal improvements, the pension law, the lottery, and an unrestricted appropriation of federal money. They substantially reduce the state governments to prefectures, subject to the dominion of the federal government, instead of being functionaries responsible to the people of the state. If the usurpation shall succeed, the expense of these cyphers will be a sufficient reason for their suppression. It was intended to establish a division of power between the natural affection which the people of each state possess for themselves, and between the natural affection which all the states possess for themselves in relation to other countries, as a better security for liberty, than a supreme power in either of the three old principles, or in any of their combinations, and as the only means of sustaining the modern doctrine of the sovereignty of the people. This principle would be subverted by investing the federal government with supreme power, in imitation of Britain, and trusting to its departments, or to geographical partialities, for controlling its supremacy, because it would take from the people the right of self-government, the only foundation of their sovereignty, and destroy its only material consequence, by depriving the responsibility of state functionaries to the people, of all its efficacy.

In this new experiment, the United States had many obstacles to surmount, and strong prepossessions to remove. The old tories were glued to a king, lords, and commons; the new, admire the same species of concentrated power, concealed under different names. The old Congress blamed the patriotick state governments, because the success of the revolutionary war was not more wonderful, and believed that, invested with supreme power, it could have astonished the world still more; the new, shutting its eyes upon the late war, and a long current of prosperity, contemplated with admiration by other nations, consider the absence of a supreme power in a combination of the three ancient political dogmas, as a great defect in our more perfect union, and has been endeavouring to remove it, with the help of its judiciary. Some learned and honest statesmen candidly appealed to the publick in defence of a supremacy according to the British model; others, under the same impression, contrived an intrigue, suppressed by Washington. The holders of a certain description of paper money to a large amount, were ripe for any revolution by which they could obtain great affluence at little cost. Arrogant men saw charms in the old forms of concentrated supremacies, not perceivable in our new principles.

Eminent members of the convention advocated the principles which the states had recently resisted. The attempt then defeated, is with equal ardour and less disguise, now renewed; and the question, whether we shall have a concentrated power, invested with a local supremacy or a limited federal government, is again to be decided, not by a solemn appeal to the people, but by Judge Construction, into whose mouth the parties interested can put what words they please.

A concentrated power over extensive territories, has unexceptionably found it necessary to establish pro-consuls, governors, or generals, supported by armies, to sustain its authority. Local powers in Congress, despatched into the states, are instruments of the same kind, requiring the same auxiliary. Had the constitution contemplated the states as subordinate instruments of a concentrated supremacy, it would have been extremely defective. It has been found hard to enforce the obedience of subaltern individuals, but it would be infinitely harder to enforce the obedience of subaltern governments, contrary to the local habits and interests of their constituents. Individual deputies are always exposed to severe punishments, and these supposed subordinate governments are not subjected to any punishment for disobedience. If the constitution had intended to impose upon the state governments in the exercise of their powers, the duty of obeying the federal government, it would have contained provisions for extorting that duty. The subordinate agents of a concentrated power, are removable, because supremacy and subordination could not otherwise exist. The state governments are not removable, because they are not subordinate, nor the federal government supreme.

The difference between a federal and a supreme government, was quite visible to the convention; and in considering the attributes of each, it saw that a power of appointing state governors, of revoking state laws, and of reversing state judgments, was necessary to establish one form; and that a reservation of undelegated state powers, undestroyed by subordination, was necessary to establish the other. By rejecting the consolidating attributes, it never intended to invest construction with a power of substantially reviving them, by conferring on the federal government, or either of its departments, a power of removing, revoking, and reversing, the acts of the reservation. The difficulty of banishing, hanging, or shooting, state governments, for violating the constitution, suggested the preferable provision for altering it, combined with its division of powers. Thus two absurdities were avoided; that of a supreme government, shackled with deputies whom it could neither punish nor remove; and that of a confederation of states, comprising an abolition of their rights. Consistency required a supremacy in the national government proposed, and its exclusion from the federal government adopted. As subordinate authorities, the states must have been subjected to the coercion of a supreme national government; with their reservation of independent local powers, this coercion was incongruous. A national form of government, not invested with a power to compel obedience, or local state powers, subjected to a limited federal government, would both be political absurdities, and therefore the former was not proposed, nor the latter established. The rejection of all the modes proposed for coercing the state governments, whilst a national government was in contemplation, proves that the constitution preferred the mutual check, to a concentrated supremacy. But the federal government may coerce a disobedient state by an army, just as one of the English balancing or collateral departments, has often endeavoured to enslave the others. This mode of compelling the obedience of state governments, being infinitely more inconvenient and dangerous, could not have been contemplated by the rejection of the modes proposed, as it would destroy the mutual check allowed by the Federalist to be intended, as a conquering general might persuade or terrify the people into an opinion, that one despot was as good as an hundred, and as the submission of conquest could not have been sought for by the rejection of the milder means of obtaining obedience, by appointing governors, revoking state laws, and reversing state judgments.

As local authorities were indispensable, the question was, which ought to be preferred; such as were responsible to the people interested to preserve local justice, and best informed as to what might advance their happiness; or such as would be subjected to the control of a national government? The former corresponded with the right of self-government; the latter with despotick, principles, because it would leave to the people of each state no substantial power to provide for their own happiness. They could not be subjected to a supremacy in the federal government, and also retain their local state right of self-government. The contrariety between the two modes of constituting local authorities, was thoroughly considered in the convention, and a preference became unavoidable, because they were incapable of reconciliation. One sustained intirely the principle of self-government; the other deprived the people of every state of so much of that principle, as was applicable to their local affairs; and it was determined that the intire, was more likely to constitute a good government and preserve the liberty of the people, than the mutilated principle. If the wisdom and patriotism of the union was again assembled to re-consider the question, the opinion, that the two systems of government are almost as far asunder as liberty and despotism, would probably be more unanimous than it formerly was, because many of the prejudices arising from old habits and the revolutionary war, which then obstructed the same conclusion, are now obliterated.

In establishing the division of powers between the federal and state governments, another principle as important, and not less true than that of uniting sympathy with power, was kept in view by the convention, namely, that great power is a great temptation to do wrong. The able expositors of the constitution having in the Federalist adverted to this axiom, united in an opinion, that a greater share of power was reserved to the states, than was delegated to the federal government; and therefore concluded that the danger of usurpation rested in that department. As neither their opinion nor inference could have any foundation, if the powers reserved to the states were controllable by the federal government, they must have believed, as they said, that each department was independent of the other within its own sphere; because, had the constitution invested the federal, with a supremacy over the state governments, the greatest share of power could not have been assigned to the latter. The anticipation of the comparative magnitude of the two primary divisions of power, to ascertain which would be most sorely afflicted with the malady of usurpation, was then chiefly conjectural; and the egregious mistake of these commentators, is both a proof that their constructions are not infallible, and also an admonition against destroying the mutual check which they commended. If experience has ascertained that the superiority of power is in the federal government, they have proved that the disposition to encroach must go with it. The axiom, that the least moderation is to be expected from the most power, decides the comparative magnitude of these primary dividends, since there is as much difficulty in discovering an instance of the usurpation of a power delegated to the federal government, by a state, as in discovering a state reserved power, not usurped or threatened by federal precedents. The whole mass of state powers are attempted to be drawn within the federal sphere, by a supremacy claiming a right to remove obstructions to its dominion; converting them, whatever may have been their constitutional magnitude, into cyphers, useful only to endow the federal sphere with an unlimited decimal increase of power. To transfer our jealousy from the encroaching sphere to that, experimentally weak, unassuming, and too submissive, would seem to violate common sense, and would certainly defeat the mutual control, eulogised by the Federalist, and established by the constitution, to ensure the moderation of power, upon which it is agreed that all the benefits of civil liberty depend.

But the modern commentators, far from believing, with the Federalist, that the state governments possess a superiority of power, contend that it resides to such an extent in the federal government, as to make it absurd for the states to struggle for rights which must be lost, or to oppose an impetus which must prevail. Giving up the idea of checking power on account of its magnitude, they urge its magnitude as a reason for suppressing the check, and submitting to its commands; expounding the constitution by Lord Shaftesbury's logick, they ridicule its attempt to reserve rights to the states in communion with the great power bestowed on the federal government; and laughing at its provisions, they yield to their subversion, because they are too feeble to withstand the usurpations of the federal government. Should the contempt thus plenteously poured out upon the state governments, unite them for the preservation of rights common to all, the barriers against the disposition of great power to usurp, may prove stronger than these facetious gentlemen are disposed to believe. If the parties actuated by conflicting principles, should happen to be described by proper names, such as consolidators and constitutionalists, or concentrators and federalists, it might induce the people to consider whether they would subscribe to the combined projects of laughing or coercing them out of their state rights, and they could easily make the charge of absurdity, urged against the constitution, recoil upon the statesmen by whom it is advanced. But consolidation avows its patriotism by talking of the sovereignty of the people, whilst assailing their state rights, and of its loyalty to the constitution, whilst appealing from it to the supremacy of construction.

> Libertas et natale solum!
> Fine words, I wonder where you stole 'um,

says Swift. Oh, for a poet to write an epigram upon this, and the following congenial motto:

> Words are very pretty things
> For patriots as well as kings.

Will it be arrogant to offer him an humble hint?

> Libertas! meaning by debate
> To pilfer powers from a state,
> And into wholesale bring a nation

At vendue of consolidation.
Libertas, also, does import
The power imperial of a court,
Supremely fixing right and wrong
By constitution of the tongue.
Natale solum, in orthography,
Distinctly intimate geography;
Or they may mean protecting duties,
To money-holders, perfect beauties.
Words, of construction are the mint,
Coining its currency without stint;
The shot with which ambition fights
'Gainst reservation of state rights.
Thus liberty and words supply
Accommodations for a———.

What a miserable poet am I, to want a rhyme! Reader, can you supply it?

Having endeavoured to ascertain the origin, progress, and consequences of a consolidating, concentrating, or national system of government; to ascertain the intention of the constitution by its words, spirit, and ratification; to prove, by the journal of the convention, that a federal government was established and a national government rejected; and to vindicate the wisdom and patriotism of that body, in both these decisions; I have only to add a hope that abler writers may gratify the publick by discussing these important subjects.

Construction

Several formidable arguments used to convict the constitution of absurdity, or to subject it to the supremacy of construction, remain to be fairly stated; that, although I am unable to answer them, they may be considered by the publick. The supremacies of construction and legitimacy are said to rest upon foundations equally solid, and to be equally omnipotent, because the word government as naturally inherits power as the word king. As men have natural rights, so have kings and governments; and supremacy not being among the natural rights of men, and yet necessary, must be among those of a government. Upon this ground it was contended in the convention that the creation of a federal government, although the old Congress never made the discovery, revoked the declaration of independence, and reduced the states to corporations. For how could a king be a king, or a government a government, without sovereignty or supremacy, any more than a man could be a man, without spirit or soul? Hence the attempt of the constitution to establish a federal government, without these natural souls, was preposterous, unnatural, and void; and when the government was born, it inherited its natural rights, like any other species of legitimacy. The authority of a great monarch sustains our philologists in taking their stand upon this doctrine. We are informed by Hume, "that at the treaty of the Pyrenees, when Louis the Fourteenth espoused a Spanish princess, he had renounced every title of succession to every part of the Spanish monarchy; and this renunciation had been couched in the most accurate and most precise terms which language could afford. But on the death of his father-in-law, he retracted his renunciation, and pretended that natural rights could not be annihilated by any extorted deed or contract." If the natural rights of kings could not be impaired by the constitutions of France, Naples, Spain, and Portugal, the natural rights of governments cannot be impaired by the same papers. If Louis could not divest himself of his natural rights, he could not be divested of them by another. If the plainest words which language could afford, were not sufficient to deprive Louis of his natural rights, words as plain could not establish the reserved rights of the states, and deprive the federal government of its natural supremacy. But as the federal government is not chargeable, like Louis, with having voluntarily imposed any restrictions upon itself, those imposed upon it by the states whilst it was in ventre sa mere, were as outrageous, fraudulent, and void, as if a nation should attempt to disinherit the heir of a king before he was born. Acts of limitation do not run against infants, much less against an embryo; and therefore all limitations imposed upon the federal government before it was born, or in its infancy, before it was able to take care of itself (as a concentrated government can always do, according to Mr. Hamilton) were contrary to natural right and void.

The natural right of a government to supremacy, is completely sustained by the natural supremacy of construction, as it could not be a government, if this supremacy of construction belonged to people who wished to control it. A profound statesman has written a celebrated treatise to establish the supremacy of construction, not hitherto quoted by the consolidators, out of pity, I presume, for their adversaries, and an aversion to killing honest but deluded people by a single blow. But whether it shall be ascribed to candour, or an apprehension that it is reserved to be produced if they are hard pressed, I shall suggest it to their recollection, and disclose it to the publick.

The code of rules alluded to, for defining the powers and rights of construction, was evidently written with an eye to the constitution of the United States; although the author, to avoid the censures of the federalists, has concealed his intention under the title of "A tale of a tub," and used the allegory of a last will, intending thereby to insinuate, that the constitution of the United States was liberty's last will. A testator bequeaths a coat to each of his three sons, with directions that they should be kept clean, and unsophisticated by patches, to imitate fashion or gratify pride, and his death-bed admonition to his children was in these words: "Sons, because I have purchased no estate, nor was born to any, I have long considered of some good legacies to bequeath you; and at last, with much care and expense, have provided each of you a new coat. Now you are to understand, that these coats have two virtues contained in them; one is, that with good wearing, they will last you fresh and good as long as you live. The other is, that they will grow in the same proportion with your bodies, lengthening and widening of themselves, so as to be always fit. Pray, children, wear them clean, and brush them often. You will find in my will full instructions, in every particular, concerning the wearing and management of your coats, wherein you must be very exact, to avoid the penalties I have appointed for every transgression or neglect, upon which your future fortunes will depend. I have also commanded in my will, that you should live together in one house, like brethren and friends, for then you will be sure to thrive, and not otherwise."

No allegory could be more exact. It exhibits the veneration in which the constitution ought to be held, its prohibitions against vice, and the subterfuges to evade them. The three coats are, the exclusive powers of the federal government, the exclusive powers of the state governments, and the concurrent powers of both. And the three sons typify a supreme power, a federal government, and a frantick democracy. Fine writers are allowed to be inspired, and if any have disclosed stronger proofs of it than Swift, in this admonition, they have never reached me. The United States, our testator, inherited *no estate.* With much *care and expense* they obtained the three coats, namely, the exclusive and concurrent powers. These coats, with good wearing, would last *fresh as long as they lived.* They would require frequent *brushing* to be kept *clean.* They would *grow in the same proportion with their bodies, lengthening and widening of themselves, so as to be always fit:* referring to new states, and the extension of the three classes of power over a larger space. In the constitution, *full instructions are contained concerning the wearing and management* of these powers. Exactness in this *respect* is necessary to avoid *the penalties of transgression,* and to secure their *future fortunes.* And the constitution is the *one house* in which the three powers must live as *brethren and friends, by which, and not otherwise, they would be sure to thrive.*

"Here, the story says, this good father died, and the three sons went altogether to seek their fortunes. I shall not trouble you with recounting what adventures they met with in the first seven years, any farther than by taking notice, that they carefully observed their father's will, and kept their coats in very good order. That they travelled through several countries, encountered a reasonable quantity of giants, and slew certain dragons." In this extract, the voluntary fraternity between the states; the seven years' adventures of the revolutionary war; the prosperity arising from keeping state and federal powers clean; our travelling into other countries, by negotiations and commerce; our encounters with the British, Hessian, and French giants; and our wars with the Indians, or dragons of the wilderness; are distinctly foretold, to prevent the misapprehension of the more essential parts of the allegory.

After this season of fraternity and adventures had past, the brothers "came up to town, and fell in love with the ladies, but especially three, the Dutchess d'Argent, Madame de Grand Titres, and the Countess d'Orgueil; or covetousness, ambition, and pride; from whom they met with a very bad reception; for on the one side, the three ladies were at the top of the fashion, and abhorred all that were below it but the breadth of a hair. On the other side, the will was very precise, and it was the main precept in it, not to add to or diminish from their coats, one thread, without a positive command in the will. Now the coats their father had left them, were, 'tis true, of very good cloth, and besides so neatly sown, you would swear they were all of a piece; but at the same time very plain, and with little or no ornament. The brothers, however, being induced by love to fall into all the vices of a town, were strangely at a loss what to do." The coming up to town, specifies the meetings of Congress; the Dutchess d'Argent, the funding, banking, and protecting-duty systems; Madame de Grand Titres, the prepossession or habit in favour of titles; and the Countess d'Orgueil, the pride of affecting supremacy. The love of men for these town ladies, and the difficulty of gratifying it, on account of the precise and close texture of the constitution, and its prohibition against altering one thread, except in the mode it prescribes, is also stated by Swift, as forciby displaying the efficacy of his rules for construction, to which he then proceeds:

"It happened, before they were a month in town, great shoulder-knots came up. Straight all the world was shoulder knots. In this unhappy case, the brothers went to consult the will, read it over and over, but not a word of shoulder-knots. What should they do? Obedience was absolutely necessary, and yet shoulder-knots appeared extremely requisite. After much thought, one of the brothers, who happened to be more book-learned than the other two, said he had found an expedient. It is true, said he, there is nothing here in this will, totidem verbis, making mention of shoulder-knots, but I dare conjecture, we may find them inclusive, or totidem syllabis. This distinction was approved by all, and so they fell to examine; but their evil star had so directed the matter, that the first syllable was not to be found in the whole writing. Upon which disappointment, he who found the former evasion took heart, and said, Brothers, there is yet hopes; for though we cannot find them totidem verbis, nor totidem syllabis, I dare engage we shall make them out tertio modo, or totidem literis. This discovery was also highly commended, upon which they fell once more to the scrutiny, and picked out the letters, s, h, o, u, l, d, e, r, when the same planet, enemy to their repose, had wonderfully contrived that a k was not to be found. Here was a weighty difficulty! But the distinguishing brother, now his hand was in, proved, by a very good argument, that k was a modern illegitimate letter, unknown to the learned ages, nor any where to be found in ancient manuscripts. Calendœ hath been sometimes writ with a k, but erroneously; for in the best copies it has been ever spelt with c. And by consequence, it was a gross mistake in our language to spell knot with a k; but from henceforward, he should take care it should be writ with a c. Upon this, all farther difficulty vanished. Shoulder-knots were made clearly out to be jure paterno, and our three gentlemen swaggered with as large and flaunting ones as the best." Great shoulder-knots are evidently typical of the national and supreme powers getting into fashion, and worn above other ornaments. Obedience to the constitution is absolutely necessary; but these powers, being very convenient, are extremely requisite. I may have been mistaken in supposing that the consolidating party had overlooked Swift's sage authority. They seem to have used it to get at their beloved ladies, without disobeying the constitution. As the letters, n, a, t, i, o, n, a, l, are all in the constitution, though the word itself is not, it has literally established a national government. The argument in the case of the letter k, has also furnished them with another important rule for construction. As neither governments, divested of supremacy, nor our federal system of dividing powers between two governments, are to be found in ancient manuscripts, and were unknown to the learned ages, they are modern illegitimate contrivances, and ought to be suppressed, for the purpose of restoring to the word government its good old meaning and supremacy inherited from antiquity.

Here I must gratify a certain feeling, not very uncommon, called vanity; and boast of my superior candour or sagacity over the commentators who have suppressed or misunderstood an authority so profound. As the word national is not in the constitution, they have clumsily sought for it by a transformation of words, not discerning that when a pebble only lay in their way, it was quite unnecessary to remove a mountain which lay out of it, and thus negligently weaken the capacity of construction to create a national government and a judicial supremacy. In like manner, by making the word constitution beget supremacy, they have reasoned on the ground, that a child of to-day might be the father of Adam. There are a great variety of constitutions, male and female, agricultural, charitable, religious, and commercial. All are made by qualities or stipulations, and none contain any thing, ex vi termini, not to be found in these qualities or stipulations. By changing the word constitution into the word supremacy, the conventional qualities of the former would be lost in the natural qualities of the latter; and the constitution, having thus lost its qualities, would be extinct. Now, instead of getting at supremacy in a mode so inartificial, had the consolidators adhered to the word government, or the word national, as containing internally, ex vi termini, the ethereal essence of power, called supremacy, neither to be defined by compact nor limited by words, their reasoning would have been sustained by the authority of the great Dean Swift; but by transforming United States into national, and constitution into supreme, they have incautiously weakened it. As the word national, totidem syllabis, was not in the constitution, and the letters n, a, t, i, o, n, a, l, were, to come at it tertio modo, was infinitely more grammatical, orthographical, and rational, than a violent metamorphosis of words, even defective in letters. The convention no doubt thought itself very cunning in rejecting the word national, proposed for its adoption, as it would imply a supreme power, according to ancient manuscripts and the learned ages; and the consolidating gentlemen, by endeavouring to seize upon Ovid's patent-right for arbitrary transmutations, have been caught in their trap; but Swift ingeniously gets them out again. Though national and sovereign, totidem verbis, are not in the constitution, both are there totidem literis; demonstrating the superior power of construction, when governed by a rule, simple, plain, and comprehensible, than when obliged to resort to the poetical license of working wonders. We all know that letters can make words; but how some words can make others, is a mystery. I am certain, therefore, of receiving the thanks of the consolidating school, for simplifying their reasoning, and vindicating the power of construction, by the useful discovery, that the constitution conveys sovereignty to the federal government, makes it a national government, and gives it any other power which commentators, who can spell, may choose to find; for they can now save themselves a world of trouble, by justifying their constructions upon the same ground used by the learned Doctor Swift, to justify the construction of their father's will by the brothers.

The words, necessary, requisite, and expedient, used by the learned brother, consign whole cargoes of arguments to our consolidating politicians, received with avidity, but without acknowledging the obligation. "Obedience to the will was absolutely *necessary,* and yet shoulder-knots appeared extremely *requisite.*" Peter, the great philologist and commentator, said he had found *"an expedient."* No anticipations could be more express than these. The constitution uses the word necessary; whatever is necessary is at least requisite, and whatever is requisite may be effected by an expedient, conformably with the constitution, as shoulder-knots were conformable to the will, because they were requisite. Hence, as a national government, judicial supremacy, banks, lotteries, roads, and canals, even if not necessary, are still requisite; and as every letter by which these words are spelled is actually in the constitution, without the perplexing absence of the letter k, it clearly follows, according to Swift, that the exercise of these, and all other requisite powers, may be effected by expedients, and that they would be more conformable to the constitution, than shoulder-knots were to the will, because that did not contain the letter k. Thus our consolidating commentators have wisely proceeded within the verge of a high authority, and prudently identify themselves with the learned Peter.

"Next to shoulder-knots, gold lace came in fashion, which seemed so considerable an alteration, as to require a positive precept. Then flame-coloured satin, for lining; then silver fringe; and, finally, an infinite number of points, tagged with silver. Upon consulting their father's will, the brothers, to their great astonishment, found these words: Item, I charge and command my said three sons to wear no sort of silver fringe upon or about their coats. However, after some pause, the brother so often mentioned for his erudition and skill in criticism, said that he had found, in a certain author, who should be nameless, that the word fringe also signifies a broom-stick, and doubtless ought to have the same interpretation. This, another brother disliked, because of the epithet silver, which could not, he humbly conceived, be applied to a broom-stick. But it was replied upon him, that this epithet was understood in an allegorical sense. However, he objected again, why their father should forbid them to wear a broom-stick upon their coats; a caution that seemed unnatural and impertinent; upon which he was taken up short, as one that spoke irreverently of a mystery; and this *expedient* was allowed to serve as a lawful dispensation for wearing their full proportion of silver fringe."

These successive fashions are obviously emblematical of the successive fashions which came up among us, called assumption of state debts, funding, banking, lotteries, and protecting duties. The infinite number of points tagged with silver, with special precision describe the multitude of manufactures thus tagged to lace capitalists with gold. Even every pin made in the United States has a tip of silver. But silver fringe was expressly forbidden. This peculiarity is stated to justify banking; the proposal and rejection of which in the convention, was equivalent to a *charge and command* against it. No emblematical description of it could have been more happy. Bank paper is fringed with silver, and the use of fringe is either to hide defects or to entrap by a bait. Fringe disfigures a good substantial coat, as banks disfigure an honest government. The prohibition in the will was positive, and if that could not prevent a requisite and expedient construction for wearing fringe, the rejection in the convention only, could not defeat the same great principle when applied to banking. As silver fringe meant a broom-stick, the banks rejected in the convention might mean mounds of earth; and therefore their rejection is only a prohibition upon the federal government to bury state rights under mounds of earth. If this idea should even be allowed to be as preposterous and impertinent as that of wearing broom-sticks upon coats, yet it may also contain some mystery. And thus it clearly follows, that the federal government may suffocate state rights by banks of paper, but not by banks of earth. In this extract, we discover that Swift foresaw the transformations of the word judiciary into the word supremacy, and of the words United States, into the word national; and authorized both, by proving that the words silver fringe might be construed broom-sticks. The idea of wearing broom-sticks over coats, is a fine illustration of supremacies for sweeping away state rights; but the application of silver fringe to unrestricted appropriations of fed-

eral money, is still closer, as silver is more graceful upon governments than broom-sticks upon coats. If, therefore, the federal
government can add to its silver embellishments, by unrestrained
appropriations, legislative judgments, bounties, pensions, banks,
and internal improvements, this authority will justify it in resorting to these or any other modes of fringing itself; because, as the
prohibition in the will against wearing silver fringe, distinctly
refers to the prohibitions in the constitution against the state
and federal governments wearing each other's powers, a mode
of getting over the first, must also be a mode of getting over the
others.

"But the gold lace seemed too considerable an alteration
without better warrant; when the learned brother, having read
Aristotelis Dialecta, and especially that wonderful piece, De
Interpretatione, which has the faculty of teaching its readers to
find out a meaning in every thing but itself, observed, You are
to be informed, that of wills, duo sunt genera, nun cupatory and
scriptory; that in the scriptory will here before us, there is no precept or mention about gold lace, concedetur; but si idem
affirmeter de nun cupatoria, negatur. For, brothers, if you
remember, we heard a fellow say, that he heard my father say,
that he would advise his sons to get gold lace to their coats. By
G—, that is very true, cried the other; I remember it perfectly
well, said the third. And so, without more ado, they got the largest
gold lace in the parish, and walked about as fine as lords."

It is impossible, after reading this extract, to doubt of Swift's
inspiration. It may be called the golden rule of construction.
Even members of the convention certainly did say, that a national
government, invested with supremacy, ought to be established.
But all well-informed politicians have often heard others say, that

governments were divine, inherently supreme, sovereigns of the people, and able to do anything but turn a man into a woman; and these nuncupatoria very clearly supply all powers overlooked by written constitutions, necessary to enable governments to come at gold. Therefore, when we have obtained the word government by a constitution, these nuncupatoria come in play, and constitute the marrow of construction. Now all the letters for spelling the words government and supreme, are really in the constitution, and moreover, both the words, in extenso, are in it, and therefore we are not obliged to find them, as the word shoulder-knot was found in the will. But each was attended with a difficulty. One is applied to the state as well as the federal government, so that both might lay claim to its comprehensiveness; and the other is used in reference to inferior federal courts. Swift foresaw and removed both these difficulties; the first by the nuncupatoria resource, as the states were called in the convention, that father of the constitution, corporations; and the other, by the inherent rights of supremacy, bequeathed to it also by nuncupatoria. The federal system having thus obtained exclusively the words government and supreme, obtains also their inherent nuncupative donations. But lest construction should be taxed with finding out a *meaning in every thing but itself,* Swift cautiously refers us to the Dialecta of Aristotle, to prove that the art de interpretatione is not fettered by the unreasonable obligation of containing in itself any meaning, to rebut the charge, and fortify his treatise on every quarter.

"The flame-coloured satin, for linings, caused them to fall again to rummaging the will, because the case required a positive precept, the lining being held by orthodox writers to be of the essence of the coat. After long search, they could fix upon nothing to the matter in hand, except a short advice of their father in the will, to take care of fire, and put out their candles before they went to sleep. This, though a good deal to the purpose, and helping very far towards self-conviction, yet not seeming wholly of force to establish a command, and being resolved to avoid farther scruple, says he that was the scholar, I remember to have read in wills, of a codicil annexed, which is indeed a part of the will, and what it contains hath equal authority with the rest. Now, I have been considering of this same will here before us, and I cannot reckon it to be complete, for want of a codicil. I will therefore fasten one in its proper place very dexterously. I have had it by me for some time, and it talks a great deal (as good luck would have it) of this very flame-coloured satin. The project was immediately approved by the other two; an old parchment scroll was tagged on according to art, in the form of a codicil, and the satin bought and worn."

It has been wittily said, "that though truth is not to be spoken at all times, it may be spoken sometimes," and under this authority it may perhaps be borne at this time. The codicil to the will, plainly alludes to the Federalist, as a codicil to the constitution. Lest the reference should be over-looked, it is very particular. The learned commentator Peter, had kept the codicil by him for some time; the learned commentators of the constitution, had kept by them their propositions for a supreme national government made in the convention. Peter's codicil talks a great deal of the flame-coloured satin; the codicil of the Federalist talks a great deal of a national or general government, and supremacy. The lining is held by orthodox writers, to be of the *essence of the coat*. The orthodox Federalist says, "that the sources of the ordinary powers of government make it national and not

federal." What an admirable concurrence is here! The departments of the federal government, being the lining of the constitution, and lining being of the essence of a coat, this lining
converts a federal into a national constitution; for a national
constitution only could beget a national government; and as the
Federalist had positively declared the constitution to be federal, it
could only be made national and supreme, by the lining of the
ordinary powers of government. The flame-coloured satin is a type of
supremacy, and that having become of the essence of the constitution, justifies its alteration by a supreme court. The constitution goes farther than the will, by declaring that codicils may
be added to it, and the house of representatives, as a part of its lining, having turned a federal into a national government, a
national supremacy acquires the power of making these codicils. As Peter, the supreme brother, so the court, the supreme
department, may make them by an exclusive right of construction. The advice in the will to take care of fire, and put out the
candles before they went to sleep, is a fine allusion to the colour
of the lining, as the flame of supremacy might consume state
rights; and also an admonition to the states to extinguish this
flame *before they went to sleep,* which they have carelessly kindled,
by putting the words government and supreme, and even the letters which spell the word national, into the constitution. As the
will required Peter's codicil to justify the requisite but prohibited satin lining, so the constitution required the codicil of the
Federalist, to justify the requisite but rejected national government. The judgments of the federal courts are the linings of federal laws. Being of their essence, they can alter the division of
powers, as the linings could essentially alter the coats. Codicils are
as requisite, necessary, and proper, for the constitution, as for the

will, to accommodate it with new fashions; and the supreme
Peter had before proved, that expedients were allowable for
effecting whatever was requisite, necessary, and proper.

"But fashions perpetually altering in that age, the scholastic
brother, weary of searching for farther evasions, and solving ever-
lasting contradictions, resolved at all hazards to comply with the
modes of the world; they concerted matters together, and agreed
to lock up their father's will in a strong box, brought out of
Greece or Rome, and trouble themselves no farther to examine
it, but only refer to its authority whenever they thought fit. In
consequence whereof, it grew a general mode to wear an infinite
number of points, most of them tagged with silver. Upon which,
the scholar pronounced, ex cathedra, that points were absolutely
jure paterno. 'Tis true, the fashion prescribed somewhat more
than were directly named in the will; however, they, as *heirs general* of their father, had power to make and add certain clauses
for *publick emolument,* though not deducible, totidem verbis, from
the letter of the will, or else multa absurda sequerentur. This was
understood for canonical, and therefore on the following Sunday,
they came to church all covered with points." The text almost
becomes too plain to be allegorical. Construction is the strong
box, brought from England, in which the constitution may be
locked up. Whether that or Greek and Latin would be most
unintelligible to the learned reader, may be doubtful; but to the
unlearned, both would be incomprehensible. By the obscurity,
those having an exclusive custody of the box, might refer to it
without the danger of contradiction, as empowering them to
wear as many points tagged with silver as they chose. This decision, pronounced ex cathedra, specifies the decision of the
supreme court, ex banco, declaring that the federal government

was invested by the constitution with a power to remove every obstruction to its wearing as many points tagged with silver as it chose. This was a compliance with the modes of the world at all hazards. Though the infinite number of these points might exceed the objects named in the constitution to which silver might be tagged, yet *as heir general* of the states, the federal government might add clauses to the constitution for publick emolument. By adhering to the will, multa absurda sequerentur, in the opinion of the learned brother; by adhering to the constitution, the same thing would happen, in the opinion of our learned department; and therefore, where powers are not to be found, totidem verbis, it may supply those necessary, or multa absurda sequerentur. And what can be more absurd, than to suffer inconveniences which may be removed by expedients?

The reader has discerned, that the sage maxims collected by as able a commentator as ever lived, are intended to constitute a complete code for settling the rights and powers of construction, though conveyed to the world by an allegory, alluding to the United States in particular; but to place his intention beyond a doubt, Swift tells us "that he treats the subject by types and figures for the benefit of mankind;" thereby giving us to understand, that it was calculated to instruct all ages in the profound art of construction.

"The learned brother now began to look big and take mightily upon him. He insisted that he was his father's sole heir. What with pride, projects, and knavery, he became distracted, and insisted that he should be called Lord Peter, monarch of the universe, and God Almighty. He invented various projects, and circulated many slips of paper for getting money, and made fine promises of an ample retribution in terra incognita. He insisted that a crust of bread was beef, mutton, veal, venison, partridge, plum-pudding, custard, and claret. When his brothers doubted this; look ye, gentlemen, cries Peter in a rage, to convince you what a couple of blind, positive, ignorant, wilful puppies you are, I will use this plain argument: By G—, it is true, good, natural mutton; and G—confound you both eternally, if you offer to believe otherwise."

Here is a positive precedent, entitling the federal government or the supreme court, to consider itself as the sole heir of the states, as the concentrated power of America, and as a political almighty. At least, it justifies its modest claim to supremacy over only a portion of the universe so inferior to Lord Peter's; and undoubtedly recognises the banking, protecting duty, lottery, and all other projects for getting money by slips of paper, as legitimate consequences of its supreme power; if attended with promises of ample retribution in the terra incognita called specie, or in the cheapness to be produced by monopolies. It proves that banks are mounds of earth, or couriers for transporting taxes, and the ten miles square the whole United States; postulates as necessary to sustain sundry laws and judgments, as that a crust was beef, mutton, veal, venison, partridge, plum-pudding, custard, and claret was, to sustain Lord Peter's supremacy. The forbearance of the federal government in not pushing its constructive powers to the extent justified by the authority, entitles it to confidence. Far less furious than the supreme Peter, it only puts people in prison, and seizes their temporal estates, and does not send their souls to hell, to convince them of the virtues of supremacy. The crust is obviously the economy passionately recommended to the people by the capitalists, who, like Lord Peter, have fine houses, fine clothes, fine victuals and drink, and plenty of money in their pockets.

"This worthy matter gave a principal occasion to a great rupture which happened among these brethren, and was never afterwards made up. The two brothers, weary of his usage, asked for a copy of their father's will, which had lain long neglected. Instead of granting them this request, he called them damn'd sons of whores, rogues, and traitors, and all the vile names he could muster up. However, they got a copy of the will; but Peter, with a file of dragoons at his heels, very fairly, by main force, kicks them both out of doors, and would never let them come under his roof, from that day to this."

The states, having long indulged and even imitated the extravagancies of the federal government, have at length bethought them of the long-neglected constitution. This arrogance has drawn upon them sundry hard names, but hitherto not so very vile, as those applied by the supreme Peter to his brethren; witness One of the People, who deserves great praise for his moderation under the same provocation by which Lord Peter was so justly incensed. It is not highly arrogant in the states to winch from the discipline of being kicked from under the roof of the constitution by supremacy, never to return? The reader will recollect, that the constitution is the house, in which the three classes of powers, federal exclusive, state exclusive, and concurrent, were placed. Peter, the great commentator, remarkable for his book-learning, and knowledge of Aristotle, is a type of constructive supremacy, remarkable for its book-learning, and knowledge of Lord Coke, who finds but a single exception to its power. But here, to shew both my candour and erudition, I shall suggest a considerable difficulty. What is meant by the file of dragoons, by whose help Peter kicks his brothers out of doors? It appears that Swift wrote his treatise upon construction in the year 1697, and that it was not published until several years afterwards. Sir Richard Steele, a contemporary author, wrote his comedy called The Funeral, in the year 1702. In this play, a file of men is said to consist of six; it being then the custom to form armies three men deep. It is therefore obvious that Swift, by a file, meant six dragoons, and Peter, who led them on, made seven. So that Swift might have intended a numerical reference to the court, as the supremacy by which the state exclusive and concurrent powers would be kicked from under the roof of the constitution. This opinion is very far from violating his rules for construction, or those adopted by our supremacy, because the verb "to dragoon," means "to persecute," and that means "to harass with penalties," and this implies "to prosecute," and that means "to pursue by law," so that we fairly come by constructive induction to the very case of pursuing state rights by suits in law and equity in the federal courts. Moreover, though the members of this court, totidem verbis, may not be dragoons, yet it is quite fair to infer from the phrase "church militant," that there may be a court militant. Civil and religious freedom make but one principle, and a militant temper, if it had never been ascertained, might as probably have been expected from civil, as from religious functionaries. On the other hand, when we consider that dragoons are people who enforce commands by guns and swords, and not by executions and sequestrations, we are forced to imagine that Swift, by the allegory of "a file of dragoons," might mean a mercenary army, with a General Peter at its head. For this interpretation also, there are weighty reasons. Lord Peter having assumed a supreme power over his father's will, resorts to the customary instrument of supremacy for enforcing his constructions; and Swift, by the analogy, might have intended to predict, that the same necessary and proper expedient would be resorted to here by supremacy, for enforcing its constructions of the constitution. Between interpretations both plausible, the learned reader will choose for himself; or he may think them both sound. Supremacy itself will certainly incline to the opinion, that it may shoot judgments from courts, or bullets from guns, as expediency or convenience may dictate; but it is unimportant to state rights, because when kicked out of doors in either mode, the text declares that they will remain there.

The tale goes on to relate "how the two brothers, named Jack and Martin, being left to the wide world, with little or nothing to trust to, whilst Lord Peter had gotten a noble house, a title, and money, called to mind their father's will, consisting of certain *admirable rules* about the wearing of their coats, resolved to alter what was amiss, and to reduce their future measures to the strictest obedience, as prescribed therein. How Lord Peter's fancies, infused into his brothers, had covered their coats with an infinite quantity of lace, ribbands, fringe, embroidery, and points, (meaning only those tagged with silver, for the rest fell off), so as to produce the most antick medley conceivable, and to leave hardly a thread of the original coat to be seen. How Jack advised Martin to strip, tear, pull, rend, and flay off all, because Peter had locked up the drink, cheated them of their fortunes, palmed his damn'd crusts upon them for mutton, and kick'd them out of doors. How Martin begged Jack not to damage his coat, for he would never get such another; and desired him to consider, that it was not their business to form their actions by any reflections upon Peter, but by observing the rules prescribed in their father's will; that he should remember Peter was still their brother, whatever faults or injuries he had committed, and therefore they should by all means avoid such a thought as that of taking measures for good and evil, from no other rule but that of opposition to him; that it was true, the testament of their good father was very exact in what related to the wearing of their coats, yet it was no less penal and strict in prescribing agreement, friendship, and affection, between them. How Martin proceeded gravely, stitch by stitch, to reform his coat, without damaging the cloth. How Jack, in pulling off the fineries from his coat, tore it to pieces, and was forced to darn it again with pack-thread and a skewer. How the resemblance between the persons, and between the finery and rags of Peter and Jack, was so great, that they were often mistaken for each other. And how Martin separated himself from them both." Lord Peter's noble house, locking up the drink, palming crusts upon his brothers for delicacies, and cheating them of their fortunes, allude to our noble capitol, the residence of the assumed supremacy; to protecting duties, locking up good liquors from all except the wealthy; to the advice of capitalists to the people (converted into commands by a number of laws) to be economical, or live upon crusts; and to banks, bounties, pensions, with other constructive powers, for cheating them of their fortunes, being the very efficacious means of the capitalist Peter for enriching himself, and impoverishing his brothers. But here the allegory, having with wonderful exactness described what has happened, dives into futurity, and guesses that the states will call the constitution to mind, and consider its *admirable rules* for wearing the three classes of powers; that the antick medley with which these powers are covered, by stitching on them inter-polations, hardly leaving a principle of the original constitution to be seen, may be removed; that though some people, like Peter, may be for hiding the federal system under the fineries of supremacy, and some, like Jack, for tearing it to pieces by the idea of an American nation, others may, like Martin, separate themselves from both extremes, and proceed prudently to restore it to its original perfection; that furious states would be obliged to darn up the rents they might make with very bad materials; that prudent states will not forget that the federal government is their brother, nor over-look the advantages of living amicably with it, under the roof of the constitution; and that the resemblance between Peter's finery and Jack's tatters, will make it hard to distinguish one from the other, because either would produce a rupture between the state and federal governments, which may never be made up. Martin's advice is adverse both to the tyrannical supremacy of Lord Peter, and the disorganizing fury of mad Jack, and clearly points out the measures by which the admirable rules of the will, or federal constitution, can be made to secure the prescribed mode of wearing the coats, that is, of exercising the federal and state powers. But whether this sage advice will be followed, or whether the supremacy of Peter, or the madness of Jack, will be preferred, are matters in the womb of time, which cannot be delivered by anticipation. Swift, however, intuitively declares, "that if the reader fairly considers the strength of what he has advanced, according to his constitution, it will produce a wonderful revolution in his notions and opinions;" meaning, that his rules for construction, when applied to our constitution (the political constitution of every individual), will change his habits of thinking.

That enough of Swift's erudite treatise for establishing the supremacy of construction over the rights and sovereignties of the states, may be left to exercise the superior sagacity of the consolidating school, and to reap the praise due to brevity, I have quoted it sparingly, like an amicus curiæ, pleading without a fee, and only solicitous to state a question fairly. But candour compels me to add, that it contains many other allusions worthy of consideration, such as, that Peter, the profound commentator and type of supremacy, first induced his brothers to consent to his constructions, and then kicked them out of doors; that Martin, the type of our federal system, would not rip from his coat the checks and balances by which it is constituted; that Jack, the type of the notion that the mode of electing the house of representatives will prevent an adulteration of the constitution, ruined his coat, was a madman, and finally chained, like a great nation subjected to a concentrated supremacy; and that the fripperies added to the coats, from time to time, with the consent of all the brothers, indicate the successive interpolations stitched to the constitution, with the consent of all our parties. These were at length used by the supreme Peter, to compel his brothers to live on crusts, were carefully removed by the federal Martin, and were furiously torn off by the frantick Jack. It is also worthy of observation, that Lord Peter does not take away the coats of his brethren, and wear them under his own. Was it because the acute Swift saw the ridiculousness of swaddling his hero, like a Dutch boor with three pair of breeches on? And did he think that the federal government, by clothing itself in powers cut out for state governments, would become such a comick, antick, jack-pudding figure, and exhibit such tumblings, bamboozlings, flounderings, and scufflings, as too much to resemble a political zany, to be shown in so grave a work? To rebut intirely the charge of designing the least suppression, by my conciseness, I acknowledge that this treatise upon construction furnishes many other arguments in favour of the consolidating school; and lest I may have failed to select the strongest, I humbly advise its disciples to distribute an hundred thousand copies of it among the people, as a complete prolegomena for explaining their constructions of the constitution.

It supplies a vast mass of precedents and argumentation for removing collisions between the state and federal governments, and for proving the efficiency of a concentrated supremacy; to which I confess that only one poor observation can be opposed, namely, that if the state and federal governments may be occasionally scratched by the mutual check resulting from the division of powers, it may still be considered as the only brier which bears the rose called liberty, able to impart that rare flavour to our political nose-gay, highly agreeable to some people, but very offensive to others.

INDEX

acts of limitation, 366
Adams, John, 56–57, 68, 260
agriculture, 34, 334
ambition, 369; consolidating projects and, 102–3; division of powers and, 244, 307; individuals and, 343; liberty and, 256, 292; monarchy and, 53; nature of, 245; power and, 246–48, 251–52; state governments and, 245, 343; state sovereignty and, 249
amendment: constitutional mode of, 14–15, 161–62, 210–12, 312–15, 346; constructive mode of, 15; state sovereignty and, 210–11
"America", 208
America. *See* United States
American nation: confederation of 1777 and, 104; constitutional amendment and, 14–15; Constitution and, 104; Declaration of Independence and, 104; federal judiciary and, 135; Madison and, 111; powers of, 109; state conventions and, 225; supremacy of, 135
American people: Constitution and, 104–5; government and, 104; powers of, 116; state conventions and, 106–7; states and, 119

anarchy, 301
Annapolis, 13, 16
Archimedes, 72
aristocracy, 8, 68, 354; capitalist, 331–32; large states and, 102–3; pecuniary, 332; population and, 270; rights of people and, 232; southern, 102
Aristotelis Dialecta, 376, 377
Aristotle, 383
arrogance: of political departments, 243; power and, 243, 246; of state governments, 264
Articles of Confederation: federal union and, 22; revision of, 13, 17, 30
"assembly", 6
"A tale of a tub", 367–89
Athens, 317
Augustus, 73
authorities, opinion and, 258–59
"authority", 143

banks, 286, 331; case involving, 94; laws for, 72, 327; power to create, 338
Bonaparte, Napolean, 343, 351
Butler, 22–23

Caesar, Julius, 247, 343
Callender, 265
capitalist aristocracy, 332
capitalists, 341

cases in law and equity: Constitution and, 167; controversies of political nature and, 175; criminal prosecutions and, 171; English judiciary and, 162; federal judiciary and, 159, 174–75; national government and, 188–89; power to try, 162, 163, 193; restriction of, 162; states and, 159–60, 164, 167–68, 384

Catharine of Russia, 291–92

censorial power, 308–13

Charles the First, 274

charts of incorporation, 34

Coke, Lord, 383

collisions: concentrated supremacy and, 308; Constitution and, 314; power moderated by division and, 308; tribunal for settling, 315–16

Columbia, 168

commerce: Constitution and, 330; federal power of regulating, 328–30; geographical interests and, 330; promotion of, 34; rights of sovereignty and, 2

commitia centuriata, 89

commitia tributia, 89

"common defence and general welfare", 4, 5

common interest, 300

compact: collisions and, 300; Constitution as, 165–67; government by, 68, 71, 226; national government and federal, 274; power and, 226–27; states and federal, 274; union and, 1

concentrated power: affections of, 247–48; collisions and, 266; control of election and, 298; divinity of kings and, 297–98;

division of power and, 298–99; division of powers and, 310; in England, 334; in federal departments, 266; federal government and, 255; geographical interests and, 353–54; laws of nature and, 250; liberty and, 251, 318; over extensive territories, 357; principles of, 293; securities against, 250–51; state rights and, 253, 271; supremacy and, 270–71; sustaining of, 291; tyranny of, 291. *See also* power

concentrated supremacy: collisions and, 308; division of powers and, 296–99; efficiency of, 389; of England, 294, 318–19; nature of, 254; over extensive territories, 292; superiority of, 254

concurrent powers, 90, 94–95, 133–34, 159–60, 329, 339–40

"confederacy", 273

"confederation", 14, 16, 18

confederation, sole government v., 82–83

confederation of 1777, 56–57; alteration of, 14; American nation and, 104; "common defence and general welfare" and, 5; "confederation" and, 16; Congress and, 6, 20, 79, 112, 121, 283; consolidated sovereignty and, 5–6; consolidation of states and, 3; judicial department and, 152; necessity of, 4; ratification of, 211; state sovereignty and, 2–3, 191, 211, 212, 213

confidence: distrust and, 327–28; government and, 328; party, 340

"Congress": "assembly" and, 6; constitutional convention use of, 20; convention and, 31; Declaration of Independence and, 6; federal union and, 20; "parliament" and, 6; in Randolph's resolutions, 20

Congress: amendment of Constitution and, 161, 274; banks and, 338; censorial supremacy in, 311; "common defence and general welfare" as ends of, 4; confederation of 1777 and, 4, 14, 20, 79, 112, 121, 283; confidence in, 328; consolidated government and, 253; consolidation of states and, 3–4; Constitution and, 4, 13, 37, 72, 109–10, 153–54, 281, 313, 324; constructions of, 15; convention recommendations of, 16–18; division of powers and, 331–33, 335; erroneous constructions and, 314–15; federal judiciary and, 36–37, 72, 153, 153–54, 155–56, 204, 287, 335; geographical interests and, 67, 305–6, 319–23, 330; geographical majority in, 134–35; Hamilton's plan for government and, 51; laws of nature and, 256; legislative powers of, 21; local interests and, 323; local powers in, 357; local powers of, 321; national, 50; national government and, 13, 24; national right of territory and, 117; national supremacy and, 319–20; negative over state laws and, 50, 192–93, 205, 286; political meaning of, 109–10; powers of, 112, 145, 158; powers of sword and, 249; public good and, 36;

regulation of law and fact by, 164–65; representation in, 118–19, 299, 303; representative character of, 6; responsibility to people of, 235; right of appeal of, 314–15; self-defense and, 286; source of power of, 121; sovereign states and, 115; sovereignty in, 78; special powers invested in, 115; state governments and, 9, 73, 229, 253; state laws and, 159, 310–11; state powers and, 340; state representation in, 342; state rights and, 1, 310; states and, 6–7; state sovereignty and, 7, 67, 71, 213–14; supremacy of, 52, 60, 72, 279–80, 281, 321–22; taxation and, 94, 122–23, 245, 286; treason and, 281; tribunals and, 145, 173; two parties of, 309–10; union and, 7; united representation of, 1

Connecticut, 214; constitutional convention and, 7; federal government and, 33; federal v. national union and, 18; national government and, 23; powers in convention of, 17

consolidated government, 222, 253

consolidated sovereignty, 5–6, 254–55

consolidating project: ambition and, 102–3; construction of, 273; in convention, 23; Declaration of Independence and, 2; state conventions and, 106–7

consolidating school: dogmas of, 220; election of president and, 344; federal government and, 81; power of construction and,

consolidating school (*continued*)
373; secrecy and, 47; sovereignties created by Constitution
and, 79–81; state rights of people and, 264–65
"consolidation", 5
consolidation, 1, 45, 53
"constitution": aggregate nation
and, 274; "confederation" and,
14, 16, 18; federal, 21; innate
powers of, 273; national government and, 274; recondite powers
and, 313; supremacy and, 372;
union of states and, 276
Constitution: amendment of,
14–15, 105, 161–62, 176, 210–
12, 274, 312–15, 346; American
people and, 104–5; cases in law
and equity and, 167, 174; censorial power established by, 312;
characters of, 165–71; classes of
power and, 339–40; collisions
and, 314; commerce and, 330;
as compact, 165–69; concurrent
power and, 180; Congress and,
4, 6, 13, 37, 72, 109–10, 161,
253, 281, 324; consolidated sovereignty and, 5–6, 209; consolidating constructions of, 61;
construction and, 367, 380–81;
constructions of, 39, 46, 47, 75,
102, 152; constructive
supremacy and, 15, 19–20;
departments of power and,
81–82; division of powers and,
197, 246, 251–52, 266–67, 302,
308, 312–14, 316–18, 326–27,
330–31, 352–53, 358; election
of president and, 345–46; executive department and, 343; federal character of, 257, 273, 275,

379; federal government and,
13, 36, 42–43, 59–60, 69–70,
79, 101, 109, 114–17, 139, 283,
373, 379; Federalist and, 76–79;
federal judiciary and, 25, 30,
148–49, 153–61; foundation of,
99, 104; framers of, 105; framing of, 7, 207; "general" and, 86,
112–13, 126; general government and, 126; geographical
interests and, 323; government
and, 16; Hamilton's construction of, 46, 131–32, 257; house
of representatives and, 341–42,
388; impeachment and, 184–85;
intention of, 52; language in,
372–79; legislative and judicial
powers and, 173; legislatures
under, 90; as liberty's last will,
367–89; limited powers and, 32;
local interests and, 324; Madison's construction of, 30, 46,
126, 132, 136–38, 257; Martin's
construction of, 46; meaning
of, 46; mixed character of government and, 195; "national"
and, 29, 86, 112–13, 126, 274,
371; national government and,
26, 59, 94, 117, 126, 198, 218,
238, 276; "necessary" and, 373;
negative over state laws and, 20,
22, 40; oath of state judges to,
170–71; "people" and, 8–9, 284;
people and, 219, 267; political
departments and, 160; potential
state opposition to, 41–42;
powers of, 273–74; powers
vested by, 88–89; preamble of,
238–39; preservation of union
and, 17; prohibitions of,
191–95, 282–85, 286–87; public

good and, 36; ratification of, 14,
38–39, 43, 59–60, 75, 76,
99–100, 104, 211, 239, 255; ratifying states and, 10; representation in, 112; republican
government intended by, 278;
rights of people and, 84–85,
238–39; stability of, 311; state
and federal legislatures under,
90; state conventions and,
105–7; state election and, 249;
state governments and, 101,
134, 238, 253, 358–59; state
laws and, 20; state legislatures
and, 105; state nations and, 15;
state rights and, 96, 221,
263–64, 361–62; states and, 14,
38–39, 42, 107, 152, 165,
199–200, 209, 284, 324; state
sovereignty and, 3, 4–5, 44, 76,
77, 100, 136, 209, 212, 213–14,
325; state supremacy and, 196;
supremacy of, 26, 27, 170–72,
179, 182, 266–67; supremacy
over, 313–14; "supreme" in,
25–26, 29; as supreme law, 26,
93; unconstitutional federal
judgments and, 182; "union"
and, 273; "united" and, 277;
United States and Congress
and, 281; war powers and, 330;
Yates's construction of, 46
constitutional convention: battle
between national and federal
government in, 29, 50–52,
70–71; change from national to
federal government in, 69;
"Congress" and, 20, 31; consolidating project in, 23; Constitution and, 38–39; "convention"
and, 14; elements of political

power and, 224–25; "federal"
and "republican" in, 62; federal
government and, 24, 30; federal
parties in, 25, 37; Hamilton's
plan of government and, 31–33;
Jefferson's absence from, 57;
judicial power and, 30, 35,
36–37; "national" and, 19–20,
29, 34; national government
and, 34–35, 38, 48–49, 51, 57,
217, 376; national government
in, 19–27; national supremacy
and, 326–27; negative over state
laws and, 29–30; political parties in, 25, 37, 49, 52–53,
55–62; resolutions of, 33–35;
secret debates of, 45, 47–48, 50,
63; state appointments of
deputies for, 7; state distinctions
and, 23–24; state ratifications
and, 15; states and, 23;
"supreme" and, 29
constitutionality, 127
constitutional laws, 93, 311
constitutional rights, 314
constitutions: supremacy of,
198–99; tyranny and, 188–89
construction: art of, 381–82; censorial power of, 312; concurrent
power of, 179–80; concurrent
rights of, 95; of Congress, 15;
Constitution and, 367, 380–81;
enforcement of, 384–85; golden
rule of, 376; judicial supremacy
and, 372; national government
and, 372; national supremacy
of, 15; powers of, 336, 367–89;
prejudice and, 46–47; principles
and, 1; rules for, 367–89; state
sovereignty and, 387–88;
supremacy of, 19–20, 26, 333,

construction (*continued*) 334, 365, 366–67; unconstitutional, 314; words and, 1, 11

"convention": constitutional convention and, 14; "legislatures" and, 9–10

corporations, states as, 21, 222–23, 226, 365

council of revision, 19, 20

crime, opinion and, 187

Cromwell, Oliver, 318

d'Argent, Duchess, 369

d'Orgueil, Countess, 369

Declaration of Independence: American nation and, 104; "Congress" and, 6; consolidated sovereignty and, 5–6; consolidating project and, 2; construction of, 4; federal court and, 200; federal government and, 365; as foundation of government, 2; framing of, 207; judicial department and, 152; language used in, 4; liberty and, 2; national government and, 21; negative over state laws and, 21; people and, 10, 267; per capita supremacy and, 201; principles of United States in, 2; public opinion and, 42; state governments and, 9; states and, 3–4, 55; state sovereignty and, 3, 42, 191, 213; state supremacy and, 196; union of states created by, 3; "United States" and, 3

De Interpretatione, 376

Delaware, 214; constitutional convention and, 7; federal government and, 33; national government and, 23; Pinckney's

motion and, 64; powers in convention of, 17

delegated powers: centrifugal tendencies and, 255; of federal government, 214; limits between reserved and, 145–46; state sovereignty and, 210

delusion, 47

democracy, 68, 102, 354

despotism, 226, 301, 319–20

Dickinson, 30, 33, 63

divinity of kings, 297–99

division of powers: ambition and, 244; collisions and, 266; in compound republic, 130–31; concentrated power and, 267–69, 296–99, 310; concurrent powers arising from, 90; Congress and, 331–33, 335; Constitution and, 197, 246, 266–67, 302, 312–18, 326–27, 330–31, 352–53, 358; domestic evils and, 292; domestic happiness and, 307; establishment of, 359–60; federal judiciary and, 132; federal legislature and, 131; foreign aggression and, 292; geographical interests and, 306–7, 321; integrity of political departments and, 182; judiciary and, 130; liberty and, 132, 140–41, 218, 227–28, 243, 266, 293, 349–50; maintenance of, 129–30; mutual check resulting from, 389; national government and, 334–36; necessity of, 131–32, 292–93, 316–17; objections to, 300–301; people and, 231, 355–56; popular supremacy and, 135; principles of, 293; representation and, 298;

state governments and,
299–301; states and, 355;
supremacy of people and, 131;
territorial lines of states and,
325–26; union and, 351; value
of, 296; wisdom of, 294–95; .
See also powers
domestic happiness: division of
powers and, 307; general government and, 67
Don Quixote, 197–98
Dutch provinces, 276, 277

election: concentrated power and
control of, 298; federal, 233–36;
federal government and, 109;
legislatures and control of, 181;
national, 234, 236; national
government and, 109; of president, 236, 341–47; right of,
233–34; state, 233–34, 249
Ellsworth, Judge, 67, 307
"empire", 209
England: capitalist aristocracy and,
331–32; division of powers in,
169; domestic regulations and,
246; judiciary of, 162; kings,
lords, and commons of, 301;
legislation in, 95; national government of, 31; national legislature and, 128; oppressions of,
330; rights of people and,
231–32; slavery and, 341;
supremacy in, 256, 267, 270,
297, 318–19, 334, 350; union
of, 1
Europe: absolute concentrated
power in, 353–54; governments
of, 300
executive: Constitution and, 343;
federal government and

supremacy of, 25; national, 19;
in national government, 23;
structure of, 52; supreme, 31, 34
"extension", 157–58

"federal": convention adoption of,
60; federal courts and, 347;
interpretations of, 58; quarrel
between "republican" and, 62;
state sovereignty and, 7;
supreme court and, 347
federal courts. *See* federal judiciary
federal departments: concentrated
power in, 266; division of
power between state and, 218,
242; mutual check of state and,
269–70; mutual independence
of, 218; supremacy of, 269–70
federal government: American
people and, 104; battle between
national and, 29, 69; collisions
between state and, 389; concentrated power and, 255; concentrated supremacy in, 294;
concurrency of legislation and,
93; concurrent powers of, 134,
179–80, 285, 368; consolidating
school and, 81; constitutional
rights and, 314; Constitution
and, 36, 42–43, 59–60, 69–70,
116–17, 161, 266, 379; constructive supremacy and, 22;
constructive supremacy of, 19;
controversies between states
and, 175–76; convention and,
24, 45–46, 50–52; corporate
character of, 222–23; Declaration of Independence and, 365;
difference between national
and, 70–71; division of powers
and, 165, 244; division of rights

federal government (*continued*)
between political individuals
and, 301; English government
and, 170; first resolution in
favor of, 30; geographical interests and, 305; impeachment
and, 184; individuals and,
119–20, 293; liberty and, 75;
mutual checks and security of,
40; mutual control between
state and, 308, 312; mutual
independence of, 152; mutual
moderation and, 307–8;
national character of, 341;
national sovereignty and, 82,
226–27; necessity and propriety
of laws and, 92; negative over
state laws and, 39–40, 116,
189–90; opposition to, 59–60;
ordinary sources of power and,
114; people and, 231, 236, 298;
powers of, 35–36, 79, 101, 109,
114–16, 139, 140, 145, 156,
214, 282, 338–39, 368; regulation of commerce and, 328–30;
representation and, 79, 109,
115; senate and, 100, 185; sole
government and, 81; sovereignty of, 373; special powers
conferred upon, 209; state governments and, 125, 171, 247,
257–58, 298, 299; state rights
and, 89–90, 115, 202–3, 230,
261–64, 268, 361–62; states
and, 42–43, 255, 338–39, 366,
383; state sovereignties and,
101; state sovereignty and,
43–44, 69, 157, 207, 223–24;
superiority of power of, 361;
supremacy of, 96, 127, 274–75,
277, 278–79, 282–83, 304,

336–39; "supreme" in, 24–25;
supreme v., 357–58; territorial
sovereignty and, 221–22; territorial state rights and, 229–30;
treason and, 240–41; tribunal
and, 144–46; Virginia resolutions and, 65. *See also* general
government; government;
national government
federalism, 62, 72, 73
Federalist: appellate jurisdiction of
judiciary and, 73; Constitution
and, 76–79, 348; division of
powers and, 228; federal constructions in, 77; federal
supremacy and, 339–40; Madison's construction of Constitution and, 30, 46, 103, 126, 132,
136–38, 257; mutual check of,
359; mutual control and, 183,
308; national government and,
77, 86; national sovereignty
and, 78–80; One of the People
and, 258; regulation of commerce and, 329; state governments and, 75–76, 214, 361;
state powers and, 360;
supremacy rights of Congress
and, 72; title of, 60
federalists, 367
federal judiciary: American nation
and, 135; appellate jurisdiction
of, 153, 164–65, 172–73; articles of union and, 52; cases in
law and equity and, 159,
174–75; censorial supremacy in,
311–12; Congress and, 72, 145,
153–56, 204, 287, 310; Constitution and, 153–61, 167, 173,
313; controversies between federal and state departments and,

180–81; controversies between states and, 174–75; controversies between states and federal government and, 175–76; Declaration of Independence and, 200; division of powers and, 132; erroneous constructions of, 152; exclusive supremacy in federal government and, 338; extension of jurisdiction of, 175; extension of powers of, 157–58, 159, 160, 163; "federal" and, 347; federal government and, 144–45; federal laws and, 379; general government and, 145–46; impartiality of, 147–51; impeachment and, 182, 183–84, 187–88; jurisdiction of, 30, 37, 39, 50–52, 151, 180, 204, 204–5; jurisdiction over individuals of, 176; limits between delegated and reserved powers and, 145–46; local interests and, 323; local power and, 321; mutual right of control of state and, 178–79; negative over state laws and, 29–30, 33, 136–37, 286–88; "original and appellate" and, 163–64; people and supremacy of, 235; as political department, 169; power of control of, 132; powers of, 161; regulation of political powers by, 147; right of construction of, 379; rights of federal and state departments and, 152–53; settling of controversies by, 126; state constitutions and, 199; state courts and, 157, 165; state governments and, 73, 162; state judiciaries v.,

143–44; state laws and, 310–11; state rights and, 50–51, 72, 185–86, 192–94, 384; state sovereignty and, 138; supremacy of, 60, 91–92, 128, 156–57, 171–72, 176–77, 187, 202–3, 279–80, 331, 347; supremacy over, 280–81; taxation and, 94; as tribunal intended, 146; tribunals inferior to, 163–64; unconstitutional laws and, 182. *See also* judiciary

federal laws: federal courts and, 379; local rights and, 295–96; states and, 295; supremacy and, 93

federal party: Congress and, 309–10; convention and, 224; monarchical and consolidating parties and, 61; principles of, 60. *See also* political parties

federal powers: limitation of, 213; mode of designating individuals to exercise, 274–75; state governments and, 321

federal rights: federal usurpation and, 243–44; national government and, 263; responsibility of house of representatives and, 237; state governments and, 229

federal treasury, 321

federal union, 17; Articles of Confederation and, 22; "Congress" and, 20; local interests and, 321; "national" and "supreme" and, 24; national union v., 18; remedying of defects of, 17; states and, 263. *See also* union

France: attempted war with, 328; *bed of justice* in, 36; concentrated supremacy in, 319; conflicting

France (*continued*)
political parties in, 269; consolidated government of, 82; division of power in, 318; love of liberty in, 351; natural rights of kings and, 366; rights of people and, 232; supreme concentrated power in, 297
fraud, 47
Fredonia, 207–8
freedom, 301–2
"freedom and independence of the states", 2, 3
The Funeral (Steele), 384

"general": application of, 137–38; Constitution and, 86, 112–13, 126; conveyance of powers and, 115; national government and, 86
"general government", 144
general government: ambition of, 246; Constitution and, 126; despotism of, 64; domestic happiness and, 67; federal election and, 235; geographical interests and, 67; people and, 219; power and, 243–44; representation and, 235; state governments and, 83–84; state sovereignty and, 244; supremacy deduced form, 235; tribunal and, 145–46; "under" and, 145. *See also* federal government; government; national government
Gengis Khan, 250
Genoa, 350
geographical interests, 304; commerce and, 330; concentrated power and, 353–54; Congress and, 67, 305–6, 319–23, 330;

Constitution and, 323; division of powers and, 306–7, 321; federal government and, 305; general government and, 67; national government and, 293, 305–6; states and, 324; violations of, 354
geographical justice, 294
Georgia, 214, 221; constitutional convention and, 7; federal government and, 33; powers in convention of, 18
Germany, 297
Gerry, 65, 67
"government": "people" and, 218–19; power and, 365; will of supremacy in another government and, 194
government: attempts to render contemptible, 265; by compact, 68, 71, 226; complete sovereignty in, 94; concentrated form of, 292; confidence and, 328; consolidated, 222, 253; creation of, 11; Declaration of Independence and, 2; division of powers and, 128–29; division of rights between people and, 301; ease and, 256; English, 33, 66, 94, 127, 195, 264, 293–94, 302–3; federal character of, 138; formation of, 162; forms of, 52; free, 57, 75, 315–16; individuals and, 120; liberty and restraints on, 349; mixed character of, 74, 100, 113, 114, 195–97; monarchical, 49, 52; natural rights of, 366; nature of, 52, 239; operation of, 162; ordinary powers of, 107, 114, 115, 379; political parties and, 53; power and,

226–27, 246; power to pass laws
and, 81–82; representation and,
195; republican, 277–78; safety
and happiness and, 117; self-,
120, 278–79; sources of powers
of, 100; supremacy in, 26, 196,
201–2, 230; unlimited, 292. *See
also* federal government; general
government; national government
Grand Titres, Madame de, 369
Great Britain. *See* England
Greece: confederation of, 350; federal diets of, 117

Hamilton, Alexander, 243; Adams
v., 260–61; centrifugal tendencies of states and, 255; coextensiveness of legislative and
judicial powers and, 177–79;
Congress and, 279–80; consolidated government and, 59,
82–83; Constitution and, 92;
construction of, 46, 52, 103,
257; control of political departments and, 147; departments of
power and, 81–82; election of
president and, 343–44, 347;
English system and, 195; federal
government and, 93; federal
judiciary and, 180–81; judicial
supremacy and, 127; legislative
authorities and, 90; mutual
right of control in state and
federal judiciaries and, 178–79;
national government of, 31,
37–38, 51–52, 71–72, 91–93,
93–94, 126–28, 242, 256–57,
333; national sovereignty and,
78–80, 197–98; political principles of, 258–59; quitting of

convention by, 38; senate and,
113; separation of powers and,
129–35, 141; signing of Constitution of, 38; state governments
and, 87–88, 109; state rights
and, 95–97, 263; state sovereignties and, 65–66; state sovereignty and, 94, 125, 139–40;
supremacy of people and, 129;
supreme legislature and, 127
Hartford convention, 110, 261–64
hereditary powers, 120
hereditary supremacy, 201
Holland, 350
house of commons, 148, 232
house of representatives: Congress
and, 52, 119; consolidated
nation and, 274; Constitution
and, 166–67, 341–42, 388; election of president and, 344–45;
establishment of, 109; federal
character of, 341–42; mode of
electing, 275, 388; national, 91;
national government and, 100,
135; as national representation,
236–37; people and, 100, 105,
107, 113, 235–36; representative
character of, 79; responsibility
of, 237; rights of people and,
186; senate v., 110–11, 113–14;
source of power of, 100, 105,
107, 113; states and, 107–8
human nature, geography and, 322
Hume, David, 365–66

impeachment: Constitution and,
184–85; federal government
and, 184; federal judiciary and,
30, 183–84, 187–88, 347; judicial fidelity and, 182; judicial
impartiality and, 187; national

impeachment (*continued*)
judiciary and, 30; senate and,
187–88; subordination of judicial department and, 197; treason and, 239–40
individual rights, 243–44, 293
individuals: ambition and, 343; federal government and, 119–20;
government and, 120; hereditary powers and, 120; political
rights of states and, 185; securing rights of, 120–21, 314;
"state" and, 7; state governments and, 120; state rights and,
303; taxation and, 122–23
"infidelity", 289
interests: common, 328; geographical, 67; local, 60; sympathy and,
327–28, 351. *See also* local
interests
Ireland, 294, 297, 304, 318, 325

James the Second, 319
Jefferson, Thomas: absence from
convention of, 57; creation of
parties by, 57; election to presidency of, 268–69; political
principles of, 258–61
Jewish experiment, 195
Johnson, 8, 273
Judge Construction, 357
judiciary: absolute sovereignty and,
83; co-extensiveness of judicial
powers and, 180; confederation
of 1777 and, 152; Congress
and, 36–37; in Constitution, 25;
Declaration of Independence
and, 152; English, 148–49, 162;
impartiality of, 147–51,
148–49, 187; impeachment and,
347; jurisdiction of, 127; legisla-

tive powers and powers of,
177–79; national, 19; national
government and, 23, 143,
196–97; negative over state laws
and, 127; permanent tenure of,
130; power of, 35; revenue and,
30; rights of federal and state
departments and, 143; subordination and, 196, 197; supremacy
of, 25, 127–28, 197, 309, 331,
372; veto power of, 20. *See also*
federal judiciary

"king", 365
"kingdom", 209
kings: divinity of, 297–99; limited,
81, 300; natural rights of, 366

Lansing, 65, 67
large states: amendment of Constitution and, 346; aristocracy and,
102–3; national government
and, 103; responsibility to states
and, 236; struggle between
small and, 101–3
laws: bank, 327; constitutional, 93;
creation of pecuniary capital by,
333–35; federal, 93; federal government and, 92; government
and power to pass, 81–82; lottery, 327; national legislature's
authority to make, 88; of
nature, 250; necessity and propriety of, 89, 91, 92; state, 93;
supremacy and, 89, 93; unconstitutional, 93, 95. *See also* negative over state laws
legislative department: co-extensiveness of judicial powers and
powers of, 180; Constitution
and powers of, 173; federal,

50–51, 105, 131; federal government and supremacy of, 25;
influence over judicial of, 178;
judicial powers and powers of,
177–79; in national government, 23; powers of, 34, 97, 161;
power to constitute tribunals of,
163–64; structure of, 52
legislatures: co-equality of, 90, 92,
92–93; control of election and,
181; control of people of, 128;
co-ordinate, 90–91; national,
19; ratification and, 9; as representatives of people, 10; state
governments and, 84; supreme,
127; unconstitutional laws and,
179. *See also* national legislature
legitimacy: ordinary powers and,
114; supremacy of, 333, 365
liberty: ambition and, 256, 292;
concentrated power and, 251,
318; Constitution as last will of,
367–89; Declaration of Independence and, 2; division of
powers and, 32, 132, 140–41,
218, 227–28, 243, 266, 349–50;
executive power and, 343; federal government and, 75; individual, 301; mutual control
between political departments
and, 200; national strength and,
349; origin of, 2; parties and,
53; power and, 291; power of,
350–51; precautions for preservation of, 183; restraints on
government and, 349; state
rights and, 305; of states, 301;
state sovereignties and, 299;
tyranny and, 57
local interests: Congress and, 323;
consolidated sovereignty and,

254–55; Constitution and, 324;
federal union and, 321; national
government and, 304, 330; people and, 323–24; power of states
over, 60; states and, 323; supreme
court and, 323. *See also* interests
lottery, 286, 327
Louis the Fourteenth, 365–66
Lyon, 265

Madison, James: American nation
and, 111; American people and,
104–5, 109, 116; centrifugal
tendencies of states and, 255;
construction of Constitution
of, 30, 46, 103, 126, 132,
136–38, 257; didactic federalism
of, 72; establishment of Constitution and, 99–100; federal
judiciary and, 91–92, 126, 128,
138, 145–46, 180–81, 203–5,
204–5, 279–80; federal powers
and, 336; general government
and, 144; geographical interests
and, 67, 305–6; house of representatives and, 166–67, 341;
judicial impartiality and, 147;
judicial integrity and, 182;
jurisdiction of judiciary and,
127; mixed character of government and, 74, 100, 195–96,
197; national government of,
51–52, 63–64, 72, 123, 135,
256–57; national supremacy
over states and, 197–98;
national system and, 59; negative over state laws and, 29;
people and, 108; ratification of
Constitution and, 104–6; senate
and, 113, 185–86; senate v.
house of representatives and,

Madison, James (*continued*)
110–11; separation of departments of government and,
128–29; separation of powers and, 129, 141; signing of Constitution of, 38; state governments and, 125; state judiciaries and, 143–44; state rights and, 263; states and people of states and, 107; state sovereignty and, 66–67, 100, 116, 138–40
Mahomet, 349
Martin, Luther, 50; construction of Constitution of, 46–48; departure of, 45–46; political parties and, 52–53, 56–58, 63
Maryland, 7, 17, 33, 67, 214
Massachusetts: constitutional convention and, 7; federal government and, 33; federal v. national union and, 18; national government and, 23, 203–4, 270; negative over state laws and, 29; Pinckney's motion and, 64; powers in convention of, 17; struggle between small and large states and, 101
Massachusetts Bay, 214
Milton, John, 242
Missouri question, 321, 327
moderation, 307–8, 360–61
monarchy, 8, 275, 354; absolute, 352; dissolution of state governments and, 227; limited, 32; principles of limited, 57; republican government and, 53
monopoly, 172, 351
Morris, Gouverneur, 68, 226, 243

Naples, 366
"national": application of, 137–38;

Congress of 1787 and, 16–17; Constitution and, 86, 112–13, 126, 274, 371; convention and, 19–20, 23, 24, 29, 34; conveyance of powers and, 115; national government and, 86; in Randolph's resolutions, 20; state rejection of, 19; "United States" and, 375
"national and state rights", 220
"National and state rights considered, by one of the people", 219
"national government", 16
national government: American people and, 104; basis for, 223–24; branches of, 22–23; cases in law and equity and, 188–89; Congress and, 13, 16–17, 20, 24; consolidation and, 45; Constitution and, 26, 59, 94, 117, 126, 198, 218, 238, 274, 276; construction and, 372; constructions hostile to, 48; constructive supremacy and, 26–27; constructive supremacy of, 19; convention and, 19–27, 42, 48–52, 57, 217, 376; Declaration of Independence and, 21; division of powers and, 334–36; election and, 109; of England, 31; federal compact and, 274; Federalist and, 77, 86; federal supremacy and, 339–40; federal v., 29, 69, 70–71; "general" and, 86; geographical interests and, 293, 305–6; Hamilton's plan for, 31–33, 37–38, 51–52, 71–72, 238, 242, 256–57, 333; house of representatives and, 100, 135; judicial power and,

196–97; judiciary and, 143; large states and, 103; laws of, 134; local interests and, 304, 330; Madison's plan for, 51–52, 63–64, 72, 135, 238, 256–57; mode of designating individuals to exercise federal powers and, 275; modes of conveying power and, 113; monarchical form of, 217; "national" and, 86; necessity and propriety of laws and, 89, 91, 128; negative over state laws and, 20, 40; One of the People and, 270; people and, 349; Pinckney's plan for, 63, 64; power and, 243–44; power to pass laws of, 94; Randolph's plan for, 64–65; rejection of, 20, 34–35, 38, 45–46, 47; republican form of, 217; right of alteration and, 26; rights and, 263; security and, 67; senate and, 113, 188–89; sovereignty and, 78–79; state governments and, 66, 87–88, 154–55, 171; state nations and, 104; state rights and, 96; states and, 18, 33, 46, 63, 70–71; state sovereignty and, 157; supremacy of, 91–94; "supreme" in, 24–25; sustaining of, 304; taxation and, 125; territory and, 118; "union" and, 289; United States and, 75; Virginia plan for, 48–49, 156; Washington and, 256. *See also* federal government; general government; government

national judiciary: impeachment and, 30; jurisdiction of, 30, 49, 50, 204–5; national peace and harmony and, 30; states rights and, 50–51. *See also* federal judiciary; judiciary

national legislature: authority to make laws of, 88; federal jurisdiction and, 347; negative over state laws and, 64, 205; negative over state laws in, 29; powers of, 48–49; power to pass laws of, 127–28; states rights and, 50–51

national sovereignty: Congress and, 319–20; consolidation of states into, 88; convention and, 326–27; federal government and, 82; national government and, 78–79; senate and, 80; slavery and, 340; state governments and, 77–79, 83. *See also* sovereignty; state sovereignty

nature, laws of, 250, 320

"necessary", 373

negative over state laws: Congress and, 50, 192–93, 205, 286; Constitution and, 20, 22, 40; construction and, 21; convention's proposals for, 42; Declaration of Independence and, 21; federal government and, 39–40, 116, 189–90; federal judiciary and, 29–30, 33, 136–37, 286–88; judiciary and, 127; Madison and, 29; national government and, 20, 40; national legislature and, 29, 64, 205; state sovereignty and, 44; supremacy and, 21

New Hampshire, 214; arrival of delegates of, 45–46; constitutional convention and, 7; first appearance at convention of, 34; powers in convention of, 17

New Jersey, 7, 17, 33, 214, 265

New York, 214; absence from convention of, 34; constitutional convention and, 7; federal government and, 33; federal judiciary and, 39; legislature of, 65; national government and, 23; powers in convention of, 17; struggle between small and large states and, 101

ninth amendment, 335

North Carolina, 214; constitutional convention and, 7; federal government and, 33; national government and, 23; powers in convention of, 18

Ohio, 168

oligarchy, 15

One of the People: claim of authority of, 255–57; doctrine of, 250; doctrines of, 256; England and domestic regulation and, 253–54; Federalist and, 258; Hamilton's plan of government and, 238; national government and, 220, 224, 238; object of pamphlet of, 270; pamphlet by, 218; "people" and, 219–20; restrictions and divisions and, 251–52; state rights and, 220–21, 228–29, 237–38; state sovereignty and, 222–24; treason and, 240–41; use of authorities of, 256–61

opinion: authorities and, 258–59; crime and, 187

ordinary powers, 114–15

Ovid, 372

parliament, 303; national sovereignty and, 78; power to pass

laws of, 94; representation in, 77–78; states and, 67; supremacy of, 53–55, 91, 168, 294, 328; united representation of, 1

patriotism, 317

Patterson, 30, 34, 64, 65

pecuniary aristocracy, 332–33

pecuniary capital, 333–35

Pennsylvania, 214; censorial experiment in, 308–11; constitutional convention and, 7; federal government and, 33; national government and, 23, 203–4, 270; negative over state laws and, 29; Pinckney's motion and, 64; powers in convention of, 17; struggle between small and large states and, 101

pension law, 331

"people": "government" and, 218–19; meaning of, 8–9; "state" and, 284

people: co-equal supremacy of legislatures and, 92–93; Congress and, 121, 235; Constitution and, 84–85, 99–100, 104, 219, 238–39, 267; control over legislatures of, 128; Declaration of Independence and, 267; destruction of rights of, 228; division of powers and, 231; division of rights between government and, 301; federal government and, 236; general government and, 219; house of representatives and, 100, 105, 107, 113, 235–36; judicial supremacy and, 235; local interests and, 323–24; national government and, 349; oppressive government and, 318; per capita supremacy of, 201; political rights of states and, 233; preservation of rights of, 266; representatives of, 10; right of election and, 233–34; right to form government of, 278; senate and, 235; sovereignty of, 10, 104, 273, 355–56; state and federal government and, 298; state constitutions and, 199–200; state governments and, 9, 84, 219, 231–33, 267, 299; state rights of, 264–65; states and, 111; state v., 108; supremacy of, 129, 131, 147, 199, 230–31

per capita supremacy, 201
perpetual union, 4
Persia, 246, 254, 270
Persian empire, 350
Philadelphia, 13, 17
Pinckney, Charles, 21, 29, 34, 63, 64, 203
Pitt, William, 265
political departments: arrogance of, 243; constitutional rights of, 243; Constitution and, 160, 180; controversies in relation to powers of, 162; division of powers and, 182; federal judiciary and, 180–81; integrity of, 32; judicial control over, 146–48; mutual control of, 183, 199, 200; state courts and, 167; state sovereignty and, 160
political parties: consolidating, 58–59, 60–61, 73; in convention, 49, 52 53, 55 62; creation of, 57, 259; dividing and concentrating power and, 269; federal, 57–59, 60–61, 224, 309–10; federalists, 367; federal

republican, 268; liberty and, 53; monarchical, 58–59, 60–61, 73, 268; national, 61; powers of government and, 53; republican, 268, 309–10; tories, 53, 267, 356; Washington and, 56; whigs, 54–55
Portugal, 232, 366
power: absolute, 354–55; allurements of, 245–46, 250–51; ambition and, 246–48, 251–52; arrogance and, 246; censorial, 308–13; classes of, 339–40; collisions and moderation of, 308; compact and, 226–27; concentration of, 227; concurrency of, 93, 336–37; departments of, 81; essence of, 372; exclusiveness of, 336–37; extensive empires and unlimited, 292; general government and, 243–44; government and, 226–27, 246; of judiciary, 35; "king" and, 365; liberty and, 291; moderation and, 360–61; national government and, 243–44; primary divisions of, 360; resistance to, 243; sympathy and, 352, 360. *See also* concentrated power
powers: classes of, 383, 386; concentrated, 250; concurrent, 90, 94–95, 133, 329, 339–40; of Congress, 115; constitutional, 172; delegated, 145–46; derived from state sovereignty, 154; exclusive, 125, 339–40; federal, 4; of federal government, 35–36; hereditary, 120; implied, 6; judicial, 172; legislative, 6, 34; liberty and restrictions of, 32; limited, 5, 21; local, 321,

powers (*continued*)
338–39, 357; mutual, 82, 145,
183–84; ordinary, 107, 114,
114–15, 379; political, 43,
224–25; prohibited, 194; public
good and sovereign, 37; recondite, 313; representation as basis
of, 195; reserved, 145–46, 209;
sources of governmental, 100;
sovereign, 4, 37; state, 250;
supreme legislative, 31; territorial division of, 292; war, 31–32.
See also division of powers
prejudice, 46–47
Presbyterianism, 1
president: centripetal tendencies
and two terms for, 256; Constitution and, 21; controversy over,
321; council of revision and, 20;
election of, 236, 341–47; geographical propensities of, 342;
important functions of, 243;
national, 91; national election of,
343; representative character of,
79; state of the union and, 276;
states and, 342, 348–49; trivial
geography of, 310
Providence Plantations, 214

Randolph, Edmund: federal union
and, 22; jurisdiction of judiciary
and, 127; "national" and, 19;
national government of, 63,
64–65; national judiciary and,
30, 204; refusal to sign Constitution of, 38; rejection of plan
of, 38; resolutions of, 20
ratification: constitutional amendment and, 15; modes of, 9,
211–12; nature of compact and
form of, 239

Read, Judge, 66
reciprocal forbearance, 97
representation: coalition between
monarchists and consolidators
and, 73; in Congress, 299, 303;
in Constitution, 112; division of
powers and, 298; federal, 340;
federal government and, 80,
109, 115; first principle of, 112;
general government and, 235;
for general purposes, 112–13;
geographical lines and, 320;
large states and, 73; national,
340; national sovereignty and,
78–79; nature of government
and, 195; ordinary powers and,
114, 115; power and, 195; powers of federal government and,
79; slavery and, 340; small states
and, 73; sovereignty and, 79; for
special purposes, 112–13; state
legislatures and, 111–12; struggle between small and large
states over, 101; supremacy and,
294
republic, 8, 130–31
"republican": interpretations of,
58; quarrel between "federal"
and, 62; right to form government and, 278
republican government, 53
republican party, 309–10
reserved powers: centripetal tendencies and, 255; limits between
delegated and, 145–46; of state
governments, 214
reserved rights: of people, 231–33;
responsibility of house of representatives and, 237; self-defense
and, 286; of states, 1; taxation
and, 286

responsibility: of Congress, 235;
federal judiciary and, 235; of
house of representatives, 237;
judicial veto and, 20
restraint, 301–2
revenue: judiciary and, 30; state
government right to raise,
87–88; state right to raise revenue, 96
Revolutionary War, 8, 9, 56
Rhode Island, 214
rights: local, 295–96; mutual, 82;
political, 244; popular, 53; positive reservation of, 42; reserved,
1; securing of individual,
120–21; of sovereignty, 2–3; of
state sovereignty, 4–5; of taxation, 94; of territory, 117–18
Roman Catholicism, 1
Roman republic, 73, 89–91
Romans, 350
Rome, 318
Russia, 246, 254, 270

Scotland, 1
secrecy, 47
sedition, 226
sedition law, 72, 232, 265, 321
self-government, 120, 278–79
senate: censorial supremacy in,
311–12; Congress and, 52, 119;
consolidating tendencies and,
186–88; election of president
and, 344; establishment of, 109;
federal government and, 100,
185; house of representatives v.,
110–11, 113–14; impeachment
and, 187–88; individuals and
state rights and, 185; national,
91; national government and,
113, 188–89; national sover-

eignty and, 80; people and, 235;
representation in, 80, 342; representative character of, 79;
rights of governments and, 186;
source of power of, 100, 107–8,
113; state and, 185–86; state
governments and, 109, 162;
state representation in, 77–78,
82; states and, 113; supreme legislative power and, 31; war
powers of, 31
Shaftesbury, Lord, 361
Sherman, 67
slavery, 340–41
small states: amendment of Constitution and, 346; federalism of,
344; senate representation of,
236–37; struggle between large
and, 101–3
sole government, 81–83
"sole purpose", 18
South America, 232
South Carolina, 214, 218, 241;
convention and, 7; federal government and, 33; national government and, 23, 270; powers
in convention of, 18; powers of
states and, 38–39; ratification of
Constitution by, 38–39
"sovereign and corporate rights",
220
sovereignty: cession of territory
and, 221–22; concentrated, 291;
in Congress, 78; consolidated,
3, 5–6, 254–55; crimes against,
240; inherent attribute of, 159;
judicial department and, 83;
national, 15; of people, 104,
355–56; of people of each state,
10; political power and, 43; regulation of commerce and rights

sovereignty (*continued*)
of, 2; representation and, 79;
rights of, 2–3; royal, 215; of
state governments, 87, 92;
union and, 2, 3, 43. *See also*
national sovereignty; state sovereignty
Spain, 1, 232, 366
"sphere", 136
"state", 208–9, 213; individuals
and, 7; meaning of, 7–8; "people" and, 284; public and, 7–8;
republic and, 8
state governments: abridging powers of, 166; ambition and, 343;
arrogance of, 264; collisions
between federal and, 389; compelling obedience of, 358–59;
concurrency of legislation and,
93; concurrent powers of,
179–80, 368; Congress and, 73,
253; constitutional rights and,
314; Constitution and, 134,
161, 238, 266–67, 358–59; controversies between federal and,
175–76; crimes against sovereignty and, 240; Declaration of
Independence and, 9; defense of
rights of, 84; delegation of
powers by, 246; designating
individuals for the exercise of
federal powers and, 274–75;
division of powers and, 165,
244, 299–301; establishment of,
11; exclusive powers of, 368;
exclusive supremacy of,
336–37; federal government
and, 125, 171, 231, 247,
257–58, 299; Federalist and,
75–76; federal powers and, 321;
federal rights and, 229; general

government and, 83–84; as
guardians of their rights, 162;
hostility in convention to, 24;
individuals and, 120; judicial
supremacy over, 73; judicial
control of, 162; legitimate control over, 89; mediatorial check
of, 227; monarchy and, 61, 227;
mutual independence of, 152;
mutual powers of, 145;
national, 235; national government and, 66, 87–88, 154–55,
171; national right of territory
and, 117–18; national sovereignty and, 83; original political
rights of, 262; as part of
national sovereignty, 77–79;
people and, 9, 84, 85, 219,
231–33, 267, 298, 299; as perfect, 170–71; powers of, 9, 101,
245; preservation of, 64; raising
of revenues and, 87–88; republican form of, 279, 287; reserved
powers of, 214; safety and happiness and, 117; senate and, 78,
109; state rights and, 228–29;
supremacy of, 202–3; taxation
and, 88, 97, 285; tribunals and,
145–46; usurpation of, 83–84
state laws, 93; censorial power
over, 309; Congress and, 159,
310–11; Constitution and, 20;
federal judiciary and, 310–11;
judicial supremacy over, 21;
negative over, 20–21;
supremacy and, 93. *See also*
negative over state laws
state legislatures: alterations of
Constitution and, 274; Constitution and, 105; federal government and territorial state rights

and, 230; general powers of,
111; power to pass laws of, 112;
representation and, 111–12;
state conventions and, 106, 212
state rights: cases in law and equity
and, 384; concentrated power
and, 253; Congress and, 303–4,
310; Constitution and, 96, 221;
federal courts and, 384; federal
government and, 89–90, 115,
230, 261–64, 268, 304, 361–62;
federal judiciary and, 50–51,
185–86, 192–94; federal legislature and, 50–51; federal
supremacy and, 122; free and
independent departments and,
155; as inherent, 219, 220–21;
interest of individuals and, 303;
liberty and, 305; national government and, 96, 263; national
judiciary and, 50–51; national
legislature and, 50–51; of people, 264–65; of preservation,
249; preservation of, 269; to
resist usurpation, 85; senate representation and, 77–78; state
governments and, 228–29; state
usurpation and, 243–44;
supremacies and, 375; taxation
and, 96–97; territorial, 229–30;
union and, 265. *See also* state
sovereignty
states: American people and, 119;
annihilation of rights of, 65;
appointment of deputies for
convention and, 7; cases in law
and equity and, 159–60, 164;
co-equal sovereignties of, 225;
common federal interest and,
320; concentrated sovereignty
and, 292; concurrent powers of,

159; Congress and, 1, 6–7, 17,
115, 340; consolidation of, 3–4,
88; Constitution and, 10, 14,
15, 38–39, 41–42, 100, 152,
199–200, 209, 324; constitutions of, 65, 198–201, 240; constructions of, 39; constructive
national checks and, 40; constructive supremacy and, 331;
convention and, 15, 23; conventions of, 105–7, 212, 225; as
corporations, 226, 365; corporations v., 222–23; debts of,
331; Declaration of Independence and, 20, 42, 55; as dependent, 61; as dependent
corporations, 21, 67, 165;
destruction of distinction of,
23–24; distinct powers of, 82;
division of powers and, 355;
federal compact and, 274,
276–77; federal government
and, 42, 42–43, 338–39, 366,
383; federal judiciary and,
174–75; federal laws and, 295;
federal union and, 263; geographical interests and, 324;
government control of, 67;
house of representatives and,
107–8; independence of, 42, 67;
individuals and, 176; judicial
supremacy and, 331; judicial
power of, 163; judicial powers
of, 157, 160; judicial supremacy
over, 156–57, 187; judiciaries
of, 143–44, 165, 167–68, 169,
178 79, 180, 182, 347; liberty
of, 301; local interests and, 60,
323; local laws of, 310–11;
"national" and, 19; national
government and, 18, 33, 46, 63,

412 Index

70–71; national supremacy over, 197–98; oligarchy of minority of, 15; parliament and, 67; pecuniary aristocracy and, 332; pecuniary controversies between, 176; people and, 107, 108, 111; political character of, 3; political union of sovereign and independent, 5; powers of, 39–40, 86, 157–59, 189–90, 209, 243, 247, 250, 339, 341, 360–61; president and, 342, 348–49; prohibitions on, 159–60, 282–85, 339; representation and, 73, 211, 342; republican equality between, 60; senate and, 77–78, 82, 100, 113, 185–86; slavery and, 341; small, 20; struggle between small and large, 101–3; supremacy of, 196; supremacy over, 15, 55; taxation and, 193; tendencies of, 255; territorial lines between, 325–26; territorial sovereignty of, 221–22; treason and, 281; union and, 324; war and, 245; writ of error and rights of, 173. *See also* state governments; state laws; state legislatures; state rights; state sovereignty

state sovereignty: affirmation of, 208; ambition and, 249; amendment and, 210–11; assertion of, 190–91; commerce and, 2; under confederation, 2–3; confederation of 1777 and, 211, 212, 213; Congress and, 7, 67, 71, 213–14; Constitution and, 3, 44, 76, 77, 100, 136, 209, 212, 213–14, 325; construction

and, 387–88; criminal state jurisdiction and, 171; Declaration of Independence and, 3, 213; delegated powers and, 210; destruction of, 116; "federal" and, 7; federal government and, 43–44, 69, 157, 207, 223–24; federal judiciary and, 138; general government and, 244; Hamilton and, 65–66; judicial power and, 157; king and, 214; language implying, 207–9; Madison and, 66–67; national government and, 157; negative over state laws and, 44; per capita supremacy of people and, 201; political departments and, 160; powers derived from, 154; powers of, 116, 209–10; powers reserved to states and, 157; prohibition of certain attributes of, 4–5; prohibition on states and, 160; rights of, 2–3, 4, 4–5; sovereignty of union and, 2, 3; state governments and, 77–78, 207; states and, 42; taxation and, 125, 284–85; territorial state rights and, 230; treaty between US and British king and, 214–15; "union" and, 5. *See also* national sovereignty; sovereignty

Steele, Sir Richard, 384
supremacy: absolute, 293; of American nation, 135; censorial, 311; concentrated, 253–54; concentrated power and, 270–71; of Congress, 52, 60, 72, 321–22; of Constitution, 170; of constitutional laws, 93; "constitution" and, 372; constructive, 15, 22,

26–27, 333, 334, 366–67; English, 53–55, 103; federal, 15; of federal government, 96, 127; of geographical majorities, 315; government and, 196, 201–2; hereditary, 201; judicial power and, 197; of judiciary, 127–28; kinds of, 201; laws and, 89, 93; of legitimacy, 333; negative over state laws and, 21; over Constitution, 313–14; over states, 15, 55; of people, 147; per capita, 15, 201; popular, 135; representation and, 294

"supreme": in Constitution, 25–26; convention debate over, 23; debate in constitutional convention over, 24; debate in convention over, 29

Swift, Jonathan, 362–63, 368–89

Swiss cantons, 276, 277

Switzerland, 350

sympathy: interest and, 327–28, 351; mutual, 328; power and, 352, 360

taxation: concurrent power of, 93, 125, 140, 158, 249, 285, 329; Congress and, 94, 122–23, 245; federal, 121–22; federal judiciary and, 94; individuals and, 122–23; mutual right of, 179; national government and, 125; pecuniary, 181; of pecuniary aristocracy, 332–33; powers of, 247–49; prohibitions on state power of, 284–85; reserved rights and, 286; restrictions of, 249; state governments and, 97; state power of imposing, 88; state rights and, 96–97; states

and, 193; state sovereignty and, 125, 284–85; war and, 122

territory: national government and, 118; national right of, 117–18; sovereignty and cession of, 221–22; state right of, 229–30

Thummim, 195

tories, 53–55, 267, 356

treason, 31, 182, 239; classes of, 240; Congress and, 281; federal government and, 240–41; impeachment and, 239–40; state constitutions and, 240; states and, 281

treaties, 88–89

treaty of the Pyrenees, 365–66

tribunal. *See* federal judiciary

Turkey, 82, 246, 254, 270

twelfth amendment, 324

tyranny: concentration of power and, 131; confounding of legislative and judicial power and, 184; liberty and, 57; men of large property and, 68; repose of, 75; sovereignties and, 80; state legislatures and, 84; supremacy of people and, 129

unanimity, 9, 212

unconstitutional laws, 94–95, 179

"under", 145

"union": Constitution and, 273; inexplicitness of, 1; meaning of, 1–2; national government and, 289; state sovereignty and, 5

union: as association of individuals, 288; as association of states, 288–89; civil, 1; compact and, 1; Congress and terms of, 7; consolidation and, 1; Constitu-

union (*continued*)
tion and, 13, 17; division of
powers and, 351; federal character of, 121, 342; individual states
as parties to, 276; perpetual, 4;
political, 1; ratification of, 14;
sovereignty and, 43; sovereignty
of, 2, 3; state and, 324; state and
federal powers and, 313; state
rights and, 265; as union of
states, 279. *See also* federal
union
union of 1777, 9, 10, 38
union of 1787, 9
"united", 2, 277
"United States": convention's use
of, 34; Declaration of Independence and, 3; "national" and,
375; nature of government and,
239
United States: absolute power and,
355; agriculture and, 334; Constitution and, 281; Declaration
of Independence and, 2; existence of, 24; general governor
of, 31–32; geography of, 319;
individual legislation and, 19;
legislature of, 34; national government and, 75; new experiment of, 356–57; political birth
of, 1–2; political rights existing
in, 221; supreme executive
authority of, 31; supreme leg-

islative power of, 31; treaty
between British king and,
214–15; *union* and, 1–2
Urim, 195
Utopia, 209

Venice, 350
Virginia, 19, 214; constitutional
convention and, 7; convention
of, 38; federal government and,
33; national government and,
23, 203–4, 270; negative over
state laws and, 29; Pinckney's
motion and, 64; plan of, 71,
156; powers in convention of,
18; struggle between small and
large states and, 101
Virginia resolutions, 48–49, 65

war: authority over direction of,
31–32; powers of, 37, 247–49,
330; states and, 245; taxation
and, 122
Washington, George, 56, 255, 256
whigs, 54–55
Wilson, 64
writ of error, 173

Yates, Judge: construction of Constitution of, 46, 47; departure
of, 45–46; notes of secret
debates of, 45, 63–70, 305, 307;
quitting of convention of, 67

Note
on the
Editors

JAMES McCLELLAN

James McClellan is the James Bryce Visiting Fellow in American Studies at the Institute of U. S. Studies, University of London. He holds a Ph. D. in political science from the University of Virginia and a J. D. from the University of Virginia School of Law. Dr. McClellan has taught American government and Constitutional law at a number of American universities and colleges. He has also been a professional staff member of the U. S. Senate, and from 1981 to 1983 was chief counsel and staff director of the Subcommittee on Separation of Powers of the Senate Committee on the Judiciary. From 1983 to 1993 he was president of the Center for Judicial Studies and editor of Benchmark, a journal of constitutional law, and from 1993 to 1998 served as the director of publications of Liberty Fund. His publications include *The Political Principles of Robert A. Taft* (co-author with Russell Kirk); *Joseph Story and the American Constitution; The Federalist. A Student Edition* (co-editor with George W. Carey); *James Madison, Debates in the Federal Convention of 1787* (co-editor); and *Liberty, Order & Justice*

CHRISTOPHER B. BRIGGS

Conservative Leadership Series editor Christopher B. Briggs holds degrees from Bowdoin College and The Catholic University of America. Currently senior book editor at the Intercollegiate Studies Institute, he is also assistant editor of *Humanitas*, a journal of the humanities published in Washington, D. C.